True Christianity

True Christianity

The Doctrine of Dispensations in
the Thought of John William Fletcher (1729–1785)

J. RUSSELL FRAZIER

◦PICKWICK *Publications* • Eugene, Oregon

TRUE CHRISTIANITY
The Doctrine of Dispensations in the Thought of John William Fletcher (1729–1785)

Copyright © 2014 J. Russell Frazier. All rights reserved. Except for brief quotations in critical publications or reviews, no part of this book may be reproduced in any manner without prior written permission from the publisher. Write: Permissions. Wipf and Stock Publishers, 199 W. 8th Ave., Suite 3, Eugene, OR 97401.

Pickwick Publications
An Imprint of Wipf and Stock Publishers
199 W. 8th Ave., Suite 3
Eugene, OR 97401

www.wipfandstock.com

ISBN 13: 978-1-62032-663-3

Cataloguing-in-Publication Data

Frazier, J. Russell.

True Christianity : the doctrine of dispensations in the though of John William Fletcher (1729–1785) / J. Russell Frazier.

xxiv + 298 p. ; 23 cm. Includes bibliographical references and indexes.

ISBN 13: 978-1-62032-663-3

1. Fletcher, John, 1729–1785. 2. Methodist Church—Doctrines—History—18th century. I. Title.

BX8276 .F73 2014

Manufactured in the U.S.A.

Scripture quotations, except for brief paraphrases or unless otherwise indicated, are from the Authorized or King James Version of the Bible.

Against Heresies. by Irenaeus, Alexander Roberts and James Donaldson, eds. Vol. 1, *Ante-Nicene Fathers, The Apostolic Fathers with Justin Martyr and Irenaeus.* © 2004 by Hendrickson Publishers, Peabody, Massachusetts. Used by permission. All rights reserved.

The Enchiridion: or On Faith, Hope and Love. by Augustine. Philip Schaff. Vol. 3, *Nicene and Post-Nicene, First Series, Augustine: On the Holy Trinity, Doctrinal Treatises, Moral Treatises.* © 2004 by Hendrickson, Publishers, Peabody, Massachusetts. Used by permission. All rights reserved.

The Covenant of Grace: A Biblico-Theological Study. by John Murray. ©1977 by The Tyndale House, London. Used by permission. All rights reserved.

The Redemption and Restoration of Man in the Thought of Richard Baxter: A Study in Puritan Theology by James I. Packer. © 2003 by Regent College Publishing, Vancouver, British Columbia. Used by permission. All rights reserved.

The Federal Theology of Johannes Cocceius (1603–1669). by Willem J. van Asselt, Raymond A. Blacketer, trans. © 2001 by Brill Academic Publishers, Leiden. Used by permission. All rights reserved.

"Gracious Accommodations: Herbert's 'Love III.'" Review of *Love III*, by George Herbert. by Anne Williams In *Modern Philology* 82, 1 (August 1984): 13–22. © 1984 by University of Chicago Press Journals, Chicago, Illinois. Used by permission. All rights reserved.

"Wesley's Trinitarian Ordo Salutis." by Corrie M. Aukema Cieslukowski and Elmer M. Colyer. In *Reformation and Revival* Journal 14, 4 (Fall 2005): 105–31. Used by permission of ACT 3 Network, www.act3network com, 2012.

"A dreadful phenomenon at the Birches." by Peter S. Forsaith. A paper presented at the Ecclesiastical History Society conference. © 2008 by the author. Used by permission of the author. All rights reserved.

Hymns on the Trinity. by Charles Wesley © 1998 by The Charles Wesley Society. Used by permission. All rights reserved.

"A Trinitarian Theology of the Holy Spirit?" by Kilian McDonnell OSB, © 1985 by the editor of *Theological Studies.*

Whitsunday Hymns. by Charles Wesley and John Wesley. Randy Maddox, ed. Bristol: Farley, 1746; The Center for Studies in the Wesleyan Tradition, Duke University.

"Strains in the Understanding of Christian Perfection in Early British Methodism." M. Robert Fraser, © 1989 by the author. Used by permission. All rights reserved.

Evangelicalism in Modern Britain: A History from the 1730s to the 1980s by David W. Bebbington. © 1989 by Taylor & Francis Books. Used by permission. All rights reserved.

Quote on page 63 taken from, *The Holiness Pilgrimage* by John A. Knight © 1973, 1986 by Beacon Hill Press of Kansas City, Kansas City, MO. Used by permission of the Publisher. All rights reserved. Visit the website at www.beaconhillpress.com to purchase this title.

Inclusive language policy: In every possible instance, inclusive language has been employed in this book. However, it is to be understood by the reader that direct quotations from older sources that use non-inclusive terminology necessitate the faithful reproduction of the original language used.

To my wife, Carla, in grateful acknowledgement of her loving and prayerful support of all of my ministry and to my children, Rachelle and Seth, in deep recognition of their love and understanding.

... la sainteté et le bonheur des premiers Chrétiens dépendoient de la connoissance expérimentale qu'ils avoient du mystère de la sainte TRINITÉ, ou le Dieu manifesté dans leur ame comme Père, Fils, et St. Esprit, ou comme Créateur, Rédempteur, et Sanctificateur. [1]

---

1. John Fletcher, *La Grâce et la Nature, Poëme*, 2nd ed. (London: Hindmarsh, 1785) 389.

Contents

Preface / xi
Acknowledgments / xv
List of Abbreviations / xviii

    Introduction / 1
1   The Milieu of Fletcher's Theology / 9
2   God of Nature and of Grace: Theological Foundations for the Doctrine of Dispensations / 35
3   The Doctrine of Dispensations: An Overview / 58
4   The Dispensation of the Father / 99
5   The Dispensation of the Son / 120
6   The Dispensation of the Spirit / 158
    Conclusion / 211

Bibliography / 223
Subjects and Names Index / 279
Scripture Index / 295

Preface

THIS BOOK IS ABOUT listening. It is born out of the conviction that the Church must listen intently to the voices of the past in order to think critically about its message, to reflect upon its mission, and to move confidently into the future. Over the course of time, voices become muted due to the passage of time, the din of the present, or to the would-be listener's perception of the speaker's insignificance.

One voice that has been mitigated through the years is that of John William Fletcher (1729–1785). Fletcher was a seminal figure among the evangelical clergy of the Church of England and in the early methodist movement in the eighteenth century. While serving as vicar in the remote village of Madeley, Fletcher was renowned for his personal piety, his dedicated pastoral labors, and his theological writings. A native born Swiss, Fletcher maintained affinities and relationships with other immigrants to England throughout his life, and this continental affinity is reflected in the sources and flavor of his theology.

Fletcher's voice needs to be heard today. I believe that the Church should listen to this seminal theologian for several reasons. First, there is a breadth and depth to his theological enterprise that is scarcely paralleled today. Fletcher provides a panoramic view of theology and continually appeals to his readers to view the minutia of controversial issues within the light of a broader vision of God's salvific work in history. His thought has an ecumenical appeal. He invites his readers not only to understand the "whole tenor" (Wesley) of Scripture, but to listen to the harmony of divine revelation in all of creation and in all of history. Second, while certain biographers resorted to hagiography, evidence still remains that Fletcher was a man of great piety and devotion to God. If his theology produced such a godly man, one would profit greatly from listening to Fletcher. Thirdly, the modern-day reader will benefit from having Fletcher as a partner in dialogue because he handled controversy deftly. Fletcher models an irenic spirit, which advances discussions in a post-modern world that values dialogue, but that increasingly is bifurcated along cultural lines. The Church should listen to Fletcher's voice lastly because he provided a practical theology that gives clear direction for pastoral and missionary practice today. For over twenty-eight years, I have served as a pastor, an educator, and a missionary. As a minister wanting to serve with integrity, I sought to integrate the practical tasks of ministry with the more theoretical aspects of Christian thought; I sought intellectual and practical integrity. In Fletcher, I found such a system. Although much of Fletcher's system is bound to the eighteenth century and to the controversies in which he was embroiled, he provided a way out of the impasse; his is an integrated system unifying both practical and theoretical. The central and unifying doctrine of his system is his doctrine of dispensations.

This book examines the doctrine of dispensations in the thought of John William Fletcher (1729–1785), analyzing principally his published and unpublished writings. During the controversy surrounding Wesley's Conference Minutes of 1770, Fletcher developed his already nascent doctrine of dispensations to provide a cogent theology of history as a polemic against hyper-Calvinism, whose system of divine fiat and finished salvation, Fletcher believed, did not take seriously enough either the activity of God in salvation history or an individual believer's personal progress in salvation.

The principal pattern of Fletcher's theology of history was based upon the doctrine of the economic Trinity, as God disclosed the divine nature in the economy of salvation through three ages of history: the dispensations of the Father, Son, and Spirit. The doctrine of divine self-disclosure occurs on both a macro level, an objective view of history or an *ordo temporum*, and a micro level, a personal faith history or an *ordo salutis*. The dispensations, while revealing the variety of God's dealings with humanity throughout history, demonstrate an inherent unity as the God of holy-love accommodates revelation to human limitations and the noetic effects of sin in order to communicate effectively to the objects of divine love. Although principally a Calvinistic doctrine, Fletcher made the doctrine of accommodation a unifying principle of his theological system providing a theology that offered correctives to both Arminianism and Calvinism and proposed a reconciling theology between the two.

The doctrine of accommodation is furthermore central to Fletcher's doctrine of ministry. As God accommodated divine revelation to human capacity, Christian ministers must accommodate the gospel to the various states of their hearers in order to move hearers toward the *telos* of the Christian life, i.e., Christian perfection. The book concludes with a survey of the application portions of Fletcher's sermons to his hearers in order to understand the way Fletcher categorized his congregants into different states of faith or dispensations, accommodating his message to them.

While not questioning all of the various polarities posited by the different interpreters of Fletcher's dialectical thought, the present book points to the more fundamental union of Fletcher's thought: the union of grace and nature that Fletcher developed in one of his most mature works, *La Grâce et la Nature*. The union of grace and nature was foundational to Fletcher's theology of history, for the Creator and Redeemer are one God. Thus, the present author argues that in Fletcher's thought grace infused all of nature and transforms fallen human nature in the period of history subsequent to the Fall.

The book questions implicitly the Wesleyan-holiness paradigm that has been used to interpret Fletcher's thought and concludes that the categories of that tradition are too narrow to conceptualize accurately the scope of Fletcher's soteriology and pneumatology in particular. In contrast to the normal Wesleyan-holiness distinction, made by many of Fletcher's interpreters, between the dispensation of the Son as the state of an evangelically regenerate believer and the dispensation of the Spirit as the state of an entirely sanctified believer, this book argues that the distinction between the two dispensations on the micro level is a difference between the "almost" and the "altogether" Christian or on the macro level is a difference between imperfect Christianity and perfect Christianity.

Acknowledgments

I WOULD LIKE TO express my sincere thanks to a number of people who have helped me with this project. First, I would like to thank my former supervisor, Rev. Dr. Herbert McGonigle who encouraged me tremendously in my studies. His enthusiasm spurred me to remain on task. I also appreciate the assistance of my current supervisor, Rev. Dr. David Rainey, who guided this project to completion.

Thanks to Donald Maciver, librarian of Nazarene Theological College of Manchester, for his very willing assistance and to Geordan Hammond, director of the Manchester Wesley Research Centre, for his encouragement and support. Thanks to the administrators and staff of NTC for their hospitality, encouragement, and guidance through the procedures.

A special thanks to Peter Nockles and Gareth Lloyd who provided invaluable information about the archives at Methodist Archives and Research Centre, John Rylands University Library of Manchester. They and their staff were very accommodating, despite my repeated requests for materials. Their assistance is deeply appreciated.

Thanks to the archivists, Clive Taylor and Russ Houghton, of the Arthur Skevington Wood Archive of Cliff College and to the administration for permission to consult the archives and to the staff for their wonderful hospitality.

Thanks to the archivists of the following repositories for their assistance and guidance during my visits: Archives d'Etat de Genève, Université de Genève; Université de Lausanne; Archives Cantonales Vaudoises of the Etat de Vaud; Cheshunt Foundation Archives, Westminster College; Wesley College, Bristol; Shropshire Archives, Shrewsbury; New Room, Bristol; Rare Book, Manuscript, and Special Collections Library, Duke University, Durham, North Carolina; The General Board of Discipleship of the United Methodist Church, The Upper Room Chapel and Museum, Nashville, Tennessee; the British Library, London; and Madeley Library.

Acknowledgments

Other archivists have answered questions, provided materials and/or tours of the facilities. Thanks is due to the following: Archives Communales de Nyon; Attingham Park, Shropshire; Wesley Chapel, London; Perkins Library, The Robert W. Woodruff Library of Advanced Studies, Special Collection Department, Emory University, Atlanta, Georgia; General Commission on Achieves and History of the United Methodist Church, Drew University, Madison, New Jersey; Wesley Center, Oxford, Westminster Institute of Education, Oxford Brooks University, Oxford; Staffordshire Record Office, Stafford; Lovely Lane Museum, Baltimore, Maryland; University of California, Santa Barbara, California; Countess of Huntingdon Connexion Archives, Rayleigh; National Library of Wales, Aberystwyth; The United Library, Garrett Evangelical Divinity School, Evanston, Illinois; Bridwell Library, Perkins School of Theology, Dallas, Texas; and Herefordshire Record Office.

Thanks to the members of the Wesley Historical Society and its various branches for valuable assistance and materials. Thanks to the Shropshire Magazine for answering questions and supplying materials.

Other friends have provided encouragement, insight and a listening ear. Peter S. Forsaith responded to my many questions and willingly provided valuable material and insights. A special thanks to him for his encouragement. Many others were willing to respond to my questions and/or to discuss theological or historical questions; among them are Rhonda Carrim, Kenneth Collins, Joanna Cruickshank, Stephen Flick, Martin Klauber, Victor P. Reasoner, Laurence W. Wood, and David R. Wilson. Thanks to all of my colleagues who have listened to me and provided feedback in discussions.

I owe a debt of special thanks to Bill and Elaine Graham who were excellent guides and hosts on a visit to Trevecka and other early Methodist sites. The visit was very informative and special to me. Thanks to the Revd Henry Morris who twice gave me a guided tour of the St. Michael's Church and provided some helpful information.

Thanks to the librarians of Lees Campus Library of the Hazard Community and Technical College for their interlibrary loan services and to the archivists and librarians of Asbury Theological Seminary for assistance with material.

I want to thank my professors Marvin E. Powers, H. Ray Dunning, Daniel Spross, William M. Greathouse among others who stimulated interest in further studies. Thanks to national leaders in Africa who helped me to learn French and encouraged me in the practical aspect of this book. Thanks to a number of missionary leaders who encouraged me initially in this project: John Seaman, John Cunningham, Don Messer, Don Gardner, and Eugénio Duarte. A special thanks to those individuals who prayed for me, including my accountability group, and for members of the local church where I now serve as pastor.

Thanks are due to my extended family who supported me and prayed for me. A particular debt of gratitude is owed to my immediate family to whom I dedicate this book. Thank you Carla, Rachelle and Seth for your support during the research and writing of this book. You have endured my absences and seclusion as I wrote. Thanks for understanding, supporting and loving me!

Above all, I want to thank God who has sustained me and given me grace. To God be the glory!

Abbreviations

ArmMag	*Arminian Magazine*
ATJ	*The Asbury Theological Journal; The Asbury Journal*
AH	Irenaeus. *Against Heresies.* Edited by Alexander Roberts and James Donaldson. In vol. 1 of *Ante-Nicene Fathers, The Apostolic Fathers with Justin Martyr and Irenaeus.* Peabody, MA: Hendrickson, 2004.
Benson-Life	Joseph Benson. *The Life of the Rev. John W. de la Fléchère compiled from the Narrative of Rev. Mr. Wesley; the Biographical Notes of Rev. Mr. Gilpin; from His Own Letters, and Other Authentic Documents, Many of Which Were Never Before Published.* 11th ed. London: Mason, 1835.
BiCentWJW	John Wesley. *The Bicentennial Edition of the Works of John Wesley.* Edited by Frank Baker and Richard P. Heitzenrater. 35 vols. projected. Nashville: Abingdon, 1984–.
Bruxelles-Sermons	John Fletcher. *Sermons.* 2nd ed. Brusells: 1836; Paris, 1853.
CH	Countess of Huntingdon
Christian-Letters	John Fletcher. *Christian Letters.* London: Hawes, 1779.
Cook-Letters	John William Fletcher. *Letters of John Fletcher.* Edited by Edward Cook. Stoke-on-Trent: Christian, 1999.
Cox-Life	Robert Cox. *The Life of the Rev. John William Fletcher, Vicar of Madeley, first American edition.* Philadelphia: George & Byington, 1836.
CW	Charles Wesley
DAP	Irenaeus, *Demonstration of Apostolic Preaching*
Fletcher-Baptism	John William Fletcher. Baptism of John and Christ. The Fletcher-Tooth Collection, The John Rylands University Library, The University of Manchester, MCA: MAM Fl. 21.11.

Abbreviations

Fletcher-Covenant	John William Fletcher. Salvation by the Covenant of Grace. 18 April 1762. The Fletcher-Tooth Collection, The John Rylands University Library, The University of Manchester, 20.3.
Fletcher-Creed	John William Fletcher. *The Fictitious and the Genuine Creed: Being "A Creed for Arminians," Composed by Richard Hill, Esq; to Which is Opposed A Creed for Those Who Believe that Christ Tasted Death for Every Man. By the Author of the Checks to Antinomianism*. 2nd ed. London: Hawes, 1775.
Fletcher-Darby	John William Fletcher. An Answer to the Objections and Queries of Mrs. Darby in her Dispute with me John Fletcher Vicar of Madeley On Thursday the 22d Nov.br 1764. To which are added some Remarks upon what she calls a faithful Declaration of that Dispute, by Way of Appendix. The Fletcher-Tooth Collection, The John Rylands University Library, The University of Manchester, 31 (Item E).
Fletcher-Discours	John William Fletcher. *Discours Sur la Régénération*. London: 1759.
Fletcher-Dispensations	John William Fletcher. Essay on the Doctrine of Dispensations. The Fletcher-Tooth Collection, The John Rylands University Library, The University of Manchester, 18.12.
Fletcher-EC1	John William Fletcher. *The First Part of An Equal Check to Pharisaism and Antinomianism*. Shrewsbury: Eddowes, 1774.
Fletcher-EC2	John William Fletcher. *Zelotes and Honestus Reconciled: or, An Equal Check to Pharisaism and Antinomianism Continued: Being the First Part of the Scripture Scales to Weigh the Gold of Gospel Truth - To Balance a Multitude of Opposite Scriptures - To Prove the Gospel Marriage of Free-Grace and Free-Will, and Restore Primitive Harmony of the Gospel of the Day. With a Preface, Containing Some Strictures upon the Three Letters of Richard Hill, Esq; Which Have Lately Been Published*. 2nd ed. London: Hawes.
Fletcher-Grâce	John William Fletcher. *La Grâce et la Nature, Poëme*. 2nd ed. London: Hindmarsh, 1785.
Fletcher-Loose	John William Fletcher. Loose Hints on the Spirit. The Fletcher-Tooth Collection, The John Rylands University Library, The University of Manchester, 17.1.
Fletcher-Last	John William Fletcher. *The Last Check to Antinomianism: A Polemical Essay on the Twin Doctrines of Christian Imperfection and a Death Purgatory*. London: Hawes, 1775.

Abbreviations

Fletcher-New	John William Fletcher. Essay on the New Birth. The Fletcher-Tooth Collection, The John Rylands University Library, The University of Manchester, 21.12.
Fletcher-Patriotism	John William Fletcher. *American Patriotism Farther Confronted with Reason, Scripture, and the Constitution: Being Observations on the Dangerous Politicks Taught by the Rev. Mr. Evans, M.A. and the Rev. Dr. Price with a Scriptural Plea for the Revolted Colonies*. Shrewsbury: Eddowes, 1776..
Fletcher-Portrait	John William Fletcher. *The Portrait of St. Paul: or, The True Model for Christians and Pastors. Translated from a French Manuscript of the Late Rev. John William de la Flechere, Vicar of Madeley, to which is Added, some Account of the Author, by the Rev. Joshua Gilpin, Vicar of Rockwardine, in the County of Salop*. 2 vols. Translated by Joshua Gilpin. Shrewsbury: Eddowes, 1790.
Fletcher-Third	John William Fletcher. *A Third Check to Antinomianism in a Letter to the Author of Pietas Oxoniensis by the Vindicator of the Rev. Mr. Wesley's Minutes*. The second edition. London: Hawes, 1775.
Fletcher-Tooth	The Fletcher-Tooth Collection
Fletcher-Vindication	John William Fletcher. *A Vindication of the Rev. Mr. Wesley's Last Minutes: Occasioned by a Circular, Printed Letter, Inviting Such Principal Persons, Both Clergy and Laity, as well as of the Dissenters of the Established Church, who Disapprove of Those Minutes, to Oppose Them in a Body, as a Dreadful Heresy: and Designed to Remove Prejudice, Check Rashness, Defend the Character of an Eminent Minister of Christ, Prevent Some Important Scriptural Truths from Being Hastily Branded as Heretical, and Stem the Torrent of Antinomianism in Five Letters to the Hon. and Rev. Author of The Circular Letter, by a Lover of Quietness and Liberty of Conscience*. 4th ed. London: Hawes, 1775.
FletcherBrian-Implications	W. Brian Fletcher. "Christian Perfection in Wesley and Fletcher with Implications for Today." PhD thesis, University of Edinburgh, 1997.
Flick-Pastoral	Stephen Allen Flick. "John William Fletcher, Vicar of Madeley: A Pastoral Theology." PhD diss., Drew University, 1994.
Fl-L1791	John William Fletcher. *Posthumous Pieces of the Late Rev. John William de la Flechere*. Madeley: Edmunds, 1791.
Fl-W1806	John William Fletcher. *The Works of the Reverend John Fletcher*. London: Edwards, 1806–1810.

Abbreviations

Fl-W1856	John William Fletcher. *The Works of the Rev. John Fletcher.* 9 vols. London: Wesleyan Conference Office, 1856–1860.
Fl-W1877	John William Fletcher. *The Works of the Reverend John William Fletcher, Late Vicar of Madeley.* 9 vols. London: Wesleyan Conference Office, 1877.
Fl-W1883	John William Fletcher. *The Works of the Rev. John Fletcher.* 4 vols. New York: Phillips & Hunt, 1883.
Genuine-Letters	John William Fletcher. *Some Genuine Letters of the Late Rev. Mr. Fletcher, Vicar of Madeley, Shropshire to Which is Added, His Heads of Self-Examination.* Dublin: Dugdale, 1788.
GW	George Whitfield
Horne	John William Fletcher. *Posthumous Pieces of the Late Rev. John Fletcher: Containing His Pastoral and Familiar Epistles, Together with Six Letters on the Manifestation of Christ.* Edited by Melvill Horne. London: Mason, 1833.
IC	Jacob Vernet. *Instruction chrétienne, divisée en cinq volumes; seconde édition, retouchée par l'auteur & augmentée de quelques pièces.* 5 vols. Geneva: 1756.
JCW	Charles Wesley. *The Journal of Charles Wesley.* 2 vols., London: Mason, 1849; Kansas City: Beacon Hill, 1980.
JB	Joseph Benson
JF	John Fletcher
JI	James Ireland
JJW	Nehemiah Curnock, editor. *The Journal of Rev. John Wesley.* 8 vols. London: Epworth, 1909–1916.
JRULM	The John Rylands University Library, The University of Manchester
JW	John Wesley
LJW	John Wesley. *The Letters of the Rev. John Wesley.* Edited by John Telford. 8 vols. London: Epworth, 1931.
Macdonald-Life	Frederic W. Macdonald. *Fletcher of Madeley.* Men Worth Remembering. London: Hodder & Stoughton, 1885.
Macdonald-Memoirs	James Macdonald. *Memoirs of the Rev. Joseph Benson.* New York: Methodist Episcopal Church, 1823.
MBF	Mary Bosanquet Fletcher
MethMag	*Methodist Magazine*
Moore-Life	Henry Moore. *The Life of Mrs. Mary Fletcher: Consort and Relict of the Rev. John Fletcher, Vicar of Madeley, Salop.* New York: Lane & Scott, 1848; Schmul, 1997.

Abbreviations

NT	New Testament
OT	Old Testament
PWHS	*Proceedings of the Wesley Historical Society*
Seymour-Countess	Aaron C. Hobart Seymour. *The Life and Times of Selina, Countess of Huntingdon.* Vol. 2/1–2. London: Painter, 1840; Elibron Classics, 2003.
Seymour-Letters	Aaron C. Hobart Seymour, editor. Letters from the Rev. John Fletcher, Vicar of Madeley Shropshire to the Right Honorable the Countess of Huntingdon with Copious Notes, Biographical and Explanatory. The Fletcher-Tooth Collection, The John Rylands University Library, The University of Manchester.
Six-Letters	John Fletcher. *Six letters of the late Rev. John Fletcher.* Bath: Hazard, 1788.
WesMethMag	*Wesleyan-Methodist Magazine*
WJW	John Wesley. *The Works of John Wesley, Complete and Unabridged.* Vol. 14. London: Wesleyan Methodist Book Room, 1872; Baker, 1991.
WTJ	*Wesleyan Theological Journal*

Introduction

A BRIEF INTRODUCTION TO FLETCHER'S LIFE

Jean Guillaume de la Fléchère was born in Nyon, Switzerland, on 12 September 1729.[1] After having studied for the ministry at the Collège and in the Faculty of Arts at the Académie de Genève, he migrated to England at approximately the age of twenty where he anglicized his name to John William Fletcher.[2] In England, he came under the influence of the Methodist movement and experienced an evangelical conversion. In 1757, he was ordained in the Church of England and became, in 1760, the vicar of Madeley where he culminated twenty-five years of ministry upon his death at the age of fifty-five.

Close relationships developed between John and Charles Wesley and John Fletcher. When controversy arose in 1770 between the Calvinist and Arminian branches of the Methodist movement over the minutes of the annual Methodist conference, Fletcher rose to defend his friend, John Wesley, from the barrage of Calvinistic writings with his *Checks to Antinomianism*. Because of his theological and polemical contributions, he has been called the "theologian of early Methodism" and is credited with systematizing its

---

1. Streiff insists that this is only an approximate date (Streiff, *Reluctant Saint?*, 3). Fletcher wrote to MBF: "The twelvth of this month will be a memorable day for me: Then began to breathe my better self and/or thy worst self, if I remember right I was baptized the 20 or there about: if 8 days old, we might have begun to breath about the same day of the same month. What if we should be baptiz'd and born of the Spirit together." (JF→MBF, 10 Sept. 1781). According to the church registry, Fletcher was baptized on 19 September 1729 by Isaac François Monod, the minister of the church at Nyon (Noms des Enfans Eb 91/4, 1).

2. Forsaith has suggested an earlier date than other biographers based upon evidence in JF→CW, 2 Aug. [1772] in which Fletcher made reference to the "Bottle Cungerer," a celebrated practical hoax that occurred in January 1749 (Forsaith, *Unexampled Labours*, 300).

theology.³ Luke Tyerman summarized his contribution saying, "He did for Wesley's theology what no other man than himself at that period could have done. John Wesley traveled, formed societies, and governed them. Charles Wesley composed unequaled hymns for the Methodists to sing; and John Fletcher, a native of Calvinian Switzerland, explained, elaborated, and defended the doctrines they heartily believed."⁴

On 15 January 1773,⁵ Wesley asked Fletcher to succeed him as the leader of Methodism; however, Fletcher died on 14 August 1785 after less than four years of marriage to the former Miss Mary Bosanquet, preceding Wesley's death. Fletcher's piety was renowned throughout the Methodist movement of his day, and he was recognized as one of the preeminent models of Christian perfection within Methodism.

SURVEY OF THE SECONDARY LITERATURE

Developments in Theology⁶

Given Fletcher's seminal contribution to early Methodist doctrine, relatively little has been written about his theology. He is often seen as simply the shadow of Wesley; few theologians have studied Fletcher as a competent theologian on his own terms. Much of what has been written about Fletcher in recent years has addressed a supposed shift between his theology and that of his mentor, John Wesley. Writers have posited that Fletcher modified Wesley's theology at several points, and some insist that even Wesley himself was induced by Fletcher's reasoning into making some adaptations. One of the suggested modifications is a greater emphasis on pneumatology in Fletcher's thought.

Due, in part, to the rise of the Pentecostal and charismatic movements, pneumatology has received significant attention in recent decades. The number of articles in the *Wesleyan Theological Journal* demonstrates this attention and has illustrated a demarcation on the doctrine of the baptism of the Holy Spirit as Wesleyan-holiness theologians have attempted to distinguish their movement from the bourgeoning Pentecostal movement. The positions may be classified in three broad categories: (1) baptism with

---

3. T. Smith, "How John Fletcher Became the Theologian," 69.
4. Tyerman, *Wesley's Designated Successor*, 346.
5. J. Wesley, *Letters of the Rev*, 6:10–12.
6. Some writers hold that Fletcher was an empiricist: Shipley, "Methodist Arminianism in the Theology of John," 147; Knickerbocker, "Doctrine of Authority in the Theology of John," 248; J. Knight, "John William Fletcher and the Early Methodist," 208.

the Spirit has been associated with conversion;[7] (2) it has been linked with entire sanctification;[8] (3) and it is viewed as an ambiguous term.[9]

While much of this mêlée has been fought on biblical and theological grounds, efforts have been made to find the historical origins of the connection between the baptism with the Spirit and a Wesleyan understanding of entire sanctification.[10] In the search for the "theological roots of Pentecostalism," Fletcher has been frequently identified as the theologian who elevated pneumatology and linked or equated the doctrine of entire sanctification with Spirit-baptism. Under the influence of Donald Dayton's work, *Theological Roots of Pentecostalism*, the theory that Fletcher was the source for Wesleyan-holiness theology of the nineteenth century that gave rise to the Pentecostal and charismatic theologies of the twentieth century became widely accepted.[11]

Another related concern is whether or not John Wesley approved or acquiesced to Fletcher's theological emphasis and the perceived link in Fletcher's thought between the doctrines of entire sanctification and baptism with the Spirit. On this issue, theologians have been rather divided as the table below demonstrates:

Table on the Various Positions of Modern Theologians on Wesley and Fletcher's Position(s)

	Wesley's Concession	**Wesley's Toleration**	**Substantial Agreement**
Position Described	Early Wesley held to a Christological dominant thought pattern but later Wesley, under the influence of Fletcher adopted an equation between baptism with the Spirit and Christian perfection.	Wesley permitted Fletcher's position in Methodism but did not adopt himself an equation of the baptism with the Spirit and Christian perfection.	Neither Wesley nor Fletcher held to an unequivocal equation between baptism with the Spirit and Christian perfection.
Adherents	Wood,[1] Neff,[2] Smith[3]	Dayton,[4] Maddox,[5] Knight,[6] Fraser,[7] Staples[8]	Reasoner[9] Fletcher[10]

---

7. Lyon, "Baptism and Spirit Baptism in the New Testament," 14–44; Reasoner, "The American Holiness Movement's Paradigm Shift," 132–46.

8. Grider, "Spirit-Baptism the Means of Sanctification," 31–50; Agnew, "Baptized with the Spirit," 7–14.

9. Deasley, "Entire Sanctification," 27–44.

10. McGonigle, "Pneumatological Nomenclature in Early Methodism," 61–72.

11. Dayton, *Theological Roots of Pentecostalism*, 35–60.

1. L. Wood, "Thoughts Upon the Wesleyan Doctrine of Entire," 88–99; L. Wood, "Third Wave of the Spirit and the." 110–40; L. Wood, "John Fletcher and the Rediscovery of Pentecost in." 7–34; L. Wood, "Pentecostal Sanctification in Wesley and Early"; L. Wood, "Pentecostal Sanctification in Wesley and Early Methodism"; L. Wood, *The Meaning of Pentecost in Early Methodism*; L. Wood, "John Fletcher's Influence on John Wesley"; L. Wood, "Pentecost and the Wesleyan Doctrine of Full"; L. Wood, "John Fletcher of Madeley'"; L. Wood, "The Biblical Sources of John Fletcher's"; L. Wood, "John Fletcher Revisited"; L. Wood, "John Fletcher as the Theologian of American."
2. Neff, *John Wesley and John Fletcher on Entire*.
3. T. Smith, "How John Fletcher Became the Theologian," 68–87.
4. Dayton, *Theological Roots of Pentecostalism*; Dayton, "Wesleyan Tug-of-War on Pentecostal Link." 43; Dayton, "Rejoinder to Larry Wood"; Dayton, "A Final Round with Larry Wood."
5. Maddox.,"Wesley's Understanding of Christian Perfection."
6. J. Knight, "John William Fletcher and the Early Methodist."
7. Fraser, "Strains in the Understanding of Christian."
8. Staples, "The Current Wesleyan Debate on the Baptism of the." Not all of the theologians in the "Wesley's toleration" position hold that Fletcher held "a simple one-to-one equation between entire sanctification and the baptism with the Holy Spirit." This category includes those who believe that "baptism with the Spirit" was an ambiguous term in Fletcher's thought that could apply to more than one experience of grace. Staples is an example of this position (Staples, "The Current Wesleyan Debate on the Baptism of the," 19–20). According to Staples, Fletcher associated the baptism with the Holy Spirit and the experience of entire sanctification but he did not equate them (ibid., 29–30).
9. Reasoner, "The American Holiness Movement's Paradigm Shift."
10. W. B. Fletcher, "Christian Perfection in Wesley and Fletcher with," 263.

Some hold that while Wesley permitted Fletcher's viewpoint within the ranks of his branch of Methodism, Wesley never acquiesced to Fletcher's position or adopted a link or equation between the two doctrines. Others argue that Fletcher influenced Wesley to concede an equation of the two doctrines and that it became the widely accepted position within Methodism and the holiness movement. Few theologians have argued that neither Wesley nor Fletcher maintained a link between the two above mentioned doctrines.

Further, Knight notes a shift under Fletcher's influence from a theocentric to an anthropocentric emphasis as Fletcher developed the doctrine of free will as a corollary of Wesley's doctrine of free grace. While Fraser agrees with Knight,[12] he insists that Wesley was not influenced on the association of Spirit-baptism and Christian perfection, pointing to a John Wesley manuscript supposedly written to criticize the use of Pentecostal language in an unpublished treatise of Joseph Benson's entitled *The Baptism of the Holy Spirit*.[13] The differences of opinions on Wesley and Fletcher

12. See Fraser, "Strains in the Understanding of Christian," chapter 7.
13. Ibid., 490–91.

emphasize the need for a re-evaluation of the theology of John Fletcher whose supposed doctrinal innovations are the subject of such controversy.

Shipley contrasted Fletcher's Methodist Arminianism with Dutch Arminianism and to some extent the major theological traditions of Western Christianity. Fletcher's Arminianism was analogous to the classical Protestant tradition including certain characteristics of the Roman Catholic position with the Protestant pattern remaining dominant.[14] Fletcher's theology is dialectical, according to Shipley; his position has been endorsed in successive evaluations of Fletcher's theology. Wiggins, who places Fletcher's writings within their historical context studying his works in chronological order,[15] concludes that Fletcher held in dialectical tension the doctrines of "grace and justice." Kinghorn argues that Fletcher failed to dissolve the dialectical tension between faith and works and held equally to their validity.[16] Davies argues that Fletcher's doctrine of election held in dialectical tension the human will and divine sovereignty and that furthermore, the dialectical, hermeneutical method of Fletcher led him to make some original contributions[17] in balancing seemingly contrary texts of scripture to show them to be complementary.[18] Fletcher's efforts as a mediator between the Calvinistic and Arminian Methodists caused him to arrive at a mediating position and to make his most significant contribution to theology.[19]

Phillip Streiff wrote a theological biography of his compatriot that has been recognized as a standard work.[20] He places Fletcher's theology within its historical context and demonstrates the influence of continental theology upon Fletcher's thought. According to Streiff,[21] Fletcher held to two covenants (contra Dayton), as did the Reformers and John Wesley: a covenant of works and a covenant of grace; Fletcher divided the latter into three dispensations: the dispensations of the Father, Son and Spirit.[22]

---

14. Shipley, "Methodist Arminianism in the Theology of John," 195–202, 364–67, 389–90, 406.
15. Wiggins, "Pattern of John Fletcher's Theology," v–vi.
16. Kinghorn, "Faith and Works," 169.
17. *Contra* Lockhart, "Evangelical Revival as Reflected in the Life."
18. Davies, "John Fletcher of Madeley as Theologian," 11.
19. Ibid.
20. Streiff, *Jean Guillaum de la Fléchère John William*.
21. Ibid., 203.
22. Ibid.

Developments in Practical Theology

Two writers have made contributions to Fletcher's pastoral/practical theology. George Lawton has evaluated Fletcher's roles in ministry and has given particular attention to his literary style. Flick provides "insight into the pastoral thought and life of John William Fletcher while vicar of Madeley parish."[23] Fletcher's understanding of ministry is analyzed according to three functions: prophetic, priestly and kingly functions.

Developments in Historical or Bibliographical Studies

Whereas the secondary literature on Fletcher's thought is very limited, biographies of Fletcher abound; however, many biographies border on hagiography or merely repeat material found in the standard biographies. Luke Tyerman and Joseph Benson, a personal friend of Fletcher's, who was assisted by Mary Fletcher, have provided for many years standard biographies for Fletcher's life and reflect an obvious loyalty to institutional Methodism. They accessed many original materials, but often truncated Fletcher's letters. Robert Cox, an Anglican minister, wrote his biography from the perspective of the established church.

The focus of Peter Forsaith's thesis is not theological, but historical.[24] The author has transcribed letters that were previously unpublished or largely inaccessible.[25]

David Robert Wilson's thesis takes the form of church history localized on Madeley studying the parish ministry and Methodism with special attention given to the ministry of John Fletcher. Wilson holds that the religious societies that Fletcher formed were an extension of his parish ministry; thus, Fletcher's brand of Methodism differed from that of John Wesley's. His principal argument is that "Fletcher's ministry at Madeley was representative of a variation of a pro-Anglican Methodism—localized, centered upon the parish church, and rooted in the Doctrines and Liturgy of the Church of England."[26]

---

23. Flick, "John William Fletcher," 10.

24. Forsaith, "Correspondence of the Revd," xiv; cf. Forsaith, *Unexampled Labours*.

25. The present writer has reviewed Forsaith's book in Frazier, Review of *Unexampled Labours*.

26. Wilson, "Church and Chapel," 7.

Introduction

SURVEY OF PRIMARY LITERATURE

Fletcher's theological treatises will be given primary consideration in this work.[27] However, the collected works are incomplete, and many manuscripts remain unpublished; these unpublished holographs will be considered in this work.[28] Under the anvil of the Calvinist controversy, Fletcher developed his doctrine of dispensations, which was nascent at least in c. 1767 when he wrote *Six Letters on the Spiritual Manifestation of the Son of God*, a posthumously published work. Another significant work, *The Portrait of Saint Paul or the True Model for Christians and Pastors* (1779), was written in French while he convalesced in Switzerland and was later translated into English. It discusses not only his doctrine of dispensations but also its connection to his doctrine of ministry.[29] His letters and his sermons will be useful in determining his understanding and application of the doctrine of dispensations.

THE SIGNIFICANCE AND PURPOSE OF THIS BOOK

Although John Wesley endorsed Fletcher's doctrine of dispensations, his teaching on dispensations has not been taken seriously by Wesley's followers. The debate over the link between Spirit-baptism and the doctrine of Christian perfection arose in part because Fletcher's pneumatology has not been studied adequately within its dispensational structure. None of the writers who have considered Fletcher's theology have given sustained analysis of his doctrine of dispensations, though widely recognized as central to Fletcher's thought. While some have discussed it, the treatments tend to be cursory or concise, falling short of a thoroughgoing analysis of the doctrine.[30]

---

27. For a full list of Fletcher's published works, see "Appendix 1: Fletcher's Published Works" in Frazier, "Doctrine of Dispensations in the Thought of John William Fletcher (1729–1785)," 289ff. The transcriptions published in the *Asbury Theological Journal* are not completely reliable and reflect the unsorted state of the archival material (*ATJ* 49/1 [Spring 1994]).

28. The thesis upon which the present work is based contains a rather lengthy transcription of one of Fletcher's holograph essays that was entitled by the present author "Essay on the Doctrine of Dispensations" (cf. Appendix 6, Frazier, "Doctrine of Dispensations in the Thought of John William Fletcher (1729–1785)," 424ff.

29. Fletcher-Portrait.

30. The following writers have given some treatment: Flick, "John William Fletcher," 152–62; Fuhrman, "Contribution of John Fletcher to," 190, 354–59; O'Brien, "Trinitarian Revisioning of the Wesleyan," 32–36; Streiff, *Reluctant Saint*, 192ff.; Wiggins, "Pattern of John Fletcher's Theology," 226–68; L. Wood, *Meaning of Pentecost in Early Methodism*, 113ff.; Wilson, "Church and Chapel," 285–96.

7

TRUE CHRISTIANITY

This book will analyze John Fletcher's doctrine of dispensations and its structure of the divine/human experience, noting how it might inform a minister's response to persons at various stages of their spiritual development. The current work is both historical and descriptive: it describes the doctrine of dispensations, but it moves beyond a mere restatement in order to analyze the historical context in which the dispensations arose. It will endeavor to avoid the two extremes of a mere recitation of the facts on one hand and the error of not taking history seriously enough on the other hand. It will attempt to interpret correctly the subject of study and as such will be principally an inductive task. The present work will not be merely a discourse in historical theology, which is the primary task, as valuable as that may be, but it will also provide some suggestions for a Wesleyan theology of ministry.

The subject will unfold in the following manner. Chapter 1 explores the influences upon Fletcher's doctrine of dispensations, including the continental and British contexts. Chapter 2 investigates the key doctrine of divine grace and nature that serve as a theological foundation for the doctrine of dispensations. Chapter 3 discusses the relationship between the doctrine of dispensations and the doctrine of divine revelation. Chapters 4, 5, and 6 will explore in greater detail each of the dispensations in the trinitarian schema of the doctrine. The conclusion surveys Fletcher's own application of the doctrine to the hearers of his sermons. It attempts to provide some practical insights to the ways a Wesleyan minister can intelligently, sensitively and more effectively minister to persons using the dispensations.

1

The Milieu of Fletcher's Theology

WHILE IT IS NOT the specific goal of this study to reconstruct the sources of the doctrine of dispensations in Fletcher's thought (if such a task would even be possible), it will be helpful to outline the historical milieu of the era preceding his emergence as a theological thinker and writer, and to suggest certain constitutional elements of his thought. At one point, Fletcher does make an explicit reference to certain writers and theologians who serve as sources for his doctrine of dispensations;[1] he, of course, assumes that the doctrine of dispensations is intrinsic within Scripture.

The majority of Fletcher's biographers erroneously trace the formative influence upon Fletcher's life and thought primarily to the Methodists.[2] While Methodists certainly had a formative effect upon the young émigré from Switzerland, they were not the only source of influence upon his life and thought. As will become evident, Fletcher was nurtured within an environment that fostered personal piety[3] and trained in an environment that was conversant with Enlightenment thought and with continental theology;[4] it was the "experimental religion" and the "living faith" of Meth-

1. Fl-W1856 1.588. Here Fletcher endeavors to defend his formulation of the doctrine of dispensations against accusations of novelty. These writers will be discussed later in this chapter.

2. R. Ferguson, "Early Methodist Piety and Polemics," 17.

3. The pietistic and mystical elements of Fletcher's thought and spirituality may be found in the Huguenot community, which Théodore Crinsoz de Bionnes, Fletcher's uncle, gathered around himself and whose leaders frequently visited him in Nyon.

4. Streiff, *Jean Guillaum de la Fléchère John William*; RS; Forsaith, "Correspondence

odism melded with the via media theology of the Church of England that formed the mature Fletcher.

THE EARLY CHURCH FATHERS

In order to understand Fletcher's doctrine of dispensations, one must grasp a seminal truth about the nature of the Christian faith: Christianity is radically historical in its very essence. Central to the Christian faith is a belief in the historicity of the Christ event. Any teaching that seemed to undermine the historical nature of the faith was contested with utmost vigor. The history of the Christian thought reveals this struggle.

One of the first heresies that presented a challenge to the Christian faith was Gnosticism, which the early church fathers believed undermined the historical nature of the Christian faith. They defended vigorously the Christian faith against the Gnostic onslaught and upheld not only the essential oneness of God but the unity of Old and New Testaments against the bifurcation of the two; they posited a covenant scheme that stressed the essential unity of salvation history and explained a Christian view on the relationship between Judaism and Christianity. When the issues of the relationship between Judaism and Christianity were no longer in the forefront, the language of covenant theology became less predominant.[5] Catholicism made no direct, significant contributions to the covenant idea in the ensuing years; however, when the rise of Protestantism "brought the question of the distinctive nature of Christianity again into the foreground,"[6] the covenant idea regained prominence.[7]

The Creeds

Fletcher's writings reveal a familiarity with the Early Church Fathers. He quoted extensively from them in *Equal Check* to defend "that the doctrines of free grace and free will . . . are the very doctrines of the primitive Church, and of the Church of England."[8] In considering the objection that the doctrine of dispensation may be too complex for plain Christians, Fletcher

---

of the Revd"; Forsaith, "'Dearer Country' the Frenchness of the Rev."

5. Brown, "Covenant Theology," 4:219.

6. Ibid.

7. It is for this reason that this chapter passes over a lengthy period in the history of the Church.

8. FL-W1883 2:199 ff.

underscored that the earliest and "simplest" creed, *The Apostles Creed*, and *The Nicene Creed* distinguish "three degrees of faith," i.e., (1) faith in the Father; (2) faith in the Messiah; (3) and faith in the Holy Spirit.[9] One of his contentions over the *Athanasian Creed* is that while the creed mentions the Christian dispensation, it neither addresses nor validates "the faith of the inferior dispensations" but only denounces any faith that is not catholic and damns all persons who do not hold to the faith of the higher dispensation. Clearly, Fletcher sees a logical connection between the economic Trinity and a three tiered progression in the lives of believers.

Irenaeus

Irenaeus of Lyons was "among the first Christian writers to seek the theological meaning of history."[10] In his response to the Gnostics, he expounded a fully developed view of history and employed the term "economy of salvation" by which he meant "'the way in which God has ordered the salvation of humanity in history.'"[11] Irenaeus emphasized the progression of the biblical story; recounting the history of God's salvific activity, he began with creation and unfolded chronologically God's redemptive purposes for humanity. His doctrine of the recapitulation of all humanity points to Jesus as the climax of history. The covenant idea plays a prominent role in Irenaeus' theology. Everett Ferguson has suggested that "Irenaeus was a covenant theologian."[12] While Irenaeus' covenant theology[13] is implicit in *DAP*, it is explicit in *AH*.[14] *Adversus Haereses* is Irenaeus' response to the Gnostic, Marcionite heresy of his day and to the form of Gnosticism purported by Ptolemaeus, a disciple of Valentinus. Irenaeus employed the covenant idea to underscore the unity and continuity of the Old and New Testaments and divine revelation.

Irenaeus' calculation of the number of covenants varies. "Sometimes he reckons four (Noah, [Abraham], Moses, Christ; more often only two."[15] When he makes reference to two covenants, he means the old and new covenants in which he recognizes an essential unity. Differences between the covenants are due to God's accommodation to humanity's weakness.

---

9. FL-W1883 1:590–2.

10. Gonzalez, *History of Christian Theology*, 174.

11. McGrath, *Christian Theology*, 323.

12. E. Ferguson, "Covenant Idea in the Second Century" 144.

13. Here the term "covenant theology" should not be understood with the same connotations as when it is applied to the Puritans.

14. Duncan, "Irenaeus of Lyon: A True Radical Orthodox."

15. W. A. Brown, cited in ibid. See *AH*, 4.11.8.

Irenaeus highlights the accommodations that God has made: "[T]he Lord remains the same, and the same Father is revealed; thus, therefore, as the one and the same Lord granted, by means of His advent, a greater gift of grace to those of a later period than what He had granted to those under the Old Testament dispensation."[16] The covenants progress from a lesser to a greater degree but maintain their continuity by sharing in "the same substance" and possessing "properties in common, but merely differ in number and size."[17] The idea of progressive revelation is essential to Irenaeus' argument for the unity of the two Testaments.

Augustine

In *The Enchiridion: or On Faith, Hope and Love*, Saint Augustine develops an *ordo salutis* and finds a link with them to "the four corresponding stages of the church's history."[18] The four stages of the human beings are classified as those before the law, those under the law, those under grace and those who have full and perfect peace. The history of the church is compared to these four stages. "[T]he history of God's people [has] been ordered according to his pleasure who disposeth all things in number, and measure, and weight. For the church existed at first before the law; then under the law, which was given by Moses; then under grace, which was first made manifest in the coming of the Mediator."[19]

THE INFLUENCE OF CONTINENTAL THEOLOGIANS

Calvin's Thought

One may be surprised to find a discussion of the influence of Calvin upon the thought of Fletcher who has been called "The Arminian of the Arminians."[20] Fletcher's birth in Switzerland and passing his formative years on the continent ensured exposure to Calvinistic theology. He, in fact, attended the Collège and Académie de Genève for about seven years.[21] How could Fletcher have exited what was once the stronghold of Calvinism with

---

16. *AH*, 4.11.3.
17. *AH*, 4.9.2.
18. Augustine, *Enchiridion*, 275.
19. Ibid.
20. D. S. Schaff, "Fletcher," 332.
21. JF→[Claude Bosanquet], [22 September 1781].

an Arminian flavor to his theology?[22] To what degree was Fletcher's thought influenced by John Calvin's thought?

Lord Eustace Percy insisted that the *Institutes* articulate "'something much more explosive than the dogma of predestination; [they] contained a philosophy of history, a statement of Christian faith in terms of divine purpose.'"[23] Calvin's philosophy of history comes to expression within his theology of the covenants. While other Reformers held to a distinction between the Law and the Gospels, Calvin espoused a positive view of the Law and emphasized the unity of the two Testaments. Although he distinguished between them, he differentiated between "their chronological position in the plan of salvation, rather than by their content."[24] Calvin stated: "The covenant made with all the patriarchs is so much like ours in substance and reality that the two are actually one and the same. Yet they differ in the mode of dispensation."[25]

Amyraut

Moïse Amyraut, a professor of theology at Saumur (1626–1664), was one of the most influential theologians in the era following Calvin.[26] He and his colleagues had a significant influence upon continental theology in the second half of the seventeenth century. Amyraut tolerated French humanism and endeavored to temper the rigid, Calvinist doctrine of predestination by positing the doctrine of hypothetical universal atonement and to harmonize reason and revelation. His theological system can be traced to John Cameron (1579–1623), a Scottish theologian, who was professor of theology at Saumur from 1618–1622.[27]

Amyraut's system was heavily dependent upon John Calvin. Brian Armstrong points out that Salmurian theology served to correct orthodox

---

22. Some historians/theologians assume that Fletcher was a Calvinist upon his departure from Switzerland (R. Ferguson, "Early Methodist Piety and Polemic," 17; Lawton, *Shropshire Saint*), 73; Kinghorn, "Faith and Works," 31–3; Tyerman, *Wesley's Designated Successor*, 346; Forsaith, "'Dearer Country' the Frenchness of the Rev.," 524; Thompson, "John Fletcher," 239; D. Smith, *John Fletcher*, 8. However, evidence does not support the assumption that Fletcher absorbed Calvinist theology from his studies at Geneva as will be shown.

23. Percy, *John Knox*, 109.

24. Wendel, *Calvin*, 209.

25 Calvin, *Institutes of the Christian Religion*, 2.10.2.

26. Bourchenin, *Études sur les Académies Protestantes en France*, 463.

27. The influence that Shipley speaks of came more probably through Richard Baxter, a disciple of Cameron (Shipley, "Wesley and Some Calvinistic," 205).

Calvinism whose emphasis upon the pre-historical, secret decrees of God did not give adequate regard to history.[28] The Calvinist orthodox doctrine of the decrees of God is an *a priori* scheme whereas Amyraut's scheme is *a posteriori*. His is a three-fold *heilsgeschichtlich* scheme that focused on the way that God has acted in history, and this is the very point of departure of Salmurian theology from orthodoxy.[29] The three-fold scheme, diverging from the usual orthodox two-fold scheme, unfolds progressively in history.[30] The economic view of the Trinity unfolds as follows: the Father conceives the plan of redemption; the Son executes it, and the Spirit applies it. Key to Amyraut's economic Trinitarian thought is his doctrine of accommodation in which God accommodates revelation to the limited capacity of the human race. His theological system reinvigorated history with meaning whereas the prevailing theological system sapped history of its meaning. Although the National Synod gave a warning against Amyraut's theology, his theology eventually triumphed in Switzerland with the consensus of theologians, Jean Frédéric Ostervald, Samuel Werenfels, and Jean-Alphonse Turrettin. Attention will now be given to the protégé of the last of these theologians.

From "Rome Protestante" to "Petit Paris"[31]

Sixteenth-century Geneva was known as the bastion of Calvinism and was one of the most, if not the most, influential centers of Protestant theology. It became known as the "Protestant Rome" and as a result of its wide-ranging influence, Protestant theology has had ever since a distinctively Calvinistic flavor. Armstrong dates the turning point: "[A]fter the French translation of Calvin's *Institutio* (1541), French Protestantism had become broadly aligned with Calvinism."[32]

Scholars have chronicled the theological shifts following the demise of Calvin and his immediate successors that took place in the Académie during the seventeenth and eighteenth centuries as the prominent theologians of Geneva began to reassess their theological heritage under the barrage of Cartesian Enlightenment thought and divest itself of scholastic Protestantism.[33] The Académie de Saumur was particularly influential in the theologi-

---

28. Armstrong, *Calvin and the Amyraut Heresy*, 52–53.
29. Ibid., 144.
30. Ibid., 145.
31. Roney attributed this phrase to Hermann de Goltz (Roney, "Introduction," 9).
32. Armstrong, *Calvin and the Amyraut Heresy*, 21.
33. See Klauber and Roney, eds., *Identity of Geneva*.

cal and philosophical shifts within continental thought and had a significant impact upon the Académie de Genève.

Jacob Vernet

One of the most influential theologians of the Académie de Genève was Jacob Vernet (1698–1789) who held the professorial chair in Belles Lettres when Fletcher began his studies in 1746.[34] He was influential not only in the Académie de Genève but also in the religious and political life of the city. He was a pastor, professor of humanities, of history and of theology and rector of the academy; his longevity of more than fifty years in these positions gave an enduring quality to his legacy. David Sorkin states that Vernet "was such an influential figure that he was the representative Genevan theologian of his day."[35]

INSTRUCTION CHRÉTIENNE

The doctrine of accommodation was particularly important in Vernet's thought and will be summarized as it comes to expression in his *Instruction Chrétienne*. While Vernet had published other works, *Instruction* "was entirely Vernet's; was written at the height of his powers; and did not undergo any revisions after the second edition."[36]

The purpose of the work was to serve as a sophisticated version of a catechism for the young noblemen who would not be content with an ordinary catechism but that would not embark on a full-fledged course in theology.[37] The major theme is that Christianity in its purest forms is nothing more than natural religion in its most mature form. Christianity is natural religion brought to its maturity. The Genevan theologian mounted a polemic against the arguments of the French humanistic philosophers by beginning at the point of the Cartesian disciple's doubt and developed in a Cartesian manner propositions that depend upon one another resulting in a theological system that used epistemology as the starting point. His purpose was to harmonize the Christian faith with Enlightenment thought and to make it palatable to the rationalists' sensibilities.

---

34. Streiff, *Reluctant Saint?*, 12.
35. Sorkin, "Geneva's 'Enlightened Orthodoxy,'" 286.
36. Ibid., 291.
37. Vernet, *IC*, 1:3, 6.

Vernet endeavored to defend the Christian faith against the attacks of the *philosophes* by meeting them on their own ground. Theoretically, Vernet held reason and revelation in a harmonious, dialectical tension.[38] However, he seemed to operate from the Cartesian principle "if reason does not affirm a principle, it is best not to believe it at all."[39] Gargett has pointed out that dark clouds appeared over Vernet's doctrine of revelation because he changed "the title of book 1 to *De la grande utilité d'une Révélation* [*Of the great usefulness of a Revelation*], whereas it had originally read *De la néccesité de la Révélation* [*Of the necessity of Revelation*]."[40] Vernet was severely ostracized for making this change by both his friends and especially the *philosophes*. Vernet endeavored to maintain the necessity of the doctrine of special revelation, but allowed for the salvation of those who had no access to revelation. Vernet could not conceive of heathen being condemned "to hell for rejecting Christ when they had never heard of him."[41]

The unifying crux of his theological system is the doctrine of accommodation that signifies the condescension of God to humanity or God's adaptation to the limits of human finitude and capacity in order that humanity could receive revelation in a way that was suitable to the human condition. While enlightened orthodox theologians had rebuffed many orthodox doctrines, Vernet endorsed the orthodox doctrine of accommodation, making at least one modification.[42] Whereas Calvin held that knowledge of God was available to humanity but natural light was not salvific, Vernet believed that natural light (i.e., knowledge from conscience and general revelation) could lead to salvation when properly received.[43] Vernet preserved a doctrine of the heathen by insisting upon the doctrine of natural light, which flowed logically from his doctrine of accommodation.

Vernet's doctrine of accommodation was so crucial to his theological system that it influenced the structure of his presentation. His argument unfolds in a way that respects the historical development of the revelatory activity of God. This is evident in his "Book VII," which is entitled "De la Religion Judaïque (Of the Jewish Religion)." He begins this chapter with a discussion of natural light and insists that humans did not make good usage of this light. God then resorts to extraordinary means in order to restore

---

38. While Vernet maintained theoretically a dialectical tension, in the final analysis reason takes precedence over revelation in his thought.

39. Here the principle is applied to Vernet not to Tronchin (Klauber, "Reason," 327).

40. Gargett, *Jacob Vernet*, 64.

41. Klauber, *Between Reformed Scholasticism and*, 383.

42. Calvin posits a doctrine of accommodation in *Institutes of the Christian Religion*, 2.16.2; 3.18.9.

43. Ibid., 1.4.1.

them to the true religion. Vernet's argument, which began with natural theology, advances to the Jewish religion and then to the Christian faith; his treatment reveals his concern to unveil the plan of divine accommodation to human limitations throughout the history of God's revelation.

What is implicit in the flow of his argument is explicit in the content of the discussion. In describing religion, Vernet employs the French words "degrez" (or degrees) and "gradation" (or progression) to describe the improvement from one successive stage of God's revelatory activity to another.[44] The existential impetus for the progression is found within man's need of "a superior direction in order not to wander."[45] The theological impetus was God's love for humanity and God's desire to reveal the divine nature fully. "At last, God *wanting to perfect again the knowledge of heavenly truths* and to manifest His mercy not only toward the Jew but toward the Gentiles sent Jesus Christ in order to be the Great Teacher and Savior of the human race."[46] God in Christ condescended ushering in the economy of grace; such condescension does not however invalidate the law.[47]

In his discussion of the law of Moses, Vernet revealed his view of the OT. He queried: "Is it permissible to call it imperfect—a law which came from heaven?" Vernet replies that the term "perfection" is a relative term and insists upon the progressive character of revelation. "Nature offers us thus a thousand productions which develop by degrees and are not achieved all at once. It is the same with revelation; it has its growth and its periods. What it could have lacked in the earliest times is not properly speaking an imperfection; it is nothing but a lower perfection."[48] In this same chapter, Vernet used the image of light in order to convey his idea of the progressive character of revelation.[49] The law of Moses should be regarded as "the dawn which preceded the full day."[50] The law was given by God to a nation still in infancy as an "introduction or preparation for more elevated teaching or more refined worship."[51] Thus, the OT is preparatory for the NT. While Vernet made distinctions between the Old and New Testaments, he held in

---

44. IC, 1:136–38, 53; 2.12, 54.

45. IC, 1:252.

46. IC, 1:253 (emphasis added).

47. In chapter 5, "Fourth Point of the Christian Doctrine, An Economy of Grace in favor of repentant sinners," Vernet addressed the condescension of God to humanity (IC, 2:57).

48. IC, 1:283.

49. One of Fletcher's favorite images for his doctrine of dispensations is light (FL-W1883, 1:142).

50. IC, 1:283.

51. Ibid.

dialectic tension the unity and the diversity of the Testaments.[52] In fact, one of the proofs of the evidence of divine revelations in the Old and New Testaments is the unity of the two Testaments. "Only a superior Wisdom would prepare so well in advance in the OT what must be accomplished under the New and to add so well in the New what was necessary to fulfill the Old. Such an edifice built little by little on the same plan, indicates a unique Author of which the grand designs embrace the past, the present and the future."[53] Following in the train of John Cocceius' (1603–1669) adherents, Vernet spurned the scholastic method of amassing proof texts in support of doctrine.[54] He held to the organic unity of the Testaments, the New unveiling what was hidden in the Old.

Vernet applied the doctrine of accommodation to the Scriptures in order to render the differences between the Old and New Testaments reasonable and to prove that Christianity was an enlightened religion for the *philosophes*. Reason took precedence over revelation. Vernet had abandoned the Augustinian principle *credo ut intelligam*; Cartesian doubt ruled the day. Theoretically, Vernet held to a harmonious relationship between reason and revelation but practically he did not.

Observations on Vernet's Thought

Under the gun of the enlightenment, Jacob Vernet endeavored to defend the Christian faith against the barrage of Enlightenment thought typified by the French humanistic philosophers who were his contemporaries and to some degree solidified the ranks of Enlightened Orthodoxy that had been essentially instigated by his mentor, Jean-Alphonse Turretin.

As the theologian who held the chair that Calvin had held over a century before him, Jacob Vernet maintained only rudiments of the doctrines that the great Reformer had held; the most dominant doctrine of these was Calvin's doctrine of accommodation. The other "Calvinistic" doctrines had been abandoned in Geneva's race to plunder the Egyptians; this was most evident in Vernet's espousal of Arminianism or Amyrauldianism. As Falletti put it, "Turretin discretely opened the gates of Geneva to [Arminianism], Vernet conferred citizenship upon it."[55] In addition, Vernet embraced a form of moderation reminiscent of the latitudinarianism of Anglicanism.

52. IC, 1:92.
53. IC, 1:85.
54. McClintock and Strong, eds., *Cyclopedia of Biblical, Theological, and Ecclesiastical Literature*, s.v. "Crisp, Tobias," 395–397.
55. This is quoted by Sorkin, "Geneva's 'Enlightened Orthodoxy,'" 289.

The Milieu of Fletcher's Theology

At times in reading *Instruction Chrétienne*, one is given the impression that the Enlightenment has reached its pinnacle in the thought and the moral character of Vernet.

David Sorkin insists that Vernet opted for the middle way theologically, politically and philosophically. His theology provided an open door for dialogue with those under the spell of rationalistic humanism of the Enlightenment era and a platform for his discussions with the *philosophes*. He sought valiantly to unify the various expressions of the Protestant Church found in France, Holland and England. One cannot understand Vernet's theology without understanding that he sought peace and reconciliation whenever possible. His theological system reflects his conciliatory spirit.

Central to his concerns were the relationship between reason and revelation. He endeavored to achieve a harmonious relationship between reason and revelation by making the doctrine of accommodation the controlling norm for his theological system.

Fletcher's Assessment of Swiss Theology

According to Fletcher's own account in a letter written to Claude Bosanquet,[56] he stayed nearly seven years at Geneva: "I was ~~for 7 years~~ sent to Geneva to pursue my studies, ~~with a view to the ministry take holy orders,~~ but But after I had stayed there ₙₑₐᵣ 7 years ~~before I entered upon the study of divinity~~, a fear of being unfit for the ministry ~~not succeeding in that holy calling way of life~~ and the ~~promises of an uncle~~ inticing offers my father's brother who was a lieut. Colonel in the Duch service, made me ~~incline to~~ for a time prefer the sword to the gown. I left the ~~university~~ academy."[57] The *Livre du Rector* of the Académie de Genève, which often records the exact date of matriculation for the students, notes that Fletcher studies in "Belles-Lettres" and the years of his studies "1746–47."[58] As Streiff states, there is no further mention in the *Livre du Rector*, which means that Fletcher's remaining years of the seven year period of study must have been at the Collège.[59] From the above, it seems evident that Fletcher left the Académie during his studies of philology, which were preparatory for formal theological studies.

---

56. Tyerman supplies the first name of Mary Bosanquet's uncle (Tyerman, *Wesley's Designated Successor*, 488–90) and the year. The addressee of the original letter is unnamed; JF→[Claude Bosanquet], [22 September 1781].

57. JF→[Claude Bosanquet], [22 September 1781].

58. Stelling-Michaud, *Le Livre du Rector de l'Académie de Genève*, 244.

59. Streiff, *Reluctant Saint?*, 14–16.

In his 24 November 1756 letter to John Wesley, Fletcher stated his reasons for not seeking ordination in his native country; one of them is doctrinal: "I went through my studies, with a design of going into orders; but afterwards, upon serious reflection, feeling I was unequal to so great a burden, and *disgusted by the necessity I should be under to subscribe to the doctrine of Predestination*, I yielded to the desires of my friends, who would have me go into the army."[60] As is pointed out above, many who have studied Fletcher's life and thought have assumed that he would have been schooled in staunch Calvinism at the Académie de Genève. However, it should now be evident from the discussion above that this was not the case. Nor would he have been required *in Geneva* to subscribe to the *Helvic Consensus Formula* since it was abrogated there in 1706 under the influence of Jean-Alphonse Turrintin. However, it was not abrogated in the Pays de Vaud until some 52 years later! The differing situations require some explanation: while there was a strong contingent of ecclesiastical leaders in the Pays de Vaud who were opposed to the *Formula* (among them were Georges Polier and Théodore Crinsoz de Bionnes), the ecclesiastics in the cantonal capital, Berne, were more Calvinistic and wielded authority over the churches in the Pays de Vaud. The *Formula* was retained in the Pays de Vaud but with a restricted scope of authority as Henri Vuilleumier explains: "[T]he stated creed was not prescribed to any one as an article of faith in which one must believe, but it was simply a rule of teaching against which no one should write or speak, and that in the interest of order and peace in the Church and in the State."[61] Although in his native Pays de Vaud the creed had "déjà tombée dans l'oubli,"[62] Fletcher would have been required to subscribe to the *Oath of Association* (later in 1746 the more moderate *Oath of Religion*), which obliged adherence to the *Formula Consensus*—a concession his conscience would not allow.[63] Perhaps his awareness of his uncle's plight in this regard was a further deterrent. In the end, the *Formula Consensus* was abrogated on 1 June 1758.[64] By then, Fletcher's roots were already deep in English soil.

60. Fl-L1791, 71; emphasis added.

61. "[L]e dit formulaire n'était prescrit à personne comme un article de foi qu'on serait tenu de croire, mais simplement comme une règle d'enseignement contre laquelle nul ne devait parler ni écrire, et cela dans l'intérêt de l'ordre et de la paix dans l'Eglise et dans l'Etat" (Vuilleumier, "Quand et Comment la Formule Consensus a-t-elle été," 472).

62. Ibid., 473.

63. Davies holds that Fletcher would have sensed a moral obligation to accept the doctrine of predestination in Geneva, which, although abrogated, was still regarded as a norm of teaching (Davies, "John Fletcher of Madeley," 7).

64. Vuilleumier, "Quand et Comment la Formule Consensus a-t-elle," 477.

The Milieu of Fletcher's Theology

In a letter to John Wesley, Fletcher mentioned another Calvinistic creed that remained intact in his Pays de Vaud. Following a reference to a young clergyman, who opened his home to Fletcher's ministry and who wanted to go to England, he adds, "He can have no Living in his own country, because he will not *swear to prosecute all who propagate Arminian Tenets*; which is more honest than the Clergy, many of whom are Arians, Socinians, or Diests, and do not scruple to take the Calvinian Oaths!"[65] Since the *Formula Consensus* had been abrogated, Fletcher may be referring to the *Confessio Helvetica Posterior* (1566 AD), which remained in force in the Pays de Vaud until 1839.[66] The creed remained in effect due to political will rather than ecclesiastical choice and did not serve as a true expression of the faith of the entire church in the Pays de Vaud. The *Second Helvetic Confession* held to a mild Calvinistic position, which maintained adherence to the predestination of the elect to salvation.[67] Fletcher was familiar with this creed, which is evidenced by the fact that he quoted it in the *Portrait of St. Paul*, which was written on Swiss soil; thus, this may have been the creed to which he made reference in the letter cited above.[68]

Presumably, Fletcher maintained an aversion to the theology of Geneva all of his life; Geneva was constantly the brunt of Fletcher's irony; as George Lawson points out, Fletcher constantly underlined the incongruities of Geneva's Calvinism by using "Logica-Genevensis," "Geneva-colossus," "Geneva-medusa," and "Geneva-purgatory."[69] It should be pointed out, however, that the brunt of Fletcher's ironic pen was not the eighteenth century Geneva but the Geneva of Calvin's day and of his immediate successors. Major portions of the Swiss church of Fletcher's day were largely influenced by Salmurian thought, Socinianism, and French humanism and maintained the creedal statements as mere relics of the reformation. Fletcher asserted in his *Historical Essay of Equal Check Part I* that the ministers of Geneva still subscribed to the French Confession of Faith (*Confessio Fidei Gallicana*, 1559 A.D.): "Servetus's heresy is thus described in the fourteenth of the 'Forty Articles of religion,' which the ministers of Geneva still subscribe, and which, if I mistake not, were drawn up by Calvin himself."[70] However, the subscription was a mere formality, and Fletcher emphasized this point asserting that while the ministers signed the creedal statement, it did not

---

65. JF→JW, 24 June 1781, Genuine-Letters, 44.
66. Archinard, *Histoire de l'Eglise du Canton de Vaud Depuis Son*, 263.
67. Schaff and Schaff, eds., *Creeds of Christendom*, 1:400.
68. Fletcher-Portrait, 2:4, 9, 80–82.
69 Lawton, *Shropshire Saint*, 60.
70. Fl-W1856, 3:355.

represent adequately their faith. Fletcher recognized this influence citing the D'Alembert's article on Geneva in the *Encyclopédie* and concluded: "What has Calvinism done for Geneva? Alas! it has in a great degree shocked and driven it into Arianism, Socinianism, and infidelity."[71]

While only conjectures may be made, there is some indication that his decision to abandon his studies may be due either to Fletcher's frustration with the liberal philosophy of the Academy and his unwillingness to be exposed any longer to Vernet's unorthodox theological views or his self-perceived ineligibility for the ministerial role. Perhaps it could have been a combination of the above.[72] A perusal of Vernet's work, *Instruction Chrétienne*, reveals that Vernet, Fletcher's professor, placed heavy emphasis upon the law; perhaps one could say that he was a moralist. It is no wonder that his student described himself in a letter to his brother, Henri-Louis de la Fléchère, as "a pharisaical philosopher." John characterized his life at eighteen years of age in the following terms: "He [the unconverted man] is a voluptuous, a worldly-minded person, or a pharisaical philosopher: or, perhaps, like myself, he may be all of these at the same time."[73] It may be perhaps a sad commentary on Geneva when Fletcher wrote in the same letter, "I was ignorant of the fall and ruin in which every man is involved, the necessity of a Redeemer, and the way by which we may be rescued from the fall by receiving Christ with a living faith."[74]

Prior to his departure from England, Fletcher was averse to signing the creedal statements of his native country to which ordination would have obliged subscription. However, the professors at Geneva, while constrained not to teach against the Calvinistic creeds, were tolerant of other traditions; despite the constraints, the professors took their academic freedom and averred doctrines, which undermined the creedal statements of the Swiss church. Conscientious as he was, Fletcher could not live with the inconsistencies and was deterred from taking orders in the Swiss church. Fletcher's concept of the scope of the atonement further deterred him: "I dare not, tho' I studied at Geneva, doom all the poor heathens to perdition, & therefore I must side here also with the Author of the Minutes."[75] Only late in life did Fletcher mention another aversion for the unorthodox theology of eighteenth century Geneva.

---

71. Ibid.

72. Yet, at one point Fletcher speaks of Vernet as the "judicious divine" (Fletcher-Portrait, 2:203) but he does not frequently quote him.

73. JF→Henri-Louis de la Fléchère, 11 mai 1755.

74. Fl-W1856, 9:438.

75. JF→CH, 7 March 1771.

THE INFLUENCE OF BRITISH THEOLOGY

After Fletcher's arrival in England, he spent the remainder of his life there with the exception of a journey in 1768 to the continent and a period of convalescence from 1778 to 1781. The friendships, the literature, and the conversion that the young émigré from Switzerland experienced on English soil had a formative influence upon him. In particular, the personal relationships that he forged with the early Methodists profoundly shaped his Christian life and thought. His preference for England was maintained throughout his life; on 18 July 1779, Fletcher wrote during his period of convalescence from Nyon of his compatriots who urged him to remain in Switzerland, "They urge much, my being born here, and I reply, that as I was born again in England, that is, *of course*, the country which, to me, is the dearer of the two."[76] This section considers the English context in which Fletcher wrote the majority of his writings.

Anglican Theology

While Fletcher's contact with the Methodist societies occurred probably early in the summer of 1753, his contact with the Church of England was no doubt soon after his arrival in England. Through the encouragement of the Wesley brothers, Fletcher, who had been reluctant to submit to ordination in his native Switzerland, submitted to ordination as a deacon in the Church of England on 6 March 1757, and a week later, he was ordained as a priest on 13 March 1757.[77] Fletcher was appointed as the curate of Madeley on 14 March 1757 serving under the incumbent, Rowland Chambers.[78] Upon Chamber's removal to Dunham, Fletcher was inducted to the living at Madeley on 17 October 1760. Ten days prior to his induction as the Vicar of Madeley, Fletcher signed a certificate of subscription to the Thirty-nine Articles of Religion and a certificate of subscription to the liturgy of the Church of England.[79]

---

76. Fl-L1791, 52.; JF→JI, 2 Feb. 1779; Fl-L1791, 270; JF→JI, 25 September 1778; Fl-L1791, 268; JF→William Perronet, 31 December 1779; Fl-W1883, 4.398.

77. Fletcher's certificate of ordination as a deacon, 6 March 1757, Fletcher-Tooth, JRULM, P4d1; and his certificate of ordination as a priest, 13 March 1757, Fletcher-Tooth, JRULM, P4d2.

78. In the document, "Mandate for Induction to Madeley," the name of the incumbant is spelled "Chambre"; other sources use the anglicized form "Chambers" (Mandate for Induction at Madeley, 7 October 1760, Fletcher-Tooth, JRULM, P4d.6).

79. Fletcher's certificate of subscription to Thirty-nine Articles, 7 October 1760, Fletcher-Tooth, JRULM, P4d7; and his certificate on conforming to the liturgy, 7

Fletcher took seriously his pledges and remained a loyal son of the Church of England throughout his life. While George Lawton argues that Fletcher was both "Methodist and Anglican," he also points out that Fletcher never repudiated Methodism "because he believed that essentially it was the religion of the Church of England Fathers."[80]

Fletcher constantly used the standards of the Church of England to defend his theological positions. In *Pentecostal Grace*, Wood makes the claim that one of Fletcher's primary resources for his doctrine of dispensations was Anglican theology: "Fletcher largely defended the doctrine on the basis of his exposition of Scripture, yet he did indicate its basis in the broader context of the history of Christian thought and especially in the theology of the Anglican church."[81] In *An Appeal to Matter of Fact and Common Sense*, Fletcher quoted from the articles, homilies, and the liturgy to support his position on the depravity of the human race.[82] He quoted the homilies because he believed that they provide "the strongest pleas . . . for holiness and good works."[83] While some of his opponents cited the articles in support of their Calvinism, Fletcher believed that the Articles were anti-Calvinistic; he pled, "O ye considerate Englishmen, stand to your articles, and you will soon shake off Geneva impositions!"[84]

Not only did Fletcher use the standards of the Church of England in his polemical writings, he also supported his position with the writings of a number of the church's prominent theologians, including Thomas Cranmer, John Davenant, James Ussher, William Laud, William Chillingworth, John Tillotson, George Bull, Jeremy Taylor, Edward Stillingfleet, William Beveridge, and others. Fletcher respected Thomas Cranmer as the architect of the Anglican standards because he felt that Cranmer preserved the same delicate balance that Fletcher maintained in his theological system. Fletcher also found the latter Caroline divines whom C. Fitz Simons Allison identifies as the "holy living" school to be comrades in the battle against antinomianism.[85]

The key feature that Fletcher emulated from the Anglican divines was the via media of their theological method.[86] As was pointed out pre-

---

October 1760, Fletcher-Tooth, JRULM, P4d8.
80. Lawton, *Shropshire Saint*, 21.
81. L. Wood, *Pentecostal Grace*, 184.
82. Fl-W1856, 2:16–17.
83. Fl-W1856, 3:4, 20–29.
84. Fl-W1856, 3:220.
85. Allison, *Rise of Moralism*, 133.
86. Balzer, "John Wesley's Developing Soteriology and the," 58.

viously, Fletcher's theological system has been described as dialectical. In endeavoring to find a middle way between two extremes, Fletcher reflected the spirit of Anglican theology.

Puritan Theology

While one finds the covenant idea in Calvin's thought, his successors developed the idea into a full fledged covenant theology.[87] The neo-Calvinism that arose emphasized covenantal theology or federal theology, which emphasized the federal headships of Adam and Christ. Everett H. Emerson argues that Calvin should not be regarded as a covenant theologian and that there are similarities between Calvin's theology and the covenant theology of the Puritans. "[C]ovenant theology flourished in the seventeenth [century] as a reaction against the abstractions of Reformed scholasticism, and as a defense against the Arminian attack on predestination. By using the covenant idea, theologians shifted emphasis from the eternal decrees of God, central High Calvinist teachings, to God's relationship with man, without abandoning predestination."[88] While there are some similarities between the covenant idea in Calvin's thought and the covenant theology of the Puritans, "[C]ovenant theology seems to undermine predestination."[89]

The Puritans' doctrine of covenants emphasized two positions on divine revelation: (1) the continuity of revelation including an emphasis upon the importance of the OT and (2) the progressive character of revelation. John Murray writes

> Students of historical theology, even those who entertain a radically different view of the history of divine revelation from that which governs the thought of classic Reformed theology, have recognized that the covenant theology marked an epoch in the appreciation and understanding of the progressiveness of divine revelation. William Robertson Smith, for example, gives the following appraisal: 'With all its defects, the Federal theology of Cocceius is the most important attempt, in the older Protestant theology, to do justice to the historical development of revelation.' Geerhardus Vos, steeped in and sympathetic towards the covenant theology, says that it 'has from the beginning shown

---

87. W. Brown makes a distinction between covenant theology and the covenant idea (W. Brown, "Covenant Theology," 4:216).

88. Emerson, "Calvin and Covenant Theology," 138.

89. Ibid., 136.

itself possessed of a true historic sense in the apprehension of the progressive nature of the deliverance of truth."[90]

The Seventeenth-Century Antinomian Controversy

During the seventeenth-century a controversy arose when certain divines radicalized certain tenets of Calvinist doctrine resulting in theological antinomianism. Tobias Crisp (1600–1643) and John Saltmarsh (d. 1647) were the principal proponents of this form of hyper-Calvinism, which rejected any role for the law in the Christian life. These antinomians emphasized a demarcation between the law and the gospel. Christ, through his atoning work, abrogated the law and so satisfied its demands that Christians no longer have any obligations to the moral law. The doctrine of free grace was overemphasized and misused to such an extent that the role of the law in the Christian life was ostracized. These divines emphasized a doctrine of eternal justification; sinners were absolutely and unconditionally elected to salvation prior to confession of sins or faith in Christ; indeed, Crisp asserted, "An elect person is not in a condemned state while an unbeliever; and should he happen to die before God call him to believe, he would not be lost."[91]

A number of Christian theologians provided rebuttals to Crisp and Saltmarsh; among the respondents were Daniel Williams (c.1643–1716), John Flavel (c.1630–1691), and Samuel Rutherford (c.1600–1661). One of the most prolific writers who contributed more than 130 books to the Puritan cause was Richard Baxter (1615–1691) who defended the Christian faith against the influences of Antinomian doctrine. He had a significant influence upon early Methodist theologians.[92]

Baxter's theology is not easily categorized due in part to his method of dichotomizing, which was influenced by Peter Ramus. The prolific author attempted to reconcile opposing viewpoints and to provide a mediating theology.[93] One of the principles of exercising moderation is his expressed dictum "'over-doing is undoing.'"[94] Baxter read widely and was influenced

---

90. Murray, *Covenant of Grace*, 3–4.

91. McClintock and Strong, eds., *Cyclopedia of Biblical, Theological, and Ecclesiastical Literature*, s.v. "Crisp, Tobias," 2:566.

92. One writer asserts that Fletcher's thought as delineated in his *Checks* corresponds "more nearly with that of Baxter than of any other divine" (Anonymous, "Fletcher's Checks," 420). See Monk, *John Wesley*, 43.

93. Packer, *Redemption and Restoration of Man in the*, 405.

94. Ibid., 20.

The Milieu of Fletcher's Theology

by different strains of Christendom. He "advocated a version"[95] of Moïse Amyraut's theology—developing a system of doctrine that was a halfway house between Calvinism and Arminianism, but he was acquainted with the Saumur theological tradition through the writings of John Cameron whose work was edited by Moïse Amyraut.[96]

Central to Baxter's theology was the *regnum Dei*, the reign of God,—a theme that Baxter exploits throughout his works. "God's moral government of man, he insisted, is the central subject of the Bible and the central topic of theology. The doctrines of sin and of the unfolding of redemption must be understood, from first to last, within a 'political' framework."[97] Baxter re-evaluated the Puritan view of history and the theology of the covenants according to his political method.[98] History unfolded in successive tripartite forms of the reign of God: the kingdoms of nature, of grace and of glory; the first two take place on earth, and the third occurs principally in heaven. The first was the rule of God over perfect humans, which endured until the fall of humanity; the second is the Kingdom of God the Redeemer whose purpose is to effect the restoration of the kingdom to the Father. While these three kingdoms are successive and chronological, they remain one kingdom.[99]

> The relevance of God's reign to the governance of human affairs is a significant concern for Baxter. God's right "of propriety and government" over humanity has a three-fold ground in the creation, the redemption, and the raising and glorifying of humanity.[100] The three-fold ground of God's right to reign corresponds to the kingdom of nature, the kingdom of grace, and the kingdom of glory which serve as an overarching structure for Baxter's theology of the covenants which is summarized in the following citation from Packer: The covenants of works and of grace are the laws of the kingdom in its first two forms, and within each dispensation three distinct subjects arise for consideration: "constitutio efficiens," God's legislation; "constitutio

---

95. Packer, *Quest for Godliness*, 157.

96. Morgan states that Baxter came to his conclusion on the universal application of the atonement before reading Amyraut but once he did, he was convinced that Amyraut was a judicious divine (*The Nonconformity of Richard Baxter*, 77). Clifford argues this same point (*Atonement and Justification*, 26). Packer writes, "Baxter always quoted from the folio edition of his works (Ioannis Cameronis . . . TA SWOMENA, edited by M. Amyraldus, J. Placaeus and L. Cappellus), which was published only in 1642" (*Redemption and Restoration of Man in the*, 198).

97. Packer, *Redemption and Restoration of Man in the*, 122.

98. Ibid., 213.

99. Ibid., 215.

100. Ibid.

effecta," the resultant state of affairs; and "administratio," which last subdivides again into three, "regimen antecedens," "actiones subditorum," and "regimen consequens." Within the framework afforded by these distinctions, Baxter proceeded to set out in tripartite analysis the whole history of God's dealings with man from the creation to the coming end of the world, the whole content of man's duty and, to conclude, a detailed dissection of the threefold summary of Christian virtue, faith, hope, and love.[101]

With these distinctive features of his soteriology, Baxter's concern was to rebut antinomianism, which prevailed in certain Calvinist camps. He desired not only to refute the blatant doctrinal antinomianism of Tobias Crisp and John Saltmarsh, but the more subtle theoretical antinomianism of John Owen. His desire to refute antinomianism and to promote practical holiness established a foundation upon which the early Methodists and particularly John Fletcher would construct their checks to antinomianism and their doctrine of Christian perfection.

"I Must Be a Baxterian"

Richard Baxter's theology, which was shaped on the anvil of the antinomian controversy, became a significant source in Fletcher's own polemic against hyper-Calvinism in the Minute controversy of the 1770s.[102] Fletcher quotes Baxter frequently[103] finding him to be a comrade in the fight against antinomianism and a source for Fletcher's emphasis on the law. Clifford comments on Baxter's views, "Baxter's neonomian scheme was his way of saying that the imputation of Christ's righteousness has not abrogated the precept of the law. Believers, therefore, are not lawless."[104] Fletcher held a high view of Baxter; he wrote to Charles Wesley: "In many things, I mu_st be a Baxterian. Him I admire_" most for _consistency & labours_ of all the divines of the last century."[105]

---

101. Ibid., 84.

102. Monk traces the doctrine of four justifications in Fletcher's thought to Baxter's influence (*John Wesley*, 122–32); see also Shipley, "Wesley and Some Calvinistic Controversies," 205–10.

103. Fletcher-Patriotism, 101ff.; Fletcher-Vindication, 78; Fl-W1883 4:405–6.

104. Clifford, *Atonement and Justification*, 96.

105 JF→CW, 21 Sept. 1771. Cf. JF→CW, 13 Oct. 1771.

John Milton

In Wesley's letter to Betsy Ritchie dated January 17, 1775, he indicates his approbation of Fletcher's doctrine of dispensations: "Mr. Fletcher has given us a wonderful view of the different dispensations which we are under. I believe that difficult subject was never placed in so clear a light before. It seems that God has raised him up for this very thing,-

> To vindicate eternal Providence,
> And justify the ways of God to man." [106]

Wesley cites these two lines from John Milton's epic poem, *Paradise Lost*. Following the restoration of the English monarchy in 1660, Milton (1608–1674) who viewed the Protectorate as the godly republic wrote *Paradise Lost* to provide justification of God's providence in the eyes of men for its collapse. "The godly government of the interregnum had been displaced by the profligate court of Charles II, and for those who had laboured for the good old cause, God's ways stood in need of justification."[107] That Wesley commends Fletcher's doctrine of dispensations is clear but precisely what he commends about it is unclear. Certainly, his commendation does not indicate the political connotations that Milton intended. However, it seems more evident that Wesley recognized the inherent logic of Fletcher's argument: when the span of history reveals inconsistencies in God's dealings with human beings, Fletcher's theology of history provides a coherency and consistency to divine providence.

In the *Checks*, Fletcher specifically quotes Milton as a source for his doctrine of dispensations: "To conclude: Milton says somewhere, 'There is a certain scale of duties, a certain hierarchy of upper and lower commands, which for want of studying in right order, all the world is in confusion.'"[108] While Fletcher doesn't seem to know the exact source, the quote is drawn from Milton's *The Doctrine and Discipline of Divorce* in which he argues for the right of a believer to divorce "an idolatrous heretic."[109] The context of Fletcher's citation of Milton follows the latter's rather lengthy argument in which he claims that Christ's command to hate and forsake family members for the sake of the kingdom (Luke 14:25) supersedes his prohibition against divorce. According to Milton, the inconsistencies between the declaration of Christ on divorce and the commands of Moses concerning divorce be-

---

106. WJW, 13:55.
107. G. Campbell, "Milton."
108. FL-W1883, 2:342.
109. Milton, *Doctrine and Discipline of Divorce*, 49.

come clear when correct hermeneutics are used. In the quote, Milton indicates that a gradation or a succession of ascending and descending steps and degrees or to use his words a "scale of duties," which when properly understood, reveal a right understanding of God's Word. Fletcher's own application of Milton's axiom is different from Milton's own application. The Vicar of Madeley pointed out that neither the "rigid Calvinists" nor the "rigid Catholics" adequately understand the historical progression of God's revelatory activity because they insist that their theological systems leads one to the conclusion that there is no salvation outside of the New Testament dispensation; this done when the rigid Catholics insist that there is no salvation outside the Church and when the rigid Calvinists insist that there is no salvation outside of "the new covenant and the election of God's partial grace."[110] An adequate understanding and application of the hermeneutical principle of which Milton spoke will enable an accurate view of the dispensations that enables one to see a unity in the seeming inconsistencies of God's dealings with humankind through a progressive development in the history of revelation; Fletcher wrote, "What that great man said of the scale of duties and commands, may with equal propriety be affirmed of the scale of evangelical truths, and the hierarchy of upper and lower Gospel dispensations. For want of studying them in right order, all the Church is in confusion."[111] Fletcher seems to reflect Milton's thought when he states the doctrine of dispensations has become "my *key* and my sword."[112] By the use of the word "key," Fletcher seems to imply the doctrine of dispensations is a valuable hermeneutical tool that opens doors of understanding.[113] The doctrine of dispensations enables him to hold in dialectical tension the various seemingly conflicting truths whose unity is evident within Scripture but not quite so apparent in the divergent traditions of the Church.

Methodist Theologians

John Wesley

In *Equal Check*, Fletcher responds to the accusation that the doctrine of dispensations is a novel invention or a theological fiction: "However, that the idea of *novelty* may not stand in the way of any of my readers, out of fifty authors, whom I may quote in support of this important doctrine, I shall

---

110. FL-W1883, 2:341.
111. FL-W1883, 2:342.
112. Fletcher-EC2, ix.
113. This concept will be explored more fully later in this book.

The Milieu of Fletcher's Theology

produce two, a Calvinist and an anti-Calvinist; not doubting but their consentaneous testimony will sufficiently break the force of your objection."[114] Fletcher's "anti-Calvinist" is no less than John Wesley whose theology will be given fuller treatment later due to the integral relationship between the two theologians. The discussion now turns to Fletcher's second witness, John Green, who can only be considered a Methodist in the broader sense of the word.

John Green: The Whitefieldian

Biographical details on the first of the two witnesses that Fletcher calls upon to corroborate the historicity of the doctrine of dispensations against novelty are scanty indeed. The Calvinist witness is the Reverend John Green (d. 1774) who authored a number of books on theological issues.[115] He served as the curate of Thurnscoe, in Yorkshire and was master of the Academy in Denmark-Street London early in 1770.[116] In the early 1740s, he labored with the Wesleys but later separated from them over theological issues, became antinomian and wrote a book to refute the doctrines of Minutes of the 1744 Conference.[117] Following his disagreements with the Wesleys,[118] he preached frequently at Norwood for the Countess of Huntingdon. According to Seymour, Green supplied the pulpit at Whitefield's Tabernacle "with great success until some misunderstanding took place, when he left them [i.e., the other ministers], and retired to Reading, in Berkshire, where he died."[119]

Fletcher quotes at length from Green's book *Grace and Truth Vindicated, or the Way to Heaven Manifested, From Scripture and Experience*. Green stated his purpose in writing as follows: "My only Intention therefore, in the following Pages; is to vindicate the Free Grace and everlasting Truth of our God: to justify his Ways to Men, and manifest the Way to Heaven; from the Sacred Scriptures and real Experience."[120] He proposes three heads: first, an account of his spiritual experience and conversion; second, some

---

114. Fletcher-EC1, 253. Green, *Grace and Truth Vindicated*, 16.

115. The Revd Green to whom Benson (Benson, *Life*, 2/2) makes reference is possibly the same Green; more evidence is needed.

116. According to the title page of his book, *Decency of Behaviour at the Table of the Lord*.

117. WJW, 2:312; BiCentWJW, 7:501; JCW, 1:428–29, 452; 2:179.

118. BiCentWJW, 11:501.

119 Seymour, *Life and Times of Selina*, 1:358, 388; 2:350.

120. Green, *Grace and Truth Vindicated*, 4.

31

"reflections upon God's Free Grace and all-wise providence towards me from my Infancy;"[121] third, he proposes to address three categories of Christians: the nominal or formal Christians, Christians and spiritual Christians.[122] In recounting his own experiences, he classifies his early experience, which was characterized primarily by a rudimentary knowledge of God and his ways among the enlightened heathen (e.g., Cornelius), but he had not yet attained perfection.[123] At this point, Green's discussion reflects the language of Hebrews 6:1ff. While the subjective aspect is not absent, the experience herein described is typified by an emphasis on the objective content (i.e., the doctrines of the Christian faith) in Green's early knowledge of God. This inferior knowledge has now been superseded by a more superior knowledge; however, the lesser dispensation should not be despised by the experience of a higher dispensation. Understanding is gradually enlightened. While babes in Christ are recipients of God's glory just as much as fathers in the faith, the larger vessels have a greater capacity for greater degrees of grace and glory.[124]

As Green unfolded the story of his spiritual growth and conversion, one finds a distinction emerging between the experience of the disciples prior to Pentecost and their experience subsequent to Pentecost. His own experiences caused him to affirm: "I now see how far a Man may go, and yet his day of Pentecost not be truly come, or he not spiritually come to Christ."[125] His experiences led him to affirm a progression in his experience of the Spirit. "I was in a Measure clean, thro' the Word spoken unto me, or sanctified by the Blood of the Covenant. I was now a *Partaker* of the Holy Ghost, and of the Fruits thereof; that is, I had a *Ray* or *Manifestation* thereof to profit withal. But, as yet, my Day of Pentecost was not fully come; I had not then received that *the Holy Ghost since* I believed, even the Spirit of Truth, which bringeth to my Remembrance, and unfoldeth the things which our Saviour before had told me."[126]

---

121. Ibid. Green's language is reminiscent of Wesley's in his Wesley's letter to Betsy Ritchie dated January 17, 1775 in which he indicates strong approval of Fletcher's dispensation. "It seems that God has raised him up for this very thing,-
> To vindicate eternal Providence,
> And justify the ways of God to man." (WJW, 13:55)

122. Green, *Grace and Truth Vindicated*, 4.
123. Ibid., 80.
124. Ibid., 88.
125. Ibid., 111.
126. Ibid., 113–14.

The Milieu of Fletcher's Theology

Green admittted three dispensations: first, a spiritual heathen; second, a spiritual Jew; third, a spiritual Christian.[127] A degree of progression is evident in these dispensations; he posited four arguments: (1) the privileges of the latter days supersedes those of the days of the prophets; (2) a greater condemnation awaits those who reject the greater privileges of the gospel; (3) the greater privileges are particularly evident in the parables of the kingdom; (4) different mansions (i.e., the Tabernacle as a type of the heavenly temple) prove the greater privileges.[128] While Fletcher did not make use of the various mansions (e.g., the court of the Gentiles, etc.) as did Green,[129] he did employ the concept of the Kingdom of Heaven having different degrees, and in particular the parable of the talents is given some treatment: the man who received only one talent is compared to the heathen who received "the true light which lighteth every man that cometh into the World."[130] The spiritual Christian in the higher dispensation is called to holiness or perfection.[131] In the third and last section of this book, Green made application of Christian principles to the various categories of readers, i.e., nominal Christians, covetous Christians, pleasure-taking Christians, etc.

SUMMARY

John Fletcher's thought parallels the covenant idea found in many Christian theologians in the history of the Christian church. He was largely in agreement with the federal school of theology of the continental theologians and Puritans whose doctrine of the covenants tended to undermine, inadvertently in some cases, the ahistorical, decretal system of hyper-Calvinism. Foundational to his doctrine of dispensations is the doctrine of accommodation, one of the few vestiges of Calvinism retained by his professor, Jacob Vernet. Fletcher remained a loyal son of the Church of England. He reflected the spirit of Anglican theology with his dialectical method. Fletcher found comrades among the Puritans and the "holy living" school of the Church of

---

127. Ibid., 117.

128. Ibid., 118–19.

129. Fletcher's use of the word "mansions" differs from Green's use of the word. Fletcher uses "mansions" drawing from John 14:2 in order to demonstrate the various degrees of rewards that correspond to the various degrees of spiritual development (J. Fletcher, *Fictitious and the Genuine Creed*, ix; Fletcher-Vindication, 60; Fletcher-EC1, 233; Fletcher-Creed, 36; J. Fletcher, John *Last Check to Antinomianism*, 243; Fletcher-Portrait, 316).

130. Green, *Grace and Truth Vindicated*, 123.

131. Ibid., 204.

England in the struggle against antinomianism. His thought also resonated with the Puritan emphasis on salvation as a process.

2

God of Nature and of Grace
Theological Foundations for the Doctrine of the Dispensations

FOR THE FIRST FIFTEEN hundred centuries of Christianity, the locus of the authority of Christian claims was principally within the Church due to the hierarchical system that developed as it reflected its cultural setting and responded to the various heresies that arose. However, during the Reformation, the locus of the authority shifted, for Protestants, from the Church to the Scriptures. In the early period of the Reformation the principal concern of Protestantism centered on soteriology; later, the central issue shifted to the doctrines of revelation and authority as the implications of Reformation thought eroded the religious authority of the Church.

Enlightenment rationalism orchestrated a crisis of the Christian faith as reason supplanted revelation in the enlightened mind. The Church, thus, grappled with the encroachment of rationalism. H. D. McDonald traces the Church's response to the first Boyle Lecture in 1692 by Richard Bentley under the title, *The Folly of Atheism and Deism even with respect of the Present Life*.[1] McDonald insists, "The idea of revelation was . . . the dominant one of the period."[2] Gerald R. Cragg states similarly, "[T]he history of eighteenth-century though is largely concerned with the problem of authority."[3]

1. McDonald, *Ideas of Revelation*, 3.
2. Ibid., 3.
3. Cragg, *Reason and Authority in the Eighteenth Century*, 2.

McDonald typified the responses to Enlightenment rationalism with the rationalism of deism at one end of the spectrum and enthusiasm at the other.[4] In an era when reason was considered the principal arbitrator of truth, philosophers, such as John Locke with his work, *The Reasonableness of Christianity* (1695), endeavored to prove the rationality of the Christian faith. According to McDonald, the result was that "Locke robbed it [Christianity] of its worth, and consequently his work which was meant to be a sword against deism became a powerful weapon in its hands."[5] Matthew Tindal, influenced by Locke's work, wrote *Christianity as Old as Creation* whose purpose was revealed in the subtitle, *The Gospel a Republication of the Religion of Nature*; it was referred to as "the deists' Bible." Tindal argued, "No special revelation can be claimed as enlarging or ennobling the revelation of nature, since this would call in question the perfection of what has been given by nature."[6] God has revealed in nature all that needs to be revealed, and rational human beings, through unaided reason, are capable of discerning truth through a study of nature and natural law. During the period, there was, thus, a heightened interest in the study of nature.

At the opposite end of the spectrum of opposing views on revelation from the rational-objective view of the deists was the mystico-subjective view of the Quakers.[7] Among others, such as the Ranters, Seekers, and Shakers, the Quakers were labelled enthusiasts by the more rationalistic Christian apologists. Enthusiasm was a rejection of the dogmatic, rationalistic, faith of the established Church, its standards, and at times the Scriptures.[8]

During the seventeenth century, a small group of scholars, known as Cambridge Platonists, posited a middle way between Scylla and Charybdis on the doctrine of revelation; they responded to Enlightenment rationalism by stressing the rationality of Christian faith. While their roots were in Puritanism, they reacted to the anti-rationalism of the dogmatism of Puritan theology.[9] Cragg describes them as follows: "They refused to divorce the rational from the spiritual. They admitted no boundaries between theology and philosophy, or between natural and revealed religion. The reason which they exalted was very different in quality from the pedestrian rationalism

---

4. McDonald, *Ideas of Revelation*, 35.

5. Ibid., 41.

6. Ibid., 48.

7. Ibid., 35.

8. McDonald points out that enthusiasm arose, at times, as a rejection of the Calvinistic doctrine of particular election: "To stress the universal influence of Christ, emphasis was placed upon the Johannine declaration that, He was the light that lighteth every man that cometh in the world" (ibid., 63).

9. Hutton, "Smith."

which satisfied the eighteenth century, but they taught their age to trust in the mind of man."[10] For them, reason and revelation were in harmony; Whichcote referred to reason as "the candle of the Lord" (Proverbs 20:27) by which he meant that the human mind was illuminated by God.[11] D.A. Rees emphasized that the seventeenth century Platonists stressed the inner life of the Spirit and demonstrated some affinities with the Quakers and their stress on an "inner light," which is not necessarily limited to Christians.[12] Thus, the seventeenth century was marked by Christian apologists who endeavored to prove the reasonableness, reality and sufficiency of the Christian revelation.

Another characteristic of the era of the Enlightenment was an emphasis on a more optimistic view of history. Coupled with such optimism was a belief in the inevitable progress of history. The emphases on reason and the idea of the progress of history could not be bifurcated. Immanuel Kant is representative of Enlightenment thinkers who viewed the goal of history as "an approach, typical of the Enlightenment that describes history as the story of humanity's progressive development from barbarism and superstition to a life of reason."[13]

While many evangelicals considered themselves exempt from its influence, Enlightenment thought affected theology in England.[14] Evangelicals too were enamored with the Enlightenment assumption of the progress of history. Due to the inextricable link of the Christian faith to history, it was impingent upon the apologists of the Church to defend the historicity of divine revelation. They viewed history as redemptive and linked the doctrines of divine providence and revelation with the idea of the progress of history. Bebbington writes, "Evangelicals reflected the later Enlightenment in their optimistic temper. The eighteenth century, and especially its second half, characteristically believed that humanity enjoyed great potential for improvement. It was the later eighteenth century that witnessed the emergence of the idea of progress, the conviction that human beings are steadily becoming wiser and therefore better."[15] John Wesley himself held to an optimistic view of the providence of God despite his pessimism of sin; God was

---

10. Cragg, *Reason and Authority in the Eighteenth Century*, 66.

11. D. Edwards, *Christian England*, 2:369.

12. D. A. Rees also stated that neo-Platonism has exerted a profound influence in the field of poetry, an observation that will have significance in a later discussion (D. A. Rees, "Platonism and the Platonic Tradition,").

13. Nash, *Meaning of History*, 72.

14. Bebbington, *Evangelicalism in Modern Britain*, 50ff. See also Rack, *Reasonable Enthusiast*, 32.

15. Bebbington, *Evangelicalism in Modern Britain*, 60.

working in history to bring about the divine redemptive end. This optimism becomes more evident as the revival spread, and is particularly evident in his late sermon, *The General Spread of the Gospel* (1783).[16]

Questions arose in this era regarding the authority of Scripture. The principles of the Reformation had undermined the Church as the religious authority and replaced it with the Scriptures. The Reformers and their successors held to the veracity of God's Word and to its centrality and authority within the Church as the rule of faith and practice. However, a problem arose: the Scriptures disclose the inconsistent, inequitable ways that God has dealt with God's people and in particular the dissonance between the Old and New Testaments. When the consistency of the established Church was replaced with the inconsistencies of Scripture, it was impingent upon the Reformers to prove the veracity of Scripture. How could they hold to the veracity of the Scripture given inherent inconsistencies? Their conviction caused them to grapple seriously with the contradictions of Scripture and to develop a theology of history that underscored the unity of God's revelatory activity. Their response to the question was a doctrine of progressive revelation, which assumes an incremental increase of the knowledge of God throughout history and attempts to explain the different ways that God dealt with humanity.

Butler's Analogy

Eighteenth century thinkers were also enamored with the idea of nature. Cragg writes, "The authority claimed by natural religion and the universal respect accorded it were among the most characteristic features of eighteenth-century thought."[17] Locke's emphasis upon reason and Sir Isaac Newton's emphasis upon the uniformity of the universe gave rise to an "assured and self-confident period" in which "it seemed clear that man's intelligence had traced God's handiwork in creation, and had detected the divine purpose both in the structure of the universe and in the operation of man's mind."[18] As noted above, Matthew Tindal posited the continuity between natural religion and the religion of the Gospel. For Tindal, natural and revealed religion were in fact "different aspects of the one rational religion."[19] Deists ennobled the revelation of nature to such a degree of perfection that

---

16. BiCentWJW, 2:485ff. Another late sermon (1787), "The Signs of the Times," reflects this same tone (BiCentWJW, 2:521ff.).

17. Cragg, *Reason and Authority in the Eighteenth Century*, 9.

18. Ibid., 9. Cf. ibid., 119.

19. McDonald, *Ideas of Revelation*, 48.

special revelation could add nothing to it.[20] Orthodox theologians reacted to the naturalism of the deists and reasserted the necessity of revelation. Fletcher found the anti-deistic writers to be allies in his polemical writings against the deists. Representative among them is Bishop Butler.

Joseph Butler (1692–1752) wrote to refute the deists among whose works Tindal's *Christianity as Old as Creation* was the most recent publication. His work, *The Analogy of Religion, Natural and Revealed, to the Constitution and Course of Nature*, "was addressed to those who conceded order and regularity in nature but were sceptical about the claims of Christianity."[21] Butler countered "[T]he deist critique by arguing both that the investigation of nature can show us more than the deists allow—such as the existence of a future life and that this life is a time of moral probation—and that the difficulties apparent in Christian revelation are analagous to the difficulties apparent in the account of natural religion offered by the deists."[22] Christianity, according to Butler, is the authoritative promulgation of the law of nature "with new light, and other circumstances of peculiar advantage, adapted to the wants of mankind."[23] However, Christianity is greater than a mere republication of the law of nature; it involves revelation: "[I]t contains also a revelation of a particular dispensation of Providence, carrying on by his [the Father's] Son and Spirit, for the recovery and salvation of mankind, who are represented in Scripture to be in a state of ruin."[24] Bishop Butler posited a Trinitarian unfolding of revelatory history and an epistemological order of divine revelation. This Trinitarian unfolding of revelation history is the foundation for the Trinitarian formula of Christian baptism. Moral obligations, which are (or morality is) the very essence of religion,[25] are revealed in the subsequent dispensations through the offices of the Trinity as well as through the relation of Persons of the Trinity to human beings:

> By *reason* is revealed the revelation, which God the Father stands to us. Hence arises the obligation of duty which we are under to him. In *Scripture* are revealed the relations, which the Son and Holy Spirit stand in to us. Hence arise the obligations of duty, which we are under to them. The truth of the case, as one may speak, in each of these three respects being admitted: that God is the governor of the world, upon the evidence of

20. Ibid., 48, 53.
21. Cragg, *Reason and Authority in the Eighteenth Century*, 114.
22. Cunliffe, "Butler."
23. Butler, *Analogy of Religion*, 191.
24. Ibid., 104.
25. Matthews, "'Reason and Revelation Joined,'" 96.

reason; that Christ is the mediator between God and man, and the Holy Ghost our guide and sanctifier, upon the evidence of revelation.[26]

Human knowledge of God, according to Butler, progresses from knowledge of the Father, a knowledge revealed through reason, to knowledge of the Son and Spirit, which is revealed through further revelation. Cragg points out that the language of Butler on reason is reminiscent of the Cambridge Platonists; Butler "spoke of 'the faculty of reason, which is *the candle of the Lord within us.*'"[27] Parallels of Butler's epistemological claims to Fletcher's thought will become evident.

The word "analogy" in the title of Butler's work refers to the analogy between "the principles of divine government, as set forth by the biblical revelation, and those observable in the course of nature, [an analogy which] leads us to the warrantable conclusion that there is one Author of both."[28] According to McClintock and Strong, the central analogy developed in Butler's work is between "the system of nature and the system of grace."[29]

FLETCHER ON GRACE AND NATURE

Fletcher reflects a profound interest in the doctrines of revelation, nature, providence, and history. These doctrines are foundational for his theological system and the doctrine of dispensations and must be considered here.[30]

One of the most mature and comprehensive expressions of Fletcher's theology appeared under the title *La Grâce et la Nature*; originally it was written and published in Switzerland under the title *La Louange*, but was later significantly expanded and published in England in 1785 under the new title.[31] The genre of literature portrayed in the poem is reminiscent of the poetry of the Cambridge Platonists. The poem with its corresponding notes forms a descant on creation based upon Psalm 148.[32]

---

26. Butler, *Analogy of Religion*, 194; emphasis original.
27. Cragg, *Reason and Authority in the Eighteenth Century*, 120.
28. *The Encyclopedia Britannica*, 11th ed., s.v. "Butler, Joseph," 885.
29. McClintock and Strong, eds., *Cyclopedia of Biblical, Theological, and Ecclesiastical Literature*, s.v. "Butler, Joseph," 937.
30. B. Gregory wrote, "Fletcher's doctrine of the dispensations was in perfect harmony with his view of the revelations of nature and grace" ("John Fletcher, the Theologian," 180).
31. Fletcher-Grâce, iv. The preface was dedicated and signed on "le 6 de Sept. 1784."
32. Ibid., xxxii–xxxiii.

God of Nature and of Grace

Wiggins gives a sustained treatment of *La Grâce et la Nature* and provides an analysis of the structure of the work that contains a total of twenty-four "chants" or cantos. The first division comprising Cantos I through X "are addressed to men in various stations of life and each is implored to praise God."[33] The second division including Cantos XI through XIV presents "animal life with the lessons of natural praise which each category offers to its creator."[34] The third division of cantos, Cantos XV through XVIII, is drawn from Fletcher's previous work, *Essai sur la Paix de 1783*, and describes the peace between France and England. "Cantos XIX through XXIV deal with a group of natural phenomena, each of which in its own being has a lesson to offer to man about the vocation of praising God."[35]

Wiggins emphasized the significance of *La Grâce et la Nature* for Fletcher's thought and its neglect in studies of Fletcher's writings: "[O]ur contention is that the poem offers an entrè [sic] into the full spectrum of Fletcher's thought and talent."[36] In giving his rationale for the new title, Fletcher exposed a concept that is key to his theological system: "If grace causes us to praise the God of all grace, Nature does not invite us any less to celebrate its invisible Author."[37] Fletcher cited from the French translation of Romans 1 to show that unbelievers failed to recognize God's glory in nature, did not glorify ("rendu grâce") God and live like atheists.

Among others, Fletcher found an ally for his views on nature in Monsieur Jean-André du Luc (1727–1817), who was a geologist, meteorologist, and author of *Lettres Physiques et Morales sur Histoire de la Terre*, which Fletcher quoted at length in *La Grâce et la Nature*. Du Luc who was, during his youth, challenged by philosophers to reconsider his belief in divine revelation decided to devote himself to the study of nature. The geologist studied the structure of the earth and found evidence for the world-wide deluge of Noah's day and for Mosaic cosmology.[38] Du Luc was surprised at the audacity of the unbelievers' attacks on and their scornful attitude toward Christianity because his study of nature led him to the conclusion: "Religion has its Basis in Nature."[39] This geologist/philosopher concluded that there was a basis for divine revelation and morality that was evident in nature

---

33. Wiggins, "Pattern of John Fletcher's Theology," 60.
34. Ibid.
35. Ibid.
36. Ibid., 35.
37. "Si la Grace nous porte à louer le Dieu de toute grace, la Nature ne nous invite pas moins à célébrer son invisible Auteur" (Fletcher-Grâce, x).
38. Ibid., 341–43.
39. "[L]a Religion a ses Bases dans la Nature" (ibid., 343).

and argued for a continual admiration of the universe on the part of human beings and of the intelligent Cause behind it. Upon quoting du Luc, Fletcher commented, "To follow the advice of this Doctor is to pass by the Beauty of the Universe to the knowledge of its Author; making devotion walk hand in hand with Philosophy: it is to unite Nature and Grace: Sweet Union which is the basis of this Poem."[40] A holograph draft letter reveals the connection that Fletcher felt with his compatriot, Monsieur du Luc.[41] Fletcher identified himself to his addressee whom he did not know personally as "an author who follows your footsteps in conducting men on the path of nature and piety."[42]

Foundational to Fletcher's theology is the concept that grace and nature are one because God is both the Author of nature and of grace.[43] In this work, nature serves two useful purposes: it announces God and instructs human beings.[44] Both the minutia of nature and the holistic view of nature reveal the attributes of God and God's grace in divine-human relations. Birds that dart under the water reveal how baptized righteous believers detest their sins.[45] The sun, as the principal source of the earth's light, indicates the Primary Cause of the Universe, and the moon reminds believers that they reflect the light of God.[46] The fruit of trees demonstrates good works, and the sap demonstrates the faith that are worthy of heaven.[47] Water in the natural world is a symbol for grace in the spiritual world.[48] In an obvious allusion to Jacob's declaration, "How dreadful is this place! this is none other but the house of God, and this is the gate of heaven" (Gen. 28:17), Fletcher extolled the whole universe as Bethel, the house of God:

> May the Universe be for us a vast Bethel;
> And may even our rocks glorify the Eternal God![49]

---

40. "Suivre le conseil de ce Physicien c'est aller par le Spectacle de l'Univers à la connaissance de son Auteur; c'est faire marcher la Dévotion d'un pas égal avec la Philosophie; c'est unir la Nature et la Grace: Douce Union qui fait la base ce Poëme" (ibid., x–xi).

41. Streiff, *Reluctant Saint?*, 15.

42. JF→[Monsieur du Luc], n.d ["before 19 Dec. 1782," RS, 15].

43. Fletcher-Grâce, 261.

44. Ibid., 140.

45. Ibid., 126.

46. Ibid., 221–23.

47. Ibid., 240.

48. Ibid., 256.

49. "Que l'Univers pour nous soit un vaste Béthel;
Et jusques sur nos rocs bénissons l'Eternel!" (ibid., 228).

God of Nature and of Grace

The universe announces the various attributes of God even in the midst of humanity's indifference:

> If God has showered Humans with his blessings,
> Object of his love, Masterpiece of his hands:
> Unique Orators on the wave and the earth,
> It is up to us to praise the Master of the thunder.
> But if for our responsibilities we are full of cowardly fear,
> Ungrateful, we forget our great Benefactor,
> Nature, in all places, by its beautiful harmony,
> Sings to God of His infinite Greatness:
> Of lifeless bodies the lightening or the virtues
> Announce to us the divine attributes of God
> Everywhere shine these names: Goodness, Magnificence,
> Order, Beauty, Light, Love, Glory & Power. [50]

Fletcher's position is not materialistic or pantheistic. In advising the philosophers to glorify God by avoiding false philosophy, Fletcher encouraged the philosophers to distinguish between nature and its Author.[51] The key correlation between nature and spiritual things is analogy. Jesus' use of the simple things of nature to illustrate spiritual things validated Fletcher's use of analogies, drawing connections between natural things and spiritual things.[52] The portions of Scripture that contain mystical elements cannot be understood accurately by a literal reading; one must penetrate beyond the literal reading for an accurate spiritual understanding.[53] In the "Discours

---

50. "Si Dieu de ses faveurs a comblé les Humains,
Object de son amour, Chef-d'œuvre de ses mains :
Uniques Orateurs sur l'onde et sur la terre,
C'est à Nous de louer le Maitre du tonnerre.
Mais, si pour nos devoirs pleins de lâche tiédeur,
Ingrats, nous oublions notre grand Bienfaiteur,
La Nature, en tous lieux, par sa belle harmonie,
Chante de l'Eternel la Grandeur infinie ;
Des Corps inanimés l'éclat ou les vertus,
Nous annoncent d'un Dieu les divins attributs :
Par-tout brillent ces noms, Bonté, Magnificence,
Ordre, Beauté, Lumière, Amour, Gloire & Puissance" (ibid., 219–20). .

51. Ibid., 74. Loyer argues correctly that Fletcher's understanding of utter transcendence of God provides a basis in Fletcher's thought for safeguarding against inappropriate language about the divine: "Fletcher teaches that in reference to God, whatever ideas or images associated with these and other words need to be evaluated on the basis of God's utter transcendence" ("'Adoring the Holy Trinity in Unity,'" 4).

52. Fletcher-Grâce, xi–xii.

53. Knickerbocker has noted neo-Platonic strains ("Doctrinal Sources and Guidelines in Early," 190).

Préliminaire: Sur le Mysticisme évangélique," Fletcher provided a key to understanding the analogical relation that he perceived between grace and nature:

> St. Paul has given us a key to evangelical mysticism, when he assures us, "that the invisible things of God are clearly seen by the things which he has made," that is, by the visible creation. And he gives the reason, saying, "That things which are seen were not made of things which do appear;" and when he declares, "that the things on earth are copies of those in heaven:" as though he had said, that all the visible and sensible objects are only dross and material copies, whose originals are spiritual and invisible. This is the foundation of that mysticism which runs through the Gospel. [54]

The influence of neo-Platonism is evident in Fletcher's hermeneutics and fundamental to his analogy between grace and nature.[55] While the influence of neo-Platonism seems implicit in the above quotation, Fletcher made it explicit by a lengthy quote from Henry More, the Cambridge Platonist, only cited here in part: "[T]he whole universe is one great emblem, or symbolic sign of the truths which are most interesting for us."[56] The goal of the poem is to emphasize the spiritual truths that natural things represent and to cause the readers to glorify the God of nature and grace.

Fletcher was quite a master at making spiritual analogies not just in his writing, but in everyday life.[57] In Fletcher's thought, the analogy between grace and nature is possible because God is Source of both as the Creator and Redeemer. Next under consideration will be the theological foundations for analogical predication.

---

54. "St. Paul nous donne la clef du mysticisme évangélique, lors qu'il nous assure que *Les choses invisible de Dieu, se voyent comme à l'oeuil dans les choses crées* et matérielles: Rom. 1.20. Et il en indique la raison, quand il nous fait entendre que *Les choses qui se voyent, ont été faites de choses qui ne paroissent point* : Heb. xi.3. Et quand il déclare, que les choses qui sont sur la terre, *réprésentent celles qui sont dans les cieux* : Heb. ix.23. Comme s'il disoit, Tous les Objets visible et sensible, ne sont que des copies grossiéres et matérielles des choses dont les Originaux sont invisible et spirituels. C'est ici le fondement du mysticisme de l'Evangile" (Fletcher-Grâce, xxx).

55. English "discussed the correspondence and differences between John Wesley and the Cambridge Platonists by exploring Wesley's editing of these writers for the Christian Library" ("Cambridge Platonists in Wesley's 'Christian,'" 161–68).

56. "[T]out l'Univers n'est qu'un grand emblème, ou un signe symbolique des vérités les plus intéressantes pour nous" (Fletcher-Grâce, xxxi).

57 WJW, 11:307–8; "Rev. John Fletcher and the Rev. C. Simeon," 326. See Tyerman, *Wesley's Designated Successor*, 551–52.

"I FIND TRUTH IN THE WORLD OF NATURE": ANALOGICAL PREDICATION IN FLETCHER'S THOUGHT[58]

John Fletcher wrote to Joseph Benson on 20 March 1774: "There is undoubtedly truth in the world, tho' what I have seen and felt from a variety of professors, has sometimes stunned my faith for half a minute, and almost made way for the hellish snare of skepticism: But I find truth in the world of nature, I see it in the starry world, I read it in the scripture, I enjoy it in a few holy souls, and I trust that I can testify to the glory of God there is a spark of it in my own breast."[59] Without doubt, Fletcher found truth in the world of nature.[60] Constant references are made throughout his writings to the world of nature.[61] Fletcher echoed the sentiment that Charles Wesley expressed in his *Hymns for Whit-Sunday*:

> Author of every work Divine
> Who dost through both creations shine,
> The God of nature and of grace,
> Thy glorious steps in all we see,
> And wisdom attribute to Thee,
> And power, and majesty, and praise.[62]

Natural phenomena are a source for illustrating divine grace in Fletcher's writings.

In order to make the point that human efforts do not invalidate the free gift of justification, Fletcher illustrated the concept with the laws of nature. When farmers respect the laws established by the "God of providence," their obedience to the laws does not invalidate the fact that harvest is the free unmerited gift of God.[63] The God of nature is the same God as the God of grace; the basic law of nature that is applied to natural phenomenon is the same basic law that is applied in spiritual matters. Spiritual hunger is analogous to physical hunger, and common sense that regulates the dispensing of food to the sick to their capacity to receive it regulates the dispensing

---

58. Lawton discusses the literary genius of Fletcher and references the many allusions and other literary devices that Fletcher employs in his works (*Shropshire Saint*, 60–63).

59. JF→JB, 20 March 1774.

60. John Wesley held that God revealed the divine nature through nature as well (*Compend of Wesley's Theology*, 36).

61. Cf. Fl-W1856, 3:453; 4:62.

62. Osborn, *Poetical Works of John and Charles Wesley*, 7:198.

63. Fl-W1856, 2:245–6.

of spiritual nourishment to sinners: "The word of God must be offered to sinners as a remedy suited to the disease of their souls; but to the faithful it must be administered as nourishing food. Hence . . . the order of grace resembles that of nature."[64] Divine governance of nature and grace are similar: "the appointed ways of providence" and "the appointed ways of grace" both require divine intervention and human effort. Writing to Walter Shirley, Fletcher illustrated the necessity of human effort in his soteriology: "[S]o sure as a farmer, in the appointed ways of providence, shall have no harvest if he does nothing toward it, a professor in the appointed ways of grace, let him talk of finished salvation all the year round, shall go without justification and salvation, unless he do something toward them."[65] Frequently, Fletcher depends upon the agrarian parables of Jesus to illustrate spiritual truths, demonstrating his penchant for connecting grace and nature.

Fletcher's response to a cataclysmic event in his parish further demonstrates his concept of the relation between grace and nature. On Tuesday, 27 May 1773, a landslip occurred along the Severn River at the boundary of the Buildwas parish and Fletcher's own parish, which significantly altered the topography of the area.[66] In July, Fletcher wrote an account of the event under the title: *A Dreadful Phenomenon Described and Improved: Being a Particular Account of the Sudden Stoppage of the River Severn, and of the Terrible Desolation That Happened at the Birches, Between Coalbrook-dale and Buildwas Bridge in Shropshire. On Thursday Morning, May the 27th, 1773. And the Substance of a Sermon Preached the Next Day, on the Ruins, to a Vast Concourse of Spectators.* As indicated by the title, the publication consisted of two principal parts. In the first part, he describes in great detail the topography of area prior to and subsequent to the landslip including measurements of the length, breadth and depth of the chasms and the redirection of the course of the River Severn.[67]

The publication repudiated a Newtonian view of mechanistic regularity of the universe, which results in a deistical world where God is uninvolved in the ongoing activities of the human affairs. Against the philosophers of the day whom Fletcher labels "disciples of Epicurus" that deny the agency of God, Fletcher asserts that God is the force behind nature.[68] Nature is not to be worshiped nor should it be considered merely as the sum of laws by which God generally rules the world. God is the agent behind "natural"

64. Fl-W1856, 6:372.
65. Fl-W1856, 2:246.
66. JF→CW, 30 May 1773.
67. Fl-W1856, 8:219ff.
68. Fl-W1856, 8:272.

God of Nature and of Grace

events. Fletcher replies with the following question: "Can any thing, then, be more irrational than the exclusion of God's immediate agency from the works of nature?"[69] God is the first cause of all things with the exception of moral evil.[70] "But let us hear God himself speaking in Isaiah: 'I am the Lord, and there is none else; there is no God besides me. I,' not nature, 'form the light, and create darkness; I make peace, and create evil.' I create natural, to punish moral evil. 'I the Lord do all these things.' Isaiah xlv. 5, 7."[71]

After determining that the secondary cause of the phenomenon is an earthquake, Fletcher states, "But whatever the second or natural cause of our phenomenon was, it is certain that the first or moral cause of it is twofold: on our part, aggravated sin; and on God's part, warning justice."[72] It seems that Fletcher has adopted Thomas Aquinas' idea of a primary cause, God, who delegates divine action to secondary causes.[73] In this system, suffering and pain are not to be associated with the first cause, "but to the fragility and frailty of the secondary causes through which God works."[74] On the very day of the landslip, Fletcher read and enlarged upon several passages from his book *An Appeal to Matter of Fact, or, a Rational Demonstration of Man's Fallen and Lost Estate*. In these citations, Fletcher pointed out that there are spiritual implications to the occurrence of the natural phenomenon: "Does not the natural state of the earth cast a light upon the spiritual condition of its inhabitants?" The "God of nature and providence" is the one who is the primary Actor and causes the natural events in order "to punish disorders of the moral world."[75] Fletcher sermonized, "God yesterday, for the first time, commanded these fields to rend the rocks in their bowels; to tear the green carpets that cover the surface; and to turn some south, others east and west: and he was obeyed. Thus, the word of the Lord, which is perpetually slighted by the generality of mankind, was instantly submitted to by the inanimate creation."[76]

Fletcher often used the word "nature" in contexts where he clearly had the doctrine of prevenient grace in view. In his observations on Romans 2:14 on the Gentiles who "do by nature the things contained in the law," Fletcher inserted the following parenthetical comment after the word "nature": "in

69. Fl-W1856, 8:272.
70. Fl-W1856, 8:272.
71. Fl-W1856, 8:273.
72. FL-W1856, 8:253.
73. McGrath, *Christian Theology*, 286.
74. Ibid.
75. Fl-W1856, 8:255.
76. Fl-W1856, 8:279.

its present state of initial restoration, without, any other assistance than that which Divine grace vouchsafes to all men universally."[77] Clearly the prevenient grace of God infuses nature, indicating a union between grace and nature; however, he also employed the word differently in other contexts. The word "nature" was sometimes used in opposition to the grace of God, specifically nature could be applied to fallen human nature. In *A Dialogue Between a Minister and One of His Parishioners, on Man's Depravity and Danger in His Natural State*, Fletcher emphasized that the disorders of the world show "that its chief inhabitant is *disgraced* by the God of nature and providence."[78] The disgracing of nature includes cataclysmic events such as "storms, inundations and earthquakes" or more common occurrences such as "lightening and thunder, burning heat and piercing cold;" nevertheless these events "concur to make this earth a vast prison for rebels, who are already 'tied and bound with the chain of their sins,' a boundless scaffold for their execution, an immense 'field of blood,' and, if I may be allowed the expression, the charnel house of the universe."[79]

On the day after the landslip, Fletcher preached a sermon to a crowd that gathered to see the catastrophe that was based on the text from Numbers 16:30–34; the sermon comprises the second part of the aforementioned publication.[80] Whereas the previous section of the publication is principally descriptive, the sermon is a theological interpretation of the event and of course an application of the gospel to the hearers. As in the previous address, God is the main actor whose purpose is to bring the inhabitants of the parish to repentance and Christian faith. The justice and the mercy of God are demonstrated in the catastrophic event, and Fletcher held these two doctrines in a dialectical tension. God has acted in judgment, but has demonstrated his mercy by not pouring out the full measure of the cup of his wrath.[81] Fletcher portrays the divine rationale: "To rouse our souls, he tosses our grounds; to stop us in our sinful career, he absorbs our highway; and to water in our hearts the withered plant of God's fear, he dams up our navigable river."[82] God has demonstrated mercy to the inhabitants by

---

77. Fl-W1856, 3:269.

78. Fl-W1856, 9:474; emphasis added.

79. Ibid.

80 This sermon was not the only sermon that Fletcher preached from the ruins. Jeremiah Bretell reported that Fletcher preached a sermon based on Psalm 46:8. The verse is a further indication of Fletcher's theme of God as the first cause: "Come, behold the works of the Lord, what desolations he hath made in the earth" (Brettell, "Memoir of the Rev.," 651).

81. Fl-W1856, 8:258.

82. Fl-W1856, 2:259.

warning them but not destroying them as they deserved.[83] Thus, both God's mercy and justice are demonstrated in this act of God. Fletcher insisted that the objective of certain songs within scripture is to demonstrate the justice and the mercy of God: "Thus, while the blessed show forth in heaven the praises of his holiness and mercy, the wicked in hell display those of his holiness and justice. Therefore, the destruction of the latter, as well as the salvation of the former, is the proper theme of heavenly songs."[84]

The world of nature displays the variety of God's dealings with creation. The sovereignty of God is demonstrated in the world of nature as Fletcher illustrated spiritual things with natural things: "Why was the lark elected to the blessing of a towering flight, and of sprightly songs, from which the oyster is so absolutely reprobated? the poor oyster, which is shut up between two shells, without either legs or wings, and so far as we know, equally destitute of ears and eyes."[85] In the same manner, the grace of God reflects a great variety in dealings with human beings. God dispenses grace in various manners and in different degrees: "God, as a sovereign benefactor, may, without shadow of injustice, dispense his favours, spiritual and temporal as he pleases."[86] The sovereignty of God results in an "election of distinguishing grace, which is the basis of the various dispensations of divine grace towards the children of men," Fletcher continued with an explanation "Christ dies to purchase more privileges for the Christian church than the Jews, more for the Jews than for the Gentiles."[87] God's partiality is evident in the distribution of divine providential blessings and also in the distribution of spiritual blessings.[88]

Consistent in his dialectical thought, Fletcher insisted that God's equality is evident as well: "The equality of God's ways does not consist in giving just the same number of gracious talents to all; but, first, in not desiring to 'gather where he has not strawed,' or 'to reap' above a proportion of 'his seed:' and, secondly, in graciously dispensing rewards according to the number of talents improved, and the degrees of that improvement."[89] The law of the harvest applies to nature as well as to grace. The law of the grace is "Use grace and have grace." "The inseparable counterpart of the axiom

---

83. Fl-W1856, 8:270.
84. Fl-W1856, 8:268.
85. Fl-W1856, 5:119.
86. Fl-W1856, 3:293.
87. Ibid.
88. Fl-W1856, 5:120. Cf. Cragg, *Reason and Authority in the Eighteenth Century*, 123.
89. Fl-W1856, 2:405–6.

[must be] admitted, 'Abuse grace and lose grace.'"[90] The law of the spiritual harvest is based upon Luke 12:48, "For unto whomsoever much is given, of him shall be much required, and to whom men have committed much, of him they will ask the more."

God uses nature to mediate grace. The subject of God's saving acts is human beings who, due to their fallen nature, have need of a "gradual display" of divine revelation: "But if you mean *Scriptural, distinguishing grace*, that is, the 'manifold wisdom of God,' which makes him proceed gradually, and admit a pleasing variety in the works of grace, as well as in the productions of nature."[91] The need for the accommodation of divine revelation is the rationale for the doctrine of nature and its connection to the doctrine of dispensations.

NATURAL THEOLOGY?

The analogies that Fletcher made raise the question of the role of *analogia entis* in the thought of John Fletcher. Is there any likeness or analogy between the finite and infinite beings in Fletcher's thought? Is there, in Fletcher's thought, an *analogia entis* providing a foundation for a natural theology? The response to this question forms a crucial divide in any theological system.

Central to this discussion is the point of divergence between the Thomists and the Protestant scholastics over the *analogia entis*. While the Thomists argue for an analogy of being between the creature and the Creator, the Protestant scholastics give the doctrine little attention.[92] John Knight argues that Fletcher sought a middle way between a "natural" theology and a thoroughgoing revelational theology.

> Fletcher did not rule out a "theology of nature" or deny the <u>ontological</u> claim of "analogia entis." That is, he was quite willing to assert that there are various levels of Being or Reality, and that Nature objectively reveals God in varying degrees. Indeed, the structure of his whole theology, which rests upon his doctrine of dispensations, is an illustration of this claim. There is a revelation of God that is peculiar to each dispensation. However, Fletcher did insist that this ontological claim of "analogia entis" can be made only from within the framework of faith. The <u>epistemological</u> claim of "analogia entis," then, is invalid. In

---

90. Fl-W1856, 2:406.
91. Fl-W1856, 3:452. Cf. Fl-W1856, 3:452.
92. Muller, *Dictionary of Latin and Greek Theological Term*, 32–33.

other words, one cannot come to understand or recognize the various levels of Reality and Revelation in Nature and history, until first he gives himself existentially to the object revelation of his dispensation. From this standpoint of existential faith, one can then interpret and understand the preceding and inferior dispensations and revelations. Thus the true or "intrinsic" knowledge of God is a Divine gift and is authenticated only in personal faith.[93]

Hence, a purely natural theology is denied. On one hand, Fletcher rejected any hint of a purely natural theology, and as a matter of fact, called it "a painted Jezebel."[94] Influenced by Enlightenment thought, Fletcher was careful, on the other hand, not to allow the pessimism that predominated Calvinistic theology to shatter the optimism inherent in natural theology. He nuanced his position on natural religion as much as he nuanced his position on the natural state of humanity. He accepted the idea of a religion of nature, but quickly clarified what he meant: "Some call it [i.e., Gentilism] the religion of nature: I have no objection to the name, if they understand by it the religion of our nature in its present state of initial recovery, through Christ, from its total fall in Adam."[95]

Despite a generally negative view of natural theology, Fletcher recognized the value of general revelation or a theology of nature. As was stated above, the natural state is a hypothetical theological construction. It was ludicrous, for him, to speak of a natural theology because he believed that all of life was infused by grace. In Fletcher's thought, unlike Calvin, general revelation could lead to special revelation. General revelation is preparatory and introductory to a fuller revelation.

The good news of God's redemptive activity is not limited by the lack of special revelation, but God makes the divine nature known through the means of heralds. "Every dispensation has had its peculiar preachers." Fletcher wrote in *A Portrait of St. Paul*.[96] The preachers that testify to the knowledge of God the Creator include the works of creation, providence,

---

93. J. Knight, "John William Fletcher and the Early Methodist," 211; emphasis original. Cf. ibid., 268–69.

94. Fl-W1856, 152. Gentilism is commonly called "natural religion," but it is appropriately called, according to Fletcher, "the gospel of the gentiles." (Fl-W1856, 5:54; contra. Kudo, Hiroo. "John Fletcher's Concept of Christian Holiness," 13). Cf. A. Wood, *Revelation and Reason*, 24.

95 Fl-W1856, 3:313; 4:78. Fletcher also spoke of a "law of nature" from which Adam and Eve fell (*Essay on the Doctrine of Dispensations* [The Fletcher-Tooth Collection, The John Rylands University Library, The University of Manchester, 18:12], 14].

96. Fletcher-Portrait, 2:171.

the dreadful scourges (famine, pestilence, war, etc.), reason, and conscience.[97] While recognizing the limitations, Fletcher wrote approvingly of the knowledge that could be gained through creation and providence, "That there is a supreme, infinite, and eternal Mind, by which the world was made, is evident from the works of creation and providence."[98] Actually, a failure to recognize the revelation of God through nature is the error of the Calvinists. They failed to recognize the all pervading love of God in the works of creation. In Romans 10 "[T]he apostle starts the great Calvinian objection: 'But how shall they believe, and call on him, of whom they have not heard?' . . . 'Yes, verily,' replies he, 'their sound went into all the earth, and their words unto the end of the world.' If you ask, 'Who are those general heralds of free grace, whose sound goes from pole to pole?' The Scripture answers with becoming dignity, 'The heavens declare the glory of God, and the firmament showeth his handy work.'[99] The primary content of the knowledge that is revealed through nature is that God exists.[100] Not only does God reveal the divine nature through external means, God also reveals through internal light; conscience and reason are also heralds of the grace of God: "'Out of Christ's fulness all have received grace, a little leaven' of saving power, an inward monitor, a Divine reprover, a ray of true heavenly light, which manifests, first moral, and then spiritual good and evil."[101] This internal light is operable in the lives of all and will lead willing persons to "the light of the world."[102] "Those who resist this internal light, generally reject the external Gospel, or receive it only in the letter and history."[103] Obedience to the light brings greater light, but persistent disobedience to the light brings eternal damnation.

For Fletcher, it was ridiculous to speak of a natural theology because in his thought all of life was infused by grace. As Knight states, "[T]here is no 'natural' man who could produce a 'natural' theology, since all men [in Fletcher's thought] have the light of 'prevenient grace.'"[104] The doctrine of grace was the foundation for all the analogies with nature.

97. Fletcher-Portrait, 2:172–73.
98. Fl-W1856, 2:399; 7:155.
99. Fl-W1856, 2:399–400.
100. Fl-W1856, 4:31.
101. Fl-W1856, 2:403.
102. I.e. Christ. J. Fletcher, *Third Check to Antinomianism*, 16.
103. Fl-W1856, 2:403.
104. J. Knight, "John William Fletcher and the Early Methodist." 210. Knight also insists that Fletcher denied an absolute revelational theology because "he thought it reduces man to a mere puppet" (ibid., 210). "Mr. Wesley far from presuming to say that an heathen can be saved by the law, or sect that he professes, if he frames his life

THE CONNECTION OF THE DISPENSATIONS TO CALVINIST CONTROVERSY

Fletcher's doctrine of dispensations arose in response to the Calvinist controversy of the 1770s within evangelicalism of the eighteenth century and cannot be understood adequately apart from this context.

While Calvin held that "a general knowledge of God may be discerned throughout creation—in humanity, in the natural order, and the historical process itself," the epistemic distance between humanity and God is so great due in part to human sin that a natural knowledge "is inadequate as the basis of a fully fledged portrayal of the nature, character, and purposes of God."[105] The proper order of human knowledge of God in Calvin's thought is important: "[T]he noetic order is from Redemption to Creation—only by faith in the Redeemer can we know him as our Creator."[106] While Calvin acclaimed the natural sciences and reason, human or natural knowledge was inadequate to lead one to a saving knowledge of God; faith, in Calvin's thought, was essential to understanding. Human nature must be regenerated to experience grace.

In the Minute controversy of the 1770s, nature was frequently counterdistinguished from grace.[107] One definition of nature is as follows: "Humankind's natural state as distinguished from the nature of grace"[108] The Calvinists of the eighteenth century emphasized such a dichotomy between nature and grace.[109]

In 1773, Sir Richard Hill (1732-1808), one of Fletcher's opponents in the Calvinist controversy, responded to Fletcher's *Fourth Check to Antinomianism* with *The Finishing Stroke*. In his rejoinder to Fletcher's doctrine of prevenient grace, Hill believed that he perceived an inconsistency in Fletcher's thought: grace and nature were two opposing principles, and one must

---

according to the light of nature, cordially believes that all the heathens who are saved attain salvation through the name, that is, through the merit and Spirit, of Christ" (Fl-W1856, 2:250).

105. McGrath, *Christian Theology*, 209-11.

106. Noble, "Our Knowledge of God according to John Calvin," 13.

107. Cf. Cudworth, *Nature and Grace*. Fletcher had a copy of this pamphlet in his personal library.

108. *American Heritage Dictionary of the English Language*, 4th ed., s.v. "nature, n."

109. Forsaith distinguished three meanings of the word "nature" in Fletcher's writings: "First it refers to the immesaurable beauty of creation, to be found in the scenery of Switzerland or of Shropshire. But second, nature is not neutral, for it is used by God as the vehicle to convey messages to humanity. Thirdly, there is a sense of 'nature' in terms of human nature: the propensity to prefer evil to good and spoil the beauty of creation" (Forsaith, "Dreadful Phenomenon at the Birches")

necessarily overpower the other. Hill wrote "[W]hat is it that must improve this universal spark of grace, this light within, since even upon your own plan every man has naturally two principles in him? If you say grace alone carries on the work and triumphs over all opposition, you fall into perseverance, and consequently into Calvinism. If you deny this, you have nothing to say but that nature improves grace."[110] Another Calvinist, John Berridge (1716–1793), also emphasized the disparity between grace and nature:

> Nature is sunk and fallen; and nature's creed is this, Video meliora proboque, deteriora sequor, I see and I approve the better path, but take the worse. Nature may be over-ruled for a time by some violent restraints; but nature must be changed, or nothing yet is done. The tree must first be made good, before the fruit is good. A filthy current may be stopped; but the brook is filthy still, though it cease to flow. The course of nature may be checked by some human dam; yet opposition makes the current rise, and it will either burst the dam, or break out other ways. Restrained sensuality often takes a miser's cap, or struts in pharisaic pride. Nothing but the salt of grace can heal the swampy ground of nature; as Elisha's salt, a type of grace, healed the naughty waters and the barren grounds of Jericho, 2 Kings ii. 20, 21.[111]

Hill insisted that one of two choices was available: the Calvinistic position in which grace overcomes nature or the Pelagian position in which nature overcomes grace[112]

The citations above underscore not only the disparity between grace and nature, but the difference between the Calvinist and Wesleyan understandings of the nature of grace. The Calvinists linked grace with the effectual call of God by means of which believers were quickened and renewed by the Holy Spirit whereas the Wesleyan view of grace emphasized grace as enablement.

Fletcher recognized that at the basis of the Calvinistic view, there is a disparity between grace and nature, and in contrast to Calvin and the Calvinists of his day, he argued for a correspondence between the two.[113] The Calvinist controversy crystallized Fletcher's thinking on the correlation of grace and nature. Fletcher anticipated the response of the Calvinists

---

110. Hill, *Finishing Stroke*, 35.

111. Berridge, *Christian World Unmasked*, 212.

112. Hill cited Wesley, "'There are still two contrary principles in believers, nature and grace'" (*Finishing Stroke*, 35). Wesley added, "True, till they are perfect in love" (WJW, 10:397). Cf. Berridge, *Christian World Unmasked*, 146–147.

113. In *Discours*, Fletcher emphasized the distinctions between grace and nature (Fletcher-Discours, 11).

to the phrase of the Minutes, "And in fact every believer, till he comes to glory, works for, as well as from, life." "How could those who were dead by nature do any work?" was the anticipated question. Fletcher's response reveals the degree to which he had inculcated the theology of Wesley.[114] The love of God, which proffered "the gospel to every creature," made salvation available or efficacious. Within this context, Fletcher quoted Romans 5:18, a favorite verse used to support the doctrine of general justification and emphasized that all were given "a talent of free, preventing, quickening grace,"[115] which enables them to work "from life." Thus, grace interpenetrates nature and overcomes it. In response to the Calvinist idea of human beings being entirely incapable of doing any good works, Fletcher queried "[D]oes not 'grace reign' to control nature?"[116] The very fact that God must intervene proves the corrupt and lost state of humanity.[117]

Despite his opponents' view, Fletcher's doctrine of general justification and prevenient grace enabled him to avoid the Calvinistic dichotomy between nature and grace. In defense of the first point of the extract of the 1770 Minutes in which Wesley argues for the need of continual faithfulness on the part of believers, Wesley cites from Luke 16:11 "if a man is not 'faithful in the unrighteous mammon,' God will not 'give him the true riches.'"[118] Fletcher perceived in the citation, "unrighteous mammon," a depreciative reference to the material and physical and in the citation, "true riches," a reference to the spiritual, divinely-bestowed grace. Although Fletcher recognized the contrast between nature and grace, he recognized an inherent comparison of the two concepts. In his vindication of this particular point of the Minutes, Fletcher recognized that man's unfaithfulness in the lesser, more mundane, material matters will forfeit the blessings of the "more noble and valuable talents of wisdom and grace."[119] Fletcher quoted approvingly from Matthew Henry's commentary on Luke 16:9:

> If we do not make a right use of *the gifts of God's providence*, how can we expect from him those present and future comforts which are *the gifts of his spiritual grace*? Our Saviour here compares these, and shows that though our faithful use of the things of this world cannot be thought to merit any favour at the hand of God, yet our unfaithfulness in the use of them may be justly

114. BiCentWJW, 3:207.
115. Fl-W1856, 2:235.
116. Ibid.
117. Fl-W1856, 2:48.
118. Fl-W1856, 2:202.
119. Cf. Henry, *Matthew Henry's Commentary on the Whole Bible*, in loco.

reckoned a forfeiture of that grace which is necessary to bring us to glory, and that is it which our Saviour here shows, Luke xvi.10–12. [120]

A correlation between nature and grace is assumed.

Previously, it was demonstrated that Fletcher was a dialectical theologian. Here again, he posited a dialectic between grace and nature that is foundational to the functional synergism of his theological system: "When a gardener affirms that he shall have no crop unless he dig and set his garden, does he manifestly set his work above that of the God of nature? And when we say that 'we shall not reap final salvation, if we do not work out our salvation,' do we exalt ourselves above the God of grace?"[121] In this instance, Fletcher does not maintain an unresolved contradiction whether real or apparent between the two opposing forces of his dialectic, but proposed a synthesis or union of the grace and nature.

His rationale for the synthesis lies in his understanding of the nature of God. God through providential watch care over creation superintends both grace and nature. Nature and grace cooperate; the gifts of divine grace and divine providence coalesce: "Believing is the gift of God's grace, as cultivating the root of a rare flower given you, or raising a crop of corn in your field, is the gift of God's providence. Believing is the gift of the God of grace, as breathing, moving, and eating are the gifts of the God of nature."[122] In his *Essay on Truth*, Fletcher wrote,

> The preceding pages represent truth as the remedy and nourishment of our souls; and I have already observed, that as we cannot take food without the continual help of the God of nature, so we cannot receive the truth without the continual assistance of the God of grace; it being the first axiom of the Gospel, that all our sufficiency and ability to do any good are of God.[123]

Because God is God of nature and of grace, truths may be found in the natural order whose purpose is to lead to the Source of these truths, i.e., Christ who is the Truth. Fletcher wrote, "When *natural* and inferior truths raise our minds to the God of *nature* and of *grace*, they answer their *spiritual* ends: but if they are put in the place of their archetypes and antitypes, 'the truth of God is changed into a lie.'"[124]

---

120. Fl-W1856, 2:230; emphasis added.
121. Fl-W1856, 3:442.
122. Fl-W1856, 4:13.
123. Fl-W1856, 4:44.
124. Fl-W1856, 4:31.

The union of grace and nature provides foundation for the correspondence between the doctrines of Creator and Redeemer and the epistemological order from creation to redemption. Against Calvin's noetic order, Fletcher would insist that knowledge of the Creator is prior to knowledge of the Redeemer because, for example, it is impossible for one to have an awareness of the need to repent of offending God without an awareness of God's existence. However, it is important to note that the prior salvific activity of God makes possible all human knowledge of the divine. Both nature and grace are legitimized in his thought, and knowledge is given a soteriological purpose. The point is essential to Fletcher's concept of dispensations: Human knowledge is by its very nature progressive, but all human knowledge has its source in prevenient grace.

SUMMARY

Fletcher has been characterized as a dialectical theologian. However, in regard to the doctrine of grace and nature, he did not propose an unresolved dialectical tension between the two doctrines as he had done with other doctrinal concepts, but a synthesis or union of the concepts. The union arose from Fletcher's conviction that the God of nature and the God of grace is one God whose grace is demonstrated in every aspect of divine works. The One whose "name and nature is love" does not permit creation to return to the chaos toward which the trajectory of the Fall tends, but God continues to recreate the world, restoring fallen creation and the ruined race. God's love for creation causes grace to take precedence in divine-human relations; prevenient grace is the keystone of Fletcher's theological system. God's acts are chronologically prior to any human activity and essential to all human action.

Order and harmony were highly valued by Fletcher. His theological writings are a composition of the variegations of divine revelation into an organized, harmonious whole that reflects all of history and the variety of God's dealings with humanity. The dispensations were a reflection of those variegations of revelation and the next chapter provides a summary of them.

3

The Doctrine of Dispensations
An Overview

IN HIS DISSERTATION, JOHN Knight argued that a theology of history is significant in Fletcher's thought. His arguments will only be summarized here. Christian faith enables one to discern meaning in history. Divine revelation unfolds in the activity of God within history, but neither revelation nor Scriptures provides a cogent philosophy of history. Fletcher did not attempt to supply the lack of a rational philosophy of history, but employed a theology of history to serve his doctrinal purpose of demonstrating the universal scope of the atonement. Knight defines a "theology of history" in Fletcher's thought as follows: "[I]t is meant that he saw by faith the clue to the meaning of history in the biblical record of God's revelation which has climaxed in Christ, and that he deliberately used this history as a theological tool."[1] All of history is Christocentric and was interpreted in the light of revelation in Christ: Fletcher's theology of history enabled him to discern its "unity, pattern, and theme" through Christ and provided an understanding of the direction, meaning, and purpose of history.[2] All periods of history before and after Christ find meaning in Christ who is the *telos* of history; the teleological purpose of history is realized existentially when human beings respond to divine revelation. Salvation history and

---

1. J. Knight, "John William Fletcher and the Early Methodist," 17.
2. Ibid., 18.

The Doctrine of Dispensations

divine revelation are both progressive and history progresses toward the goal: Christ.[3]

Thus, history has a goal and a purpose, and its anthropological *telos* is the restoration of humanity in the image of God. A connection between the doctrine of providence and a theology of history is evident. God is concerned with the conservation, preservation, and government of the world and exercises care through divine redemptive activity. In Fletcher, history has purpose and significance because God is intricately concerned with creation.

PARALLELS WITH FEDERAL THEOLOGY

Parallels of Fletcher's thought with federal theology have been acknowledged.[4] A summary of Willem J. van Asselt's work, *The Federal Theology of Johannes Cocceius (1603-1669)*, will provide an overview of the salient features of federal theology, which will supply the structure for the present discussion of Fletcher's theology of history. In federal theology, the idea of covenant has a "constitutive significance" and is central to the entire theological system.[5] The characteristics of federal theology include a pietistic spirit, a focus on practical truth as manifested in salvation and on the relation between revelation and history.[6] Cocceius conceptualized the dynamic of history, first, as an *ordo temporum*, "which proceeds linear-historically, from beginning to end, and from the preceding to the subsequent,"[7] and secondly, as an *ordo salutis*, the temporal order of events in the salvation of a sinner. Thus, Cocceius' understanding of history retains both objective and subjective dimensions. However, van Asselt issues a word of caution regarding the way one conceives these two dimensions of his view of salvation history: One should not set salvation history over against the order of salvation or assign priority to one or the other dimensions of Cocceius' thought; because the one thing Cocceius does not do is to reduce salvation history to the *ordo salutis* (or vice versa). Nor does he subordinate one to the other. It is more accurate to speak in terms of correspondence or *analogy* between salvation history and the order of salvation.[8] Van Asselt categorizes

---

3 Ibid., 19.

4 Ibid., 21. Cf. ibid., 174; and O'Malley's preface in L. Wood, *Meaning of Pentecost in Early Methodism*, v.

5 Van Asselt, *Federal Theology of Johannes Cocceius*, 1.

6 Ibid., 1-2.

7 Ibid., 297.

8 Ibid., 308.

previous interpretations of Coccceius as either evolutionary or synthetic and commends a pneumatological model as the best for interpreting Cocceius' thought. The activity of the Holy Spirit beginning with creation and continuing throughout history in the revelation of Jesus and the dawning of the kingdom of God is "the most important factor for the maintenance of historical continuity in Coccceius' thought."[9] Coccceius held in dialectical tension the doctrines of creation and soteriology. Van Asselt summarizes, "Coccceius' understanding of *profectus* (progress) in dealing with both the (objective) history of revelation (*ordo temporum*) *and* the (subjective) faith history (*ordo salutis*) is by definition a pneumatological category that precludes all monistic interpretations."[10] Coccceius' theology of history defies easy categorization and the model that enables accurate understanding of its complexity is the pneumatological model, which retains, in particular, the dialectic of God as Creator and of God as Redeemer.

Federal theology accentuates the covenantal history in the unfolding of God's redemptive activity. Federal theologians advocate two covenants: the covenant of works, which governed relations with supralapsarian Adam and was abolished after the Fall ushering in a new order of affairs, and the covenant of grace. The substance of the covenant of grace remains stable over the period of history, but the administration of God's saving activity is historically distinguished because God accommodates revelation to fallen human nature and finitude. The history of salvation demonstrates progress due to its accommodative nature; however, Coccceius, van Asselt insists, did not hold to progressive revelation, but maintained a progress of salvation history.[11]

While parallels may be seen between Fletcher's thought and federal theology, the primary purpose of the above survey is to provide a structure for the discussion of Fletcher's theology of history. Under discussion now is the first of these dimensions of history, the *ordo temporum*.

Ordo Temporum: An Objective View of History

In Fletcher's thought the *ordo temporum* consists of two covenants: the covenant of works and the covenant of grace. The covenant of works was established with supralapsarian Adam[12] alone and demanded absolute

---

9. Ibid., 301.

10. Ibid., 310.

11. Van Asselt asserts, "Coccceius recognizes a progressive history of salvation, but not a progressive revelation" (ibid., 296).

12. Supralapsarian means before the Fall.

obedience: "Nor does this covenant make any allowances for deficiencies, or pass by one transgression, great or little, without pronouncing the threatened curse."[13] The covenant of grace was established with infralapsarian Adam[14] in behalf of the whole human race as a redemptive accommodation to fallen humanity.

The covenant of grace unfolded in three successive ages of history: the dispensations of the Father, Son, and Spirit. The dispensation of the Father began after the Fall with the promise of a Redeemer that was made to Adam and all the human race and was renewed repeatedly throughout OT history.[15] The dispensation of the Son was opened by John the Baptist, culminated with the earthly ministry of Jesus, and anticipated a more spiritual dispensation.[16] The promise of the dispensation of the Son crystallized on the day of Pentecost when the disciples were baptized with the Holy Spirit; the period that began on that day awaits the promise and culmination of the second coming of Jesus.[17]

The above model of the dispensations focused on the theological, Trinitarian pattern of God's salvific activity in history. A second overarching pattern emerges, which provides an anthropological structure that is occasionally threefold: heathens, Jews, and Christians;[18] at other times, it is four-fold: gentilism, Judaism, the gospel of John the Baptist, and the perfect gospel of Christ.[19] These differing patterns reveal the variegations of the activity of God in history.

Other soteriologies did not view the redemptive activity of God with sufficient breadth; they focused exclusively on God's saving activity in Christ and paid scant attention to the activity of the Father and the Spirit.[20] For Fletcher, the problem was not just an overemphasis on the work of one Person of the Trinity, but the neglect of God's salvific activity in those periods of history. Fletcher believed that the Triune God was active in history in the periods prior to as well as after the Christ event.[21]

---

13. Fl-W1856, 3:373.
14. Infralapsarian means after the Fall.
15. Fletcher-Portrait, 2:138–139. Cf. Fletcher-Dispensations, 73.
16. Fletcher-Portriat, 2:139–140.
17. Fletcher-Portrait, 2:144.
18. Fl-W1856, 4:329.
19. Fl-W1856, 5:54–57.
20. Fl-W1856, 5:198.
21. Thus, Fletcher asserted the doctrine of appropriation, denying a chronological modalism.

The Calvinist position, according to Fletcher, bifurcated God into Creator and Redeemer; God was not sufficiently concerned with all of creation to attempt its redemption. Against the asperity of the Calvinist doctrine of particular election and reprobation, Fletcher argued that God, as Creator and Redeemer, was sufficiently concerned for all of creation, and divine love infused all of nature and creation. Because God loves every creature, God did not defer redemptive activity to some future intervention thereby relegating those who lived prior to the intervention to damnation, but God demonstrated divine love for all creation by salvific activity in every period of history. The Protoevangelium reveals that the atonement extended to Adam who was a beneficiary of "the free everlasting gospel," which Christ preached in paradise.[22] God, as Redeemer, has acted in every period of history to redeem creation. To argue otherwise is to bifurcate God the Creator from God the Redeemer or to question the love of God for creation—something Fletcher did not do. Thus, as was argued previously, the union of grace and nature is foundational for Fletcher's understanding of his doctrine of dispensations. Grace and nature are united because God the Creator and God the Redeemer is One. Salvation history, then, is significant in Fletcher's thought.

Ordo Salutis: A Faith History

"Dispensation," at its most basic meaning, involves two activities: first, it involves the activity of God in dispensing or distributing proportionately grace to human recipients according to their capacity to receive. Secondly, the recipients are responsible to appropriate existentially the extrinsic revelation. Thus, the dual activity of the doctrine of dispensations is fundamental to the functional synergism of Fletcher's system. The doctrine of dispensations has therefore two aspects: it signifies the activity of God in history and the subjective appropriation by human beings of the extrinsic revelation.[23]

The doctrine of dispensations reflects the "saga of salvation"[24] or a narrative theology of salvation. Salvation history occurs at two levels: a macro or universal level, which entails the divine effort to redeem humanity, and a micro or personal level in which the doctrine of dispensation functions as an order of salvation. The micro scheme reflects the macro scheme.[25] As in

---

22. Fl-W1856, 2:402.
23. Cf. Langford, *Practical Divinity*, 1:45.
24. Flick, "John William Fletcher," 155.
25. Cf. J. Knight, "John William Fletcher and the Early Methodist," 10.

federal theology, the personal history of believers was analogous to salvation history; the two are not synonymous because as John Knight asserts, the internal dispensations "transcend the categories of space and time."[26] In *The Holiness Pilgrimage*, Knight confirms, "Fletcher was convinced that the spiritual pilgrimage of individual men in each of the dispensations is a recapitulation or microcosm of the way God is working in all of history."[27]

The doctrine of dispensations reflects both the progressive nature of God's revelation in the history of humanity and the progressive nature of God's restoration of individual human beings in the image of God with the goal of Christian perfection.[28] John Knight defined dispensation in Fletcher's thought as

> facets of knowledge of God, by which all men—since every man has some knowledge of God—may be classified. While there are infinite degrees of the knowledge of God, there are three main stages of divine knowledge, or three distinct dispensations—that of the Father, Son, and the Holy Spirit. Each dispensation has an external and an internal aspect. The former is cognitive and depends upon the actual information or content concerning God which may be granted to man. The latter aspect is personal or existential and relates to man's commitment to what has been revealed cognitively to him.[29]

John Knight insightfully provided a hermeneutical principle for interpreting Fletcher's theology of dispensations: "[W]hen Fletcher spoke of the audience of the dispensations (Jew, Gentile, etc.), he could mean the audience of either the external or the internal dispensation or both. The context must be studied to determine his precise reference."[30] The personal or existential aspect of Fletcher's doctrine of dispensations appears in the one of his earlier works, which will now be examined.

Spiritual Manifestation of the Son of God

One of Fletcher's earliest sustained treatments on the doctrine of dispensations appears in his work *Six Letters on the Spiritual Manifestation of the*

---

26. Cf. ibid., 14.

27. J. Knight, *Holiness Pilgrimage*, 66. Knight reflects the language of Wiggins ("Pattern of John Fletcher's Theology," 232).

28. Fletcher wrote, "We grow rich in grace by degrees. as Children, beasts, plants" (JF→sermon, Ephesians 3:8).

29. J. Knight, "John William Fletcher and the Early Methodist," 8.

30. Ibid., 14.

Son of God (1767). These letters are a polemical treatise against Sandemanianism.[31] Robert Sandeman (1718–1771) came under the influence of John Glas, a dissenting minister who repudiated the idea of national covenants, and the former wrote *Letters on Theron and Aspasio* in response to James Hervey's *Theron and Aspasio*.[32] Sandeman argued that justifying faith is merely intellectual assent to the revelation of God in Christ.[33] In Sandeman's words, "All who believe the same truth, who have the same notion of divine grace, or who understand these words *Jesus is the Christ* in the same sense as the apostles, have equally precious faith with them."[34] Faith was not subjective appropriation of trust in Christ but an objective, mental assent to the gospel.

Fletcher's concern over Sandemanianism arose because the doctrine had encroached into Methodism. In the 1760's, Benjamin Ingham, an Anglican clergyman and a close associate of the Wesleys, and the churches in his connection, came under the influence of Sandemanianism.[35] Ingham, in fact, defended Sandemanian teaching in a book published in 1763 entitled, *A Discourse of the Faith and Hope of the Gospel*.[36] Close connections were maintained between Ingham and the Calvinistic wing of Methodism; Ingham's wife, Lady Margaret, was a sister-in-law to Lady Huntingdon.[37]

Fletcher indicated to Lady Huntingdon that their doctrinal discussions on the spiritual manifestations of Christ had caused him to meditate on the subject that became foundational to his treatise, *Six Letters on the Spiritual Manifestation*.[38] Fletcher intimated that the work was polemical in nature: "I have found both comfort and profit in setting upon paper the reflections I have been enable[d] to make upon the mysterious subject; and they have, through mercy, set my soul more than every against the rampant errors of Sandemanianism."[39] The intended recipient of the treatise is unclear. However, the connections with the Inghamite Society are too obvious to ignore. The respectful tone of the letter "Sir," the references to "our" church, and

---

31. Streiff, *Reluctant Saint?*, 103ff.
32. See Hervey, *Theron and Aspasio*.
33. Sandeman, *Letters on Theron and Aspasio*, 2:301.
34. Ibid., 2:ii.
35. Rose, *Dictionary of Evangelical Biography*, s.v. "Ingham, Benjamin," 591.
36. Podmore, "Ingham."
37. Schlenther, *Queen of the Methodists*, 21–22, 83. However, there is no evidence that CH was carried away by this wind of doctrine.
38 Fletcher wrote, "Some of our conversations upon the manifestations of the Son of Man to the heart have led me into many an hour's consideration. The Holy Ghost alone can clear up the points to pursue" (JF→CH, 24 Nov. 1767).
39. JF→CH, 24 Nov. 1767.

The Doctrine of Dispensations

Fletcher's repeated references to the Anglican standards indicate that the recipient may have been an Anglican clergyman.[40] Fletcher indicates in the opening of the first of the six letters that he had recently seen the recipient of the letters and the letter assumes a friendly tone.[41] The limited evidence indicates that the recipient of the *Six Letters* was an Inghamite and was perhaps Benjamin Ingham himself.

One of the primary themes of the letters is the experimental knowledge of the Son of God. The issue was addressed from a historical viewpoint: Since those who lived in the period prior to Christ did not have the same cognitive knowledge as those who have lived since Christ, does the limited knowledge of the former enable their experiential knowledge of the Son of God? Despite the apparent lack of availability of cognitive knowledge in the period of history prior to the coming of Christ, Fletcher argues that sufficient knowledge was available for a spiritual manifestation of the Son of God or for intrinsic knowledge. Indeed, one of the themes of letters five and six is the emphasis on the manifestation of the Son of God or "Jehovah Jesus" in all ages. The limitations of the cognitive, noetic revelation do not limit the universality of the work of God. Fletcher surveyed the various manifestations in the Old and New Testaments to prove that "in every age of the church, God hath favoured the sons of men with peculiar displays of his presence."[42] The proffered salvation was qualitatively the same in every era of history but with variations in degree. The title of the treatise, then, reveals Fletcher's concern to prove that the second Person of the Trinity was working redemptively in all periods of history.

While, at first, this would seem to flatten history and to weaken the cross of Christ that is at the center of the Christian view of history, Fletcher argued conversely by asserting a progressive view of salvation history. The revelation of God is adapted progressively to the limitations of humanity or as Fletcher stated it, "to the various states of the church."[43]

Spiritual Senses

In the first letter, Fletcher insisted upon the experimental knowledge of God rather than a mere intellectual knowledge of God. Fletcher spoke of a spiritual manifestation of God to human beings through what he called

---

40. Fl-W1856, 9:10–11.
41. In 1760, Fletcher briefly considered an offer to tutor Benjamin and Lady Margaret Ingham's son (JF→CW, 26 September 1760).
42. Fl-W1856, 9:36.
43. Fl-W1856, 9:28.

"spiritual senses." His objective in the first letter is to prove these spiritual senses "by the joint testimony of scripture, our church, and reason."[44] In suggesting the idea of spiritual senses, Fletcher was consistent with John Wesley's position as expressed in the latter's *An Earnest Appeal to Men of Reason and Religion*.[45] Wesley, reflecting the empiricism of the age, postulated that the operations of the Holy Spirit may be known not through the five natural senses but through the spiritual senses that are operative through the power of faith.[46] Fletcher asserted that in the fall Adam lost the experimental knowledge of God and the natural state of human beings is such that they are "incapable of perceiving spiritual things, as a person in a deep sleep, or a dead man, of discovering outward objects."[47] Thus, the source of the experimental knowledge of the Redeemer is not to be found within human capabilities, but in divine grace.[48] Fletcher argued that the exercise of the spiritual senses "is peculiar to those who are born of God."[49] However, this does not negate what is said above regarding the possibility of salvation prior to the advent of Christ because God revealed the divine nature to the OT characters by condescending to their natural senses, not their spiritual senses. In the patriarchal period, the cognitive content of revelation was very limited and tended to consist of principally external manifestations but was nevertheless sufficient because the manifestations provided for an experimental knowledge of the Son of God. In his discussion of Wesley's concept of spiritual senses, Theodore Runyon points out that the intervention of God is essential to bring to life the spiritual senses: "[T]here must be a re-creative intervention of the divine Spirit if the veil of ignorance is to be lifted and the spiritual senses reawakened. Regeneration is a divine creative act that calls the dead to life, and new birth opens a new world of sensitivity to spiritual reality."[50] For Fletcher, this is true as well: regeneration enables the five spiritual senses.[51]

---

44. Fl-W1856, 9:5.

45. BiCentWJW, 11:56. Cf. BiCentWJW, 11:57; Blevins, "Pneumatology in John Wesley's Theological Method," 107.

46. Collins, *Theology of John Wesley*, 142.

47. Fl-W1856, 9:6.

48. Fl-W1856, 9:14.

49. Fl-W1856, 9:5.

50. Runyon, *New Creation*, 77.

51. Fl-W1856, 9.6ff. Fletcher wrote of the awakened sinner, "With regard to God, they do not have any Spiritual sensation. The man who sleeps has eyes but is incapable of seeing objects. The sleeper has ears does not hear at all. He has hands but does not feel at all. He has a mouth but cannot taste" The original appears in French: "Mais a lEgard de Dieu ils nont aucune sensation Spirituelles. L'homme qui nest pas regénéré

The Doctrine of Dispensations

Regeneration as an Epistemological Event

The solution for the rationalistic, objective knowledge of the Sandemanian clergyman, which falls short of the experimental knowledge of Christ, is not any extraordinary manifestation but the baptism with "the Holy Ghost and spiritual fire . . . the common blessing which can alone make a man a Christian, or confirm him in the faith."[52] Fletcher emphasized heart knowledge in this treatise without mitigating the significance of head knowledge; the new birth enables not only the spiritual senses but also understanding. Early Methodist epistemology restricted the dictum of Augustine, "*Crede, ut intelligas*," to an experimental and relational faith. Runyon states, "Justification and regeneration are therefore, in addition to everything else, an *epistemological* event that opens up a new way of knowing."[53]

Fletcher stressed regeneration or the new birth, and at the same time, he emphasized the degrees of spiritual development. Does the emphasis on degrees (incremental change) not undermine the emphasis on qualitative change? Kenneth Collins points out the significance of qualitative change in Wesley's thought: "The new birth, then, as evidence of the new creation, marks the beginning not simply of an incremental change, not merely one of degree, but a qualitative change which issues in a distinct kind of life."[54] In Fletcher's thought, regeneration is defined broadly; there are various degrees of qualitative change in the process of salvation. He wrote, "Regeneration differs but in degree of strength & soundness."[55] The first qualitative change occurred after the pronouncement of the Protoevangelium by the implantation of the "seed of regeneration" in the human race. It consisted of the restoration of Adam's reason and conscience and by consequence provided a capacity in human beings for responding to further overtures of grace: "The first man, to whom the promise of redemption was made, contained in himself the whole of his posterity; and *this promise*, wonderfully *powerful*, as being the *word of God* (Heb. iv. 12), had an indescribable effect upon the whole human race, implanting in man a *seed of regeneration*, a *Logos*, a *reason*, a *conscience*, a *light*, in short, a *good principle*, which, in every sincere

---

endormi a des yeux a des yeux mais ne saurait decouvrir les objets . . . Le dormeur a des oreilles mais il nendent point. Il a des mains in ne sen sert point il ne sent point. Il a une bouche mais il ne peut Gouter" (JF→sermon, Ephesians 5:14a). Cf. J. Fletcher, *Discours Sur la Régénération*, 16–17.

52. Fl-W1856, 9:24.

53. Runyon, *New Creation*, 80 (emphasis original).

54. Collins, "The New Creation as a Multivalent Theme in John," 85.

55. J. Fletcher, The Test of a new Creature, September 1758, The Fletcher-Tooth Collection, The John Rylands University Library, The University of Manchester, 36.6.

inquirer after truth, has been nourished by the grace of God, and seconded by the pious traditions of Patriarchs, Prophets, Apostles, Evangelists, or true Philosophers."[56] The seed of regeneration effected the qualitative change thereby making all human beings response-able.[57] Another qualitative change is spiritual regeneration, which makes the believer holy. Wiggins affirms the need for such a qualitative change in Fletcher's thought: "The most crucial distinction he drew was that between outward reformation and Christian regeneration. Outward reform may come through the strength of preventing grace, reason, and reflection, but never regeneration."[58]

In response to the Sandemanian's objection that "God favoured the patriarchs and Jews with immediate revelations of himself, because they had neither the gospel nor the scriptures,"[59] Fletcher argued from his concept of progressive history of salvation that the experience of Christians superseded the experience of the patriarchs. However, there is undeniably continuity between the dispensations: the same God who revealed the divine nature by immediate manifestations to the patriarchs would continue to do so to believers in the present dispensation. Otherwise, one would say,

> As for thy sacred book, thou knowest that sometimes the want of money to purchase it, the want of learning to consult the original, the want of wisdom to understand the translation, the want of skill or sight to read it, prevent our improving it to the best advantage, and keep some from reaping any benefit from it at all. O Lord, if, because we have this blessed picture of thee, we must have no discovery of the glorious original, have compassion on us, take back thy precious book, and impart thy more precious self to us, as thou didst to thy ancient people.[60]

At the conclusion of his argument, he reinforces his insistence in the progressive nature of salvation history: "St. Paul declares, that though the Mosaic dispensation was glorious, that of Christ exceeds it in glory."[61] It is much preferable to see the manifestation of God's presence than to merely read about it in a book. The particular manifestations of Christ "far from ceasing with the Jewish, have increased in brightness and spirituality under the Christian dispensation."[62]

56. Fletcher-Portrait, 2:308.
57. Dunning, *Grace*, 152.
58. Wiggins, "Pattern of John Fletcher's Theology," 105.
59. Fl-W1856, 9:44.
60. Fl-W1856, 9:46.
61. Ibid.
62. Fl-W1856, 9:44.

Having laid the epistemic foundations for the life characterized by the grace of God in Fletcher's thought, some characteristics of the doctrine of dispensations will be discussed in order to further elucidate it.

CHARACTERISTICS OF THE DOCTRINE OF DISPENSATIONS

Prevenient Grace as a Foundational Doctrine

In order to understand the doctrine of dispensations, one must understand that the doctrine of the love of God and its concomitant doctrine of prevenient grace is the keystone of Fletcher's theological system.[63] Like other early Wesleyan Methodist theologians, Fletcher held to the doctrine of total depravity like his Calvinist counterparts, but unlike his opponents, Fletcher held to the doctrine of prevenient grace, which enabled him, as did they, to ascribe all blessings to grace: "From the Creator to the creature, all blessings are and must for ever be of grace, of mere grace."[64] Two different types of grace are evident: original grace and gospel grace.[65] Original grace is the grace that Adam had before the fall that "flowed from God, as Creator and Preserver, to innocent, happy creatures."[66] Gospel grace is the evangelical, transforming grace given by God as Redeemer and Comforter to guilty humans.[67]

Prevenient grace is a category of gospel grace, not of original grace. The doctrine took a central place in the discussions during the Calvinist controversy. When Richard Hill accused John Wesley of giving his imprimatur to Fletcher's doctrine of free will and of denying and affirming at the same time the doctrine of free will,[68] Wesley, in his *Remarks on Mr. Hill's Review*, retorted, "This may prove that Mr. W. contradicts Mr. F., but it can never prove that he contradicts himself. But, indeed, both Mr. F. and Mr. W. absolutely deny natural free-will. We both steadily assert that the will of man is by nature free only to evil. Yet we both believe that every man has

---

63. J. Knight agrees, "The foundation stone of the doctrine is prevenient grace, which Fletcher accepted as being Scriptural" ("John William Fletcher and the Early Methodist," 178).
64. Fl-W1856, 3:369; 3:394.
65. Cf. Fl-W1856, 3:303.
66. Fl-W1856, 3:369.
67. Ibid. Cf. Fl-W1856, 3:417.
68. Hill, *Review of all the Doctrines Taught by the Rev.*, 129.

a measure of free-will restored to him by grace."[69] According to Fletcher, his Calvinist opponents and the Wesleyan Methodists agreed on a number of issues regarding free will: 1) the will is always free; 2) apart from the prevenient grace of God, humans are free only to sin; 3) the freedom to do right has its source in the redeeming grace of God.[70] The difference between the two camps was that whereas Fletcher's opponents held to the doctrine of divine fiat, which automatically produced saints, the Wesleyans insisted upon the probationary state and the moral responsibility of human beings.

When discussing prevenient grace, Fletcher was rather optimistic regarding its effects: "[T]he blessing which we have in Christ is far superior to the curse which Adam entailed upon us; we stand our trial upon much more advantageous terms than Adam did in paradise."[71] The blessing that is restored through prevenient grace is the capacity to receive grace, "a power to believe and repent;" this capacity extends to every member of Adam's race.[72] Prevenient grace provided all human beings with the capacity to cooperate with the grace of God.[73]

Not only does prevenient grace enable cooperation with the measure of grace dispensed, but it also facilitates human capacity to grasp the knowledge of God that is communicated through nature. Prevenient grace provides foundation for the analogy that Fletcher conceived between grace and nature.

Mildred Bangs Wynkoop in her book, *A Theology of Love* characterized Wesley's anthropology as historical, personal, dynamic, and social.[74] Wesley rejected Calvinist anthropology with its static, inert being in favor of a dynamic anthropology; in Wesley's view human beings were vital participants in history, not mere "lumps of clay." Wesley's doctrine of prevenient grace protected his view of human beings as vital participants in the grace of God and "a real living involvement in grace."[75] Prevenient grace enabled human beings to be "response-able,"[76] i.e., able to respond to the grace of God as moral agents in the divine-human relationship. Knight depicts Fletcher as the corruptor of the mature John Wesley's theology: "[B]ecause he was convinced that Fletcher had held so well these ideas together, after 1770

69. WJW, 10:392.
70. Fl-W1856, 3:188.
71. Fl-W1856, 3:127–28.
72. Fl-W1856, 2:402.
73. Fl-W1856, 3:305.
74. Wynkoop, *Theology of Love*, 79–87.
75. Ibid., 80.
76. Dunning, *Grace*, 152. Dunning uses the nominal form "response-ablility."

he frequently emphasized works and free will almost to the exclusion of grace."[77] However, Knight failed to recognize the foundational significance of grace to Fletcher's thought. As was pointed out in the previous chapter, Fletcher did not bifurcate grace from his anthropology; in Fletcher's thought, the grace of God had intervened in order to reverse the human situation. An overemphasis on human free will to the exclusion of divine grace would have been inconsistent with Fletcher's concept of the union of grace and nature. God's grace infused all persons in all periods of history. The Wesleyan view of human personhood is grounded in history. The doctrine of dispensations provides a theology of history in Fletcher's thought, a subject that will be discussed more fully below.

Dispensations as Noetic and Existential

Shipley argued that one of the major contributions of Methodism was that "it rediscovered and reasserted the intrinsic authority of the Divine revelation."[78] Divine revelation, in Fletcher's thought, included both subjective and objective aspects; human knowledge of the divine was both noetic and existential. For Fletcher, the empirical revelation within the human consciousness through the presence of the Holy Spirit is "primary and intrinsically authoritative."[79] The extrinsic authorities are nature and the Scriptures,[80] which are "secondary and extrinsically authoritative."[81] According to Shipley, "empirical revelation is fundamentally authoritative and is of primary significance for [Fletcher's] theology."[82]

Shipley's categories are helpful in their broadest application, but not in understanding every facet of Fletcher's doctrine of revelation. The difficulty of understanding Fletcher's concept is that both revelation and reason have subjective and objective aspects. However, it must be noted that revelation is not inherent or intrinsic to fallen human nature. Reason in Fletcher's thought is not intrinsic to fallen humanity: "[R]ight reason," Fletcher said, "is a ray of 'the light that enlightens every man who comes into the world;'

---

77. J. Knight, "John William Fletcher and the Early Methodist," 382.

78. Shipley, "Methodist Arminianism in the Theology of John," 132; emphasis original. Cf. McDonald-Ideas, 264.

79. Shipley, "Methodist Arminianism in the Theology of John," 140.

80. Ibid.

81. The Church may serve in a secondary sense as an extrinsic authority with the Anglican standards taking principal place.

82. Shipley, "Methodist Arminianism in the Theology of John," 138.

and a beam of the eternal *Logos*, the glorious 'Sun of Righteousness.'"[83] Reason, thus, has its source in the prevenient grace of God and is not inherent to fallen humanity. Chronologically, a subjective revelation, "the seed of supernatural grace,"[84] precedes objective revelation as the Second Person of the Trinity is "the light which enlightens every man which cometh into the world" (John 1:9). This corresponds with the idea of regeneration as an epistemological event discussed above. The extrinsic revelation of irresistible prevenient grace restored the light of reason, which enables human beings to make judgments about chronologically subsequent extrinsic revelations. The epitome of all extrinsic revelation is the empirical, Christian revelation of God, but not all humans will attain to such an experience due to their geographical location or place in history, which limits them from the Christian extrinsic revelation of God in Christ; nevertheless their existential appropriation of the measure of truth available to them by means of faith and obedience to the "light which enlightens every man" ensures their salvation. The limitations of extrinsic revelation do not limit the universality of the work of God. Despite the limited availability of cognitive knowledge in the period of history prior to the coming of Christ, Fletcher argues in *Six Letters on the Spiritual Manifestation of the Son of God* that sufficient knowledge was available for a saving, intrinsic knowledge of the Son of God. Shipley summarized, "The salvific revelation is universal in scope; it is qualitatively the same in its historical manifestations though variable in degree."[85]

In saving knowledge, reason and revelation work harmoniously and given time and opportunity lead to the highest experience available in this life, i.e., Christian perfection. Fletcher guided his readers between Scylla and Charybdis, advising them to avoid "the wild rocks of superstition and enthusiasm" on one hand and "the opposite rocks of Deism and profaneness" on the other.[86] The purpose of *An Appeal to Matter of Fact and Common Sense* is stated, "To point out the happy medium which they have missed and call them back to the narrow path, where reason and revelation walk hand in hand, is the design of these sheets."[87] In another place, he cried, "Let reason and revelation hold out to thee their consentaneous light."[88]

---

83. Fl-W1856, 2:8. JB held that JF was influenced by Chevalier Andrew Michael Ramsay (JF→MBF, 5 August 1788).

84. Fl-W1856, 2:74.

85. Shipley, "Methodist Arminianism in the Theology of John," 128.

86. Fl-W1856, 2:7.

87. Ibid. Cf. LJW, 5:364.

88. Fl-W1865 3:323.

The Doctrine of Dispensations

Frequently, Fletcher appealed to the extrinsic revelation of Scripture and made use of external proofs such as miracles and prophecy to validate his arguments.[89] Yet, extrinsic knowledge alone is insufficient; it is not saving knowledge. Consequently, Fletcher railed against the rationalism of his day by appealing for an "experimental knowledge."[90] John Knight emphasized the importance of intrinsic knowledge in Fletcher's thought:

> Yet such [extrinsic] knowledge is not redemptive, i.e., does not of itself bring salvation. This knowledge is presented to man's God-given capacity to reason. To it man may give either mental assent or rejection. As such it is a mere object of the mind. In this sense, the initial gift of God may be spoken of as external or objective. Such knowledge cannot become "saving" until it is believed with one's entire being and is existentially apprehended by the faith of obedience. Salvation-knowledge is more than mental comprehension; it is the commitment of the total self to the Divine Being.[91]

The work of the Spirit was the primary paradigm by which Fletcher emphasized the importance of empirical knowledge. Ever the evangelist, Fletcher's emphasis upon the work of the Spirit was a call to the rationalist to move beyond the cognitive content of the lower dispensations to experience the fullness of the Godhead. A unique contribution of Fletcher's doctrine of dispensations is to amalgamate external knowledge and internal knowledge into one system.

A Comprehensive and Balanced View of Soteriology

One of the outstanding characteristics of Fletcher's theological system is its comprehensive character. Benjamin Gregory recognized the breadth of Fletcher's theological system: "Fletcher perceived the composite character of the rays of Revelation, and could not bear to see them decomposed, to cast a lurid and phantasmagoric glare on the tenets of a sect or school."[92] Despite Benjamin Gregory's laudation, it must be emphasized that Fletcher's works were principally polemical and as such, lack the comprehensive scope

---

89. Fl-W1856, 2:99–101.
90. Fl-W1856, 9:4.
91. J. Knight, "John William Fletcher and the Early Methodist," 192–93.
92. Gregory, "John Fletcher, the Theologian," 36–37. In the same article, Gregory wrote that "the grandest qualities of a Master in Israel are those which most signally distinguished the theology of Fletcher—namely Breadth, Boldness and Balance" (Gregory, "John Fletcher," 33).

of a systematic theology. His primary concern was similar to the sentiment of Wesley who wrote in a letter to Christopher Hopper in 1788, "I have only one thing to do, to save my own soul and those that hear me."[93] The doctrine of dispensations focuses on Fletcher's soteriological concerns and reflects the breadth to which Gregory referred by providing a comprehensive view of soteriology that includes the whole gamut of God's saving activity in human history and looks toward the *eschaton*. Shipley reflects an understanding of the comprehensive nature of Fletcher's dispensations, "Salvation is for the Wesleyans . . . a comprehensive term, the full description of which may require consideration of the whole span of an individual life and, ultimately, the totality of human history in all of its vicissitudes as related to an unlimited series of grace-events."[94]

In one of Fletcher's most mature writings, *The Doctrines of Grace and Justice*, he discussed the scope of the doctrine of dispensations and its connection to the grace and justice of God. Fletcher perceived this treatise to be the end of the controversy with the Calvinists: "I hope however the Lord will spare me to publish my end of the controversy, which is a double dissertation upon the Doctrines of Grace and of Justice, which I hope will reconcile all the candid Calvinists and Arminians, and will be a means of pointing out the way in which Peace and harmony might be easily restored to the Church."[95] Fletcher offered correctives to the extremes of "rigid Calvinism" and of "rigid Arminianism" in the form of two axioms that compose his dialectic. The first axiom, "Our salvation is of God," serves to correct the extreme Arminians who stress the capabilities of fallen human beings to such an extent that the gracious activity of God in redemption is denigrated. The second axiom, "Our damnation is of ourselves," corrects the extreme Calvinists who stress the sovereignty of God to such a degree that God is identified as the author of sin. Fletcher attempted a mediating position between these two extremes and in doing so, defined the gospel as follows: "The gospel, in general, is a divine system of truth, which, with various degrees of evidence, points out to sinners the way of eternal salvation, agreeable to the mercy and justice of a holy God; and therefore the gospel is an assemblage of holy doctrines of grace, and gracious doctrines of justice."[96] Fletcher quoted Mark 16:16, "He that believeth and is baptized shall be saved; but he that believeth not shall be damned," to prove his proposed dialectic

---

93. WJW, 12:319.
94. Shipley, "Methodist Arminianism in the Theology of John," 222.
95. JF→CW, 11 May 1776.
96. Fl-W1856, 5:53.

between the doctrines of grace and justice.[97] In the historical essay of the *Equal Check*, Fletcher wrote, "It is equally clear from Scripture and reason that we must believe in order to be saved consistently with God's mercy; and that we must obey in order to be saved consistently with his holiness. These propositions are the immovable basis of the two gospel axioms."[98] The foundation for the dialectic of the doctrines of grace and justice is the essential nature of God as holy-love: "[Fletcher] concluded two things: one, that a dispensation of grace always accompanies a demand of justice; two, that a just distribution of grace is followed always by a gracious demand of justice in any dispensation."[99] Fletcher, like his mentor, John Wesley, held that the essential nature of God is holy-love.[100]

As Wesley stated in a letter, Fletcher's doctrine of dispensations attempts in the words of Milton,

> To vindicate eternal Providence,
> And justify the ways of God to man. [101]

While a study of history reveals the inconsistencies of God's dealings with human beings, Fletcher's doctrine of dispensations provides a coherency and consistency to the doctrine of divine providence. God's essential nature of holy-love remains a constant throughout all of history and in God's dealings with humanity. Against the Arminians who would impugn the gracious activity of God by stressing the free agency of humanity and its role in salvation, Fletcher emphasized the prior, loving activity of God in all of history to redeem humanity. Against the Calvinists who would impugn the holiness of God with their doctrine of particular predestination, Fletcher emphasized the equity of God's dealings in every period of history. Thus God is blameless; the dispensations demonstrate God's grace and justice in the divine regulation of human affairs in so far as human beings can understand God's ways.

Despite Fletcher's attempt to "justify the ways of God," the doctrine of dispensations still retained a mysterious element because the dispensing activity of God in human history evinces the inequalities of life. Fletcher drew from the parable of the talents to illustrate that God distributes differently in different dispensations: "the Christian has five talents, the Jew

---

97 Fl-W1856, 5:54–56.

98. Fl-W1856, 3:353. Cf. Fl-W1856, 4:159–60.

99. Fuhrman, "Contribution of John Fletcher to," 91.

100. Cf. ibid., 94, 64. Fletcher's thought is consistent with that of John Wesley's; cf. Collins, *Theology of John Wesley*, 22.

101. WJW, 13:55.

two, and the heathen one."[102] The equality of God is demonstrated in two ways: first, a reward is available for all dependent upon the faithful stewardship of the talent; second, "proportionable improvement" is a possibility under each dispensation.[103] It must be pointed out as H. D. McDonald summarizes Wesley's sermon "The Imperfections of Human Knowledge," "The inequalities of life are not its injustices, since the reason for them lies in the mysterious purposes of God. The sure fact is that times and seasons are in His hands."[104]

As W. R. Davies emphasized, "God's sovereignty was exercised argued Fletcher, in his distribution of talents of grace."[105] Fletcher recognized the significance of the doctrine of the sovereignty of God to the Calvinist system and did not completely dispense with it. The doctrine of grace and justice results in a unique dialectic in Fletcher's thought and was "the most valuable contribution," according to Davies, which he made to eighteenth century theology.[106] Fletcher made a significant contribution because of the comprehensive nature of his theological system.

Accommodation and Salvation History

The source of redemptive activity is God alone. God initiates the redemption of lost humanity. "God's initiative to reach out to human beings is decidedly missiological: he makes himself known so that he can be known."[107] As the initiator of salvation, the God of love considers the subjects of divine saving action and their limitations and frailties that are characteristic of human nature. The disparity between the infinite, transcendent God and finite, frail humanity is a reality of the divine-human relationship. The doctrine that describes God's gracious consideration of human frailty in order to overcome the distance in the divine-human relation is called "accommodation." Edward A. Downey Jr., in his book entitled *The Knowledge of God in Calvin's Theology*, defines the doctrine of accommodation as "the process by which God reduces to human capacities what he wills to reveal of the infinite mysteries of his being, which by their very nature are beyond the powers of the

---

102. Fl-W1856, 2:405.
103. Fl-W1856, 2:405–6.
104. McDonald, *Ideas of Revelation*, 247.
105. Davies, "John Fletcher of Madeley as Theologian," 693.
106. Ibid., 691. Cf. Davies, "John Fletcher of Madeley as Theologian," 407.
107. Corrie, *Dictionary of Mission Theology: Evangelical Foundations*, s.v. "Revelation," 339.

mind to grasp."[108] Central to the doctrine of accommodation is the God of love who knowing humanity's limitations and the noetic effects of sin acts in accordance with them in order to communicate effectively.

Downey who analyzes the doctrine of accommodation within the thought of Calvin, simplifies the varieties of accommodation to two: "(a) the universal and necessary accommodation of the infinite mysteries of God to finite comprehension, which embraces all revelation, and (b) the special, gracious accommodation to human sinfulness."[109] In Calvin's system, the doctrine of accommodation implies two offices of the Son of God:

> For there are two distinct powers which belong to the Son of God: the first, which is manifest in the architecture of the world and the order of nature; and the second, by which he renews and restores fallen nature. As he is the eternal *Speech* of God, by him the world was made, by his power all things continue to possess the life which they once received; man was endued with an unique gift of understanding, and though by revolt he lost the light of understanding, yet he still sees and understands, so that what he naturally possesses from the grace of the Son of God is not entirely destroyed. But since by his stupidity and perverseness he darkens the light which still dwells in him, it remains that a new office be undertaken by the Son of God, the office of Mediator, to renew by the Spirit of regeneration man, who had been ruined.[110]

In Calvin's thought, the proper order of human knowledge of God is important: "[T]he noetic order is from Redemption to Creation—only by faith in the Redeemer can we know him as our Creator."[111]

However, in Fletcher's thought the order is reversed. Against Calvin's noetic order, Fletcher would insist that knowledge of the Creator is prior to knowledge of the Redeemer because, for example, it is impossible for one to have an awareness of the need to repent of offending God without an awareness of divine existence. Whereas Calvin's system overrides any personal or salvation history by divine fiat, Fletcher's order respects the historical sequence of divine revelation.

History is significant in Fletcher's thought. Both personal faith histories and salvation history have real significance. God accommodated

---

108. Downey, *Knowledge of God in Calvin's Theology*, 3.
109. Ibid., 4.
110 Calvin, *Calvin's Commentaries*, on John 1:5, in loco.
111. Noble, "Our Knowledge of God According to John Calvin," 13.

revelation to humanity due to the limited human capacity to receive revelation.[112] Fletcher's doctrine of dispensations is the means by which he communicated the unfolding progress of God's revelatory activity. The dispensations are truly dispensations of grace whereby grace is dispensed according to the dictates of humanity's capacity.[113] Because of human limitations, accommodation becomes a series of divine actions that aim at the goal of "full" revelation. God desires to reveal as fully as possible but only as fully as human beings are capable of receiving. The issue, then, is not the supremacy of divine revelation; God desires to reveal fully and supremely. However, the timing of revelation is significant; revelation is dispensed in apportioned measures and at appropriate times according to the dictates of human capacity to absorb it. The fuller revelation does not invalidate the earlier revelations; the latter are only incomplete and find their fulfillment in subsequent history.

History is the only proper context for the accommodating activity of God. Implicit in the doctrine of accommodation is the idea of the progress of salvation history. Anne Williams stated, "The human mind could no more comprehend the grace of God than a thimble can contain the ocean—and yet God has, through history, made himself progressively better understood by man, as human capacities have been rendered ever readier to receive him."[114] She adds that "the doctrine of accommodation also stipulates a progressive revelation of divinity to man throughout history, a development analogous to that from childhood to maturity."[115]

The noetic order is significant: God cannot be understood in any other way. The noetic order of human understanding of God is foundational for Fletcher's doctrine of dispensations—the unfolding of God's self-disclosure in history. In Fletcher's thought, God is known in sequence as Creator, Redeemer, and Sanctifier. The dispensation of the Father must of necessity precede the dispensation of the Son. The cognitive knowledge made available

---

112. Fletcher quoted from Joseph Alleine who affirmed the doctrine of accommodation. "'The terms of mercy'—he should have said, The terms of eternal salvation—'are brought as low as possible to you. God has stooped as low to sinner, as with honour he can. He will not be thought a factor of sin, nor stain the glory of his holiness; and whither could he come lower than he hath, unless he should do this? He has abated the impossible terms of the first covenant'" (Fl-W1856 3:265).

113. A phrase from Wesley's comments on 2 Cor. 3:9 reveals an understanding of God's accommodation in the history of salvation: "But how can the moral law (which alone was engraven on stone) be the ministration of condemnation, if it requires no more than a sincere obedience, *such as is proportioned to our infirm state*?" (emphasis added).

114. Williams, "Gracious Accommodations," 14.

115. Ibid., 15.

The Doctrine of Dispensations

by the prior dispensation is foundational for the existential experience of the succeeding one.[116] The history of God's self disclosure respects the noetic order of the human mind. "There is an essential difference between the holy faith of Adam in a state of innocence, and the justifying, sanctifying faith of a penitent sinner: for Adam only stood and worked by faith in God as Creator; but we rise, stand, and work, *chiefly* by faith in God as Redeemer and Sanctifier."[117] This corresponds with one of the normal patterns of the dispensations: the dispensations of the Father, Son and Spirit. The idea of sequence is very important in Fletcher's thought.

Progressive View of Salvation History

While the term "dispensation" does have a temporal significance and in some theological systems indicates a static view of time,[118] Fletcher's view of time is dynamic, rather than static.[119] His dynamic view of history intersects with his doctrine of progressive salvation history.[120] However, it must be emphasized that Fletcher did not hold to the view of progressive revelation with its modern connotations, but held rather to the idea of a progress of salvation history. For Fletcher, the sequence of history itself is revelatory.

It has been acknowledged that the idea of progress is fundamental to Fletcher's doctrine of dispensations. In fact, progression is evident in the history of God's revelatory activity who reveals divine nature progressively as Father, then as Son and later as Spirit. Fletcher used "the *gradual* displays of 'the manifold gospel grace of God'" to speak of the progress of salvation history and "the different states of advancement in the christian faith."[121] He used many images in order to convey the progressive, unfolding nature of the divine dispensations.[122] In response to the objection to Fletcher's position that the possibility of the salvation of heathens under the inferior dispensation negates any need for further revelation, he used the image of light, one of his favorite images for a progressive view of salvation history:

116. Fl-W1856, 4:119–20.

117. Fl-W1856, 4:94.

118. Fletcher's doctrine of dispensations has very little resemblance to the dispensations of modern dispensationalism of the Plymouth Brethren despite Fletcher's inclusion in Ehlert's *Bibliographic History of Dispensationalism*, 41–42.

119. Cf. L. Wood, *Meaning of Pentecost in Early Methodism*, 372; Flick, "John William Fletcher," 155.

120. Lawton, *Shropshire Saint*, 90.

121. Fletcher-Portrait, 2:151.

122. Fl-W1856, 2:399; emphasis added.

"Or to answer by a comparison: If we see our way by starlight, what need is there of moonshine? If by moonshine, what need of the dawn of day? If by the dawn of day, what need of the rising sun? The brightness of Divine dispensations, like the light of the righteous, 'shines more and more unto the perfect day.'"[123] Light is Fletcher's favorite metaphor for the doctrine of prevenient grace and conveys the centrality of the doctrine of grace to his theological system.[124]

A progressive view of salvation history raises a number of issues and a discussion of them will enable a clearer understanding of Fletcher's thought. How can one reconcile the idea of the progress of history with the doctrine of original sin?[125] Fletcher's optimism regarding history was based upon the activity of God within history and specifically upon the prevenient grace of God. Progress, in Fletcher's thought, is particularly evident in salvation history when humans cooperate with the grace of God and not history as a whole as Nash conceives it. Fletcher portrayed the prospects of natural man in very bleak terms and saw evidence of an erosion of the morals of the Christian faith.[126] However, natural man was a theological construct: "[W]e believe that no child of Adam is a natural man in the Calvinian sense of the word, (that is, absolutely destitute of all saving grace,) except he who has actually sinned away his day of grace."[127] Divine overruling providence has intervened in history to reveal what cannot be discovered through unassisted nature.[128] What William Cannon pointed out about Wesley's view of history holds true for Fletcher's view as well; God has overruled history and overrules events to accomplish the divine will: "God will not save man without man's consent, for freedom is indigenous to human nature as God originally created it. Nonetheless, whether man obeys or disobeys, God is still the Lord of history, capable even of making the wrath of men to praise him."[129]

Another issue is whether or not Fletcher employed the concept of progress to the OT as a hermeneutical tool.[130] In Fletcher's thought, the

---

123. Fl-W1856, 2:251.

124. Fletcher used many other metaphors to illustrate the progressive nature of history: Fl-W1856, 2:397; FL-W1883, 2:340; Fletcher-EC1, 152, 232, 170, 253; Fletcher-Vindication, 59; Fletcher-Creed, 36.

125. Nash, *Meaning of History*, 82.

126. Fl-W1856, 3:305, 7:91–92.

127. Fl-W1856, 3:305.

128. Fletcher-Portrait, 2:213–16.

129. Cannon, "Methodism in a Philosophy of History," 41.

130. Fletcher did not use the idea of progress as in liberal Protestant hermenutics (Bright, *Authority of the Old Testament*, 187).

idea of progress in salvation history arises from the Scripture, and he did not violate, in his opinion, the principles of hermeneutics in the application of the interpretive lens, the doctrine of dispensations to Scripture. Lawton writes, "He did not work it out critically regarding the Scripture itself, but in applying it to non-biblical, non-christian history, he shows himself more enlightened than many of his contemporaries. All history has value, though not all equal value."[131] Thus, progressive revelation is not an accurate description of Fletcher's concept because the doctrine of dispensations was not a hermeneutical tool as the modern use of the term indicates; progressive history of salvation is a more accurate understanding of his scheme.[132]

There is an integral connection between the doctrine of accommodation and a progressive view of salvation history. At the heart of the doctrine of accommodation is the God of grace who knowing humanity's limitations accommodated divinity to human beings in order to communicate effectively. God reveals progressively as human capacities are prepared to receive and understand God's nature and salvific purpose. Anne Williams pointed out the integral connection between a progressive view of history and the doctrine of revelation: "[T]he doctrine of accommodation also stipulates a progressive revelation of divinity to man throughout history, a development analogous to that from childhood to maturity."[133]

The purpose of divine accommodation to the human condition was pedagogical. Glenn Burt Hosman writes of Wesley's view of history: "In almost romantic language, Wesley has described his view of history. History, when most fully understood, reveals God's Truth. History is instructive of the doctrines of religion, and it inspires one toward gratitude to God and goodness to man. In other words, History is the record of the dialogic relationships of God and man, and man and neighbour, if indeed they can be so dichotomized."[134] For Fletcher, history itself was pedagogical when humans respond to the grace of God. Faith is by nature pedagogical, and instruction and growth in grace require history. In Chapter VII of the *Fourth Check*, Fletcher argued against the Calvinistic doctrine of finished salvation, which was based upon the words of Christ upon the cross "It is finished" by positing the necessity of history for the remaining work of Christ, including the resurrection and ascension, as a basis for the ethical admonitions of the

---

131. Lawton, *Shropshire Saint*, 90.

132. Fletcher, like Coccieus, "recognizes a progressive history of salvation, but not a progressive revelation" (Van Asselt, *Federal Theology of Johannes Cocceius*, 296).

133. Williams, "Gracious Accommodations," 15.

134. Hosman, "Problem of Church and State in the Thought of," 188.

Bible, and the development of Christian virtues.[135] History is the context for the redemptive activity of God in which He affects the transformation of human beings.

DEGREES AND THE PROGRESSIVE NATURE OF GRACE

Progression is evident in both the macro and the micro aspects of history, i.e., in the lives of individuals as they progress in their knowledge of the Triune God. The progressive nature of the dispensations hinges upon the initialness of objective revelation and the subsequentness of subjective or empirical revelation: God reveals; humans respond to divine revelation. Fletcher wrote, "[F]aith is more or less operative according to the quality of the truth presented to us; according to the power of the Spirit of grace impresses it upon our hearts; and according to the earnestness with which we receive, espouse, and welcome it to our inmost souls."[136] In history, God has revealed the divine nature progressively to humanity; the noetic aspect of the revelation precedes the empirical revelation.[137] Such an order points to the primacy of divine revelation over the subjective experience of revelation. John Knight writes, "It is clear that for him all knowledge of God is dependent on revelation, on God's initiative."[138] Consequently, empirical revelation is contingent upon the extrinsic revelation which, by its historical quality, is progressive. Empirical revelation is, then, by nature progressive. Thus, the progression of revelation occurs both historically and existentially.

Hence, Fletcher's *ordo salutis* was progressive as was Wesley's.[139] In the manuscript, *The Test of a new Creature*, Fletcher stresses the instantaneous and progressive nature of grace: "Many look on finished holiness as instantaneous; all grace is instantaneous. But what is given in a moment is enlarged & established by dilligence & fidelity. That which is instantaneous in its decent is progressive in its increase."[140] Both Wesley and Fletcher made much use of the concept of degrees of spiritual development.

---

135. Fl-W1856, 3:71–86, 6:67–69.

136. Fl-W1856, 4:35.

137. Cf. Wiggins, "Pattern of John Fletcher's Theology," 41.

138. J. Knight, "John William Fletcher and the Early Methodist," 192.

139. Cf. O'Malley, "Pietistic Influence on John Wesley," 65, and Collins, *Theology of John Wesley*, 285.

140. J. Fletcher, The Test of a new Creature Being queries proposed to some supposed perfect in love, September 1758, Fletcher-Tooth, JRULM, 36.6, 8. "The Test of a New Creature" in the published Works follows largely the version that is written in Mary Fletcher's hand, i.e., The Test of a New Creature Being Questions of Examination for the Spiritually Minded, September 1758, Fletcher-Tooth, JRULM, 36.6. Mary Fletcher

Fletcher avoided flat interpretations of Scripture that imported the meaning of a word from one context to another. In *Five Letters to the Reverend Mr. Fletcher*, Richard Hill accused his opponent of positing that dead men work for life[141] because Fletcher vindicated the phrase of the Minutes "working for life,"[142] advocating what Hill perceived to be works righteousness. Employing the skills that are reminiscent of the scholastic theologians, Fletcher replied in *The Third Check* nuancing the terms "spiritual life" and "spiritual death" and described their various degrees.[143] In Fletcher's thought, there are many different categories of degrees of spiritual development: degrees of justification;[144] degrees of perfection;[145] degrees of light;[146] degrees of the manifestation of the Spirit;[147] degrees of sin,[148] etc. Though Fletcher's opponents accused him of "'inventing' sorts of faith 'by the dozen,'"[149] he adamantly refused to flatten the meanings of words giving them only one sense that applied in all contexts. This hermeneutical principle is the basis for his multiplication of degrees. One of these degrees now demands special attention.

Degrees of Truth

In Fletcher's thought, there are varying degrees of truth. A superior truth does not invalidate an inferior truth. The cognitive content of the various dispensations is progressive. Understanding of truth unfolds in a trinitarian manner.

1. <u>Dispensation of the Father</u>: In the dispensation of the Father, the essential truth is the existence of God, "God is." He places emphasis on *God the Creator*.[150]

---

wrote, "Many look on finished holiness as instantanious, all Grace is instantanious: but what is given in a moment is inlarged and Established by diligence and fidelity. that which is instantaneous its decent is *perfective* in its increase" (emphasis added).

141. Hill, *Five Letters to the Reverend Mr.*," 8.
142. Fl-W1856, 2:234–35.
143. Fl-W1856, 2:429.
144. Fl-W1856, 2:433–34.
145. Fl-W1856, 2:434.
146. Fl-W1856, 4:33.
147. Fl-W1856, 2:441.
148. Fl-W1856, 2:463.
149. Fl-W1856, 4:94.
150. Fl-W1856, 4:37.

2. <u>Dispensation of the Son</u>: Here Fletcher places emphasis upon the atoning work of Christ; the central truth is "God is love." *God the Redeemer* is at the forefront.[151]

3. <u>Dispensation of the Spirit</u>: The indwelling presence of the Spirit of God is the focus of the third dispensation. "God is mine in Christ." His emphasis is upon *God the Sanctifier*.[152]

The quality of the existential relation that one has depends upon the objective data available. Saving faith applies the cognitive content of revelation. Fletcher defines saving faith in the following manner: "justifying or saving faith is believing the saving truth with the heart unto internal, and [as we have opportunity] unto external righteousness, according to our light and dispensation."[153] Fletcher defines faith as "believing heartily."[154] Faith is only effective when it is receiving grace and returning love,[155] and by returning love, Fletcher means doing good works. His definition of faith is very general and may be applied to the cognitive content.

The quality of the operation of faith depends upon the quality of truth embraced: "[A]s some wines are more generous, and some remedies more powerful, so some truths are more reviving and sanctifying than others."[156] The existential relationship may not rise above the cognitive content,[157] and if the cognitive content of one dispensation is not embraced existentially, one cannot make any spiritual advances. The degrees of faith correspond with the degrees of truth. Knight summarizes, "One is judged at any given moment according to the truth revealed to him, i.e., to his reason, in his dispensation. For example, had Peter died immediately following his acknowledgement of Jesus as the Son of God, he would have been saved, although at that time he had not yet heard of the resurrection. Indeed, it was not yet truth, not having yet occurred."[158]

A clarification should be made about the above discussion. Truth for Fletcher was not relative in the sense of "lacking absolute quality."[159] Truth

---

151. Ibid.
152. Ibid.
153. Fl-W1856, 4:11–12.
154. Fl-W1856, 4:11.
155. Fl-W1856, 4:56.
156. Fl-W1856, 4:34.
157. Fl-W1856, 4:15–16.
158. J. Knight, "John William Fletcher and the Early Methodist," 202–3.
159. Davies asserts, "Truth, Fletcher claimed to be a relative term in the sense that different dispensations had different revelations given to them of what truth consisted in" ("John Fletcher of Madeley as Theologian," 208). But, this does not indicate "lacking absolute quality."

is personified in Jesus who said "I am the way, the *truth*, and the life" (John 14:6); however it is not limited to the historical person of Jesus. Truth is not caught in time; it is embodied in the Son of God and thus, transcends the historical period of Jesus' earthly ministry. As a result, truth is disclosed in various degrees within history.

In his *Essay on Truth*, Fletcher quotes at length "two of the most judicious divines of the last century,"[160] whose quotations unfold his own view of truth. According to the first writer, John Flavel, in his *Discourse on Mental Errors*, truth must be embraced wholeheartedly; the condition of the one who chooses not to embrace truth is painted vividly by Flavel as allowing "Satan to ride the fore horse, and guide that which is to guide the life of man!"[161] The next quote from John Goodwin places even more emphasis upon spiritual digression when one does not receive the truth. Goodwin employs the term *degree* to describe this digression, a term that Fletcher employed frequently to describe the progress of one who receives the truth: "All error . . . being seated in the understanding, secretly and by degrees infuseth a proportionable malignity into the will and affections, and occasioneth unholy dispositions."[162] What is important to notice here is that Fletcher acknowledged that when truth is not embraced, degeneration rather than progress results. The crux of the issue is one's attitude toward the truth. This, however, affects a personal faith history rather than the history of salvation.

One Gospel: Different Degrees

While God's saving activity appears in various degrees in history, salvation history cannot be divided into various unrelated parts. While there are many different degrees, Fletcher constantly insisted that there is only one gospel, and the dispensations are different degrees of the same gospel. Many other modifiers of the noun "gospel" were such as "Gentile," "Jewish," and "Christian." However, the gospel is one, and Christ is the foundation for each of the dispensations.

> I declare, once more, that I make no more difference between the faith of a righteous heathen, and the faith of a father in Christ, than I do between day-break and meridian light: that the light of a sincere Jew is as much one with the light of a sincere Christian, as the light of the sun in a cold, cloudy day in March, is one with the light of the sun in a fine day in May: and that the

160. Fl-W1883, 1:576.
161. Fl-W1883, 1:577.
162. Ibid.

difference between the saving faith peculiar to the sincere disciples of Noah, Moses, John the Baptist, and Jesus Christ, consists in a variety of *degrees,* and not in a diversity of *species.* [163]

In this manner, Fletcher retained the unity of God's redemptive purpose in all of the various dispensations. Unity is evident in all of the dispensations because of the revelatory activity of God in history who is the cause and source of mercy; the unity of the divine salvific purpose is evident in various degrees, the demand of works in every dispensation, and the rewards for those works.[164] "The three dispensations have one common end. They mutually tend to manifest the different perfections of the Supreme Being, to raise man from his present low estate, and to perfect his nature."[165]

The progressive nature of the dispensations accounts in part for the cohesiveness of Fletcher's system. Fletcher understood the dispensation as "the *gradual* display of the manifold gospel grace of God."[166] Fletcher uses many images in order to convey the progressive, unfolding nature of the dispensations.[167] With his concept of the progress of salvation history, Fletcher retained the unity of the OT and NT despite their diversity.

The *Telos* of History: Christian Perfection

Fletcher's doctrine of Christian perfection maintains the unity of the *ordo temporum* and the *ordo salutis*; the goal of God's redemptive work is the perfection of the human race and of individual believers. Perfection is given an escatological orientation in Fletcher's view of salvation history whose *telos* is Christ.[168]

Fletcher posited degrees of perfection, which he linked to the various dispensations. Perfection was available in every dispensation of grace, but all degrees of perfection were relative.[169] There are four degrees of perfec-

163. Fl-W1856, 4:94, emphasis added.

164. Ibid.

165. Fletcher-Portrait, 2:166.

166. Fl-W1856, 2:399.

167 Wesley's thought reflects the same idea of progression, according to John Knight ("John William Fletcher and the Early Methodist," 114).

168. Ibid., 19.

169. Fletcher distinguished between "sorts" of perfection and "degrees" of perfection. The only sort of perfection that was absolute was the absolute perfection of God. In *The Last Check*, Fletcher discussed these different sorts of perfection: the absolute perfection of God, the perfection of archangels, the perfection of angels, the perfection of glorified saints, the perfect Christians, gentile's perfection, Jew's perfection, the perfection of infant Christianity, the perfection of adult Christianity, the perfection

tion: the perfection of gentilism; the perfection of Judaism; the perfection under the dispensation of John the Baptist; and the perfection of the Christian dispensation.[170] Each subsequent dispensation results in a more meaningful experience, a greater understanding of God, and a greater piety as the believer advances toward Christlikeness and perfect love. Even Christianity, as a religion, is more perfect than other religions because it advances the piety of its adherents. In *La Grâce et la Nature*, Fletcher wrote, "[W]e must insert here that it is *the most perfect* of all the Religions, & that it guides men to *the most sublime* vertues."[171] The piety of the believers was one of Fletcher's primary concerns and the doctrine of Christian perfection plays a significant role in his theological system in the struggle against antinomianism.[172] Fletcher believed that maintaining the goal of Christian perfection protected believers against antinomianism.

When love is the *telos* of Christian life, certain benefits result.[173] The teleological view of the Christian life has some practical implications that are not preserved in other traditions: "Hence it is evident, that the doctrine we maintain, if it is properly guarded, far from having a necessary tendency to lull people asleep, is admirably calculated to excite every penitent to faith, prayer, the improvement of their talent, and the perfecting of holiness."[174]

In each dispensation, there is always openness to new light and for a superior revelation. The heathen or the Jew or the imperfect Christian cannot remain (provided opportunity to advance) in inferior dispensations. Fletcher insists that the heathen cannot take shelter in the dispensation of the Father. In his address to the antichristian moralist, he wrote, "Do you act a reasonable part when you take shelter under the dispensation of the heathens, from the blessings that pursue, and from the light that surrounds you, in this Christian land? If I may allude to the mysterious divisions of Solomon's temple — will ye obstinately remain in 'the court of the Gentiles,' when you are graciously invited to enter into 'the holy place,' with true Christians? Think ye, that because righteous heathens are saved without the explicit knowledge of Christ, *ye* may be saved upon *their* plan?"[175]

---

of disembodied spirits, and the complete perfection of glorified saints (Fl-W1856, 5:461–63).

170. Fl-W1856, 5:466–67.
171. Fletcher-Grâce, 354.
172. Cf. Lindström *Wesley and Sanctification*, 100.
173. Ibid., 99, 101.
174. Fl-W1856, 4:101.
175. Fl-W1856, 4:77.

THE DOCTRINE OF DISPENSATIONS AND FLETCHER'S DOCTRINE OF THE TRINITY

In general, the Western church, under the influence of Augustine, placed greater emphasis on the unity of God emphasizing "the relation of the three persons in terms of their mutual fellowship," whereas the Eastern church emphasized the distinction of the three persons or the *hypostases* of the Godhead.[176] When theologians do not give adequate emphasis to the distinction between the persons of the Trinity, the roles of the persons of the Trinity appear to be reduced.[177]

Early Methodist Trinitarian Pneumatology

Albert Outler argued that Wesley's doctrine of grace and the *ordo salutis* is "explicitly pneumatological and implicitly trinitarian."[178] Outler advocated a greater focus on Wesley's trinitarian pneumatology that does not bifurcate Christology and pneumatology.[179] Outler draws upon an article written by Kilian McDonnell who underscores the lack of a full-orbed witness of the Scripture to the Holy Spirit, but points out that the triadic emphasis in the NT is the basis for the present understanding of the doctrine of the Trinity.[180] The economy of salvation reveals the Triune God; H. Ray Dunning asserted that it was the experience of the early Christians that produced the doctrine of the Trinity: "They encountered Him as always and everywhere (Father); as there and then (in Jesus Christ); and as here and now (Holy Spirit)."[181] While the person and ministry of the Spirit are equal with the person and ministry of the Son, "the Spirit is an interpretive perspective which informs the whole of theology, operating at the center of the Christological moment."[182] The Spirit operates in a hermeneutic role, interpreting the history of God's revelatory activity: McDonnell asserts that the Holy Spirit has a "contact function:" "In functional terms (obviously not ontologically) the Spirit is the point of contact between God and humankind

---

176. McGrath, *Christian Theology*, 324.
177. Cf. Coppedge, *God Who Is Triune*, 108.
178. Outler, *Wesleyan Theological Heritage*, 167.
179. Cf. Vickers "Albert Outler and the Future of Wesleyan Theology," 57. Note the trajectory of recent scholarship in Wesley studies to read Wesley's soteriology in light of the Eastern tradition (Rainey, "John Wesley's Doctrine of Salvation in Relation," 55).
180. McDonnell, "Trinitarian Theology of the Holy Spirit?," 203, 205.
181. Dunning, *Grace*, 90.
182. McDonnell, "Trinitarian Theology of the Holy Spirit?," 226.

... The Spirit who is experienced in history is that point of contact between God and humankind, the point where 'the perfect Father' through the Son touches history and therefore the Church, but in another direction the Spirit is the point of entry into the mystery of Christ through which the mystery of the Father is attained."[183] Knowledge of God is communicated through means of the Spirit who is (not spatially) but functionally immediate to human beings because of the Spirit's role in salvation history. The mission of Christ and the Spirit are central and equal, but are not the same. McDonnell points out a distinction, "The doctrine of the Spirit is a methodological center, not a material center. If Jesus is the 'what,' the Spirit is the 'how.'"[184] The Spirit mediates knowledge of Jesus and the Father; valid experiences of God are mediated by the Holy Spirit and center upon God's revelation in Christ. McDonnell writes, "[T]here is no experience of the Spirit except through Christ. Or, cast in more philosophical terms, every experience of the Spirit is materially, not formally, the experience of Christ."[185]

Wesley's Trinitarian Ordo Salutis

That Wesley reflected a penchant for a trinitarian pneumatology is evident from his views of the Trinity; his Trinitarian thought reflects a focus on the economic Trinity. Wesley made a distinction between the fact and the manner of the Trinity and insisted on the former due to his penchant for biblical language over speculative theology.[186] Collins points out, "Wesley was principally concerned with what theologians today call the 'economic' Trinity, that is, God as revealed in the economy of salvation, along the *ordo salutis*, rather than with the 'immanent' Trinity, the relations within the Christian Godhead, a topic that Wesley always deemed to be far too speculative."[187] In the economy of salvation, God has revealed the divine nature in history as Father, Son and Spirit; Collins writes, "[T]he name 'Father' designates the origin of the revelation, the Son, the historic Mediator, and the Holy Spirit,

---

183. Ibid., 208.
184. Ibid., 215.
185. Ibid., 206.
186. Cf. Rainey, "John Wesley's Doctrine of Salvation in Relation," 58.
187. Collins, *Theology of John Wesley*, 146. Cf. Collins, "Reconfiguration of Power," 171. Fletcher did not avoid employing the idea of the immanent Trinity to support his argument for the doctrine of the Trinity (J. Fletcher, A pocketbook "Spiritual Extracts," Fletcher-Tooth, JRULM, 20/11; J. Fletcher, Check to Socinianism and Arianism, Fletcher-Tooth, JRULM, MAM Fl. 17).

the *present reality* of this revelation."[188] Wesley's penchant for an economic Trinity is reflected in a Trinitarian *ordo salutis*.

Cieslukowski and Colyer argue that the normal pattern of the *ordo salutis*, which entails an emphasis on prevenient grace, convicting grace, justifying grace, sanctifying grace, and perfecting grace is anthropocentric rather than theocentric and that a trinitarian pattern is more consistent with Wesley's unfolding pattern of human participation in salvation: "[G]race is the *personal* activity of the *triune God* on our behalf. Grace is always christocentric and Trinitarian. It is centered in the life, ministry, death, and resurrection of Jesus Christ, but it always involves all three Trinitarian persons, not only throughout Jesus Christ's life, death, and resurrection but also throughout the order of salvation."[189] Cielukowski and Colyer criticize Fletcher and other Methodist theologians for developing an "inadequate serial account of the Trinity in relation to the economy of salvation . . . appropriating justification to Christ and sanctification to the Spirit."[190] However this is a gross misrepresentation of Fletcher's doctrine of dispensations. The dispensations do not represent a succession of the activity of the triune persons in salvation history or a chronological modalism, but Fletcher's doctrine of dispensations conceives a Trinitarian pattern of the disclosure of God in history as God accommodates divinity to the human condition, which results in various degrees of the knowledge of God.

Fletcher's Essential and Economic Trinitarianism

While much of Fletcher's theology of history centers on an economic Trinity, he did not deviate from the orthodox doctrine of the essential Trinity.[191] In his note entitled *De ce Dieu TROIS-FOIS Saint announce la Bonté* on the poem *La Grâce et la Nature*, Fletcher stated clearly that God has revealed His *essence* to humanity as the Father, Son, and Holy Spirit: "The whole difficulty amounts therefore to believing that God, who knows his nature, in order to help us understand the magnificence of our salvation, and the price

---

188. Collins, *Theology of John Wesley*, 145.

189. Cieslukowski, "Wesley's Trinitarian *Ordo Salutis*," 118.

190. Ibid., 121.

191. Loyer argues that in Fletcher's response to Joseph Priestly, Fletcher's "primary aim is not to give a rational account of the nature and attributes of God (the so-called immanent Trinity) but to reflect on God's actions in salvation history (the so-called economic Trinity) and the implications of those actions for the life of faith" ("'Adoring the Holy Trinity in Unity,'" 19). Again Loyer states, "His basic approach is to ground the doctrine in the divine economy, as conveyed in Scripture, and thereby to locate it in the context of vital, experiential religion" (ibid., 20).

of our Redemption, has condescended to reveal to us that in this adorable Nature, he is three Principles so completely united, that they form a Trinity of Subsistances, without dividing the Unity of the Substance or the divine essence."[192] Fletcher grounded the doctrine of economic Trinity upon an ontological Trinity. While Fletcher did indicate a preference for using the term "subsistences,"[193] he did not avoid using the term "Person" in reference to the Trinity as do the *Thirty-Nine Articles*.[194]

The ontological Trinity is the foundation for Fletcher's doctrine of economic Trinity. Against above mentioned authors' suggestion, Fletcher held to the doctrine of appropriation, which "insists that the works of the Trinity are a unity; every person of the Trinity is involved in every outward action of the Godhead."[195] In an unpublished manuscript that served to rebut the writings of Edward Elwall, who was an Ebonite, Fletcher argued at length for the doctrine of appropriation; each person of the Trinity was involved in all outward actions of the Trinity: creation, redemption, incarnation, Jesus' resurrection, resurrection of human bodies, in ongoing Christian ministry, revelation of the truth, development of Christian graces, justification, regeneration, adoption, sanctification, establishment in holiness and glorification.[196] While the activity of each Person of the Trinity is evident in salvation history, Fletcher's doctrine of the unity of God does not permit any division either in the nature of God or in divine works.[197] He explained,

---

192. "Toute la difficulté se réduit donc à croire que Dieu, qui connoit sa nature, pour nous faire comprendre la grandeur de notre salut, et du prix de notre Rédemption, a daigné nous révéler que dans cette adorable Nature, il est trois Principes si parfaitement unis, qu'ils forment une Trinité de Subsistances, sans rompre l'Unité de la Substance ou de l'Essence divine" (Fletcher-Grâce, 357). Fletcher's application of the term "Principes" rather than employing the term "Personnes" to the Father, Son and Holy Spirit is reminiscent of the usage of the Cambridge Platonist, Ralph Cudworth (*The True Intellectual System of the Universe*, 546–632). A parallel with the Cambridge Platonists is also evident when Fletcher linked various virtues to each Person of the Trinity: "[L]e Père es particulièrement un *Principe* de *Vie*, le *Fils* un *Principe* de *Lumière*, et le St. Esprit un *Principe* de *Charité*."

193. Fl-W1856, 7:158–59, 167.

194. Loyer's criticism is based upon a mistranslation from the French original to English ("Adoring the Holy Trinity in Unity,'" 7). As Fletcher was apt to do, he has coined a term "la Trinité des Subsistances" (Fletcher-Grâce, 357). The French original is clear that Fletcher held to one divine substance and three subsistencies. Fletcher held that "subsistencies" is the best way to translate the word υποςσταοι' (Fl-W1856, 7:158).

195. McGrath, *Christian Theology*, 326.

196. John Fletcher, Check to Socinianism and Arianism, Fletcher-Tooth, JRULM, MAM Fl. 17. For further evidence of the doctrine of appropriation, see Fletcher-Portrait, 2:167.

197. Loyer admits that Fletcher appears to equate the divine offices with the divine persons, but does not arrive at a conclusion as to whether or not Fletcher actually

> [F]or these three distinctions are expressive of the three grand degrees of the faith, "whereby we inherit all the promises" of God, and "are made partakers of the Divine nature." They are not descriptive of faith in three gods, but of the capital manifestations of the triune God, in whose name we are baptized; and of the three great dispensations of the everlasting Gospel, namely, that of the heathens, that of the Jews, and that of spiritual Christians; the dispensation of Abraham being only a link between heathenism and Judaism; and the dispensation of John the Baptist or of Christianity begun, being only a transition between Judaism and Christianity perfected. [198]

The activity of each Person of the Trinity was evident in all outward acts of the Godhead.[199]

The doctrine of essential or ontological Trinity guards against the division of the work of the Persons of the Trinity into isolated activities. The doctrine of the Trinity is revealed by means of divine accommodation to the human condition and assumes a historical or economic nature.[200] The word "condescension" is a key term employed for the doctrine of accommodation. God, knowing the divine nature "has condescended to inform us that, in his adorable nature, there are three principles so perfectly united, that they form a trinity of subsistences, without breaking the unity of the substance, or divine essence."[201] The condescension of God in which God has revealed the divine nature as Triune has occurred in history by means of the dispensation of the Father, the dispensation of the Son, and the dispensation of the Spirit. Fletcher emphasized an economic Trinity against the Calvinistic doctrine of predestination whose stress on divine fiat stripped history of its meaning. Hence, Fletcher's system validated the significance of both personal faith history and the history of salvation.

In the Minutes controversy, Fletcher mounted a polemic against the Calvinist doctrines, which he believed thwarted true Christian piety. The Calvinistic doctrine of absolute predestination with its corollary doctrine

---

makes such an equasion ("'Adoring the Holy Trinity in Unity,'" 11). However, Loyer acknowledges in a footnote Fletcher's defense of orthodox doctrine.

198. Fl-W1856, 4:122.

199. Cf. L. Wood, *Truly Ourselves*, 203.

200. L. Wood writes, "As opposed to this, Fletcher advocated an economic view of the trinity that extends back to Irenaeus, *Against Heresies*, and was further developed in the writings of John Coccejus and Bengel and then more systematically developed in the history of redemption school of theology in the nineteenth century associated with J. C. K. von Hofmann and Oscar Cullmann in the twentieth century" (*The Meaning of Pentecost in Early Methodism*, 126).

201. Fl-W1856, 8:510.

of finished salvation frustrated the good works of believers and personal faith history.

While the above appears explicitly in his writings, Fletcher's economic Trinitarianism mounts a polemic against Calvinistic doctrine of the absolute predestination that is more implicit than explicit. The Calvinistic/Augustinian doctrine of predestination is rooted in the supralapsarian decree of God; "[T]he individual and his destiny are rooted in eternity, while Christ and the community appear only in history to serve the outworking of the eternal decree."[202] In the Anglican standards, "Christ and his community have their rooting in God's eternal decree, while the individual and his destiny appear only in history as the working out of that decree."[203] Oliver O'Donovan points out the ramifications of the two doctrines of predestination: the Calvinist doctrine of predestination causes a certain ambiguity on the doctrine of the Trinity because it divorces salvation history (the economy of salvation) from the supralapsarian decree. In *The Thirty-Nine Articles* "the doctrine of predestination arises directly out of the doctrine of the Trinity and demonstrates that the history of salvation is the true expression of God's eternal trinitarian existence."[204] In Fletcher's polemical writings against his opponents, the economic Trinity takes greater prominence in an attempt to temper their Calvinistic overemphasis on the ahistorical, supralapsarian Trinitarian pact.

While Wesley emphasized the economic Trinity, he did not apply formally a Trinitarian structure to the *ordo temporum*. Fletcher formalized Wesley's latent economic Trinitarianism and applied it to the *ordo temporum* and further melded it to Wesley's Trinitarian *ordo salutis*.[205]

"MY KEY AND MY SWORD"[206]

As alluded to above, the doctrine of dispensations served a polemical purpose. Fletcher asserted the polemical function of the doctrine of the dispensations calling it "my key and my sword":

---

202. O'Donovan, *On the Thirty-Nine Articles*, 86.
203. Ibid.
204. Ibid., 87.
205. Recent scholarship has stressed the economic Trinitarian theology of Charles Wesley: Vickers, "'And We the Life of God Shall Know,'" 329–44; Vickers, "Albert Outler and the Future of Wesleyan Theology," 56–67; Vickers, "Charles Wesley's Doctrine of the Holy Spirit," 47–60.
206. Fl-W 1856, 4:37. Cf. Flick, "John William Fletcher," 329.

> As I make my appeal to true Protestants, I lay a particular stress upon the *Scriptures*. And there I find a doctrine which, for a long succession of ages, has been *partly* buried in the rubbish of popery and Calvinism: I mean the doctrine of the various *dispensations* of divine grace toward the children of men; or of the various *talents* of saving grace, which the Father of lights gives to heathens, Jews, and Christians. To the obscurity in which this doctrine has been kept, we may chiefly impute the self-electing narrowness, and the wide-reprobating partiality of the Romish and Calvinian Churches. I make a constant use of this important doctrine. It is it chiefly which distinguishes this tract from most polemical writings upon the same subject. It is my key and my sword. With it I open the mysteries of election and reprobation; and with it I attempt to cut the *Gordian* (should I not say the *Calvinian* and *Pelagian*?) knot. [207]

My Sword: The Polemic of the Doctrine of Dispensations

Donald K. McKim argued that the Puritans' theology of history was appropriated from the Calvinist/Augustinian tradition, which emphasized "the transcendence of God and his immanence within the historical process."[208] As was argued previously, Fletcher held that the immanence of God was evident within nature; however, his doctrine of grace protected his system from the Calvinist scheme of history in which "all events are governed by God's secret plan"[209] or in which "God so attends to the regulation of individual events, and they all so proceed from his set plan, that nothing takes place by chance."[210] While Fletcher was in general agreement with the Calvinist doctrine of general providence of God, he did not concur with the Calvinist doctrine of the special providence of God, which devalued personal history.[211] Against Richard Hill's doctrine of finished salvation, Fletcher argued from the passage of Scripture, "the just shall live by faith," that salvation is not so finished as to invalidate the life of faith subsequent to the new birth.[212]

---

207. Fletcher-EC2, viii–ix.
208. McKim, "Puritan View of History," 237.
209. Calvin, *Institutes of the Christian Religion*, 1.16.2.
210. Ibid., 1.16.4.
211. Cf. J. Knight, "John William Fletcher and the Early Methodist," 16.
212. Fl-W1856, 3:80.

The Doctrine of Dispensations

In the same vein of thought, Fletcher argued against Mr. Hill's assertion of the impossibility of the perfection of Christian virtues in the present life for the possibility of perfection of Christian virtues in the present life. The present life is the context for perseverance of Christian believers, for example, as well as the development of the remaining Christian virtues.[213] Both a universal or macro history and a personal or micro history were given significance and value, in Fletcher's thought, and were viewed as the sole forum for the development of Christian virtues. The context for God's redemptive activity is history: "The salvation of people takes place always within history, for people are the components of history, either those who make it or else have it made for them by others who lead them and cause them to fit into their grandiose schemes."[214] Against a fixated, decretal theology of history, which appeared to devalue the significance of human history and decisions, Fletcher valued history and advanced that human beings through grace-assisted free will were real participants in history. Fletcher asserted that the Calvinist position on predestination, which "predetermines in advance the outcome of every man's destiny, undercuts the significance of time, and drains historical decision of its meaning."[215] Fletcher illustrated the absurdity of such a theology of history: "[Y]ou have recourse to the mysterious doctrine of the decrees; and because 'all events are present unto God, and were so from eternity to eternity,' you affirm that 'the glorification of the elect is as much finished as their predestination.' By the same rule of Geneva logic, I may say, that because God has decreed the world shall melt with fervent heat, the general conflagration is as much finished as the deluge."[216]

However, it should be noted that Fletcher employed his theology of history as a polemic against other theological systems. According to John Knight, Fletcher employed his theology of history against the Arminian position for undercutting the meaning because "it removes the element of the transcendent and Divine, and thereby becomes mere humanism."[217] The idea of degrees of faith in the early Methodist thought was a reaction to the finished salvation idea of the Calvinists.[218] The theology of history was important in Fletcher's dialectical system: "Through his doctrine of dispensations, and his 'theology of history,' he endeavored to hold together the sovereignty of God and the freedom of man so as to view history as

---

213. Fl-W1856, 6:67–69.
214. Cannon, "Methodism in a Philosophy of History," 37.
215. J. Knight, "John William Fletcher and the Early Methodist," 21.
216. Fl-W1856 3:73.
217. J. Knight, "John William Fletcher and the Early Methodist," 21.
218. Fraser, "Strains in the Understanding of Christian," 102.

meaningful to man both because of his free choice, and because all history is under the control of God."[219]

My Key: The Hermeneutics of the Doctrine of Dispensations

On 4 December 1775, John Fletcher wrote to the Revd Charles Wesley, "I hav see the end of my controversial race."[220] During the same year, Fletcher wrote of the benefits that he had received from the controversy: "As a Protestant, I hope I have much more esteem for the Scriptures in general, and in particular for those practical parts of them which the Calvinists had insensibly taught me to overlook or despise: and this increasing esteem is, I trust, accompanied with a deeper conviction of the truth of Christianity, and with a greater readiness to defend the Gospel against infidels, Pharisees, and Antinomians. As a preacher, I hope I can do more justice to a text, by reconciling it with seemingly contrary scriptures."[221]

Fletcher's dialectical method becomes evident in his *Scripture Scales* where he placed passages of Scripture in two columns with one column depicting a truth of Scripture and the other column depicting another apparently opposite truth. In the prefatory epistle of the *Scripture Scales*, Fletcher confessed to the novelty of his method: "My method so far as I know is new."[222] Fletcher attempted to portray the whole range of biblical truth. He confounded his opponents with a consistent use of the *analogia fidei*, using the general sense of Scripture to interpret the more ambiguous passages. The *analogia fidei* "presupposes a sense of the theological meaning of Scripture."[223]

> Once the literal and figurative language of Scripture is recognized, one can demonstrate the unity and harmony of Scripture by showing that the Old Testament is the historical precursor of the New Testament and that the New is the historical fulfillment of the Old. When Fletcher interprets Scripture, his intention is to do it reasonably and consistently with the context. He sees this intention as one of the principal differences between Protestants and Roman Catholics. This means that each particular passage of Scripture must be interpreted in accordance with the general tenor of the Bible. The theologian must compare Scripture with

---

219. J. Knight, "John William Fletcher and the Early Methodist," 21.
220. JF→CW, 4 December 1775.
221. Fl-W1856, 3:325.
222. Fl-W1856, 4:136.
223. Muller, *Dictionary of Latin and Greek Theological Terms*, 33.

Scripture and use the many plain passages to interpret the few obscure ones. A theologian must not distort a passage of Scripture to make it fit his preconceived notions. [224]

The *Scripture Scales* serves a similar function: when the preponderance of clear texts testifies to a particular truth, these passages outweigh the purported truth of a smaller number of ambiguous passages. "And do we not deserve that our candour or good sense should be suspected, when we go about to persuade the world, that half a dozen strained verses of St. Paul, put in the favourite scale of a Geneva balance, are sufficient to outweigh fifty plain texts of the apostle, and the best half of the Bible, which testifies, directly or indirectly, that though the final justification and eternal salvation of adult persons are not by the merit, yet they are by the evidence or instrumentality of good works?"[225] There are then various degrees of truth because of the progressive nature of divine revelation; truths revealed in the superior dispensations are more coherent and advanced.[226] Fletcher revealed the importance of the doctrine of dispensations as a hermeneutical key to his system: "Milton says somewhere, 'There is a certain scale of duties, a certain hierarchy of upper and lower commands, which for want of studying in right order, all the world is in confusion.'" Fletcher explained the connection between Milton's citation and the doctrine of dispensations: "What that great man said of the scale of duties and commands, may, with equal propriety, be affirmed of the scale of evangelical truths, and the hierarchy of upper and lower gospel dispensations. For want of studying them in right order, all the church is in confusion."[227] Only a proper understanding of the dispensations can correct the theological errors of the Church and restore the harmony of the apostolic Church.

While the literal language of Scripture was important, Fletcher also used a typological method to interpret Scripture. Knickerbocker has identified correctly the neo-Platonic roots of Fletcher's typological approach: "The basis of this literary mysticism is explained in Platonic terms which Fletcher finds in the writings of Paul. Metaphors, comparisons, and allegories are simply verbal copies of original spiritual truths."[228] The encounter occurs at two levels: first, a literary mysticism places truth on a level where even the ignorant and unlearned can grasp; secondly, "this mysticism serves as a veil

---

224. Knickerbocker, "Doctrinal Sources and Guidelines in Early," 191.
225. Fl-W1856, 3:151.
226. J. Knight, "John William Fletcher and the Early Methodist," 199.
227. Fl-W1856, 5:183.
228. Knickerbocker, "Doctrinal Sources and Guidelines," 190.

to conceal these truths from false sages."[229] Fletcher's typological approach to the OT has at its very foundation the doctrine of accommodation. It is accommodated language.

As the extrinsic view of history has an intrinsic side, Scripture also objectifies the internal spiritual experience of the spiritual manifestation of the Son of God. Knickerbocker wrote, "Christian experience internalizes and spiritualizes the truths of Scripture which have previously been external and literal. As it does this, Christian experience confirms the primary authority of Scripture."[230] Scripture, for Fletcher, is principally a means of grace that enables the attentive reader to encounter the God of Scripture.

---

229. Ibid., 191.
230. Ibid., 201.

4

The Dispensation of the Father

The Anthropological Pattern and the Dispensation of the Heathen

Studies of Fletcher's theology have recognized the variegated patterns of the doctrine of dispensations. They have concentrated largely on the trinitarian pattern of God's salvific activity in history and its relation and application to the related stages of spiritual pilgrimage of individuals. However, such studies have widely ignored a second overarching pattern of Fletcher's view of history.[1] While the above mentioned trinitarian pattern recognized a *theological* structure of history, the second pattern provided an *anthropological* structure of history. The former unfolds chronologically in the dispensations of the Father, Son, and Spirit; the anthropological structure portrays the dispensation of heathens, the dispensation of Jews, and the dispensation of Christians.[2]

The second pattern that the current author has labeled the anthropological pattern due to Fletcher's categorization of human beings is found principally in contexts where Fletcher emphasized his polemic against the doctrine of particular predestination. The focus is on the redemptive purpose of God in history: the love of God issues in a general redemption of all of humanity regardless of the geographical or historical bounds. Divine accommodation is significant in this context because God must accommodate divinity to humans in order to communicate with and redeem humanity.

---

1. A third pattern emerges in Fletcher's polemic against works-righteousness.
2. Fl-W 1859, 4:329.

The theological pattern appears principally in the contexts of Fletcher's arguments against the doctrine of antinomianism. Fletcher emphasized the teleological dimensions of personal and salvation histories and the transformative activity of God to bring history to its destined end. Against theoretical and practical lawlessness, Fletcher depicted the goal of salvation history as the restoration of fallen humanity in righteousness.

The distinctions above emphasize the differences between the two patterns. Indeed, there is a tension between accommodation of God in history and the teleological dimension of history; a contrast is evident between depraved condition of humanity to which God accommodated the divine nature and the goal of Christian perfection toward which God desires to lead humanity. The contrast underscores the sufficiency, significance, and power (optimism) of grace within Fletcher's thought.

At the same time, these two structural patterns of history are categories for roughly the same periods of history. For example, the dispensation of heathenism is roughly corollary to the dispensation of the Father, and the dispensation of Christians is roughly corollary to the dispensation of the Spirit. Thus, the two patterns should not be bifurcated from the anthropological pattern, but neither should they be considered synonymous.

THE DISPENSATION OF THE HEATHEN

In order to understand accurately Fletcher's doctrine of dispensations, one must grasp the dispensation of the heathen. The question regarding the fate of the heathen is really a continental divide between the Calvinists and the Wesleyans. Because Fletcher has given the Methodist movement the most sustained polemic against Calvinism, his writings contain a significant resource for the development of a Wesleyan position on the heathen.

What is the fate of the heathen? Is salvation possible for those who have never heard of Christ? Fletcher was obligated to answer these questions because he held to a general redemption against the Calvinist doctrine of particular predestination.

The Love of God

Fletcher viewed the love of God not as accidental, but as essential to the very nature of God. Whereas Calvinists view divine love as an expression of God's will, which results in the doctrine of particular predestination, Fletcher believed that the essential nature of God is love. God's love, thus, is

The Dispensation of the Father

not discriminating, but is universal in its scope. Because the love of God is all embracing, the grace of God extends to all.[3]

In Wesley and Fletcher's thought, God's creative activity and providential care over creation are grounded in the love of God as has been demonstrated in the two previous chapters. God is intimately related to all of creation. Divine love permeates all of the created order. In discussing the seals of the dispensations in an unpublished essay on the dispensations, Fletcher wrote that the rainbow of Noah's day was the seal of the dispensation of the Father indicating that "the Father's dispensation of mercy still ~~peculiarly~~ extends to all nations times and places."[4] As was discussed previously, Fletcher, in contrast to Calvinist theologians of his day, held that grace and nature were united. Divine love encompasses all of creation; thus, God's grace infuses nature.

Original Sin and the Plight of the Heathen

Fletcher's union of grace and nature raises questions about whether or not Fletcher took original sin seriously. Did he soften the orthodox view of original sin in order to conceptualize the salvation of the heathen? Fletcher, in fact, held to an Augustinian view of original sin.[5] As Wesley before him, Fletcher argued that the doctrine of original sin is "a leading principle in Christianity" without which the atoning work of Christ would not have been necessary.[6] Undermining the doctrine of original sin undermines the atonement. Thus, the doctrine of original sin is crucial to the entire Christian system: "This doctrine [of original sin], then, being of such importance, that genuine Christianity stands or falls with it."[7]

Fletcher acknowledged that "God created man in his own image, and after his likeness"; however, Scripture provides the sad account of the fall of the human race.[8] In *An Appeal to Matter of Fact and Common Sense*, which was addressed to "the principal inhabitants of the parish of Madeley, in the county of Salop," he combs the scriptures for proof of the doctrine of original sin. His purpose was to prove the seriousness of the corrupt nature of humanity to these "principal inhabitants" who were mere nominal Christians in order to lead them to a vital Christian experience. He supports

3. Fl-W1856 2:401.
4. Fletcher-Dispensations, 18/12.
5. Cf. Davies, "John Fletcher of Madeley as Theologian," 379.
6. Fl-W1856 2:9.
7. Ibid.
8. Fl-W1856 2:10.

his argument with citations from the *Thirty-nine Articles*, the *Homilies*, and the *Common Book of Prayer*.[9] Fletcher painted such a dark and foreboding picture of the state of humanity describing the natural state as a real and authentic condition. He portrayed in explicit detail the condition of the world and its principal inhabitant; the natural phenomena (the irregularity of climates and seasons, hurricanes, earthquakes, etc), the irregularities at childbirth, a mother's suffering in birthing a child, human ignorance of divine matters, humanity's lack of dominance over the animal world and vegetation, the inhumane work conditions, the difficulty of labor, the inequities in human relations, and the pangs of death all testify to the sinfulness of humanity.

Fletcher maintained allegiance to the ninth article of the Church of England, "On Original Sin," which "affirms the Augustinian idea of a *reatus* attached to the possession of *vitium*."[10] David C. Shipley asserts that Fletcher did not hold to a mere privation of original righteousness as did the Dutch Arminians, but to the deprivation of original sin.[11] His position was that humanity is *totally* depraved.

The will, conscience, and affections are all "warped from our original rectitude."[12] The will is able only to do that which is evil.[13] Shipley wrote, "It is impotent: when we see what is right, instead of doing it with all our might, we frequently remain as inactive, as if we were bound by invisible chains; and we wonder by what charm the wheels of duty thus stop against our apparent inclination; till we discover, that the spring of our will is broken, or naturally works the wrong way. Yes, it is not only able to follow the good, that the understanding approves; but the full of perverseness to pursue the evil, that reason disapproves.[14] In addition, the fickleness of human conscience renders it an unreliable guide.[15] At times, it is slow to reprove; at other times, it is unreasonably scrupulous or obstinately refuses to recognize the right.[16] Like the conscience, human affections are equally fickle.[17]

9. Fl-W1856, 2:16ff.

10. Shipley, "Methodist Arminianism in the Theology of John," 196.

11. Ibid., 37ff.

12. Fl-W1856, 2:58.

13. Fletcher using the words of the text, "except the Father which sent me draw him," wrote "Man neither will nor can come" (JF→sermon, John 6:44 a).

14. Fl-W1856, 2:58.

15. Reason and conscience were considered as the "two unsullied fragments" of the moral image of God, which "were more and more darken'd, and impaired by the ~~by the~~ overflowings of ungodliness" (Fletcher-Dispensations, 13).

16. Fl-W1856, 2:58–59.

17. Fl-W1856 2:59.

The Dispensation of the Father

Original sin is seminally transmitted to the progeny of Adam. Fletcher uses the concept of an acorn that unfolds and multiplies its original properties to all of the trees and acorns that derive from it. Not only did every human being exist seminally in Adam, but Adam is the federal head of mankind.[18] Thus, the corruption of original sin is transmitted both seminally and federally to all members of the human race.

In the discussion above, it is evident that Fletcher held to Augustinian concept of the *reatus* and the *vitium*. The *vitium* issues in the *actus*: the prevalence of sin demonstrates the universality of the *vitium*. Humanity's proneness to sin is verified not by one accident or single event, but by the "continual repetition of the same event."[19] Fletcher provides a greatly detailed catalog of sins in order to substantiate his argument for the prevalence of sin and the reality of original sin. Irrational and cruel amusements, drunkenness, dancing, card playing, and cruel sports are manifestations of the corruption of the sinful nature.[20]

Fletcher summarizes several of the above mentioned aspects of original sin: "We may then conclude, that a moral depravity, which comes upon us by the wilful choice of a parent, in whom we seminally and federally existed,—a depravity which cleaves to us by an obstinate neglect of the infinitely precious means provided to remove it,—a depravity which works now by our own personal choice, and to which we daily give our assent by the free commission of sins that are avoidable, leaves us not only accountable, but inexcusable before God."[21] Fletcher held without question that all human beings were in a natural state; he affirmed the orthodox position of the Church on original sin: "Hence it appears, that persons of various constitutions, ranks, and education; in all nations, religions, times, and places; are born in such a state, and with such a nature, that they infallibly commit many sins in thought, word, and deed."[22] Fletcher's position on the plight of the heathen apart from the grace of God is clear: all human beings are totally depraved and are liable to eternal damnation. However, does God leave the heathen in this deplorable, miserable condition?

---

18. Fl-W1856 2:114–15.
19. Fl-W1856, 2:77.
20. Fl-W1856, 2:77ff.
21. Fl-W1856, 2:117.
22. Fl-W1856, 2:49.

TRUE CHRISTIANITY

Divine Love in Redemption History

Fletcher's views on original sin were largely consistent with the Calvinists of his day; however, wide differences occurred between them in their understandings of the extent of the atonement. His opponents emphasized the doctrine of limited atonement whereas Fletcher held to a general redemption or the universal extent of the atonement because it is grounded in the all-encompassing love of God. In a sermon on Ephesians 3:19, Fletcher wrote that the breadth of God's love includes "All nations—ages—place,—from pole to pole."[23] In vindicating the Minutes of the Conference of 1770, Fletcher was obligated to provide an explanation of the extent of the atonement. In considering the plight of the heathen, there are two concerns regarding the extent of the atonement: one is geographical; the other is historical. If God is a God of love as Fletcher asserted, how did divine love that issued in redemptive action toward every person on the planet apply to those who were beyond the geographical limits of the community of faith that heralded the news of God's redemption? What is the plight of those who lived and died prior to the advent of Christ?

General Redemption

As is stated above, the God of love accommodates divine revelation in order that all human beings might be saved. In contrast to the particular predestination of the Calvinist Methodists, the Wesleyan Methodists stressed the doctrine of general redemption, which was the compulsion of early Wesleyan Methodist evangelism. Just as the love of God is unlimited, so the scope of God's saving activity is unlimited. Confusion results when one does not recognize the salvific activity of God within all ages of human history. Fletcher acknowledged, during the Calvinist controversy, that the doctrine of general redemption implied what he called a "general gospel." If Christ died for all, the logical consequence, according to Fletcher, is that salvation was and is made possible to all human beings in all ages of history and all places within the world. The Calvinists limited the scope of God's redemptive activity to the elect, and the issue of the providing rationale for the salvation of the heathen was a moot point for them: the Calvinist God was under no obligation to provide salvation for all human beings; since, in their scheme salvation was only for the elect.[24] However, since Fletcher

---

23. JF→sermon, Ephesians 3.19.

24. What is argued here is that logic did not obligate the Calvinists to defend the possibility of salvation of the heathen. Certain Calvinists did defend the possibility of

refuted the doctrine of limited atonement and asserted an unlimited atonement, it was impingent upon him to provide some explanation of the means of divine provision for all human beings in all periods of history and in all places.

Fletcher confessed to having been confused himself on the subject due to his own Calvinistic leanings by confining redemption to the last two dispensations, i.e., "the Jewish and Christian gospel."[25] The scope of Fletcher's doctrine of atonement led him to insist upon the ageless and universal scope of the divine provision of the atonement.[26] Within the same context, he cited many passages from scripture that point to the universal efficacy of the atonement, e.g., Revelation 14:6.

As stated previously, the doctrine of general redemption obligated the early Methodist theologians to provide some explanation of the plight of the heathen. The Minutes of the Conference of 1770, of course, did not supply a full-orbed clarification, but gave only a terse reply: "But who among those that never heard of Christ [is accepted of God]? He that feareth God, and worketh righteousness, according to the light he has."[27] Fletcher, in his vindication provided the rationale for Wesley's remarks by grounding them in the love of God. The love of God is demonstrated in providing "the gospel to *every* creature" including those who have never heard of the name of Christ.

General redemption, God's salvific activity, includes the heathen, both those who seem to be beyond the geographical limits of the community of faith that heralds the news of God's redemption and those who lived and died prior to the advent of Christ. According to Fletcher, God, out of love, accommodated revelation to the heathen in an effort to redeem them. After citing biblical passages that support the idea of general redemption, Fletcher posited the maxim upon which his doctrine of dispensations is based: "If 'Christ tasted death for every man,' there is, undoubtedly, a gospel for every man, even for those who perish by rejecting it."[28] A doctrine of general redemption effects a general gospel. In Fletcher's thought, the term "gospel" is not limited to the dispensation of the Son or to the NT era, but includes all of the dispensations of God's grace or redemptive activity in history.[29]

---

the salvation of the heathen (Hill, *Five Letters to the Reverend Mr.*, 18).

25. Fl-W1856, 3:375.

26. Ibid.

27. Fl-W1856, 2:203.

28. Fl-W1856, 2.396.

29. Fletcher stated, "This doctrine [of dispensations] may appear strange to those who call nothing gospel but the last dispensation of it" (Fl-W1856, 2:397).

TRUE CHRISTIANITY

Not only is the gospel a general gospel, but it is an everlasting gospel. Because God is the God of love who endeavors to compass the salvation of all people regardless of geographical location or place in history, the gospel is called "the everlasting gospel." For this reason, Fletcher clarified faith as that which "is common to, and essential under, all the *dispensations of the everlasting gospel in all countries and ages*."[30] He recognized that the unifying purpose of history was the salvation of humanity.

General Justification

However, how can those who are in such a corrupt condition be redeemed? While Fletcher held to the pessimism of sin, he held equally to the optimism of grace. The grace of God that has its source in the love of God overcomes the effects of sin that have been transmitted by nature (i.e., the natural transmission of sin) to all human beings. Fletcher wrote, "Is it not possible that heathen should, *by grace*, reap some blessings through the second Adam, though they know nothing of his name and obedience unto death; when they, *by nature*, reap so many curses through Adam the first, to whose name and disobedience they are equally strangers?"[31] The doctrine of general redemption involves the doctrine of nature because God is active in redeeming all of nature.

The primary blessing that the heathen reap through the second Adam is general justification, one of four justifications in Fletcher's thought.[32] In his response to Richard Hill, Fletcher described general justification: "We believe that Jesus Christ died for the whole human race, with an intention, first, to procure, absolutely and unconditionally, a temporary redemption, or an initial salvation, for all men universally."[33] General justification is distinct from justification by faith in that the former is unconditional, and the latter is conditioned by the faith of the recipient. General justification is temporary: "We believe that, in consequence of the general and temporary redemption procured by Christ for all mankind, every man is unconditionally blessed with a day of grace, which the scripture calls, 'accepted time' and 'the day of salvation.'"[34] Thus, the God of love acted in behalf of all human

---

30. Fl-W1856, 3:437; emphasis added.

31. Fl-W1856, 2:249; emphasis added.

32. Gunter limited the efficacy of Fletcher's concept of general justification to infants (*Limits of "Love Divine,"* 275, 255). For this reason perhaps, Gunter accuses Fletcher of moralism.

33. Fl-W1856, 3:296.

34. Fl-W1856, 3:297.

beings in order to provide a "level playing field," a fair and equitable state of grace that provided the liberty for all to respond to further divine overtures of grace. The source of human free will is the grace of God.[35] General justification reverses temporarily the trajectory of the fall.

While the doctrine of general justification is largely deduced from the doctrine of the love of God, Fletcher found scriptural foundation for the concept of general justification in Romans 5:18."[36] There is an inextricable link between the doctrines of general justification and prevenient grace; God, through prevenient grace, provides general justification, which makes possible and is foundational for advanced degrees of faith and good works. Grace, at this juncture, operates irresistibly.[37] Here grace functions as a power that overcomes the effects of Adam's sin; the biblical language reflects the optimism of grace inherent in early Wesleyan Methodist theology: "where sin abounded, grace did much more abound" (Romans 5:20).

It may appear to some that there is a logical inconsistency in Fletcher's thought in regard to the original sin; in *An Appeal to Matter of Fact and Common Sense*, Fletcher described the natural state of humanity as a real and authentic condition whereas in other works he argued that prevenient grace infused nature making the natural state of humanity a theoretical formulation.[38] In *Appeal*, Fletcher described the *status purorum naturalium*, the condition of human nature unaided by grace.[39] In the contexts where nature seems to be merely a theoretical formulation, Fletcher was often addressing the Calvinists who failed to see the full range of the salvific activity of God. Furthermore, Fletcher described the natural state that was for him a theoretical formulation and gave illustrations of humanity when it rejects grace. The fuller implications of nature without grace cannot be known because nature is not without grace; however, the condition of human beings who resist grace is illustrative of nature apart from grace. Fletcher clarified in his dialogue with Richard Hill: "[W]e believe that no child of Adam is a

---

35. Fl-W1856, 3:447.

36. Fl-W1856, 2:250; 3:303.

37. Ibid., emphasis added. Cf. Collins, *Theology of John Wesley*, 80.

38. Fl-W1856 2:42–43.

39. Fletcher advanced six arguments to prove "that every man before he be is a new creature by f faith in J. C. is in a damnable state yea is condemned already": (1) humans must be lost because God intervienes to save them; (2) fallen human beings are slaves of sin and need a Redeemer; (3) in admitting the need to work out one's salvation with fear and trembling, one acknowledges one's condemnation; (4) one's prayers for mercy reveal that one is under condemnation; (5) the hope of pardon for sins indicates a recognition of one's condemnation; (6) the recognition that Jesus died for the sake of sinners rather than for his own sins makes it clear that fallen humanity is under a state of condemnation (JF→sermon, John 3.18).

natural man in the Calvinian sense of the word, (that is, absolutely destitute of all saving grace) except he who has actually sinned away his day of grace."[40]

The Light of Christ

The most complete self-disclosure of God was in Jesus Christ. If God is willing to save the heathen apart from the explicit knowledge of Christ, does the salvation of the heathen undermine the significance of the revelation of God in Christ? How can the exclusive claims of Jesus (e.g., John 14:6) be reconciled with any idea of the possibility of the salvation of the heathen? How is redemption possible for those who lived prior to the Christ event? Once again the doctrine of accommodation of God that was discussed above is significant here. Given the distinctions between an infinite God and frail, finite humanity, God was obligated to accommodate revelation in order to reveal the divine nature. God in Christ condescended to the level of human understanding in order to communicate effectively. The revelation of God in the incarnation is the greatest extent of God's accommodation; the incarnation of Christ was paradoxically the fullest revelation of God and the greatest accommodation of God to humanity.

As previously stated, the idea of accommodation by its very nature introduces the concept of time. Christ is, for Fletcher, the center point of history and pervades all of history. Fletcher viewed the atoning work of Christ as a prolepsis whose benefits are effectual prior to (as well as following) the event itself. His saving act provides general justification through prevenient grace for all persons no matter their place in history. Christ is the meritorious cause of salvation of all persons who are saved in all dispensations. "For Christ, the light of men, visits all, through a variety of degrees and dispensations."[41] Though the gospel may be manifested in different degrees, it is indeed *one* gospel.[42]

Fletcher, frequently used the image of light to convey the extensiveness of revelation, citing frequently John 1:9 to support his claims. The light is not a natural light, but is a supernatural light "which Christ graciously affords them [the heathen], in the dispensation they are under."[43] Christ, the Light, overcomes the debilitating effects of sin on human reason. Right

---

40 Fl-W1856, 3:305. "Fletcher believed that all men are <u>saved</u> until they reject their dispensation of grace" (Fuhrman, "Contribution of John Fletcher to," 63).

41. Fl-W1856, 2:250.

42. Fl-W1856, 2:397.

43. Fl-W1856, 2:250.

reason, Fletcher defines, as "a ray of 'the light that enlightens every man who comes into the world;' and a beam of the eternal Logos, the glorious 'Sun of Righteousness.'"[44]

In providing a Christological interpretation of the faculty of human reason, Fletcher serves as a conjunctive theologian by providing a mediating position between extreme emphases on reason and revelation. Reason is essential to revelation and is given Christological import. His purpose in *Appeal* is "to point out the happy medium . . . where reason and revelation walk hand in hand."[45] In this manner, Fletcher preserved the normative character of God's revelation in Christ and the validity of the non-Christian's knowledge of God.[46] The light of reason becomes a force that enables those who respond to the light to be saved. As discussed previously, light was one of Fletcher's favorite images for the progress of salvation history.

The Lowest Degree

As was stated above, the light has increased in its intensity throughout the history of humanity, and the fuller revelation of the evangelical gospel is essential to the partial revelation of the earlier periods of humanity's history. In a sermon on Haggiah 2:7, Fletcher wrote "4. the Desire of Nations <u>all stand in need of him</u> Jews, turks, Christians—young old Good bad, prof[l]igate moral men the onely saviour, the onely name under heaven, the onely way the onely door—One can do without health wealth friend honour learning not without Christ."[47] Fletcher made full use of the imagery of light in comparing and contrasting the various dispensations. For Fletcher, Christ is the light that "lightens every man;" although the light appears in differing degrees of intensity, it is the same light.[48]

Thus, Fletcher emphasized the continuity and the differences between the dispensations. While light in any dispensation is always the light of Christ, it does not shine with the same intensity in all periods of history. The dispensation of the heathen is compared to the dawning light; the dispensation of Judaism is compared to morning light, and the dispensation of Christianity is compared to the meridian light.[49] The light dawns gradually

44. Fl-W1856, 2:8.
45. Fl-W1856, 2:7.
46. Fl-W1856, 3:302.
47. JF→sermon, Haggiah 2:7. Cf. M. Fletcher, "Watchwords," 25–26, and Fletcher-Dispensations, 42.
48. Fl-W1856, 4:94.
49. Fl-W1856, 4:33.

and progressively in history. However, not only does Fletcher compare and contrast the objective periods of history, but also the subjective experiences of the individuals under those dispensations.

While not the same measure of grace lavished upon Christians, a lesser degree of grace is available to heathens. Fletcher queried, "And have I not proved from scripture, that the very heathens are not without some light and grace to work suitably to their dispensation?"[50] Clearly God was active in redeeming history as is evident from Fletcher's interpolation of the words of Jesus in John 10:16, "'Other sheep have I which are not of this' Jewish and Christian 'fold.'"[51] Heathenism is, then, the lowest dispensation, but the knowledge available in the dispensation is foundational for subsequent dispensations.

The Nature of a Believing Heathen's Faith

What is the specific content of the faith of believing heathens? Since the heathen have no awareness of Christ or of the redemption provided by him, what is the objective content of the faith?

In order to defend the possibility of the salvation of the heathen, Fletcher was obligated to demonstrate continuity between the faith of the heathen and evangelical faith. The dispensation of the heathen is an inferior dispensation, but the cognitive content that is disseminated in the lower dispensation is essential to the superior dispensations. The content of the faith of the heathen is significantly different from the faith of the Christian. However, the difference is principally one of degrees; both were salvific. The benefits of believing depend largely upon the quality of truth embraced by the believer.[52] In section one of his *An Essay on Truth*, Fletcher pointed out that the Church of England's and Wesley's definitions of saving faith were accurate, but not comprehensive enough because they were definitions of faith in the Christian dispensation only and did not account for faith in previous eras of history. He argued that since Abraham's faith was valid faith, faith in any dispensation could be valid though the content of the faith may not have specific knowledge of Christ's atonement: "And if you desired to know what I mean by 'saving faith,' and I replied, 'It is a supernatural belief that Christ has actually atoned for my sins upon the cross,' would you not ask me, whether Abraham, the father of the faithful, who would

---

50. Fl-W1856, 2:236.
51. Fl-W1856, 4:35–36.
52. Fl-W1856, 4:35.

The Dispensation of the Father

have believed a lie if he had believed this, had only damning faith?"[53] After raising questions about the applicability of the Protestant definition of evangelical faith to all dispensations, Fletcher redefined saving faith providing "a definition of faith adequate to the everlasting gospel."[54] His redefinition is as follows: "'Justifying or saving faith is believing the saving truth "with the heart unto" internal, and, as we have opportunity, unto external "righteousness," according to our light and dispensation.'"[55]

Fletcher makes a distinction between the cognitive content of faith and the existential aspect of faith. The cognitive content of the faith is very limited in the dispensation of the heathen; it is restricted to the existence of God and God's pending judgment of the world. Fletcher defined the cognitive content of faith of the believing heathens as follows: "'There is a God, who will call us to an account for our sins, and who spares us to break them off by repentance.'"[56] While the existence of God is the principal truth gained in the dispensation of the heathen, other truths such as the fall and degeneracy of humanity, and the need of a Mediator and a propitiatory sacrifice may be known as well.[57]

The Conditions

Though God desires to save all human beings, God does not save all the heathens en masse; the same redemptive activity may have very different results depending on the individual response; it may reveal either God's grace or God's justice. The result depends on the response of the individual. When the conditions are met, the heathens are saved, which is evident in Fletcher's definition of saving faith: "'justifying or saving faith is believing the saving truth with the heart unto internal, and, as we have opportunity, unto external righteousness, according to our light and dispensation."[58] However, when the heathen reject the truths imparted by general revelation, the truth of God is changed to a lie.[59]

Fletcher maintained the continuity between the faith of the heathen and evangelical faith by insisting that the conditions for both were essentially the same. The conditions for saving faith, which he called catholic faith

53. Fl-W1856, 4:11.
54. Fl-W1856, 4:11.
55. Fl-W1856, 4:11–12.
56. Fl-W1856, 4:19.
57. Fl-W1856, 4:79.
58. Fl-W1856, 4:11–12.
59. Fl-W1856, 4:31.

under all the dispensations are believing and working righteousness.[60] It is important to notice that the conditions are two: first, faith is required, but the content of the faith is significantly different from the faith required in the Jewish or Christian dispensation. Under the dispensation of the Father, the object of saving faith is faith in Christ as the Light of the world (not in Christ as the Mediator):

All the heathens that are saved are then saved by a lively faith in Jesus, the light of the world; or, to use our Lord's own words, by 'believing in the light' of their dispensation, before the day of their visitation is past, before total darkness comes upon them, even the night when no man can work.[61]

Secondly, good works are required; the believing non-Christian must "work righteousness." In Fletcher's thought, works of righteousness must always accompany faith or else it is not valid faith. The role of good works was significant because it guarded against the theoretical and practical antinomianism. Fletcher cannot conceive of saving faith apart from works; he compares the faith to the beating of the heart and good works to the pulse of the circulatory system in the human body.[62] When one fervently embraces the truth of a dispensation, the faith of the dispensation is conceived. Faith may be characterized by doubt or a lack of assurance, but one consistent characteristic of saving faith is that it works by love.[63] Fletcher made it clear that salvation of the heathen is possible when these two conditions are met.[64]

As was stated previously, Fletcher rejected, along with the Reformers, *status purorum naturalium*, the condition of human nature unaided by grace, and the idea of any such state prior to the fall because even prior to the fall, human capacity for doing good rested upon the grace of God.[65] While Fletcher rejected the idea of *meritum de condigno*,[66] he, in contrast to the Reformers and in agreement with Thomas Aquinas,[67] accepted the idea of *meritum de congruo* because human capacity for doing good works was based upon prevenient grace and its concomitant doctrine, general justification. Fletcher did not consider the *meritum de congruo* (or half merit) as truly deserving of grace, but it received grace because of God's mercy.[68] The

---

60. Fl-W1856, 3:437.
61. Fl-W1856, 2:251.
62. Fl-W1856, 4:50.
63. Fl-W1856, 4:36.
64. Fl-W1883, 1:237.
65. Muller, *Dictionary of Latin and Greek Theological Terms*, 289.
66. Cf. Fl-W1856, 3:408.
67. *Summa Theologica* I-II, Q. 114, a. 3.
68. *Contra* Gunter's supposition of moralism (*Limits of "Love Divine,"* 256).

basis for the divine mercy was the covenant of grace that was established by Christ with Adam after the Fall; the covenant of grace and particularly the doctrine of prevenient grace are foundational for the idea of good works in Fletcher's thought.[69] Thus, good works were essential in every dispensation. The believing heathen was capable of good works due to the prevenient grace of God. Though Fletcher emphasized salvation by works, the good works were not to be understood as meriting salvation: "[O]ur works, that is, our repentance, faith, and obedience, have no part in properly meriting or purchasing our salvation from first to last, either in whole or in part; the properly meritorious cause of our eternal, as well as intermediate and initial salvation, being only the merits, or the blood and righteousness of our Lord and Saviour Jesus Christ."[70] While good works did not merit initial evangelical justification in Fletcher's system, they were essential as evidence of it and as conditional for final justification (provided opportunity). In this manner, Fletcher launched a polemic against theoretical antinomianism and provided objective criterion for the judgment of those who did not have access to the knowledge of subsequent dispensations.[71] Obedience is required of all persons in all dispensations.

While obedience is required of all persons under all dispensations, divine expectations are conditioned by the measure of grace dispensed. God accommodates the conditions of salvation and divine judgment to the measure of grace bestowed and in doing so, demonstrates grace and justice. God's equality is manifested because God tailors graciously divine expectations according to the knowledge received or the grace distributed in the various dispensations. "Of him to whom little is given, little shall be required; but much shall be required of them that have received much;" the equality of God's way not consisting in giving to all men a like number of talents, any more than making them all archangels; but in treating them all equally, according to the various editions of the everlasting Gospel, or law of liberty; and according to the good or bad uses they have made of their talents, whether they had few or many."[72] However, divine judgment is equitable because God is using the same standard for all persons in all dispensations; God requires of all persons in all dispensations faith and good works: "Because no one is a real believer under any dispensation of Gospel grace, and of consequence no one can be saved who does not good works,

69. Fl-W1856, 3:257.

70. Fl-W1856, 4:375.

71. Fletcher made it clear that the basis of the judgment will be works: "Proofs of which the sentence will rest. Not <u>faith</u> but <u>works</u>. Not only works of <u>piety</u>, but of <u>charity</u>. Not only sins of <u>com.</u> [commission] but of <u>omission</u>" (JF→sermon, Matthew 25.46).

72. Fl-W1856, 3:452.

i.e. who does not truly repent, believe, and obey, as there is time, light, and opportunity."[73]

While obedience is expected of the heathens, not all respond appropriately.[74] Only those who respond rightly to the light are saved. God's condemnation of those who reject the light is just because God provided a means of escape that the heathens rejected.

It is at the juncture of acceptance or rejection of the light that the distinction between the cognitive content of the dispensations and the faith in the truth of their dispensation becomes most apparent: "O! who can describe the needless perplexities of those wilful unbelievers that have the truth of their dispensation clearly brought to them, and yet like Thomas resolutely set themselves against it saying, 'I will not believe?'"[75]

Progress in Personal Experience

In the above discussion on the idea of progress in history, the focus was primarily on the salvation history; the discussion now turns to consider the idea of progress in personal experience. Having attained saving faith, may the believing heathen rest in that faith? Believing the truth of the dispensation of the heathen is preparatory for receiving superior truths. Fletcher admonished the moral men not to take refuge in the dispensation of the heathen.[76] Refusing to believe in the lower dispensations incapacitates one to believe in the higher dispensations.[77]

Fletcher clarified that the noetic order is significant not only for the order of revelatory truths to humanity but also for the personal appropriation of salvation. He illustrated the progress in personal experience with a ladder whose lower rungs signify the truths of inferior dispensations and whose higher rungs indicate truths of superior dispensations. It is impossible for individuals to leap to the middle or top rungs of the ladder; they must move up the laddar incrementally one rung at a time.[78] Biblical accounts of conversion experiences demonstrate the idea of progress as well as the growth and development of plants and trees. As Fletcher stated, "The most sudden conversions imply this gradual transition."[79]

73. Fl-W1856, 4:375.
74. Fl-W1856, 4:22.
75. Fl-W1856, 4:28.
76. Fl-W1856, 4:77.
77. Fl-W1856, 4:107.
78. Fl-W1856, 4:19.
79. Ibid.

As was stated previously, Fletcher promoted the validity of personal history as an essential argument against Calvinism. The Calvinistic doctrines of particular predestination and effectual calling circumvent the personal struggle that Fletcher deemed concomitant with the spiritual progress. Chapter 10 of the Westminster Confession, *Of Effectual Calling*, states, "This effectual call is of God's free and special grace alone, not from any thing at all forseen in man; who is altogether passive therein, until, being quickened and renewed by the Holy Spirit, he is thereby enabled to answer this call, and to embrace the grace offered and conveyed in it."[80] The Calvinist *ordo salutis* placed effectual calling, which is analogous to regeneration (as indicated in the creedal statement by the phrase "quickened and renewed"), prior to all human response. Regeneration, thus, occurs prior to any human response such as faith or repentance in the Calvinist system. In Fletcher's *ordo*, repentance and faith precede regeneration. Fletcher's emphasis on the noetic order validated the learning experiences of spiritual struggle and of personal, spiritual histories.

THE DISPENSATION OF JEWS

Divine Election and Proportionate Grace

The dispensation of the Father was frequently divided into two dispensations: the dispensation of the heathen and the dispensation of the Jews. The discussion now turns to the latter.

Whereas the dispensation of heathenism is all inclusive, the scope of the other dispensations is much narrower. The more limited scope is connected with divine election and proportionate grace.[81] Grace is not given indiscriminately. "We do not believe that grace is indiscriminately given to all men."[82] Fletcher illustrates with the parable of the talents.

In concessions with his opponents, Fletcher asserted that God was partial in the distribution of the benefits of salvation. The Calvinist system is right in viewing God as partial: God has demonstrated partiality in choosing the Jews to a special covenant and reprobated the Gentiles from the covenant of peculiarity. However, the Arminian system is correct in viewing God as impartial: God impartially seeks the salvation of all human beings, but the salvation is not in the same degree. Sufficient grace is bestowed upon all human beings in order that they may be saved; however not all human

---

80. Schaff and Schaff, eds., *Creeds of Christendom*, 3:624–25.
81. Fl-W 4:249–50.
82. Fl-W1856, 3:300.

beings receive the same measure of grace. God is partial in the geographical and historical distribution of salvation, favoring some locations and/or ages with more of divine grace than others. Fletcher pointed out the importance of what he called distinguishing grace: "We believe, moreover, that although Christ 'tasted death for every man,' yet, according to his covenants of peculiarity or distinguishing grace, he formerly showed more love to the Jews than to the Gentiles, and now shows more favour to the Christians than to the Jews, and to some Christians than to others; bestowing more spiritual blessings upon the Protestants than upon the Papists; more temporal mercies upon the English than upon the Greenlanders, &c."[83] As in Calvinist thought, distinguishing grace is the sovereign prerogative of God.[84] However, God's salvation is impartial in that all are recipients of some measure of grace. On the other hand, the Arminians are right in saying that God is impartial in judgment. God impartially judges all who refuse absolutely the divine overtures of grace. Thus, human beings, through their own free will, are the source of their own damnation.

The dispensation of the heathen, discussed previously, is a general dispensation or a general covenant that was made to infralapsarian Adam for all human beings. The conditions of salvation under the dispensation of the heathen are faith and good works. These conditions remain intact under subsequent dispensations; however, what distinguished the Jewish dispensation from the dispensation of gentilism is the added condition of election.[85] The two subsequent covenants of Judaism and Christianity are considered covenants of peculiarity because they were applied to peculiar or elect groups of people.[86] The covenant made with Adam was ratified or reissued at different points in history to various OT characters and was made principally with the Jewish nation and is called "the old testament:" the second covenant of peculiarity was made with the Christian church and is called "the new testament."[87]

The consistency of God's dealings with humanity appears in that God demonstrates God's essential nature of holy-love throughout every period of history. The consistency of salvation history appears in the consistency of the demonstration of the essential nature of God as holy-love. The inconsistency of salvation history appears in the geographic and historical distribution of grace. All are recipients of grace but not all receive the same measure

---

83. Fl-W1856, 3:297.
84. Fl-W1856, 3:298.
85. Fl-W1856, 5:130.
86. Fletcher also held to three covenants of peculiarity (Fletcher-Dispensations, 3).
87. Fl-W1856, 5:176–77.

The Dispensation of the Father

of grace. Dispensing grace demonstrates God's nature in the world: God's nature is one of holy love. Grace is democratized but not equally.

Grace, by its very nature, considers its recipients (or object) and is, thus, dispensed according to the capacity of humanity to receive. There is a certain order to dispensing: creative grace, justifying grace and sanctifying grace. While God is partial in love to the degree that God dispenses grace in different measures, God is impartial in judgment.[88] "God does not reap where he has not sown" is the scriptural dictum that Fletcher quoted frequently to support his point. The law of the harvest is applicable. God does not anticipate the same results in every dispensation because God has not dispensed grace in the same measure in every dispensation. However, God has dispensed enough grace in every dispensation to anticipate from all human beings a measure of faith and works appropriate to their respective dispensation. Thus, God, in Fletcher's mind, judges all people impartially, using the same standard of judgment. God is impartial in judgment because God holds all humans to the same standard of judgment, and God is partial in love because God dispenses benefits differently in the various dispensations of salvation history. Thus, Fletcher vindicated the early Methodist concept of the essential nature of God as holy-love.

Classification of Believers under the Dispensation of the Father

As outlined above, the believers under the dispensation of the Father fall under two broad categories: the heathen and the Jews. While the distinctions have been noted above, there are some commonalities between the experiences of believers in these two categories. In the *Essay on the Doctrine of Dispensations*, Fletcher argued that the spirit of such believers is characterized by the fear of God.[89] They regard God as a "righteous Lawgiver" and a "severe Judge."[90] Operating out of duty and servile fear of God rather than love for God, their disposition is compared to that of a servant's rather than a son's. The dispensation of the Father is compared to Hagar in the Pauline allegory found in Galatians 4. The believers under the dispensation of the Father are known by two marks: "(1) a fear of God rather mixt with terror

---

88. Cf. Fl-W1856, 3:298.

89. Ibid. "That ~~dispensation~~ economy being chiefly a dispensation of stern justice, the <u>fear of God</u>, as a ~~severe~~ righteous Lawgiver and ~~infl[illegible]~~ severe Judge, is in general the spirit and temper of those who ~~continue under it~~ are under that dispensation. They have the disposition of <u>servants</u>, rather than that of children; they act more from the <u>inferior</u> motives of duty and ~~fear~~ servile fear, than from the nobler motives of gratitude and filial love" (Fletcher-Dispensations, 30).

90. Fletcher-Dispensations, 29.

and bondage than with joy and liberty; And (2) A rash severity both towards themselves and others, which makes them deal much in ~~condemnation~~ threatnings and wrath."⁹¹ Fletcher made a psychological observation of the worshippers under the dispensation of the Father; the spirit of believers under the dispensation of the Father reflected the stern and harsh disposition that they perceived of God in the dispensation of the Father:

> You may look for rigorous justice, but for little mercy, from worshippers under that dispensation. They are severe Parents, austere Masters, harsh Preachers, inexorable judges. They cannot bear contradiction, and yet they love to contradict others: ~~they are~~ Stern and overbearing toward their inferiors; and their eye is chiefly evil towards their ~~equal and~~ superiors; ~~it is~~ and they look at their equal rather to ~~discover~~ spy faults than ~~virtues~~ to discover virtues. ~~They are~~ Lavish of censures, they are very ~~and~~ sparing ~~of~~ in their praises; and you may expect from them ~~praises, Expect rather~~ stateliness, reserve ~~cold looks~~, and even frowns, ~~than~~ rather than smiles, and ~~the~~ preventing love. ⁹²

CONCLUSION

While it has been asserted that Fletcher was "the Arminian of the Arminians,"⁹³ the fundamental elements of his theological system resonated with the basic structure of Calvinistic thought in at least three ways. First, Fletcher stressed the doctrine of total depravity of the human race. Second, Fletcher's thought resonated with Calvinistic theology in the centrality and chronological primacy of the role of grace in divine-human relations. Third, parallels are evident between the role of the doctrine of accommodation in both Fletcher's writings and in Calvinistic theology. Fletcher's doctrine of the dispensation of the Father elucidates both disparity and congruity with the Calvinistic thought. The difference in Fletcher's theology and Calvinistic theology was the point of departure; for Fletcher it was divine love.

With the doctrine of the love of God as the *terminus a quo*, Fletcher developed the doctrine of the redemptive purpose of God throughout history. God out of love accommodated revelation and salvation to the human object of redemption. While the effects of the Fall were far reaching, God in Christ overcomes those effects in order to redeem humanity. The centrality

---

91. Fletcher-Dispensations, 30.
92. Ibid.
93. D. S. Schaff, "Fletcher, John William," 4:332.

and prominence of Christ in history ensured its Christocentric import and the possibility of salvation for all humanity. The response required of worshippers under the dispensation of the Father entailed a measure of faith and obedience appropriate to the cognitive revelation of that dispensation.

In the following chapter, the continuity and discontinuity of the dispensation of the Father with the dispensation of the Son will be demonstrated principally through the law. Furthermore, the content of the dispensation of the Son will be studied.

5

The Dispensation of the Son

LIMITING THE REFORM

PROTESTANTS REACTED TO THE system of indulgences in Roman Catholicism and perceived in Catholicism an overemphasis on good works as a means of establishing righteousness before God. As a result, the Reformers stressed the doctrine of *sola fide* or justification by faith alone, which asserts God justifies and pardons sinners on the basis of faith alone in Christ without regard for effort or work on their part. Another of the central tenets of the faith of the Reformers was the related doctrine of *sola gratia*, which asserted the grace of God alone is the hope of sinners' salvation without any reliance on good works as the Catholics suggested. While the Reformers attempted to restore the Church to scriptural Christianity as they perceived it, their cry *sola Scriptura, sola gratia, sola fide* relegated the doctrine of good works in some instances to an insignificant role in Protestant soteriology. Indeed, some Protestants consigned good works and the moral law to a position that was less than Scriptural and promoted antinomianism.[1]

If John Fletcher is known at all, he is recognized for his role as a polemicist in the *Minutes* controversy of the eighteenth century and as the

---

1. Antinomianism is the belief that the moral law is no longer valid or binding for believers by virtue of their faith.

vindicator of John Wesley against the attacks by the hyper-Calvinists. His most important theological works are known as *Checks to Antinomianism*; the title itself reveals his concern for holiness of heart and life. The preservation of the role of the law in the Christian life was one of his central concerns. Fletcher waged a battle against antinomianism and attempted to restore the delicate balance that he felt was lost by an overemphasis on faith to the neglect of works. As such, Fletcher's theological system was an attempt to limit the impact of an overemphasis of Protestant theology upon the Church.

Antinomianism: Practical and Theoretical

Fletcher was convinced that the eighteenth-century church needed a radical reorientation in its thinking about the law. He wrote, "[I]t appears, if I am not mistaken, that we stand now as much in need of a reformation from antinomianism, as our ancestors did of a reformation of popery."[2] According to Fletcher, one of the principal sources of the threat was hyper-Calvinism. It is no mere coincidence that Fletcher's opponents in the *Minutes* controversy were all Calvinists. They were particularly susceptible to antinomianism because they "drew the conclusion that mankind is so totally depraved that there is absolutely no participation in his personal justification and righteousness."[3] At the beginning of the *Minutes* controversy, Fletcher's intention was to defend Christendom against the encroachment of antinomianism; however, in his *Third Check* written in reply to Richard Hill, Fletcher explained his rationale for a new focus: "My design was to oppose antinomianism alone; but the vigorous stand which you make for it upon Calvinian ground obliges me to encounter you there, or to give up the truth which I am called to defend."[4]

The target of Fletcher's criticism was hyper-Calvinism, which emphasized forensic justification of the elect by the imputation of the alien righteousness of Christ to the believer as finished salvation.[5] Fletcher characterized the position that stressed the role of faith to the neglect of good works as "solifidian."[6] Fletcher's whipping boy was the hyper-Calvinist

---

2. Fl-W1856, 2:392.

3. Gunter, *Limits of "Love Divine,"* 37. Gunter does not apply this statement to the Calvinists specifically; he only applied it to those whom he called "fideists."

4. Fl-W1856, 2:393.

5. Cf. Fl-W1856, 3:209.

6. From the Latin *sola fide* meaning "faith alone," Fletcher constructed the word "solifidian" to indicate a person or an idea that placed an overemphasis on faith alone

Tobias Crisp (1600–1642).[7] Crisp who sought to overturn the moral conventions of the Puritan *ordo salutis* posited a soteriology that rejected even faith as a condition of salvation.[8] Crisp privileged justification over sanctification, and in his thought, justification was *sola gratia* and completely forensic rather than a transient act that played out in time as in the Puritan scheme.[9] Further, he held that the Puritan soteriology was legalistic, and that the observance of the law as a "charter of righteousness" should be rejected.[10]

Fletcher encountered similar characteristics in the hyper-Calvinism of his day. During the *Minutes* controversy, Fletcher found valuable allies in John Favel (d. 1691) and Richard Baxter (among others) who had mounted polemics against antinomianism in the intra-Calvinist controversy of the previous century.[11] Fletcher's response to the hyper-Calvinists assumed a similar structure as that of the seventeenth-century moderate Calvinists.

Not only was the threat of theoretical antinomianism real, but the practical antinomianism was a threat to the methodists as well, including both the Calvinistic and the Wesleyan wings of Methodism.[12] In *A Race for Eternal Life*, Fletcher described his extract of Bunyan's sermon as a polemic against both Calvinism and Arminianism, but particularly against antinomianism among the Arminians: "This extract is published: (1) To stir up lazy and inconsistent Arminian professors, who assert, that we should work out our own salvation with all diligence; and yet neglect doing it: And (2) to convince of partiality, the contentious Calvinists, who quarrel with their brethren, for preaching consistently the very same doctrine, which is inconsistently maintained by their orthodox teachers, among whom pious John Bunyan stands in the first rank."[13]

Antinomian practices were also prevalent in the parish churches. According to Fletcher, both parishioners and ministers were affected by theoretical and practical antinomianism.[14] According to Fletcher, preachers

---

often to the neglect of good works.

7. Cf. Fl-W1856, 2:385.
8. Parnham, "The Humbling of 'High Presumption,'" 61.
9. Ibid., 67.
10. Ibid., 54.
11. Cf. Fl-W1856, 3:48.
12. Schlenther, *Queen of the Methodists*, 136; Fl-W1856, 2:218; Gunter, *Limits of "Love Divine*," 13–34, 42.
13. J. Fletcher, *Race for Eternal Life*, iii.
14. Fl-W1856, 2:343–66.

fomented antinomianism in their hearers by not declaring the whole truth of the Word of God.[15]

In redressing theoretical and practical antinomianism, Fletcher developed a thorough-going defense of the validity of the law (and specifically the moral law in light of the abrogation of the ceremonial law), the validity of the Old and New Testaments and their relation to one another, the validity of God's saving activity during the OT era including the relation of the dispensation of the patriarchs to subsequent dispensations, the supremacy of salvation under the New Covenant over the Old, the proper roles of the law and of grace in salvation, and the relation of the law of paradisiacal innocence to the Mosaic law.

The Validity of the Old Testament

In Fletcher's thought, the moral law remained obligatory for those in superior dispensations. How could Fletcher retain the ascendancy of salvation in the NT over that of the OT while insisting on an obligatory status for the law that had served as the means of entrance into the covenant relation of the Jewish religion? If the law had been abrogated under the NT, how could Fletcher retain an obligatory status for the law in the Christian life? How could Fletcher maintain the disparity between the inefficiency of the Mosaic dispensation and the efficiency of the Christian dispensation to achieve a moral, ethical, and spiritual transformation, and at the same time, maintain the continuity of God's work in salvation history? What is the Christian understanding of the OT? What is the relationship of the OT to the New?

Matthew R. Schlimm asserts that in the seventeenth and early eighteenth centuries, a number of academics, some of whom were within the church, devalued the authority of the OT. While some theologians labeled its contents as "irrational and superstitious," "Deists at the fringes of the church worked to demolish the Old Testament's sacred status to rubble."[16] Schlimm recognizes that Wesley diminished the worth of the OT, but he did not devalue it for the same reason as did the enlightenment thinkers. The latter devalued the OT because it did not measure up to their standards of rationality, whereas Wesley devalued it "for not measuring up to the New Testament."[17]

While Schlimm recognized that Wesley used the doctrine of dispensations as a lens for understanding the discontinuity of the Old and New

15. Fl-W1856, 2:349.
16. Schlimm, "Defending the Old Testament's Worth," 30.
17. Ibid., 50.

Testaments, Schlimm does not explain that the doctrine of dispensations were also a means of understanding the continuity of the two testaments.[18] Wesley's designated successor championed the doctrine of covenants and dispensations as a means of maintaining the continuity and discontinuity of the Old and New Testaments. For Fletcher, the covenants and dispensations were a lens to view salvation history and the relationship of the OT to the New. The two related doctrines enabled Fletcher to recognize the validity of God's saving activity in all ages of history because God was the Agent in every age who envisioned the redemption of humanity. The consistency that may be observed in history is due to the consistency of God's love and redemptive purpose toward the human race. The inconsistency that may be observed is due to the fallenness of humanity and God's willingness to accommodate saving activity to the object of divine affection. This chapter will explore Fletcher's views on the subject.

A DELICATE DIALECTIC

Fletcher Corrected His Understanding of Salvation History

Foundational to an accurate understanding of salvation history is the preservation of a delicate dialectic upon which Fletcher constructs his theological system. The subtitle of *The Scripture Scales* reveals Fletcher's concern for balance: "to weigh the gold of gospel truth,—to balance a multitude of opposite scriptures,—to prove the gospel marriage of free grace and free will,—and restore primitive harmony to the gospel of the day."[19] Alternatively, the "two axioms of the gospel," as he expressed it, may be stated thus: "First, our salvation is of God," and "Second, our damnation is of ourselves."[20]

Shattering the dialectic leads to a misunderstanding of the gospel, to antinomian practices and doctrine, and to a misapplication of Scriptures and of ministerial practices.[21] Confusion on the dispensations and the doctrines of grace and justice has resulted in many errors within the Church.[22] Clarity comes as one restores "the primitive harmony and fulness to the partial gospels of the day."[23]

---

18. Ibid., 46.
19. Fl-W1856, 4:124.
20. Fl-W1856, 5:65–66.
21. Fl-W1856, 5:172; 2:214.
22. Fl-W1856, 5:174.
23. Fl-W1856, 5:183.

The Dispensation of the Son

Fletcher himself admits to misunderstanding God's redemptive purpose in history. Richard Hill, an opponent in the Calvinist controversy, capitalized on what he perceived to be inconsistencies between one of Fletcher's manuscript sermons that he had preached at his parish church in Madeley in 1762 and his later work in the *Checks*. In his work entitled *The Finishing Stroke*, Hill related to his opponent, "I have in my possession a manuscript sermon, which you preached in your own parish church."[24] At first Hill conceived of publishing the manuscript sermon in its entirety, but upon second thought he decided to quote only portions of it. Fletcher's sermon decried works righteousness and emphasized faith as the only means to justification. Hill's purpose was to set the principal emphasis of the sermon, *sola fide*, in opposition to the emphasis on good works found in Fletcher's *Checks*.

Fletcher responded to Hill's charge of inconsistency in *Equal Check to Pharisaism and Antinomianism, Part I*. The preface contains a confession: "With respect to the Discourse [Sermon], I must mention what engages me to publish it. In 1771 I saw the propositions called the 'Minutes.' Their author invited me to 'review the whole affair.' I did so; and soon found, that I had 'leaned too much towards Calvinism,' which, after mature consideration, appeared to me exactly to coincide with speculative antinomianism."[25] In his 20 April 1773 letter, Fletcher communicated to Charles Wesley his decision to publish the manuscript sermon: "My Equal Check will contain 3 pieces besides a dedicatory epistle to Mr. Hill. An historical essay on the harmony of the two gospel precepts <u>believe</u> & <u>obey</u> and on the danger of parting them. The Sermon guarded with additions & notes which I preached last sunday exactly eleven years after I preached it the first, viz April 18. Then some remarks on Mr. Hills <u>Finishing stroke</u>, taking in his shows of argument, & fol groundless charges of dishonesty &C."[26] Richard Hill did not take a kind view to Fletcher's interpolations; he wrote, "I have no objection to it as you propose to print it. As to your explanatory notes, and additions in brakets [sic], you know, Sir, that by these you may easily make the sermon speak what language you see proper. *Clarke* and *Priestly* by explanatory notes and additions in brackets, can explain away the divinity of Christ; *Socinus* his attonement [sic], &c. &c. *Taylor* the corruption of human nature."[27] The modifications that Fletcher made to this sermon will now be analyzed.

---

24 Hill, *Finishing Stroke*, 44. On the date of the sermon, see Fl-W1856, 3:328–30; Fletcher-Covenant.

25 Fl-W1856, 3:329. Cf. Fl-W1856, 3:362.

26 JF→CW, 20 Apr. 1773. Fletcher clearly indicated the "3 pieces" refer to the three portions of the same publication (contra. UL, 307).

27 Hill, *Three Letters written by Richard Hill*, 15–16.

Modifications to His Sermon "Salvation by the Covenant of Grace"

Fletcher published the sermon on Romans 11:5-6 with interpolations in brackets to balance his earlier statements with his more mature theology and in doing so, nuanced his earlier theology to reflect his more mature understanding. The edited sermon, *The Guarded Discourse* as it was called,[28] was much longer than the original; it was, in fact, so long that Fletcher was obligated to preach it on two different Sundays, April 18 and May 9, 1773.[29] The modifications of the sermon may be classified under the following categories.

Degrees of Grace

In a footnote where the word "gospel" is inserted before the word "grace," Fletcher distinguished between different degrees of grace,[30] and specifically distinguished between gospel grace and original grace. Gospel grace is the evangelical, transforming grace given by God as Redeemer and Comforter to those who trust in Christ whereas original grace was given to Adam before the fall and flowed from God as Creator and Preserver. A study of the original manuscript sermon reveals that Fletcher made modifications to the original, most of which were reproduced or expanded by Fletcher in the published edition. However, the manuscript interpolations exceed, occasionally, those that were published. Following the words "of God's way of saving sinners merely through Jesus Christ,"[31] Fletcher added, "according to the covenant first made with Adam after the fall."[32] Again in the original manuscript, the Vicar of Madeley delimited with the insertions the concept of grace to include the idea of human activity: "'By grace,' says St. Paul, 'ye are' [initially] 'saved through faith, and that not of yourselves, it is the gift of God'"; and again, "seeing we can do no good works before we are [at least] in a state of [initial] salvation."[33] Fletcher nuanced the concept of grace in order to emphasize the varieties of God's grace in history. In his thought, the

---

28. Fletcher-FC1, vii.

29. Fletcher-EC1, title page.

30. Fl-W1856, 3:369. Fletcher gave directions on growing rich in grace and emphasized the degrees of salvation: "1. We grow rich in grace by degrees as Children, beasts, plants. 2. Few are equally righ in all graces. They excell most in the grace opposed to their sin. & in that they excercise most" (JF→sermon, Ephesians 3.8 b).

31. Fl-W1856, 3:367.

32. J. Fletcher, Covenant with God, 24 August 1754, The Fletcher-Tooth Collection, The John Rylands Library, The University of Manchester, MAM P4d15.

33. Ibid. Cf. Fl-W1856, 3:386.

The Dispensation of the Son

doctrine of the love of God that was discussed previously permeates all of history, and the doctrine of initial, general justification was deduced from it.

Fletcher endeavored to ensure an appropriate identification of the various degrees of divine blessings to the correct dispensations. For example, assurance of salvation is reserved for the Christian dispensation.[34] Fletcher argued that an explicit knowledge of Christ is unnecessary to salvation in the inferior dispensations and to assert otherwise is to doom to hell all those who do not have this explicit knowledge.[35] Thus, Fletcher stressed the value of the various degrees of grace in the nuanced sermon.

A Greater Emphasis on the Righteousness of Christians

In the revised sermon, Fletcher placed a greater emphasis on the expectation of righteousness of Christians than he did in the original manuscript sermon. The emphasis is evident in five ways. First, Fletcher demonstrated a more positive view of good works than he did in the manuscript sermon. When Paul denounces good works, Fletcher pointed out that such works should be modified as "pharisaical" rather than "good."[36] Fletcher limited the Pauline denunciation of works righteousness to those done in a self-righteous spirit or a ritualistic, formalistic or external adherence to the law. By limiting Paul's denunciation to a self-righteous attitude, he heightened the need for good works and righteousness in the Christian life. Second, the revised sermon stresses the importance of good works by distinguishing between merit and proper merit. Fletcher frequently added the words "proper" as an adjective of "merit" in the published edition of the sermon to refine the meaning of the word "merit" and to preserve the idea of the conditionality of good works for final justification. Fletcher sought to distinguish between the "'good works,' so called, of unhumbled pharisees, and the genuine obedience of penitent believers."[37] In response to those who asserted that he preached against good works, Fletcher differentiated between "preaching against the [proper] merit of good works, and preaching against good works themselves."[38] His latter interpolation indicates his desire to distinguish between merit of condignity and merit of congruity; the former was totally unacceptable whereas the latter was important to Fletcher's doctrine of final justification. In this matter, Fletcher insisted on the importance

34. Fl-W1856, 3:379.
35. Fl-W1856, 3:380.
36. Fl-W1856, 3:367–68.
37. Fl-W1856, 3:399.
38. Fl-W1856, 3:407.

of humanity's faithful obedience and supported Wesley's *Minutes*, which sparked the controversy.[39] Third, Fletcher previously had asserted that one should do good works in order "to be justified before men" but later he added the phrase "[now, and before the Judge of all the earth in that great day]."[40] With this interpolation, Fletcher made good works conditional to final justification, and once again, supported the *Minutes* of the Methodist Conference. Fourth, Fletcher nuanced generalizations made in the manuscript sermon about the pervasive power of sin in order to delimit the scope of them and emphasized the optimism of grace and the doctrine of Christian perfection.[41] Without the alterations in the edited sermon, certain phrases tended toward antinomianism.[42] On the atonement, Fletcher wrote: "John xvi.8 . . . shows him the all-sufficiency of the Saviour's [merits or] righteousness, to swallow up his [former sins, and] unrighteousness; and the infinite value of Christ's meritorious death to atone for his [past] unholy life."[43] Fifth, Fletcher ensured that any observations on the atoning work of Christ would not be taken as a reference to the imputation of Christ's righteousness to the believer.[44]

The Doctrine of Covenants in Fletcher's Thought

In *The Guarded Discourse*, Fletcher made a number of revisions to his views on covenant theology and salvation history. He broadened the concept of salvation history recognizing the variety of ways that God deals with humanity. He admitted to being confused previously on the breadth of God's saving activity in history and on the doctrine of dispensations: "This and the preceding clauses are added, to guard the doctrine of the gospel dispensations, of which I had but very confused views eleven years ago."[45] This new understanding of salvation history included the doctrine of the heathen, which was discussed previously.[46]

In the edited sermon, Fletcher revised many of his earlier statements by adding the words "covenant of" prior to the words "works" and "grace."

39. Fl-W1856, 3:371.
40. Fl-W1856, 3:418.
41. Fl-W1856, 3:374, 377, 379.
42. Cf. Fl-W1856, 3:379.
43. Ibid. In this section and the following, the bracketed phrases appear in the original.
44. Ibid.
45. Fl-W1856, 3:375. Cf. Fl-W1856, 3:376, 389.
46. Cf. Fl-W1856, 3:377, 380.

Fletcher employed covenant theology to clarify his position on the role of faith and works.[47] As stated previously, Fletcher held that God had established two covenants with human beings: the first covenant, the covenant of works, required "an absolute, unsinning, universal obedience," and the second covenant, the covenant of grace, provided freedom from the constraints or bondage of the law of innocence through the atoning work of Jesus Christ.[48] In *The Guarded Sermon*, salvation is not the mere occurrence of grace or works; the interpolation adds the idea of the terms of a relationship established by God in which humanity stands before God: the covenants are domains or spheres of influence. The covenants of works and grace, as stated above, were historical, occurring within the *ordo temporum*. However, they required the existential response in the *ordo salutis*; the rejection of the dispensations that one is under causes one to shift from the domain of the covenant of grace to the covenant of works where salvation is impossible.

In the supralapsarian period, salvation is impossible under the covenant of works due to the sinfulness of humanity because it requires perfect obedience. The covenant of grace includes the terms of the relationship that God established after the Fall and demonstrates the accommodation of God who tempers the terms of the relationship to the finite capacity of sinful humanity. Fletcher often employed the idea of the covenant of works to underscore the inability of fallen humanity to maintain the terms of the relationship that God had established with Adam in the Garden. He wrote "I solemnly declare and publicly affirm: 1. That there is no salvation to be attained by [the covenant of] works since the fall."[49] Fletcher used the doctrine of the covenant of grace in contexts where he wanted to emphasize the optimism of grace in the restoration of the divine-human relationship. In his concept, grace and works were more than an instance or occurrence, but they are domains or spheres under which one lives.[50] One's relationship to God is determined in part by the measure of grace dispensed; the external and objective measures of divine revelation determine the internal and subjective appropriation by humans.

As discussed above, Fletcher's doctrine of the covenants demonstrates a two-fold view of history. However, he also seemed to hold to a tripartite view of history. In 1777, Fletcher wrote in *The Reconciliation* of a three-fold

47. Fl-W1856, 3:369; J. Knight, "John William Fletcher and the Early Methodist," 285.

48. Fl-W1856, 3:377.

49. Fl-W1856, 3:388.

50. Keck describes Paul's concepts of law and grace as a sphere of influence that he defined as "to have one's existence shaped by a controlling factor outside the self" (*Paul and His Letters*, 89).

TRUE CHRISTIANITY

structure of history; the three "grand" covenants are gentilism, Judaism, and Christianity. What is the difference between the bipartite and the tripartite views of history?

The word "covenant" is used exclusively of the bipartite view where as both "covenant" and "dispensation" may be used of the tripartite view. In the following citation, Fletcher employed both terms interchangeably: "These three grand covenants give birth to gentilism, Judaism, and Christianity,—three divine religions, or dispensations of grace."[51] The following diagram depicts Fletcher's view of salvation history:

SALVATION HISTORY

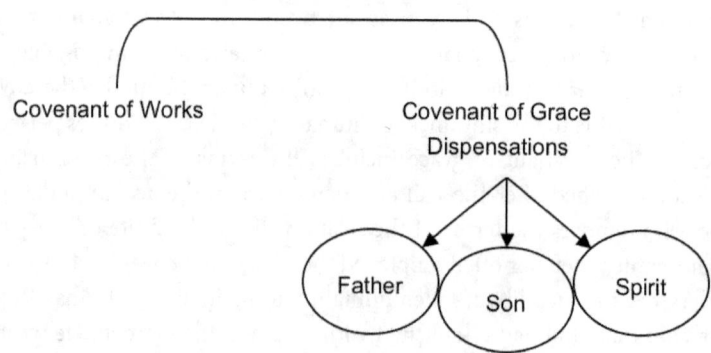

The bipartite view encompasses both pre-Fall and post-Fall history whereas the tripartite view covers only the post-Fall history. The term "covenant" is generally a more comprehensive term in Fletcher's thought than the term "dispensations."[52] For Fletcher, the doctrine of the covenants is a more comprehensive category than the doctrine of dispensations; the tripartite view of history, the doctrine of dispensations, are subsumed under the second covenant, the covenant of grace.[53] While both terms refer principally to the *ordo temporum*, covenant refers to the terms of the divine-human relationship established by God.[54] Dispensations deal with dispensing grace in the way and manner that God deems appropriate. The concept of dispensations became significant for Wesley during the *Minutes* controversy. In

---

51. Fl-W1856, 5:177.

52 Fletcher at times appeared to use the two terms interchangeably (Fletcher-Dispensations, 3).

53. Streiff, *Reluctant Saint?*, 203.

54. Cf. Fl-W1856, 3:297.

another context, the present writer makes a distinction between the dispensation and covenant:

> "Dispensation" is often employed by Wesley in polemics against antinomianism, or when he wants to address the doctrine of sanctification and to preserve the validity of the moral law while recognizing that the law no longer serves as the mode of entry into justification. The notion of covenant is employed by Wesley in contexts where he wants to emphasize the doctrine of justification and to reinforce the impossibility of justification by works. Covenants emphasize the continuity of salvation history, but the concept is somewhat static and does not normally allow for the variations within salvation history. Dispensations provide a platform for the continuity of the Testaments in a dynamic format, and for an emphasis on the progression of history. Thus, Wesley's theology of history distanced itself to some degree from covenantal language and employed dispensational language in response to Calvinism.[55]

Indeed, Fletcher was influential in the usage of the language of dispensations in the early Methodist defense against Calvinism.

According to Fletcher, the error of the Calvinist divines resulted in "confounding the covenants of creating and redeeming grace" and reducing them to two:[56] "the one a covenant of non-redemption, which they call 'the law,' and the other a covenant of particular redemption, which they call 'the gospel.'"[57] He perceived a wide chasm between law and grace in the thought of his opponents.[58] Fletcher held that the Calvinist position confused a distinction between the Adamic law and the Mosaic law, which he considered crucial, and linked the law with the covenant of works and the gospel with the covenant of grace. In this context, Fletcher emphasized the disparity that he perceived in Calvinist theology between the effects of the law and those of the gospel. The disparity between law and the gospel was, for Fletcher, logically impossible as was any reconciliation between his view of divine love with the partial love that effected the salvation of some and the reprobation of others.

While Fletcher did not concur with the Calvinist distinction between law and grace, he drew a line of demarcation between the covenant of works

---

55. Frazier, "John Wesley's Covenantal and Dispensational View of Salvation History," 52. The observation is based upon John Deschner (*Wesley's Christology: An Interpretation*, 114).

56. Schaff and Schaff, eds., *Creeds of Christendom*, 3:616–618.

57. Fl-W1856, 5:177.

58. Hill, *Five Letters to the Reverend Mr.*, 7.

and the covenant of grace: "We must be wholly saved by the covenant of works, or by the covenant of grace; my text showing most clearly, that a third covenant made up of [Christless] merits [according to the first] and divine mercy [according to the second] is as imaginary a thing in divinity, as a fifth element made up of fire and water could be in natural philosophy."[59] This was the very mistake that his opponents made. They "jumble" the Adamic or the Creator's law with the Mosaic or the Redeemer's law. The covenants differ widely: "[T]hese two laws, or covenants, are as different from each other as a covenant made with sinless man, without a priest, a sacrifice, and a mediator, is different from a covenant made with sinful man, and ordained in the hand of a mediator, with an interceding priest and atoning sacrifices."[60]

Thus, in Fletcher's thought, the moral law is consistent with the covenant of grace; it is an accommodation of the original divine purpose for humanity, but this accommodation is only a temporary state of affairs. While God accommodated revelation to the fallen human condition in the Protoevangelium, accommodation becomes less necessary as God transforms human hearts and leads believers toward Christian perfection.

Fletcher's opponents erred because they did not make a distinction between the Adamic law and the Redeemer's law, resulting in an amalgamation of the law and the gospel, which was a theological construct and was a confusion of the two. However, a problem arises. Patrick Streiff points out accurately that Fletcher did not set one divine attribute against another: "In his criticism of the Calvinistic position, Fletcher maintained that one attribute of God cannot be cancelled out by another."[61] However, Fletcher seemed to pit the creative activity of God against the redemptive activity of God when he made the above mentioned demarcation. Despite the apparent contradiction, the crux of the matter is the Fall: a demarcation between the creating grace and redeeming grace was made because redemption would not have been necessary had humanity not fallen. Wiggins wrote of Fletcher's view of redeeming grace: "[I]f man had not fallen and been depraved, God would have had no occasion to reveal fully his nature as Redeemer. This was a crucial factor in Fletcher's development of his theory of dispensations and it allowed him to argue that man under the covenant of grace is actually in a more exalted status than man as he was originally created."[62] Redeeming grace was an intervention into history. There is both

59. Fl-W1856, 3:411–12.
60. Fl-W1856, 5:177.
61. RS, 203.
62. Wiggins, "Pattern of John Fletcher's Theology," 133.

The Dispensation of the Son

continuity and discontinuity. The grace of God demonstrates the continuity of the plan of God: God's loving purpose has been consistently demonstrated throughout history. God's purpose toward humanity has always been a loving one; it became redemptive when Adam fell. Redeeming grace is the divine accommodation to human fallenness. Thus, divine accommodation and grace are inextricably linked. Fletcher saw both the continuity of God's redemptive plan and the progress of redemptive history:

> 1. Before the fall, the free grace of our Creator gave us in Adam holiness, happiness, and a power to continue in both. 2. Since the fall, the free grace of our Redeemer indulges us with a reprieve, an accepted time, a day of visitation and salvation; in a word, with a better covenant, and a "free gift, that is come upon all men unto" [initial] "justification of life." Romans v. 18. 3. That nothing may be wanting on God's part, the free grace of our Sanctifier excites us to make a proper use of the free gift, part of which is moral liberty.[63]

In his *Guarded Sermon*, Fletcher sought to preserve the unity of the law and gospel and the unity of the Old and New Testaments, and accomplished it, in part, by demarcating between the covenant of works and the covenant of grace. His opponents were criticized for confusing the moral law with the covenant of works.[64] The differentiation between the covenant of works and the covenant of grace is important for a correct understanding of Fletcher's views on the function of law in the life of believers.[65] Both the covenants point to the gracious activity of God in establishing a relationship with humanity. The covenant of works points to original sin and the failure of Adam to maintain the terms of the relationship that God has established with humanity in the Garden. The covenant of grace stresses the gracious activity of God who accommodates the terms of the relationship to the infralapsarian condition of humanity. The following table will enable a clearer understanding of the distinction between the two covenants.

Covenant of Works	Covenant of Grace
before the Fall	after the fall

---

63. Fl-W1856, 5:447.

64. Fl-W1856, 3:383.

65. Fletcher wrote, "The law given in our first state, & the law required by the Gospel, the covenant of works, & the covenant of faith are different. Whatever example we see in Jesus, & whatever he promised his followers, are indispensible requisites of gospel salvation" (J. Fletcher, The Test of a new Creature Being queries proposed to some supposed perfect in love, September 1758, Fletcher-Tooth, JRULM, 36.6, 2).

God as Creator and Preserver	God as Redeemer
original grace	gospel grace, evangelical transforming grace
in post-fall, salvation is impossible under these terms	perfection is possible according to the dispensation one is under
emphasis on original sin	emphasis on the optimism of grace
perfect obedience	"accommodated" obedience
fulfilled by Christ	not fulfilled by Christ

In order to grasp further the demarcation between the covenant of works and the covenant of grace, the law of paradisiacal innocence will be considered.

THE ATONEMENT AND ACCOMMODATION OF THE LAW

The Law of Paradisiacal Innocence

The Methodists of the eighteenth century took seriously the gap between the depravity of the human race and the righteousness demanded of believers. Fletcher's opponents in the Calvinist controversy overcame logically the disparity by positing the doctrine of finished salvation. Fletcher refuted the doctrine of finished salvation and criticized his opponents "who vainly imagine that Christ has fulfilled the terms of the second covenant for us, and talk of finished salvation, just as if our Lord had actually repented of our sins, believed in his own blood, and fulfilled his own evangelical law in our stead."[66] Fletcher denied that Christ fulfilled all of the believer's requirements toward the law and took issue with the Calvinists by insisting that Christ fulfilled the first, but not the second covenant.

Hill accused Fletcher of being "strongly tainted with the Pelagian leaven: for you go all along upon the supposition that fallen guilty man who is by nature a child of wrath and born under the curse, has no more forfeited all right and title to the favor of God, by his fall in Adam, than a young sucking infant has forfeited all right and title to its mother's care."[67] The criticism was unjust. Fletcher held that God made salvation possible under either the covenant of works or the covenant of grace. However, salvation was possible under the covenant of works to supralapsarian Adam alone; the depraved condition of infralapsarian humanity made it impossible to satisfy

---

66. Fl-W 1856, 3:376.
67. Hill, *Finishing Stroke*, 23.

the required "perfect human obedience" of the covenant of works.[68] Christ fulfilled the requirements of the first covenant in behalf of all persons, but not the terms of the second covenant.[69]

The redeeming grace of God was demonstrated in the protoevangelium in which God accommodates revelation to human capacity. Fletcher wrote: "At that first promulgation of the gospel, what St. Paul calls the 'law of faith,' and St. James, 'the law of liberty,' took place. This gracious law has been in force under all the dispensations of the everlasting gospel ever since."[70] God demonstrates grace in accommodating to the frailties of humanity and no longer requires of humanity the innocence or perfection required of Adam.[71]

Kenneth J. Collins discussed Wesley's concept of the law and specifically the objective and subjective re-inscriptions of the law. Wesley emphasized that the law was given at three different times: first, to the angels; second, to Adam and Eve; third, the law was re-inscribed on the hearts of humanity. The agent of the re-inscription of the law is Christ. Collins summarized John Deschner's thought: "[T]he initial re-inscription of the law through prevenient grace (objective) occurs irrespective of human volition while the latter re-inscription of the law upon the heart of the believer cannot occur without the consent of the will."[72] Fletcher's thought parallels the thought of Wesley. Though Fletcher did not speak explicitly of the re-inscription of the law, he did imply the idea through the means of prevenient grace immediately after the Fall.

The Moral Law

Fletcher, in his revised sermon, further clarified the concept of the law by distinguishing between the paradisiacal law and the Mosaic law.[73] Fletcher's modifications portrayed the harshness of the paradisiacal law and the impossibility for fallen humanity to attain its conditions.[74] The paradisiacal law made "no provision for repentance, neither did it offer sinners the help of a sacrificing priest, or interceding mediator."[75] Christ as mediator "has

68. Fl-W1856, 4:12.
69. Fl-W1856, 3:377.
70. Fl-W1856, 3:263.
71. Ibid.
72. Collins, "Wesley's Platonic Conception of the Moral Law," 122.
73. Fl-W1856, 3:368, 389.
74. Fl-W1856, 3:372.
75. Fl-W1856, 3:373.

fulfilled the Adamic law of innocence for us" but has not fulfilled "his own evangelical law of gospel obedience to which we must stand or fall, when by our words we shall be justified, and by our words we shall be condemned."[76]

The moral law remains valid.[77] Fletcher asserted the immutability of the moral law,[78] which remains obligatory for all persons in all dispensations; more specifically, the law of liberty or the law of Christ remains a standard for moral conduct.[79]

Under the moral law, different levels of obedience are anticipated. Whereas the paradisiacal law demanded perfect obedience, the law that Fletcher called variously "the law of liberty," "the law of faith," and "the law of Christ," was accommodated to the human condition with the "first promulgation of the gospel," the protoevangelium.[80] The various degrees of obedience are linked to the various degrees of knowledge: "Innocent man with unimpaired powers, could yield perfect obedience, to 'the law of innocence;' therefore that law made no allowance, no provision for any deficiency in duty. Not so 'the law of liberty;' for although it allows no wilful sin, yet it does not reject sprinkled, though as yet imperfect, obedience... It graciously receives from an heathen, the obedience of an heathen; and from a babe in Christ, the obedience of a babe."[81] The following schema depicts the contrast between the law of innocence and the law of Christ or the law of liberty.

law of innocence	law of liberty[A]
given to Adam in Eden	given to Adam after the fall
demands absolute perfection	demands relative perfection
no allowances, no provisions	allows imperfect obedience
	St. Paul's terminology: "the law of faith" St. James' terminology: "the law of liberty"[B]
abrogated	remains in force[C]

A. Fl-W1856, 3:264.
B. Fl-W1856, 3:263.
C. Fl-W1856, 3:263.

76. Fl-W1856, 3:377–78. However, at times, a comparison was made between the two (Fl-W1856, 3:368, 374).
77. Fl-W1856, 3:208.
78. Fl-W1856, 2:123.
79. Fl-W1856, 3:263; 2:341.
80. Cf. Fl-W1856, 3:263.
81. Fl-W1856, 3:264.

Fletcher's opponents did not adequately distinguish between these laws: "The amiable, practicable law of Christ was perpetually confounded with the terrible, impracticable law of innocence."[82]

Correctly understood, the evangelical or Mosaic law was accommodated to frail and finite humanity. The early Wesleyan Methodists' understanding of the accommodated nature of the law did not pass unnoticed by their opponents. Fletcher felt obligated to defend his position against John Berridge who claimed that the understanding of accommodated nature of the law denigrated the law.[83] The law of liberty should not be taken as lenient because it "requires us to love God with all our heart, and our neighbour as ourselves, according to the light of our dispensation, and the talent of power we have received from above"[84] Ever seeking the middle way between two extremes, Fletcher argued that supralapsarian humans were not capable of perfect obedience. "Innocent man with unimpaired powers, could yield perfect obedience, to 'the law of innocence;' therefore that law made no allowance, no provision for any deficiency in duty. Not so 'the law of liberty:' for although it allows no wilful sin, yet it does not reject sprinkled, though as yet imperfect, obedience."[85]

Fletcher was not alone in this understanding of the accommodation of the law; Wesley too agreed. A phrase from Wesley's comments on 2 Corinthians 3:9 reveals his understanding of God's accommodation in the history of salvation: "But how can the moral law (which alone was engraven on stone) be the ministration of condemnation, if it requires no more than a sincere obedience, *such as is proportioned to our infirm state*?"[86]

The Validity of the Law and the Mosaic Dispensation

Reasserting the role of the law in the Christian life, as Fletcher did, was not accomplished without its difficulties. The question might be posed as follows: How could Fletcher reassert the role of the law, which stressed the role of the believer's obedience in salvation, without devaluing the doctrine of grace, which emphasized the divine initiative in salvation? His contemporaries criticized Fletcher for falling into the trap of moralism.[87]

82. Fl-W1856, 3:350.
83. Fl-W1856, 3:262–73.
84. Fl-W1856, 3:263.
85. Ibid.
86. J. Wesley, *Explanatory Notes upon the New Testament*, in loco; emphasis added. Cf. Collins, "Wesley's Platonic Conception of the Moral Law," 121.
87. Gunter, *Limits of "Love Divine,"* 256, 275.

Fletcher himself was concerned about the way his writings would be understood. He addressed "Zelotes," a caricature of the hyper-Calvinists who zealously overemphasized solifinidian teachings, in order to appease their concerns over what they perceived to be legalism in his thought. The hyper-Calvinists identified, according to Fletcher, the moral law of Moses with the covenant of works whereas Fletcher classified it under the covenant of grace. The moral law is functional under both the Christian and Jewish dispensations.[88] Fletcher refused to compare the Decalogue and the covenant of works, but he asserted that the law of Sinai "was a peculiar edition of God's evangelical law adapted to the Jewish commonwealth, and not an edition of the Adamic law of innocence."[89] In Fletcher's thought, there were three editions of the moral law that correspond to the three dispensations of divine grace.[90]

Quoting favorably from John Flavel, Fletcher noted that the Scripture uses the term "law" in two different ways. First, it is used comprehensively to indicate the whole Mosaic economy, including the ceremonial as well as the civil law; second, it is used of the law abstracted from the promises of grace.[91] Thus, only in the former sense does the law find place within the life of the believer. The Mosaic law benefits believers in the dispensations subsequent to the dispensation of the Father because it fosters the fear of God, which "is the great ingredient of godliness under every dispensation of divine grace."[92] Obedience under this dispensation tends to be principally external and interrupted.[93]

One of the problems was his opponents' negative view of the law. Fletcher upheld the moral law of Moses and believed that the spirit of antinomianism "represented God's commandments as grievous, and the keeping of his law as bondage."[94] The antinomians confused "the heavy yoke of the circumcision and ceremonial bondage" with "the easy yoke of Jesus Christ."[95] When properly understood, the covenant of grace "keeps a just medium between the relentless severity of the first covenant, and the Antinomian softness of the covenant trumpeted by some Calvinists."[96]

88. Fl-W1856, 4:184.
89. Fl-W1856, 4:180.
90. Fletcher-Dispensations, 13–26.
91. Fl-W1856, 4:186–87.
92. Fletcher-Dispensations, 5.
93. Fletcher-Dispensations, 10.
94. Fl-W1856, 2:308.
95. Ibid.
96. Fl-W1856, 3:208.

Fletcher asserted that all of the biblical writers uphold the validity of the moral law.[97] But what about Paul's criticism of the law? How does Fletcher reconcile his insistence on the immutability of the law with the Pauline declarations regarding the Christian's death to the law (e.g., Romans 7:1–7, 1 Corinthians 7:39; Galatians 2:19)? The Christian is dead to the law in the following senses: First, the Christian believer is dead to the Levitical law. Second, the ceremonial law is no longer valid for Christian believers.[98] The believer is, thirdly, "dead to the curse attending his past violations of the moral law; for 'Christ hath delivered us from the curse of the law, being made a curse for us.'"[99] Fourthly, believers do not commend their obedience to God as meritorious of salvation.[100]

The latter argument emphasizes the importance of a right attitude toward the law. Paul condemns the Jews not for obeying the law but for their attitude toward the law, i.e., pharisaical obedience.[101] Fletcher employed the word "evangelical legality." He explained what he meant by the phrase: "The legality contended for in these letters is not a 'stumbling at Christ,' and a 'going about to establish our own righteousness' by faithless works. This sin, which the scripture calls 'unbelief,' I would no more countenance than murder. The evangelical legality I want to see all in love with, is a cleaving to Christ by a faith which 'works righteousness;' a 'following him as he went about doing good;' and a showing, by St. James's works, that we have St. Paul's faith."[102] Evangelical legality describes the proper attitude toward the law; briefly, it may be summarized as "faith working by love." The proper attitude recognizes the centrality of Christ and His atoning work to obedience; so, a Christological orientation to the law is maintained.[103]

The Superiority of the Christian Dispensation

The Christian dispensation is superior to the Mosaic dispensation because Christ secured grace "under all the gospel dispensations" and because the ceremonial and ritual aspects of the Mosaic dispensation were annulled.[104] To conclude that the Mosaic dispensation was founded on a curse, as the

97. Fl-W1856, 4:182.
98. Collins, "Wesley's Platonic Conception of the Moral Law," 125.
99. Fl-W1856, 2:339.
100. Ibid.
101. Fl-W1856, 4:181.
102. Fl-W1856, 2:337.
103. Fl-W1856, 4:202–3.
104. Fl-W1856, 4:189.

Fletcher's opponents concluded, is a mistake, however; the Christian dispensation was only founded on better promises.[105] "Christ's dispensation remaineth; but that of Moses 'is done away.' 2 Cor. iii.11. Christ's dispensation is 'the ministration of the Spirit;' but that of Moses is 'the ministration of the letter, of condemnation, of death,' not only because it eventually killed the carnal Jews, who absurdly opposed the letter of their dispensation to the spirit of it, but also because Moses condemned to instant death blasphemers, adulterers, and rebels."[106]

THE CONTENT OF THE REVELATION IN THE DISPENSATION OF THE SON

Wiggins pointed out, "Historically, the Age of the Son was the shortest period, and Fletcher spent less effort in clarifying his understanding of it."[107] The dispensation of the Son comprises the era that began with the miraculous conception of Christ and ended with his ascension. Thus, the principal source for the content of the revelation of the era is the four gospels: "it appears that the 4 Gospels contain the History of the Son's Economy."[108] The content of the revelation of the dispensation of the Son centers upon the good news of the Redeemer: "Under the Son's dispensation the capital command runs thus, Get acquainted with God thy Redeemer Remember him, and love him with all thy heart.—You believe in God the Father your Creator said the Son, believe also in me."[109]

The terms of the covenant of peculiarity of Judaism are "set aside," and "the dispensation of the Son is grafted upon that of the Father."[110] This expresses succinctly the view of the continuity of the saving activity of God in the history of the OT and in the Christ event. He furthermore acknowledged the cognitive content of the preceding dispensation is foundational to the further knowledge of the dispensation of the Son.

Fletcher argued that the gospel could not be confined to an explicit knowledge of the atoning work of Christ because the disciples prior to Pentecost did not have such knowledge. An explicit knowledge of the atoning work of Christ "is the prerogative of the Christian Gospel advancing toward

---

105. Fl-W1856, 4:190.
106. Fl-W1856, 4:189.
107. Wiggins, Pattern, 261.
108. Fletcher-Dispensations, 72. This does not deny that all of the scriptures bear witness to Christ (Fl-W1856, 8:419).
109. Fletcher-Dispensations, 6.
110. Fletcher-Dispensations, 3.

perfection."[111] The position that an explicit knowledge is essential to salvation invalidates the faith of those who have not had an explicit knowledge. At this juncture, Fletcher was thinking not only of those who lived prior to the historical event of God's revelation in Christ, but also of those who were unaware of it in the present, i.e., "all the righteous Jews, Turks and heathens."[112] Fletcher believed that such an explicit knowledge was not necessary to salvation. At first glance, this seems to diminish the work of Christ; however, Fletcher's intent was to heighten the saving activity of God prior to the Christ event and saving activity of Christ in all of history.

For Fletcher, Christ is the center of history. What Kenneth Collins wrote of Wesley's Christology remains true for Fletcher's thought as well: "The prevenient action of the Most High, based upon the life and work of Jesus Christ, is not limited by time, culture, or space, but its benefits have already been richly enjoyed by those who have lived centuries before the advent of the Messiah or by those even today who have never heard the name of Christ. In a real sense, Jesus of Nazareth, the Jew from Galilee, is at the very center of salvation history."[113] An understanding of the pervasive nature of the work of Christ in all of history leads to a Christological interpretation of history in general and of the OT in particular. While the dispensation of the Son is the shortest era chronologically, the centrality and prominence of Christ in history pervades all other eras of history, making each a chapter of the gospel. The dispensation of the Son is superior nonetheless to the preceding dispensations.

THE PERSONS OF JOHN THE BAPTIST AND CHRIST

The Ministry of John the Baptist

The superiority of Christ over the preceding dispensations is evident in the distinction made between John the Baptist (and his disciples) and the believers under the post-Pentecost dispensation. This distinction was evident in Wesley's thought. Wesley differentiated between John the Baptist and Christian believers: "The least true Christian believer has a more perfect knowledge of Jesus Christ, of His redemption and kingdom, than John the Baptist had, who died before the full manifestation of the gospel."[114] The righteousness of regenerated Christian believers was greater than the

---

111. Fl-W1856, 3:380.
112. Ibid.
113. Collins, *Theology of John Wesley*, 87.
114. J. Wesley, *Explanatory Notes upon the New Testament*, Matthew 11:11.

righteousness attained under the legal dispensation because "'the law maketh nothing perfect.'" As will become evident, Fletcher maintained the above distinctions that Wesley held.

In Fletcher's *Essay on the Doctrine of Dispensations*, he discussed three covenants of peculiarity that correspond to some degree with the three dispensations.[115] The first covenant of peculiarity was made with the Jews under the Age of the Father, but the covenant was peculiar to them and did not include the Gentiles who lived in the same age. The two other covenants of peculiarity correspond more directly to their respective dispensations. The seal of the covenant of peculiarity of the dispensation of the Son is water baptism.[116] Fletcher made a distinction between John's baptism and Christ's baptism.[117]

The distinction between John's baptism and Christ's baptism enables one to understand the distinction between the dispensations. The baptism of John the Baptist was of an earlier dispensation and should not be confused with either Christian baptism or the baptism of Christ; John did not baptize in the trinitarian formula, but made disciples "for himself calling people to repentance & the forgiveness of sins."[118] Like John's ministry, the baptism of John must decrease in order that the baptism of Christ might increase.

Water Baptism and the Dispensations

Once a clear line of demarcation had been drawn between John's baptism and Christ's baptism, one could more easily understand the implications of Christian baptism and the dispensations. Christian baptism consists of water baptism and baptism of the Spirit; both of which were means of grace.

Fletcher pointed out the commonalty between the two: "And tho' the distinction of the birth of water and that of the Spirit, necessarily imply a distinction between imperfect infant christianity and adult christianity yet strictly speaking infant christianity is as much one with [perfect] adult christianity as a the child grown up into a man makes but one and the same Jesus lying in the a manger was is one and the same individual with the chil man Jesus fighting the battle of truth agains the pharisees and the Herodians."[119]

115. Fletcher-Dispensations, 3.

116. Ibid.

117. Cf. Steele, *Love Enthroned*, 105.

118 Fletcher-Darby, 48.

119. J. Fletcher, unidentified manuscript containing in part arguments for two baptisms. Fletcher-Tooth, JRULM, 18/13.

The Dispensation of the Son

Controversy with the Quakers over Baptism

In a controversy early in Fletcher's parish ministry, he gave expression to his views on distinctions between water baptism and Spirit-baptism. During Fletcher's time, the Quaker community in the Madeley parish was small in number, but was very influential. The most influential Quaker family in Madeley was the Darby family, of whom Patrick Streiff observes, "The Darby family had built up Coalbrookdale, possessed a large landed property in Madeley, and was involved in wider partnerships in the coal and iron industries."[120] Abiah Darby, the widow of Abraham Darby II, was the principal teacher among the Quakers in Madeley during the eighteenth century. Frequently, she and John Fletcher attended the other's meetings, and on 22 November 1764, Mrs. Darby recorded the following in her diary, "A great weight came upon me to go to the Meeting of the Priest of this Parish and his followers . . . where I had been before at considerable distances of time . . . I then stood up and desire leave to speak . . . and argument ensued . . . which lasted some hours."[121] The argument covered a number of Mrs. Darby's objections to the creed and practices of the Church of England: to the Athanasian creed, to tithes, to maintenance for parish priests, to water baptism and to the Lord's Supper. Fletcher wrote a polemical tract in response to her objections and circulated it throughout his parish to interested parties. His rebuttal reveals his early theology of the sacraments and particularly his views on baptism.

According to Fletcher's account, Darby raised the question as to whether or not the baptism that Fletcher administered was the baptism of Christ who baptized with the Holy Ghost and fire. Fletcher insisted that the baptism that he administered was initiated by Christ and was "the outward sign & means" of Christ's baptism.[122] The command of Christ, the example of the apostles, and the consentaneous practice of the universal Church provided Fletcher with grounds for continuing the practice of baptism. Mrs. Darby's protégé, Daniel Rose, insisted that the baptism that Christ initiated was baptism with the Spirit and not water baptism. Fletcher responded, "[O]ur Saviour spake of <u>Outward</u> Baptism, made up of <u>water</u>, . . . as the means of conveying the <u>inward</u> Grace."[123] Fletcher concluded that when the word "baptism" is used without other qualifiers, it always means

---

120. Streiff, *Reluctant Saint?*, 121.
121. Darby, "Extracts from the Diary of Abiah Darby," 91; cf. Lawton. "Abiah Darby—Holy Woman," 23–24.
122. Fletcher-Darby, 28.
123. Ibid., 35.

water baptism, but Spirit-baptism is not in opposition to water baptism.[124] While Christ commissioned his ministers to baptize with water, Christ alone retains the prerogative of baptizing with the Spirit. Fletcher identified water baptism with the outward sign and baptism of the Spirit with inward grace; however, there was but one baptism as Paul insisted in Ephesians 4:5: "[B]aptizing with water is generally a means or a seal of our being baptized with the holy Ghost."[125] However, this was not always the case; Saint Peter for example cautioned the primitive Christians in 1 Peter 3:21 not to rest in the outward sign of water baptism without the inward grace.[126] Water baptism is not absolutely necessary to salvation, but baptism with the Spirit is absolutely necessary to salvation.

Different Measures of Grace

According to Fletcher, the doctrines of baptism of water and baptism of the Spirit should not be opposed to one another because the former is the precursor of the latter; baptism of water is not different in kind, but is only different in degree from baptism of the Spirit.[127] In a document entitled "Baptism of John and Christ," Fletcher argued that water baptism was the outward sign of which Spirit-baptism is the inward grace.[128] Thus, both baptisms communicate grace but not the same measure of grace.

Anticipating rebuttals employing Pauline teaching on one baptism (Eph 4:5), Fletcher advanced five arguments: first, Paul would not contradict the other biblical writers who distinguish between the baptism of water and that of the Spirit. Secondly, the teaching of Paul in the Epistle to the Ephesians would not contradict his practice in the city of Ephesus where he baptized with water and later prayed that those same believers would be baptized with the Holy Spirit (Acts 19:2,6). Thirdly, if water baptism is essentially the same as Spirit-baptism, the words of Scripture are irrational. Fourthly, when Paul asserts one baptism, it is incorrect to suppose that he opposed a distinction between the two baptisms. Fifthly, Paul opposed

---

124. Ibid.

125. Ibid., 44.

126. Ibid., 38–39.

127. John Fletcher, unidentified manuscript containing in part arguments for two baptisms. Fletcher-Tooth, JRULM, 18/13.

128 J. Fletcher, Baptism of John and Christ, The Fletcher-Tooth Collection, The John Rylands University Library, The University of Manchester, MAM Fl. 21/11.

The Dispensation of the Son

double baptism of the sort of the Anabaptists.[129] Elsewhere, Fletcher emphasized the demarcation between the two baptisms.

In another context, one baptism with "two branches" was emphasized. The full baptism of Christ is characteristic of the Christian dispensation and "has two branches, the baptism of water, and the baptism of the Spirit, or of celestial fire."[130] While Christ distinguished between water baptism and the baptism of fire, the two are essentially one; their essential oneness was evident in Jesus' own baptism: "they meet in ~~his~~ our Lords person, for while he was baptiz'd in Jordan with water by ~~St.~~ John, he was also baptiz'd ~~by his~~ with the H. G. [Holy Ghost] by his father."[131]

Each branch of baptism is connected to a particular grace or privilege of the Christian dispensation. In the manuscript identified as "Loose Hints on the Spirit," Fletcher quoted the collect for Ash Wednesday as an example of a prayer suitable for those who want to be born of water "or to stand in the penitential grace" of which water baptism is the seal.[132] As a sample prayer for those who want to be born again of the Sprit or "to stand fast in the grace of spiritual regeneration," Fletcher quoted the collects from Quinquagesima Sunday or Shrove Sunday and the collect for purity as appropriate prayers.[133] Thus, the grace of spiritual regeneration was associated with the birth of the Spirit whereas Fletcher associated "born again of water" with penitential grace and an external religious experience.

Water baptism is an outward sign that points to the inward grace of a death unto sin.[134] However, the rite does not automatically communicate the grace of regeneration; this point is crucial to the distinction between water baptism and Spirit-baptism. On 4 July 1764, Fletcher wrote,

> This change proceeds not from the power of man, . . . but from the Spirit of the Living God. And our blessed Lord attributes this Spiritual production to the Holy Ghost, saying—"So is every one that is born of the Spirit." Baptismal water is in itself, no other than common water, but is used as a shadow of heavenly things, and can perform no spiritual operation. Faith in Christ

---

129. Ibid.

130. Fl-W1856, 5:467.

131. Fletcher-Baptism.

132. J. Fletcher, Loose Hints on the Spirit, The Fletcher-Tooth Collection, The John Rylands Library, The University of Manchester, MAM Fl 17.1.

133. Ibid.

134. Fletcher argued in his letter to Rev. Prothero that water baptism "pleads for" spiritual regeneration (JF→[Rev. Prothero], 25 Jul. 1761). John Wesley argued that in adults, the birth of water does not always accompany the birth of the Spirit (BiCent-WJW, 2:197).

> Jesus is the gift, and the sole gift of God, and he is the object, author, and finisher, whereby the believing soul feeds, delights, and trusts there in, as his very life, joy, hope, righteousness, salvation, glory, and eternal felicity.[135]

The outward sign may be received without receiving the inward grace as is evident in the following admonition: "~~If you~~ No sooner will you have discerned that this is the ~~y~~ deplorable state of christians in general, than you will endeavour to ~~rise~~ awake out of sleep, ~~and arise from the dead~~, that Christ may give you light to see the kingdom of God. You have received the form of ~~baptism~~ water-baptism, cry ~~for~~ t to God for the power of it, 'a death unto sin, and a new birth to preparatory righteousness.'"[136] Fletcher insisted that true righteousness is evident in those who have been "born again of the Spirit."[137] Thus, baptism of the Spirit and birth of the Spirit communicated the grace of spiritual regeneration, but water baptism did not necessarily communicate that grace although it pointed to the grace of spiritual regeneration. Theoretically, water baptism implied the grace of spiritual regeneration, but did not automatically render the recipient of the rite regenerate. Fletcher did not confuse the *res* with the *signum* and thereby avoided the doctrine of *ex opere operato*.[138]

Some of the shortcomings in the experience of certain believers may be due in part to the lack of teaching or emphasis on the doctrine of Spirit-baptism. In certain segments of Christendom, the outward sign may be received while the inward grace is theoretically denied: "Thousands of paedobaptists, and anabaptists, contend for the ~~form and~~ shell of water baptism, whilst they deny a real death unto sin, which is the kernel of that divine ordinance."[139] Even the Church of England has not maintained adequately the distinction between water baptism and Spirit-baptism:

> I wish our church had ~~been~~ carefully maintained in all her offices, the capital distinction between the baptism of repentance, and that of the Spirit: But candor obliges me to confess, that ~~our~~ a degree of ~~Augustinian~~ the confusion, ~~remains yet in some of them~~ which St. Augustin, and others brought into the doctrines

---

135. JF→CH, 4 July 1764.

136. Fletcher-Loose; cf. McPherson, "Early Methodist Teaching on Water and Spirit," 4.

137. "But the mischief does not stop here. Myriads of pharisees oppose their own earthly hypocritical righteousness to the heavenly, inspired righteousness, ~~of the~~ which fills the souls of those who are born again of the Spirit" (Fletcher-Loose).

138. Cf. BiCentWJW, 2:196–97; Collins, *Theology of John Wesley*, 263.

139. Fletcher-Loose.

of ~~grace~~ the gospel, remains yet in some parts of her liturgy. Thus, as soon as ~~an infant or an adult person~~ a child is baptized <u>with water</u>, she says: "We yield thee hearty thanks, most merciful Father, that it hath pleased thee to regenerate this infant <u>with thy Holy Spirit</u>."[140]

However, Fletcher later pointed out that the liturgy for the water baptism of adults maintained an appropriate distinction between being born again of water and being born again of the Spirit because the baptismal liturgy includes the prayer for the candidates: "<u>Give thy Holy Spirit to these persons</u>."[141] Below, the subject of two degrees of regeneration, which is connected to these two branches of baptism, will be discussed.

THE PRIVILEGES BELONGING TO THE DISPENSATION OF THE SON

The central focus of the above discussion has been the *ordo temporum* and specifically the distinctions between the ministry of John the Baptist and the ministry of Christ, illustrated through the rite of water baptism, which was administered by John the Baptist and by the disciples of Christ, and the baptism with the Spirit, which Fletcher identified as the baptism of Christ. Making these distinctions enables one to discern the distinctions between the dispensation of the Son and the dispensation of the Spirit. In the following material, the *ordo salutis* is the primary focus and specifically the privileges belonging to the believers under the dispensation of the Son.

The Law of Christ

The experience of believers under the dispensation of the Son is superior to the experience of believers in the preceding dispensation and is inferior to the succeeding one. In Fletcher's discussion of the various editions of the law, he noted the superiority of the law of Christ over the first edition of the law. The superiority of the second edition of the law resides in its "stronger Motives and better Promises." The former edition of the law was dispensed with "emblems of <u>stern</u> Justice" whereas the second edition of the law was

---

140. Fletcher-New, 21/12. In his 7 March 1778 letter to Mary Bosanquet, Fletcher mentioned "a treatise on the birth of the Spirit which treatise is not yet published" (JF→MBF, 7 March 1778). The treatise to which he makes reference and the "Essay on the New Birth" may be one and the same.

141. Fletcher-New.

dispensed with "emblems of <u>sweet</u> Mercy," which accounts for the first edition being called law and the second edition being called grace.[142] Fletcher identified the Christian Decalogue as the commands to repent and believe the Gospel, the eight Beatitudes and Jesus' command to love. The promises of obedience to the law of Christ are better because they are founded by a more excellent Mediator.

As Priest, Christ freed humanity from the bondage of the paradisiacal law, and as King, Christ established the evangelical law of love or the law of Christ. Eldon Ralph Fuhrman is correct in affirming that "the nature of the law in force determines the meaning of sin."[143] As was pointed out previously, Christ fulfilled and abolished the paradisiacal law that demanded pre-Fall perfection. Concerning the former law Fletcher never once made any claim that it could be fulfilled this side of paradise; concerning the latter law, the evangelical law of love, he insisted that it was both possible and necessary to keep it, even in spite of many involuntary imperfections."[144] In a response to Rowland Hill, Fletcher made it clear that though the paradisiacal law was fulfilled by Christ, the law of Christ or the moral law was still in effect for the believers under the Christian dispensation: "Had he not just before, verse 12, admitted 'the law and the prophets' into his Gospel dispensation, saying, 'All things which ye would that men should do unto you, do ye even so unto them, for this is the law and the prophets?'"[145]

Response to the Law under the Dispensation of the Son

Were the believers under the dispensation of the Son capable of fulfilling the demands of the law of Christ? In the *Essay on the Doctrine of the Dispensations*, Fletcher described the measure of obedience of believers under the dispensation of the Spirit. While the obedience of such believers is "more spiritual, free, and vigorous"[146] than the obedience of believers under the dispensation of the Father, the believers under the dispensation of the Son "share . . . both . . . in the severity of the law, and in the sweetness of the gospel."[147] These believers "are in part <u>spiritual</u> and in part <u>carnal</u>."[148] Paul's description in Romans 7 is an accurate description of worshippers under

---

142. Fletcher-Dispensations, 15.
143. Fuhrman-Contribution, 74.
144. Ibid.
145. Fl-W1856, 3:110.
146. Fletcher-Dispensations, 10.
147. Ibid., 31.
148. Ibid.

the dispensation of the Son. Fletcher wrote, in an apparently early letter, that his own experience coincided with the experience described in Romans 7.[149] Worshippers under the dispensation of the Son vacillate between the mind serving the law of God and the flesh serving the law of sin.[150]

Pardon of Sin

Despite the above description, Fletcher attributed certain high privileges to the dispensation of the Son; one of the principal privileges was pardon of sin: "Great privileges and blessings belong to this economy of grace; the forgiveness of sins in particular."[151] Justification was linked to the dispensation of the Son whereas sanctification or regeneration was linked to the dispensation of the Spirit.[152] Fletcher wrote in some notes, which he had prepared for his response to Dr. Priestly: "Before ~~Christ~~ our holy Religion was mutilated by mistaken Divines, and ~~by~~ worldly-minded Christians, it ~~contain'd~~ included the Dispensations of the Father, ~~and~~ of the Son, ~~and~~ of the Holy ~~Ghost;~~ Spirit; it led sinners ~~first from the~~ thro' a penitential fear of ~~God~~ the Father, and thro' a justifying faith in the Son, to the sanctifying comforts of the Holy Ghost: It was a clear revelation of God in Trinity, and it stood unshaken upon that very foundation which you endevour to sap ~~with an every increasing and on~~ in all your theological Publications."[153] Thus, justification was one of the privileges available to believers under the dispensation of the Son.

While justification was available in the dispensation of the Son, was regeneration also available? Fletcher held to the doctrine of double regeneration. Regeneration could be defined in two senses: first, he spoke of new birth in the lower sense or partial regeneration. The pre-Pentecost disciples were only regenerate in part.[154] The first degree of regeneration was chiefly external and was associated with water baptism. The second degree of regeneration was internal and is associated with Spirit-baptism, which will be discussed more fully in the following chapter on the dispensation of the Spirit.

---

149. JF→C.B., n.d.
150. Fletcher-Dispensations, 31.
151. Ibid., 39.
152. Cf. JF→CW, 10 May 1757.
153. J. Fletcher, A Scriptural Vindication First Letter, Fletcher-Tooth, JRULM, 17/21.
154. Fl-W1856, 6:459–60.

TRUE CHRISTIANITY

The Doctrine of Assurance

Another privilege of the believers under the dispensation of the Son was a measure of assurance. One of Fletcher's concerns is the failure of divines to recognize the variety of God's dealings with human beings. This is evident in his doctrine of assurance. Divines failed to recognize the various degrees of assurance available to believers under the various dispensations. Fletcher's scope is much broader than many writers:

> [M]y subject has obliged me to consider it [the doctrine of assurance] also according to the dispensations of John the Baptist, Moses, and Noah. Believers, under these inferior dispensations, have not always assurance; nor is the assurance they sometimes have so bright as that of adult Christians. Matt. xi.11. But, undoubtedly, assurance is inseparably connected with the faith of the Christian dispensation, which was not fully opened till Christ opened his glorious baptism on the day of pentecost, and till his spiritual kingdom was set up with power in the hearts of his people. Nobody, therefore can truly believe, according to this dispensation, without being immediately conscious both of the forgiveness of sins, and of the peace and joy in the Holy Ghost.[155]

Not only did Fletcher criticize the divines for their failure to recognize the varieties of assurance, he also cautioned the evangelicals who asserted that no one has faith but those who have the assurance of faith.[156] In his *Essay on Truth*, Fletcher criticized Sir Richard Hill who maintained that "there is no true faith, but an explicit faith in Christ and no explicit faith in Christ, but the faith of full assurance."[157] Fletcher argued that faith cannot be confined to evangelical faith, nor does faith always include the full assurance of faith. He queried, "Is it scriptural to rank among absolute unbelievers a penitent who thus humbly and obediently waits for the faith of full assurance,—the faith of Christianity in its state of perfection?"[158] The faith of a penitent was considered an improvement over the disbelief of non-believers but was not yet the faith of post-Pentecost disciples.

In the *Third Check*, Fletcher discussed the various degrees of acceptance and divine favor. All heathens have the day of divine favor or a "day of salvation" (2 Corinthians 6:2), which if responded to positively, leads to a

---

155. Fl-W1856, 331–32.
156. Fl-W1856, 4:99.
157. Fl-W1856, 4:107.
158. Fl-W1856, 4:110.

higher acceptance in which they receive "tokens of increasing favour," which is mixed "with some love of complacence and delight."[159] Faithful Jews are accepted "in a superior manner" having a "greater grace here, and greater glory hereafter."[160] The disciples of John the Baptist and Christians who have not been baptized with the Holy Spirit "are yet more highly accepted . . . [and] are great in the sight and favour of the Lord."[161] This latter description may be applied to believers under the dispensation of the Son who have a measure of assurance. The blessing of assurance for believers under the dispensation of the Son is inferior to that of believers under the dispensation of the Spirit: "Great privileges and blessings belong to this economy of grace [i.e., the dispensation of the Son]; the forgiveness of sins in particular; for tho' the full, clear, and abiding severe witness testimony of pardon is only enjoy'd under the dispensation of the Holy Ghost, yet the knowledge and sense of pardon belong also to the Son's Dispensation."[162] Full assurance awaits the dispensation of the Spirit.[163]

There seems to be further warrant for a distinction between the assurance of believers under the dispensations of the Son and the Spirit. Although not identifying it as such, Kinghorn pointed out that Fletcher distinguished between 'believing in Christ' and being 'sealed by the Spirit.'[164] The sealing with the Spirit is associated with the day of Pentecost. Fletcher also made a distinction between sealing our faith according to the truth of the particular dispensations and "God's sealing the truth of our faith with the seal of his power"; the latter evidently refers to the day of Pentecost and is distinguished from the experience of the disciples under the dispensation of the Son.

159. Fl-W1856, 2:431.
160. Ibid.
161. Ibid.
162. Fletcher-Dispensations, 39.
163. L. Wood confused an accurate understanding of Fletcher when he stated: "What is further surprising is that Fletcher defines Christian perfection in terms of 'the Spirit of adoption' and 'the birth of the Spirit.'" He should have stated that "the Spirit of adoption" characterizes the believers under the dispensation of the Spirit, and "the birth of the Spirit" is the means of entrance into this dispensation. Woods does acknowledge however that the believers under the dispensation of the Son have the Spirit of bondage (*Pentecostal Grace*, 188–89). Fletcher wrote, "The pious Jews, and the believing disciples of John wh were children of God under their dispensation, and consequntly they had the Spirit of God—the spirit of adoption: but not according to the fulness pentecostal fulness of the Christian Church" (JF→MBF, 7 March 1778).
164. Kinghorn, "Faith and Works," 102. The source for Kinghorn's claim is the 1 November 1762 letter to Miss Hatton for which there is no extant manuscript.

The assurance available to the worshippers under the dispensation of the Son is not of such a nature to secure believers in "a lukewarm, Laodicean state, short of the assurance and 'the kingdom of God.'"[165] This assurance is sufficient to enable them to avoid on one hand "chilling, despairing fears" and on the other hand "false, Crispian comforts."[166]

A Measure of the Spirit

In Fletcher's thought, there is a distinction between the relationship of believers to the Spirit under the dispensation of the Son and the relationship of believers to the Spirit under the dispensation of the Spirit.[167] The former experience the Spirit as a Monitor whereas the latter experience the Spirit as a Comforter. In another place, Fletcher described what he means by the word monitor: "[A] divine reprover, a ray of 'true' heavenly 'light,' which manifests first moral, and then spiritual, good and evil."[168]

In another context, Fletcher identified the reception of an "inferior measure of the Spirit" with the administration of water baptism at which time the Church "has acknowledged that they are 'regenerate.'"[169] The office of Confirmation "is chiefly intended to implore for her children the abundant measure of the Spirit."[170]

While believers under the dispensation of the Son had a measure of the Spirit, they did not have the abundant measure of the Spirit. The measure of the Spirit available to those under the dispensation of the Son is the Spirit of Bondage not the Spirit of Adoption.[171] Such a believer is a child of God in a lower sense but does not have the constant witness of the Spirit.[172]

Fletcher found significance in the words that Jesus spoke of the Spirit "whom the world cannot receive, because it seeth him not, neither knoweth

---

165. Fl-W1856, 4:96–97.

166. Fl-W1856, 4:103.

167. Fl-W1856, 2:442.

168. Fl-W1856, 2:403.

169. Fletcher-New, 91. The transcription in the ATJ omits the excision "after the candidates have been baptized with water and have received the inferior measure of the Spirit, which she supposes always attends the due administration of water baptism" (Fletcher-New, 91; L. Wood, ed., "'An Essay on the Doctrine of the New Birth' by John Fletcher," 54).

170. Fletcher-New, 91.

171. Fletcher-New, 68.

172. Believers under the dispensation of the Son share "in both the severity of the law and in the sweetness of the Gospel" and in both "the bondage . . . of Mount Sinai" and "the liberty of Mount Sion" (Fletcher-Dispensations, 31).

The Dispensation of the Son

him: but ye know him; for he dwelleth with you, and shall be in you" (John 14:17). Fletcher made much of the distinction between the prepositions "with" and "in" in this verse. The disciples in the pre-Pentecost era knew the Spirit for "he dwelleth with you," and they received the promise of the indwelling Spirit "and [he] shall be in you."[173] The pre-Pentecost disciples experienced an inferior measure of the Spirit; they knew the Spirit as a Monitor. However, the post-Pentecost disciples experienced the Spirit in a superior measure as the Comforter. Or, to employ the biblical language on assurance discussed previously, the disciples under the dispensation of the Son experience the Spirit as the Spirit of Bondage whereas the disciples under the dispensation of the Spirit experience the Spirit as the Spirit of Adoption.[174]

CLASSIFICATION OF BELIEVERS

As discussed previously, the classification of believers was one of the important features of Fletcher's thought. The classification of believers under the dispensation of the Son is no exception. One of these was mentioned immediately above, i.e., the pre-Pentecost disciples. A comparison-contrast with the preceding and succeeding dispensations enables a better understanding of Fletcher's dispensational scheme.

Pre-Pentecost Disciples

In 1759 when Fletcher was preaching among the Francophone immigrant communities in London, he was accused of preaching "une doctrine dangereuse."[175] In his prefatory address of his *Discours Sur la Régénération*, he recommends three works to the readers, which he presumably translated, "because even though I am not the author of them [the writings], they contain the sentiments that I would like to see engraved on our hearts as they were on the heart of the Saint Paul."[176] These three works are *La Nature & le Dessin du Christianisme*, *Le Salut par la Foi*, and *Réveille toi, toi qui dors*.[177] What is significant at this juncture for the current discussion is that

173. Fl-W1856, 6:460; cf. 7:51.
174. Fletcher-New, 68.
175. Fletcher-Discours, [2].
176. "[P]arce que quoi que je n'en fois pas l'auteur ils ne contiennent que les sentimens que je voudrois voir gravés dans nos cœurs comme ils l'étoient dans celui de St. Paul" (ibid.).
177. Forsaith asserted that Fletcher translated Wesley's sermon "Salvation by Faith"

in his translation of Wesley's sermon *Salvation by Faith*,[178] Fletcher omitted several sentences that seem to disparage the faith of the disciples prior to Christ's ascension. The portion of Wesley's sermon that Fletcher omitted is as follows: "And when long after, supposing they had some already, they said unto him, 'Increase our faith,' he tells them plainly that of this faith they had none at all, no, not as a grain of mustard seed: 'The Lord said, If ye had faith as a grain of mustard seed, ye might say unto this sycamine tree, Be thou plucked up by the roots, and be thou planted in the sea; and it should obey you."[179] Fletcher omitted this portion because he presumably felt that it disparaged the pre-ascension faith of the disciples and undermined the progressive divine revelation to human beings.

The experience of the pre-Pentecost disciples was often synonymous with the experience of the Jews and the disciples of John. They were described as carnal believers who had not yet experienced the full liberty from the law of sin and death:

> [T]hose who are not yet do not keep this unity of the Spirit in the bond of peace, or, which is the same thing, those who are not yet made free from the law of sin and death, by the law of the spirit of life, do not yet know by experience what most essentially distinguishes the new Testament from the old: they are yet carnal as the Jews, the Disciples of John, and and Christ's own Disciples before the day of Pentecost; or, as like the Galatians, when after having begun in the Spirit, they ended in the flesh']; lik and, as the "carnal Corinthians, they walk again as men.[180]

The experience that differentiated these believers from the experience of believers in the dispensation of the Spirit was of course the baptism of the Spirit that was historically subsequent. The indwelling presence of Christ by the Spirit is "the most glorious mystery of the gospel" and anything less than this indwelling presence places one in one of the previous dispensations, living "not in a spiritual, but in a carnal state."[181] As was pointed out previously, the experience of believers under the dispensation of the Son was considered a sub-Christian experience or at best of nominal Christians.

---

and possibly more ("A Swiss Among the French Churches," 20). The Arthur Skevington Wood Archive Library of Cliff College holds a number of Wesley's sermons that Fletcher apparently translated into French.

178. J. Wesley, *Le Salut par la Foi, Traduit de l'Anglois*, 6.

179. BiCentWJW, 1:120.

180. Fletcher-Dispensations, 26.

181. Fl-W1856, 2:213.

Nominal Christianity

Peter Forsaith asserted correctly that Fletcher's *Checks to Antinomianism* must be studied within the historical and social context of the parish in which they were written.[182] The Madeley parish was "remarkable for little else than the ignorance and profaneness of its inhabitants."[183] Fletcher's doctrinal writings were not only addressed to the theoretical and practical antinomianism within society as a whole, but served to check the tide of antinomianism within his own parish, suggests Forsaith.[184]

Fletcher was concerned with professors of the Christian faith whose lives did not demonstrate Christian character.[185] David R. Wilson observes, "[I]t appears that the pastoral task in Madeley was not merely maintaining an Anglican hegemony, but continuing the work of the Reformation."[186] In *Equal Check*, Fletcher addressed the "baptized heathens" and called them to repentance: "Baptismal water was applied to your body, as a figure of the grace which purifies believing souls. Ye received, and continue to bear, a Christian name, that binds upon you the strongest obligations you can possibly be under to partake of Christ's holiness, and to lead a sober, Christian life."[187] Believers who lived below the dispensation of perfect Christianity were considered nominal Christians rather than true Christians.[188] In an early sermon on Matthew 5:20, Fletcher wrote of the carelessness of nominal Christians:

> If we consider the carelessness with which nominal Christians work out their salvation we shall be ready to think ~~we shall be apt to think~~ that nothing is easier than to enter into the ki. of H [kingdom of Heaven]. Instead of doing it with fear & tr [trembling]: according to St. P. advice, their neglect even of the outward duties of religion, or the hapiness and coldness some of them, show that they are still in a natural state dead in their Original and in many actual sins, children of wrath and consequently far from the kingdom of heaven.[189]

---

182. Cf. Forsaith, "John Fletcher: A Failure in His Parish," 8; Forsaith, "Dreadful Phenomenon at the Birches," 9, 11.

183. Benson-Life, 4/3.

184. Forsaith, "John Fletcher: A Failure in His Parish," 12.

185. Wilson, "Church and Chapel," 254–55, 278.

186. Ibid., 256.

187. Fl-W1856, 4:67.

188. Fl-W1856, 4:92–93. Fletcher wrote, "Some are in him by external profession without fruit, Others by real union bearing fruit" (JF→sermon, John 15:4).

189. JF→sermon, Matthew 5:20.

TRUE CHRISTIANITY

Fletcher's concern is evident in other sermons in which he warned his hearers of trusting in the rite of baptism for salvation.[190] In a sermon entitled "To the Ungodly how to attain saving grace," Fletcher addressed those who asserted their hope in the doctrine of baptismal regeneration, and he placed the following condition upon their faith: "if you stand to your Baptism"; however, he warned them that if they did not remain faithful to their baptismal vows "tis the first thing that will damn you."[191] In another place, when parishioners argued for baptismal regeneration, Fletcher insisted on a distinction between the inward part and the outward part of baptism, i.e., Spirit-baptism and water baptism respectively.[192]

CONCLUSION

The central precept of the dispensation of the Son is the redemption procured by Christ, which abolished the paradisiacal law of perfect obedience and the ceremonial law while retaining the validity of the moral law for the Christian life. Christ's atonement has abolished the covenant of works and established the covenant of grace as God accommodates revelation to the limitations of depraved humanity. The experience of believers under the dispensation of the Son results in a faith that is principally external. The rite of water baptism is the seal of the covenant of peculiarity, but does not automatically result in the evangelical regeneration of believers. At this stage, believers under the dispensation of the Son are justified, but not spiritually regenerated and have an intermittent assurance of their faith and a measure of the Spirit.

Fletcher classified the pre-Pentecost disciples under the dispensation of the Son because of their limited knowledge of the atoning work of Christ. Another category of believers under the dispensation of the Son was nominal Christians. As the vicar of the Madeley parish, Fletcher encountered nominal Christians who had received the rite of water baptism, but who had not experienced the *res*, the thing that the rite signified. The vicar pressed

---

190. By June 1764, Fletcher was applying to his congregants the distinction between water baptism and baptism with the Spirit that he had made in the controversy with the Quakers. Baptism was increasing important in his thought. Fletcher wrote, "By keeping taking up ones baptismal vow by not denying but being true to ones baptism" (JF→sermon, Colossians 3.4 b).

191. JF→sermon, "To the Ungodly how to attain saving grace."

192. Fletcher wrote, "IV. Baptism is my Regeneration & I was baptized. Yes but distinguish between ye inward & outward part, the Spirit & water, what Xt. & John gives, what Cornelius & Simon receive. 1 Pet: 3.21. Eph: v.26" (JF→sermon, "Temptations which hinder Conversion with their Remedies").

upon his parishioners the necessity of the baptism with the Spirit as the means of accomplishing evangelical (or spiritual) regeneration. It is the subject of the dispensation of the Spirit that the present work will now address.

6

The Dispensation of the Spirit

Historical, Objective Aspects

The *ordo temporum* consists of three ages of history: the dispensation of the Father, the dispensation of the Son, and the dispensation of the Spirit. Other soteriologies did not view the redemptive activity of God with sufficient breadth; they focused too exclusively on God's saving activity in Christ and paid scant attention to the activity of the Father and the Spirit.[1] The problem was not just an overemphasis on the work of one Person of the Trinity to the neglect of another Person, but the salvific activity of God in those periods of history was neglected as well. Insufficient understanding of the dispensations results in deficient Christian experience.

Balance characterized the doctrine of dispensations. Fletcher was at points concerned not to elevate the dispensation of the Spirit to the degree that it negated the significance of the previous dispensations. A manuscript contains notes written in both John and Mary Fletcher's handwriting. John entitled the document "Poll[y]'s Remarks,"[2] which discusses the role of Enoch in salvation history as mentioned in the Epistle of Jude. Mary Fletcher queried, "What Spirit was it so bore this Witness was it not the holy ghost & were he not saved or pardond by faith [in] the mesiah to Come?—if so might not his ~~he~~ heart be purified by faith in the holy ghost—to be given?

1. Fl-W1856, 5:198.
2. Polly was a hypocorism for his wife, Mary.

if his heart was purified by faith—was it not the temple of God? and if God dwelt in his heart by faith did not the trinity dwell their [therein]?"³ John replied to his wife's observations, "Your dispensation of the Holy G. ~~must be~~ is the highest as if the H.G. was higher than the Father & the Son."⁴

Methodist theologians have taken care to maintain a distinct economy of the Spirit.⁵ However, one of the difficulties in understanding the dispensation of the Spirit has been distinguishing it from the dispensation of the Son while still retaining a balanced view. In the *ordo temporum*, the dispensation of the Son is the shortest, and while the historical limits of the era are clearly defined, the distinction between the two dispensations in the *ordo salutis* is not always clear.⁶ Perhaps further exacerbating clarity is the position that the dispensation of the Spirit is summation of salvation history, including all the previous dispensations in their full maturity, and that all the dispensations retain their unity. Another difficulty is the understanding of the contrast between the Mosaic dispensation and the Christian dispensation. In order to preserve the role of the law in refuting antinomianism, Fletcher drew a close connection between the Mosaic dispensation and the Christian one.⁷ The dispensation of the Father included the dispensations of heathenism and Judaism. However, when Fletcher discussed the privileges of worshippers under the dispensation of the Son, he included frequently the pious Jews under the dispensation of the Son rather than under the dispensation of the Father or of Judaism. Wesley's dispensational pattern avoided such ambiguity because while Wesley contrasted the dispensation of the Spirit with Sinai, he did not distinguish the dispensation of the Spirit from the dispensation of Christ (at least not on the *ordo temporum*).⁸

Previously, it was noted that Fletcher in his translation of Wesley's sermon *Salvation by Faith*, omitted Wesley's remark, "they had none at all," which disparaged the faith of the pre-Pentecost Jewish disciples. Fletcher recognized the validity of their faith, but on the other hand he recognized its incompleteness. He was in full agreement with Wesley's assertion that true Christian faith involves a confidence in the merits of the atoning death and

---

3. John Fletcher and Mary Fletcher, Poll[y]'s Remarks. Fletcher-Tooth, JRULM, 17.22.

4. Ibid.

5. Pope, *Compendium of Christian Theology*, 326.

6. Cf. Steele, *Love Enthroned*, 100.

7. Fletcher wrote, "I am now sure that the Mosaic dispensation was nothing but Gospel in embrio" (JF→CW, 5 July 1772).

8. Fuhrman, "Concept of Grace in the Theology of John," 214.

TRUE CHRISTIANITY

resurrection of Christ—something the disciples could not produce prior to Christ's ascension.[9]

The Ascension of Christ:

The doctrine of the ascension of Christ was particularly important in Fletcher's thought. The Johannine emphasis on the glorification of Jesus Christ as a prerequisite to the outpouring of the Spirit is a paramount idea (John 7:39; 16:7).

> Our Lord was not only to be baptiz'd with his own blood before he could procure the baptism of the H. G. for believers but he was to ~~enter ascend~~ go into heaven as the high priests did went into the holiest and plead the merit of that blood ~~before at the rig~~ for to obtain the ~~g~~ promised Spirit. He ascended up on high, he has received gifts for men ~~even f~~ that the Lord God the H. S. might dwell in them. Observe if he ascended up to receive that Gift it was never bestow'd before his ascension.[10]

The ascension, glorification and intersession of Christ were historical preconditions to Pentecost: "[T]o look for the baptism of the Holy Ghost before Christ intersession in glory before his ascension into heaven before his exaltation at his fathers right hand before his resurrection, or before his death is absolutely unscriptural."[11] The order of salvation history was paramount in Fletcher's thought. Thus, Pentecost typifies the summation of salvation history. Frequently, Fletcher epitomized Pentecost not merely as the perfection of believers, but as the perfection of Christianity itself or the perfection of the Church. The outpouring of the Spirit retains a Christological dimension; it is identified with the fulfillment of Christ's Kingdom. The recipients of the democratization of the Spirit on the day of Pentecost included not only the apostles but also holy women, and it was not limited furthermore by the historical confines of that day, but the gift of the Spirit is the common privilege for everyone who has lived subsequently.[12]

---

9. BiCentWJW, 1:121.

10. Fletcher-Baptism.

11. J. Fletcher, various fragments cut from the Checks, Fletcher-Tooth, JRULM, MCA: MAM Fl. 18.

12. Of course, not everyone receives the gift of the Holy Spirit.

The Dispensation of the Spirit

Subjective Aspects

One of the issues that has divided theologians recently in Wesleyan-holiness circles has been whether or not Fletcher and Wesley had a Christological or a pneumatological focus in their theology. However, Fletcher emphasized continuity between and progression of the extrinsic knowledge of the dispensation of the Son and that of the dispensation of the Spirit.[13] The extrinsic knowledge of the post-Pentecost disciples was not significantly quantitatively different from their extrinsic knowledge immediately following Jesus' ascension; what was significantly different for them was their intrinsic knowledge. Believers under the dispensation of the Spirit internalize the extrinsic knowledge that was available to the pre-Pentecost disciples. The superiority of the dispensation of the Spirit over the dispensation of the Son lies principally in its efficacy; it makes efficacious and spiritual the knowledge that was available to the pre-Pentecost disciples (John 14:26). Thus, the dispensation of the Spirit makes application of the cognitive content of the two previous dispensations. Fletcher wrote in his commentary on *La Grâce et La Nature*: "For regeneration, without which no one will see the Kingdom of heaven, is nothing more than the restoration of the soul in the happy state, where, formed in the image of God, it has not only the *Life* of the *Father*, as being in the soul the principle of life, but also the *Light* of the *Son* to enlighten its reason, & the *Love* of the *Holy Spirit* to regulate its will."[14] The deeper meaning of the dispensations of the Father and the Son is internalized (intrinsic knowledge) in the dispensation of the Spirit as the Spirit controls the will. Thus, Fletcher and Wesley spoke of the *internal kingdom*.

The foundation for Fletcher's development of these ideas seems to be 2 Corinthians 3 and Wesley's *Notes* on this passage where Paul contrasts the Mosaic and the Christian dispensations. The present writer wrote in another context:

> The Mosaic dispensation is characterized by a veiled and limited revelation and as a "ministration of death," and a "ministration of condemnation." The principle agent of the dispensation is the "letter" of the law which results in condemnation and death . . . Whereas the agent of the Mosaic dispensation was the *letter* of

---

13. Fletcher-Dispensation, 7.

14. "Car la régénération, sans laquelle personne ne verra le Royaume des Cieux, n'est autre chose que le rétablissement de l'âme dans l'heureux état, où, formée à l'image de Dieu, elle avoit non-seulement la *Vie* du *Père*, pour être en elle un principe de vie, mais encore la *Lumière* du *Fils*, pour éclairer son entendement ; & la *Charité* du *Saint Esprit*, pour régler sa volonté" (Fletcher-Grâce, 312).

the law, the agent of the Christian dispensation is the *Spirit* who effects the transformation of believers. The Christian dispensation is superior to the Mosaic dispensation precisely because the agent of the Christian dispensation is superior to the agent of the old one. The empowering Spirit of God enables an inner righteousness which is reflected in external conduct.[15]

The dispensation of the Spirit is superior precisely because it effects the transformation of the Christian dispensation.

Fletcher's doctrine of dispensation retains a Christological focus. For Fletcher, Christ is not only the apex of the *ordo temorum*, but he is also central to the *ordo salutis* even in the periods of history prior to and following the Christ event. However, saving faith does not involve explicit knowledge of the Christ event or the faith of full assurance.[16] As with the branches of a vine, some human beings have a more immediate union with Christ than do others: "there being as many ways of being in Christ as there are dispensations of grace."[17] However, there is a more restricted or "confined" meaning of the phrase "in Christ," which is restricted to the dispensation of the Spirit: "it means a being so fully acquainted with, and so intimately united to Christ, as to enjoy the privileges peculiar to the Christian dispensation, like Cornelius, when he had believed the Gospel of Christ, and was baptized with the Holy Ghost."[18]

The work of the Spirit enables the spiritual revelation of Christ, moving the believer beyond the mere historical or doctrinal understanding and beyond mere mental assent. Of the dispensation of the Son, Knight writes, "this Christianity is yet 'imperfect.' It is received by baptism of water, and the Redeemer is apprehended, in some measure, by sense, i.e., by a faith which merely respects the history of the Gospel."[19] In a footnote, Knight adds, "This faith is more than mental assent to the biblical account of Jesus' life and death. It is a genuine commitment to the way of life portrayed by the Gospel historians. Nonetheless, this faith is inferior because it fails to bring about a completely personal and internal transformation within the believer."[20] Fletcher wrote of the believer under the dispensation of the Spirit: "He views experimentally, as well as doctrinally, the suitableness of the Redeemer's offices, the firmness of his promises, the sufficiency of this

---

15. Frazier, "John Wesley's Covenantal and Dispensational View," 44–45.
16. Fl-W1856, 4:108.
17. Fl-W1856, 4:217.
18. Ibid.
19. J. Knight, "John William Fletcher and the Early Methodist," 181–82.
20. Ibid., 182.

righteousness, the preciousness of his atonement, and the completeness of his salvation."[21] This is the great privilege of the dispensation of the Spirit over the dispensation of the Son. In order to understand the dispensation of the Spirit, the development of the doctrine in Fletcher's thought will now be traced, beginning with Fletcher's association with Trevecka College.

FLETCHER'S EARLY THEOLOGY

"No One in the College Knew the Lord"

In *The Meaning of Pentecost in Early Methodism*, Wood argues that Fletcher held to an inextricable connection or unequivocal link between the doctrines of the baptism of the Spirit and entire sanctification and that he persuaded John Wesley to adopt such a view.[22] Wood's argument for a functional equivalency in Fletcher's thought confuses an accurate understanding of the dynamic and breadth of the doctrine of the baptism with the Spirit. The early Fletcher held that baptisms (plural) of the Spirit make one a Christian and continue the process of sanctification whose goal is the perfection of the believer in love. Thus, baptism of the Spirit is the means to the end, perfect love, and the means should not be conflated with the end.

During the winter of 1770–1771, a furor arose at Trevecka College over the doctrine of the baptism of the Holy Spirit, which eventually resulted in the dismissal of the master of the college, Joseph Benson, and the resignation of its president, John Fletcher. An undated letter from Benson to John Wesley expressed his concerns over the uproar and provides insight into the situation after his return from Oxford to Trevecka.[23] Having experienced remission of his sins, Benson was convinced of "something vastly superior" and assured Wesley of his belief in Christian perfection.[24] Although he sought sanctification, he did not possess it, but did not seek the experience intently because he assumed sanctification was progressive and found only biblical examples who denied perfection. Benson described an encounter that led to a more intense period of seeking: "Abt. a Year ago it was often suggested to my mind 'I have not ye Spirit!' The reason was my experience did by no means answer the plain texts of scrip. whch described

---

21. Fl-W1856, 18.

22. Staples, "Current Wesleyan Debate on the Baptism of the.," 29.

23. JB→[JW], [before 28 December 1771]. The letter is fragmented, gives no evidence of a postmark, and is missing pages or the continuity of thought. It may be the draft of the letter to which Wesley responded on 28 December 1770.

24. Jones does not identify Benson's conversion date ("Pulpit," 20).

the state of those who were possessed of it."²⁵ Benson purposed to devote his stay at Oxford to seeking sanctification but was deterred by other avocations. He returned to the College with the same purpose. He related the developing crisis that unfolded upon his return: "When I got home I found all things apparently in a strange situation. Mr. Fletcher had been very close with the students & insisted upon it neither himself nor they were believers. This had almost disposed some [students?] to leave the College. These were hard sayings. Others acknowledged they had only the drawings of the Father. My Lady asserted no one in the College knew the Lord. Most of them had experienced very clearly the pardoning of sin. This they stood to. I was distressed what to do."²⁶ Benson had discussed with Fletcher his concerns on the differences between weak faith and strong faith.²⁷ His own faith, he testified and faith of many others at the college was weak. Benson was very distressed until he read Wesley's sermon on Christian perfection and noted Wesley's distinction between the superior privileges of the Christian believers over those of the Jews. Benson's consideration of this sermon led him to the following truths:

1. A person may believe on Christ for the remission of sins & yet not have recd [received] in the proper sense the Holy Spirit.

2. The receiving the Holy Ghost is that great privilege of the new Covenant which distinguishes it from & renders it vastly superior to the Old.²⁸

Benson cited numerous passages of Scripture that address the outpouring of the Spirit. In citing John 14:17, Benson added a parenthetical comment, which became significant for the developing doctrinal peculiarities that arose during the furore at the College: "ye know him because <u>he abideth with you</u> (this he did already) & shall be in you I will not leave you orphans. I come unto you."²⁹ Following the rather lengthy citation of verses, Benson described the state of many "Children of God" whom both he and Wesley knew that had received remission of sins, but did not enjoy the normative New Testament privileges until "The Lord who is faithful to his promises, came suddenly to their hearts & made them the Temples of indwelling God."³⁰

25. JB→[JW], [before 28 December 1771].
26. Ibid.
27. Cf. LJW, 5:281.
28. JB→[JW], [before 28 December 1771].
29. Ibid.
30. Ibid.

The Dispensation of the Spirit

John the Baptist and Jesus' disciples announced the coming kingdom of God but "never mention it as actually commenced till at ye day of Pent[ecost]." Benson continued by describing an application of this dispensational scheme to the lives of individuals:

> In the meantime people were directed to prepare for it by repenting & believing the Gospel, whereby they recd [received] remission of sins, their hearts drawn out in love to God & a degree of peace & joy in believing. And is not this all that th[e] generality now look for or experience. Is not this all, that those calld Gospel ministers know any thing at all abt. or point out to others. Are they any more than John's disciples? Like Appollos who "taught diligently ye things of Jes[us] knowing only ye Baptism of Jn." They indeed exhort people to a conformity to ye will of God, but how? not by declaring & maintaining they must receive the H. Ghost to dwell in their hearts, or they can never attain to such a conformity, & that in a very different manner from sh. they have hitherto experienced.[31]

Benson further applied his dispensational scheme to the Church of his day and expressed his thanks to Wesley for new insight into the Scripture. He concluded his letter with an appeal to Wesley: "Oh my dr [dear] Sir, I am convinced I am only one of John's disciples I have hitherto known nothing of ye grand characteristics & distinguishing privilege of Xtians. And yet I have pretended to preach the Gospel without the Spt of X?! And in some degree God may have been <u>wth me</u> & bless'd his own word as far as it was truly set forth. What might we expect if he was <u>in</u> us!"[32]

Fletcher was the impetus behind the soul-searching at the College.[33] Benson alluded to it: "Mr. Fletcher had been very close with the students & insisted upon it neither himself nor they were believers."[34] In his biography of Fletcher, Benson venerated the College president: "[A]fter speaking awhile in the school room, he used frequently to say, 'As many of you as are athirst for this fullness of the Spirit, follow me into my room.' On this, many of us have instantly followed him, and there continued for two or three hours, wrestling like Jacob for the blessing, praying one after another till we

---

31. Ibid.

32. Ibid.

33. Fraser holds that Fletcher held to a rigid form of perfectionism ("Strains in the Understanding of Christian," 345).

34. JB→[JW], [before 28 December 1771]. It appears that Fletcher was attempting to do at Trevecka what the Wesley brothers had done at Oxford to revitalized Christianity by radicalizing the distinctions between "almost" and "altogether" Christians (BiCent-WJW, 1:110–11).

could bear to kneel no longer. This was not done once or twice, but many times."[35] Further corroboration of the intense spiritual cross-examination comes from one of Fletcher's letters to the Countess in which he expressed his concern for the students: "that a day of Pentecost would make them what they did not appear to me to be as yet—Christians and preachers."[36] The Treveckan Fletcher held that the result of the Pentecostal outpouring of the Spirit was the inauguration of the spiritual blessings of the kingdom of God for the people of God.

Fletcher's dispensational scheme was nascent. On 12 February 1772, Fletcher encouraged Benson's search for the "great promise" of the Father, the outpouring of the Holy Spirit.[37] Fletcher admonished: "Keep up Jewish till you have Christian faith."[38] These admonitions reveal the marked distinction between the benefits of the believers under the two Testaments. His letters reveal his concern for greater spiritual passion among both the Trevecka students and his own parishioners.[39] The distinction between water baptism and Spirit-baptism that Fletcher had expounded in his dispute with Abiah Darby were foundational for the fracas over the baptism of the Spirit at the College.[40]

Fletcher often lamented his spiritual condition and classified himself under the Jewish dispensation or short of genuine Christianity. On 30 November 1762, he described his spiritual condition much like Benson had described his: "A faith accompanied with the love of God spread abroad in my heart by the 1st Spirit can alone make me happy & Christian."[41] On 24 November 1771, he wrote, "I am quite clear I shall die only a disciple of John unless I receive the baptism you so well describe."[42] On 30 May

---

35. Benson-Life, 5/20. Cf. JF→JW, 15 October 1785.

36. Tyerman, *Wesley's Designated Successor*, 181. Cf. JF→CH, 12 Apr. 1769.

37. Cf. Jones, "Pulpit," 67. Benson modified his views later as will be discussed later.

38. JF→JB, 12 February 1772.

39. JF→GW, 28 May [1768]; JF→CH, 10 Nov. 1768, and JF→CH, 10 Feb. 1769.

40. In the autumn of 1770 during the absence of the master, Fletcher assigned the students the following: "3. Draw a parallel between John's Baptism & Christ's and prove the supremacy of the latter over the former ... 5. Draw up an address to Jesus for the ... [gift] of the Holy Ghost urging the strongest reason you can think of to engage him to grant it you ... 6. Try in a letter to convince on who has not the spiritual Kingdom set up in his soul [illegible strikethrough] that he never had the true Christian Faith, or is back slidden" (JF→CH, Autumn 1770). Here Fletcher contrasted John's baptism with Christ's baptism; however, as was seen previously, Fletcher contrasted John's baptism with Christian water baptism (Fletcher-Darby, 47–49).

41. "Une foi accompagnée de l'amour de Dieu repandu dans mon coeur par le 1r. esprit peut seule me rendre hereux & Chretien" (JF→CW, 30 Nov. 1762).

42. JF→CW, 24 Nov. 1771.

1773, Fletcher wrote to Charles Wesley, "I see nothing will do for us but a day of Pentecost: without it we shall live and die jews, and our neighbours heathens."[43]

The theology that arose at the College during the period placed a marked distinction between the pre-Pentecost disciples and the post-Pentecost disciples. The former experienced remission of sins, but not all of the privileges of NT believers. They received water baptism, but had not yet been baptized with the Spirit. They experienced a measure of the Spirit (a dwelling with), but had not yet experienced the indwelling of the Spirit.[44]

Ecumenicism at the College and Pentecostal Language

Trevecka College was founded upon methodistical ecumenical principles.[45] The pneumatological language was sufficiently broad to encompass a variety of spiritual experiences and was well suited for its ecumenical platform. As superintendent, Fletcher observed the lack of spiritual vitality and emphasized primitive Christianity and the goal of the Christian life in order to revitalize the student body for effective Christian service.[46]

As indicated previously, the phrase, "baptism of the Spirit," was not inextricably linked to Christian perfection; it was an equivocal term and was not to be equated exclusively with Christian perfection.[47] The emphasis on pneumatological language was a pastoral accommodation in keeping with College's ecumenical platform, which would communicate effectively to the Calvinistic Methodists who were prejudiced against the terminology of perfection.[48] The hope was that full sanctification would be experienced

---

43. JF→CW, 30 May 1773.

44. One of the queries in the "Epworth Document" is "'Has there not been a larger measure of the Holy Spirit given under the Gospel than under the Jewish dispensation?'" (Baker, "John Wesley on Christian Perfection," 56).

45. Harding, *Countess of Huntingdon's Connexion*, 219.

46. "The first and grand point to be kept in view at Lady Huntingdon's College is to maintain and grow in the spirit of faith and power that breaks through the Acts of the Apostles, and was exemplified in the lives of the primative Christians" (JF→CH, 1 Jul. 1769).

47. It was doubtlessly linked, but not *equated* with Christian perfection. Fraser holds that the link was first made in 1758 in "The Test of a New Creature: or Heads of Examination for Adult Christians." According to Fraser, Fletcher continued to use the metaphor "describing the essential divine event at the initiation of the Christian life" until 1767 (Fraser, "Strains in the Understanding of Christian," 347, 354). However, there are several other instances after 1767 when Fletcher employed baptism of the Spirit as an initiatory experience as indicated below.

48. Fraser, "Strains in the Understanding of Christian," 363, 380.

by the students regardless of the terminology used. After the controversy had subsided, Fletcher expressed to Charles Wesley his hope that the use of pneumatological language would make "the doctrine [of Christian perfection] more intelligible to and defensible against all opposing friends."[49]

Due to the influence of Puritans, like Richard Baxter and John Goodwin, the Calvinist Methodists were predisposed to a pneumatological emphasis.[50] The Countess of Huntingdon herself appreciated the emphasis on the baptism of the Spirit.[51] On December 28, 1770, John Wesley wrote to Benson who was seeking sanctification in the midst of the College's crisis. Certain phrases in Wesley's letter hint at a bellicose spirit at the College: "let neither men nor devils tear it from you," "the experience of a thousand believers [i.e., witnesses to Christian perfection]," "I have no time to throw away in contending for words, especially where the thing is allowed," and "with all zeal and diligence confirm the brethren." Notwithstanding his doubts, Benson, schooled by his president, was apparently having some success in leading some of his students to evangelical conversion and to anticipate deliverance from all sin. The conflict did not endure because Benson was dismissed from the College, leaving on New Year's Day 1771.[52]

The Calvinistic Methodists would not countenance any idea of Christian perfection.[53] Criticism of the doctrine of baptism of the Spirit was mounting at the College during the winter of 1770–1771 and continued into the spring. Although Fletcher and Benson did not equate baptism of the Spirit and Christian perfection, some of their opponents did.[54] Following Benson's departure, Walter Shirley attacked the doctrine of baptism with the Spirit. In a letter to Benson dated 22 March 1771, Fletcher referred to a

49. JF→CW, 14 August 1774.

50. Wood, *Meaning of Pentecost in Early Methodism*, 25.

51. A high emotive experience (Schlenther, *Queen of the Methodists*, 177) and the need for a heightened spirituality was frequently emphasized (Seymour-Countess, 2:111–12; JF→CH, 10 Nov. 1768; JF→CH, 10 Feb. 1769; JF→CH, 12 Apr. 1769; JF→Mrs. Leighton, 19 Nov. 1768).

52 Schlenther, *Queen of the Methodists*, 197. JB cited approvingly from Wesley's biography of Fletcher in which Wesley gave the rationale for the dismissal as Benson's failure to hold to the "doctrine of absolute predestination" (Benson-Life, 5/23). JF intimated to JB, "Pray, what arts who were made use of to find you guilty? Was Arianism brought upon the carpet? I have it under Mr. Wms hand that My Lady on Xmas day acquainted him ~~of her fears lest you should be the~~ she was convinc'd you was the main spring of hinderance to the life & power of religion in the college– And that they were busily talking about your discharge in the parlour when you came from Breckon into the Room" (JF→JB, 10 January 1771).

53. Cf. LJW, 5:155.

54. A distinction should be made between equating and linking. A link between the two terms is evident, but an equation is not.

treatise written by Benson and Shirley's assault: "what you had wrote upon the baptism of the Holy Ghost was taken to pieces, & Mr. Shirley maintain'd that the Prophecy of Joel Act:2. had its compleat fulfilling on the day of pentecost, and thus he turn'd the streams of living waters into <u>imperceptible dews,</u> nemine contradicente [none contradicted], but 2 who made one or 2 feeble objections: So the point was (in my judgment) turn'd out of the College after you and abus'd under the name of <u>perfection</u>."[55]

Walter Shirley criticized the doctrine of Spirit-baptism as perfection and convinced the students of his cessationist position. Fletcher was troubled.[56] He described the central point of the doctrine not as perfection, but as "Internal conversion by the power of the Holy Ghost dwelling in the heart by faith."[57] Although Lady Huntingdon had originally appreciated the emphasis on Spirit-baptism, she grew to resent what she perceived as a connection between it and Christian perfection. After Fletcher preached on "the good old doctrine," the Countess gave a "charge" against perfection the next day in his absence, Fletcher reported to Benson.[58]

Fletcher who remained president of the College acknowledged that the opponents' criticism of Christian perfection would not abate his search for whole-hearted love for God and the fullness of the Holy Spirit.[59] Rupture was imminent. In his written response to the 1770 *Minutes* per Lady Huntingdon's request, Fletcher provided some reasons for his resignation, one of which is the abandonment of the doctrine of Spirit-baptism: "His want of freedom in the College since the grand point to be maintain'd there (the baptism of the Holy Ghost and the day of power) hath been given up either in whole or in part."[60] The refuge that the students found in the Calvinistic doctrine of perseverance was a barrier to the spiritual growth and vitality about which Fletcher felt so passionate.[61] Fletcher related to Wesley that Lady Huntingdon had asked each student to write a response to an extract of the conference *Minutes* and informed Wesley of his resignation.[62]

---

55. JF→JB, 22 March [1771]. Schlenther wrote of a change in CH's views on the Spirit (*Queen of the Methodists*, 107).

56. Tyerman, *Wesley's Designated Successor*, 184.

57. JF→JW, 18 Mar. [1771].

58. JF→JF, 22 Mar. 1771.

59. "[N]o body shall prevent my following after an intire [sic] devotedness of heart to God ~~and~~ a loving ~~of God~~ him with all my heart, & a being fill'd with the H. Ghost & with power, by baiting my christian hopes and priviledges under the name of Christian perfection" [JF→JW, 20 Feb. 1771].

60. JF→CH, [9 Mar. 1771].

61. Tyerman, *Wesley's Designated Successor*, 184–85.

62. JF→JW, 18 Mar. [1771].

Fletcher had been attracted originally to College's catholicity, but when it adopted the doctrinal provincialism of Calvinism, Fletcher was disappointed.[63] On this point, Fletcher wrote: "I fear we are going, or already gone from our plan of catholicism at the College."[64] One of the underlying issues was the eclectic nature of Lady Huntingdon's theology. Maintaining any clear direction in the College was difficult due to the Countess of Huntingdon's "cyclothymic" temperament.[65] Thus, in March, Fletcher resigned from the College.[66]

Fletcher resigned frustrated with the spiritual tone of the college. During intense cross examination of the students and himself, he had disallowed all claims to evangelical conversion when one did not demonstrate the normative privileges of the dispensation of the Spirit. He had attempted to heighten the spiritual vitality of the students in order to prepare them for effective ministry; however, in doing so, he disparaged his and the students' spiritual state. When Lady Huntingdon sided with Shirley's cessationist views and the students apparently imbibed the view of finished salvation, Fletcher was perturbed; he felt that he could no longer fulfill his vision for primitive Christianity at the College. His dispensational distinctions were forged in the furnace of the College.

The distinctions that Fletcher made between the dispensation of John and the dispensation of the Spirit raise questions about Fletcher's soteriology. Where does evangelical regeneration fit in his *ordo salutis*?

Discours Sur La Régénération

In 1759, Fletcher published *Discours Sur La Régénération* in which he unveiled his early views on regeneration.[67] His description of regeneration emphasized the great contrast between the states of humans prior to and following regeneration. Clearly the righteousness of a Pharisee, like Nicodemus, was insufficient for entry into the Kingdom of God. Fletcher compared the spiritual birth to physical birth, illustrating the spiritual state prior to regeneration with the state of a pre-born child. He wrote, "However, there may be some principles of life and spiritual movement before being

---

63. Tyerman, *Wesley's Designated Successor*, 182.

64. JF→JW, 20 February 1771.

65. Schlenther, *Queen of the Methodists*, 179.

66. JF→CH. 7 March 1771. Forsaith holds that Fletcher left campus on 15 March (UL, 273).

67. The treatise was translated into English by Henry Moore, but has not been translated in its entirety; for this reason, the present writer relies upon the French original.

regenerated."⁶⁸ Despite any good desires and efforts toward God, one is devoid of spiritual life until one is born again.⁶⁹ Fletcher pontificated on the difference between human attempts at self-reform and the spiritual transformation that is accomplished by baptism of the Holy Ghost. He wrote of "the difference which exists between the reformation of a Pharisee and the Regeneration of a Child of God: Some degree of prevenient grace, of reason, and of reflection is sufficient for the first, but nothing less than the baptism of the Holy Spirit and a real participation in the death and resurrection of Jesus will effect the second."⁷⁰ In this same discourse, he exhorted the true penitents: "Yes, you will also be baptized of the Holy Spirit for remission of Sins, & justified freely by faith, you will have peace with God by our Lord Jesus Christ & you will rejoice in God your Savior with a joy unspeakable and full of glory."⁷¹ Baptism of the Spirit alone could suffice for the remission of sins and the justification of the believer.

In the *Discours,* Fletcher distinguished between justification and sanctification and clearly stated that the first revelation of Christ does not destroy the body of sin.⁷² The doctrine of regeneration has two grand operations; the first is justification or the remission of sins, which is the beginning or basis for the second part of regeneration, i.e., sanctification.⁷³ "For in the same moment that a sinner receives the faith without pretense, the faith that justifies, at the same moment that the Spirit of God witnesses to him that his sins have been forgiven him, he receives the power to love much, because he feels that God has much forgiven him; and the love of God being shed abroad in his heart, causes an extraordinary transformation in all the powers of his soul, and makes him to feel, though in a low degree, the effects of the new birth described in the second part of this discourse."⁷⁴ At the

---

68. "Cependant il peut avoir quelques principes de vie et de mouvement spirituel avant que d'être régénéré" (Fletcher-Discours, 15).

69. Ibid., 15.

70. "[L]a différence qu'il y a entre la réforme d'un Pharisien, et la Régénération d'un Enfant de Dieu: Quelques degrés de grace prévenante, de la raison, et de la réflection suffisent pour la première, mais il ne faut pas moins pour la seconde que le baptême du St. Esprit, et une participation réelle à la mort et à la résurrection de Jesus" (ibid., 31).

71. "Oui, vous serez aussi baptizé du St. Esprit en rémission des Péchés, & justifié gratuitement par la Foi, vous aurez paix avec Dieu par notre Seigneur J. Ch. & vous vous réjouirez en Dieu votre Sauveur d'une joie ineffable & glorieuse" (ibid.).

72. Ibid., 34.

73. Ibid.

74. "Car à l'instant qu'un pécher reçoit *la foi non feint, la foi qui justifie* ; à l'instant que l'Esprit de Dieu lui témoigne que ses péchés lui sont pardonnés, il reçoit le pourvoir *d'aimer beaucoup, parce* qu'il sent que *Dieu lui a beaucoup pardonné* ; et *l'amour de Dieu étant* ainsi *répandu dans son cœur,* cause une révolution extraordinaire dans toutes les

new birth, the believer's sins are forgiven, and the process of sanctification is begun.[75] However, Fletcher qualified his previous statements by asserting that the body of sin is not destroyed in this "first revelation of Christ in the soul of the sinner."[76] Above, regeneration has two operations of the Spirit, justification and sanctification, which occur at the same moment.

The new birth, in a low degree, does not destroy the body of sin, but ushers in a process that does. As David and Paul discovered, sanctification is not normally the work of a short duration, but it is a progressive work of a long duration. The goal of sanctification is not identified in pneumatological language[77] but in the language of Ephesians 3:19, "the fullness of God." Furthermore, the fullness of God was given specific moral and ethical content, clearly defined as the love of God and others, the highest point of the sanctification of believers:

> We, therefore, define sanctification as the powerful operation of the Holy Spirit on the heart of a justified sinner, by which he receives the power to go *from faith to faith*; by which *enlightened more and more, in order to see the glory of God in the face of Jesus Christ* and *transformed* day by day *in the image of the Lord* that he lost in Adam, he senses himself internally *changed from glory into glory until he is filled with all the fullness of God*. That is to say, until he *loves God with all his heart, with all his soul, with all his mind and with all his strength and his neighbour as himself, as Christ loved him*, which is the highest point of the Sanctification of the Believer and by consequence his complete Regeneration.[78]

---

puissance de son ame, et lui fait ressentir, quoi que dans un bas degré, les effets de la renaissance décrite dans la seconde partie de ce discours" (ibid.).

75. Ibid.

76. "[C]ette prémière révélation de Christ dans l'ame d'un pécheur" (ibid.).

77. It is acknowledged that the circumstance of sanctification is pneumatological as in the phrase "the powerful operation of the Holy Spirit," but the substance or the goal is not.

78. "Nous définissons donc la Sanctification cette opération puissante du St. Esprit sur le cœur d'un Pécheur justifié, par la quelle il reçoit la force de marcher *de Foi en Foi* ; par la quelle *illuminé* de plus en plus, *pour voir la gloire de Dieu dans la face de J. C.* et *rénouvellé* de jour en jour *à l'image du Seigneur* qu'il avoit perdue en Adam, il se sent intérieurement *changé de gloire en gloire, jusqu'à ce qu'il soit rempli de toute la plénitude de Dieu*. ; C'est à dire, jusqu'à ce qu'il *aime Dieu de tout son cœur, de toute son ame, de toute sa pensée, et de toute sa force ; et son prochain comme lui même, comme Christ l'a aimé*, ce qui est le plus haut point de la Sanctification du Fidéle, et par conséquent sa Régénération complette" (ibid., 35).

Fletcher broadened the concept of regeneration to include the idea of a complete sanctification or "Régénération complette."[79] Thus, regeneration is not complete until the believer is filled with the love of God, indicating that Fletcher held to a progressive view of regeneration.

Fletcher's Developing Doctrine of Regeneration

In *Spiritual Manifestation of the Son of God* (1767), Fletcher distinguished between the ordinary and the extraordinary manifestations and argued that while the outpouring of the Spirit on the day of Pentecost was accompanied with extraordinary manifestations, baptism with the Spirit was the common experience of all Christians: "That they should be baptized with the Holy Ghost and spiritual fire was not extraordinary, since it is the common blessing which can alone make a man a Christian, or confirm him in the faith."[80] Fletcher admonished: "Acknowledge, that so sure as you want the regenerating knowledge of Christ, you want the manifestation of his Spirit, without which he can never be known savingly."[81] While baptism with the Spirit was the sole experience that constitutes one a Christian, Fletcher spoke in other contexts of imperfect Christians who have not been baptized with the Holy Spirit.[82] By imperfect Christians, Fletcher meant those who had received the rite of baptism without the reality to which the baptismal rite pointed.

In *An Appeal to Matter of Fact and Common Sense* (1772), Fletcher lamented the spiritual ignorance of sinful humanity that failed to distinguish between the means of grace and the grace itself: "How weak, how dark in spiritual things! How few idiots are there but can distinguish between the shadow and the substance, the cup and the liquor, the dress and the person! But how many learned men, to this day, see no difference between water baptism and spiritual regeneration, between the means of grace and grace itself, between 'the form' and 'the power of godliness!'"[83] The rite of water baptism without the grace of Spirit-baptism resulted in external Christianity rather than the true spiritual regeneration to which the rite pointed. As Fletcher stated, "[O]ur regeneration cannot be a mere metaphor, or a vain ceremony; our spiritual birth must be real and positive."[84]

---

79. Ibid.
80. Fl-W1856, 9:24.
81. Fl-W1856, 9:25.
82. Fl-W1856, 4:116.
83. Fl-W1856, 2:55.
84. Fl-W1856, 2:133.

TRUE CHRISTIANITY

In his *Essay on Truth* (1774), Fletcher, after reading Wesley's sermon *Scriptural Christianity*, was persuaded of the following:

> 1. That till a man is thus born of the Spirit," he "cannot see the" Christian "kingdom of God;"—he cannot be under that glorious dispensation of divine grace, which Christ and the apostles spake of, when they preached, "Repent, and believe the gospel, for the kingdom of heaven is at hand." 2. That whosoever has not in his breast the above-described kingdom, that is, "righteousness, peace, and joy in the Holy Ghost," and does not bring forth its excellent fruits in his life, either never was a spiritual Christian, or is fallen back from the ministration of the Spirit into the dispensation of the letter, or the bare form of godliness, if not into open wickedness.[85]

In *Discours*, Fletcher formulated the doctrine of progressive regeneration. In the sermon on 2 Corinthians 5:17, he made clear with his interpolations two degrees of regeneration: ritual regeneration and spiritual regeneration.[86] Fletcher denied that the unregenerate according to the fully Christian sense of the word could possess "the *lively* hope."[87] The effects of the Spirit, "lively" or "exhilarating" hope, are linked with the presence of the Spirit. The pre-Pentecost disciples cannot possess the lively hope because they are "regenerate in part" (not spiritually regenerate).[88] An undated manuscript document classifies the pre-Pentecost disciples as not fully regenerated: "he [the Lord] never gave ~~any~~ believers to understand (while he was on earth) that they were fully ~~converted or~~ regenerated on the contrary he preached to them conversion ~~Joh~~ Matt: 18:3 & a new birth of the Spirit Joh. 3.7. ~~He never~~ Far from intimated they ~~were~~ had the indwelling Spirit; he always spoke of it as a blessing they were strangers to."[89] In the same document, Fletcher connected the new birth with the baptism of the Spirit: "In short we see in them that if any man is in Christ by the Baptism of the Spirit he is indeed a new creation old things are pass'd away behold all things are become new."[90] With great respect for the Anglican standards, Fletcher maintained that water baptism produced a partial regeneration, but not a true spiritual regeneration.

---

85. Fl-W1856, 4:109.
86. Fl-W1856, 8:364–65.
87. Fl-W1856, 6:459; emphasis added.
88. Fl-W1856, 6:459–60. See *The Test of a New Creation* (Fl-W1856, 9.87–92).
89. Fletcher-Baptism.
90. Ibid.

The Dispensation of the Spirit

Several summary remarks may be made about Fletcher's doctrine of regeneration. First, there is a greater tendency after his dispute with Abiah Darby to distinguish between water baptism and Spirit-baptism, perhaps conceding that not all of his baptized parishioners were fully converted. Second, Fletcher's respect for the Anglican standards led him to maintain the doctrine of baptismal regeneration, but his commitment to evangelical tenets and specifically to the evangelical conversion of adults caused him to posit a fuller and more spiritual doctrine of regeneration and to depict infant baptism as a formal rite. Third, baptism of the Spirit was the means of effecting regeneration. Knight agrees with this assessment of Fletcher's thought, "Regeneration can be effected, and completed only by 'the baptism of the Holy Ghost,' and a real participation of the death and resurrection of Jesus."[91] Fourth, regeneration is progressive in Fletcher theology. The mature Fletcher formulated two degrees of regeneration: in water baptism, baptismal candidates were partially regenerated through the rites of the church; Spirit-baptism effected a real spiritual transformation. Fifth, in Fletcher's thought there is a temporal distinction between justification and spiritual regeneration.[92] According to Mark Olson, this is also characteristic of Wesley's theology. The pre-Pentecost disciples were "clean" before God (i.e., justified), but were not yet born again; Wesley believe the latter occurred at Pentecost.[93]

Previously, it was noted that as president of Trevecka College, Fletcher categorized himself, Benson and the students not as "altogether" Christians, but as "almost" Christians. They did not have genuine Christian faith and had not received the indwelling of the Spirit. In his later writings, Fletcher introduced a distinction between the pre-Pentecost and the post-Pentecost disciples; based upon John 14:17, the former experienced the Spirit dwelling with them, and the latter experienced the indwelling of the Spirit. At this juncture, the source for these distinctions will be considered.

---

91. J. Knight, "John William Fletcher and the Early Methodist," 302. L. Wood admitted that Fletcher maintained that "entrance into 'the kingdom of the Holy Ghost' (i.e., into perfect Christianity) is made by the 'new birth'" (*Pentecostal Grace*, 189).

92. In 1757 when writing the *Discours*, Fletcher formulated the doctrine of progressive regeneration, but at that time, his view that baptism with the Spirit was the means for effecting conversion seems to lead logically to a temporal distinction between justification and regeneration in the *ordo temporum* since the Jesus' disciples did not experience baptism with the Spirit prior to Pentecost. This becomes evident when he applies his more developed dispensational scheme, but is not evident in *Discours*. In *Discours*, he links baptism with the Spirit and justification, but in the *ordo salutis* (Fletcher-Discours, 31).

93. Olson, "Roots of John Wesley's Servant Theology," 124.

Charles Wesley and the Trinitarian Hymns

Fletcher acknowledged to Charles that Charles' hymns had a significant impact upon his doctrine of dispensations: "I want sadly both your prayers & advice. I shall introduce my, why not your doctrine of the Holy Ghost, & make it one with your brothers perfection. He holds the truth, but this will be an ~~addition to it~~ improvement upon it, if I am not mistaken. In some of your pentecost hymns you paint my light wonderfully. If you do not recant them we shall perfectly agree."[94] Two collections of hymns serve as possible sources for these "pentecost hymns."

Hymns on the Trinity (1767):[95]

Charles Wesley's *Hymns on the Trinity* emphasize not merely an intellectual understanding but an inward experience of the Trinity.[96] The Trinity was experienced in history as God progressively revealed the divine nature, and human beings must retrace history existentially in order to know the highest expression of God.

In the section on "The Divinity of the Holy Ghost," the hymnist identified the new birth with an operation of the Spirit.[97] On John 14:17, Wesley further distinguished between the indwelling of the Spirit and the Spirit's dwelling with humans.[98] In Hymn LXIII, a personal day of Pentecost brings about the permanent indwelling of the Spirit in the hearts of humans.[99] The indwelling Spirit is the means by which God indwells believers and reveals the Triunity of God (Hymn LXVI) and without the Spirit, one cannot believe savingly in the Triune God (Hymn LXXII). The indwelling of the Spirit is connected inextricably to the ministry of Christ in Charles' thought. Each person of the Trinity is involved in creation and in the ongoing creative activity of the new birth of believers. However, it is principally the work of the Holy Spirit to witness to the work of grace and to "Seal and preserve us

---

94. JF→CW, 24 November [1771].

95. C. Wesley, *Hymns on the Trinity*. References to the hymns will employ the hymn numbers rather than page numbers in parentheses.

96. Sigler, "Charles Wesley and the Power of Poetic Theology," 13. Cf. O'Brien, "Trinitarian Revisioning of the Wesleyan," 69.

97. Wesley, *Hymns on the Trinity*, 39.

98. Ibid., 41–42.

99. Ibid., 42.

to that day" (Hymn CVI).[100] Believers experience the Triune indwelling of God:

> The Father, Son, and Spirit dwell
> By faith in all his saints below,
> And then in love unspeakable
> The glorious Trinity we know
> Created after God to shine,
> Fill'd with the Plenitude Divine.[101]

Whitsunday Hymns:

In 1746, John and Charles Wesley published *Hymns of Petition and Thanksgiving for the Promise of Father*, which became known popularly as *Whitsunday Hymns*. Wesley posited a personal Pentecost (Hymn I), which was available to sinners (Hymn IV):

> Sinners, lift up your hearts,
> The PROMISE to receive!
> Jesus himself imparts,
> He comes in man to live;
> The Holy Ghost to man is given;
> Rejoice in God sent down from heaven.[102]

The Pentecostal outpouring was available to sinners upon trusting the merits of Christ's atoning work (Hymn VI). One of the characteristic features is the distinction between the abiding presence of the Spirit and the transitory visitation of the Spirit. In Hymn VII, which is based upon John 14:16, this distinction is made clear:

> He visits now the troubled breast,
> And oft relieves our sad complaint,
> But soon we lose the transient guest,
> But soon we droop again, and faint,
> Repeat the melancholy moan,
> Our joy is fled, our comfort gone.
>
> Hasten him, Lord, into our heart,
> Our sure inseparable guide;
> O might we meet and never part,

---

100. Ibid., 68.
101. Ibid., 82.
102. C. Wesley and J. Wesley, *Whitsunday Hymns*, 7.

TRUE CHRISTIANITY

> O might he in our heart abide,
> And keep his house of praise and prayer,
> And rest, and reign forever there. [103]

Wesley emphatically stated that the Holy Spirit resides in "all his saints" and "in all his people" through "faith's internal sense."[104]

In his poetic rendition of John 14:16–17 (Hymn IX), the world does not receive the Holy Spirit and are strangers to the Spirit's inward work.[105] The first person plural pronoun is employed to indicate those who experience the Spirit dwelling with them, but as the prayer of the fourth stanza indicates that they have not experienced the indwelling Spirit:

> But we know by faith and feel
> Him, the Spirit of truth and grace,
> *With us* he vouchsafes to dwell,
> With us, when unseen, he stays;
> All our help, and good we own
> Freely flows from him alone.
>
> Yet alas, we cannot rest
> Help'd with an *external* guide,
> Till the transitory guest
> Enter, and *in* us abide:
> Give him, Lord, thy Spirit give,
> In us *constantly* to live.
>
> Wilt thou not the promise seal,
> True and gracious as thou art,
> Send the Comforter to dwell
> Every moment in our heart?
> Yes, thou *must* the grace bestow,
> Jesus said It shall be so![106]

Individuals who have not experienced the full measure of the indwelling Spirit experience a measure of the Spirit's presence. To them, the Spirit is a transitory guest as was noted above in Hymn VII.[107] However, Christ prom-

---

103. Ibid., 10.

104. Ibid., 11.

105. Wesley's sermons make it clear that the Pentecostal experience makes one a Christian (Newport, *Sermons of Charles Wesley*, 218, 221).

106. C. Wesley and J. Wesley, *Whitsunday Hymns*, 12.

107. Mrs. Richardson, though she was justified, experienced the Spirit as a Guest (C. Wesley, *Short Account of the Death of Mrs.*, 4). Fletcher lamented to Charles Wesley

ises the democratization of the abiding, indwelling presence of the Holy Spirit, which reveals all the Godhead (Hymn XI). Wesley underscored the integral connection between the work of Christ and the work of the Spirit (Hymn XXIII).

One distinctive of Charles's thought is the doctrine of the divine indwelling: "For Charles, the end or purpose of divine indwelling is nothing less than the hallmark of the patristic doctrine of the economic Trinity, namely, that human persons might become 'partakers of the divine nature' (2 Peter 1:4)."[108] Charles asserted that the indwelling Spirit is the mark of true believers: "This experimental knowledge, and this alone is true Christianity. He is a Christian who hath received the Spirit of Christ. He is not a Christian who hath not received him."[109] As stated previously, Charles Wesley made a distinction between those who experienced the Spirit dwelling with them and those who experienced the indwelling Spirit. The former, then, are not true Christians who experience a measure of the Spirit, but not the indwelling of the Spirit.

The Spirit as the Means of Indwelling God

On 28 December 1764, Fletcher added an appendix to his "An Answer to the Objections of Mrs. Darby" to rebut a treatise that she had written entitled, "Faithful Declaration" in which she asserted, "The Holy Spirit is always in man, either as a reprover or Comforter, while the day of his visitation lasteth."[110] While acknowledging the omnipresence of the Spirit, it is unscriptural, asserted Fletcher, to hold that the unconverted always have the Spirit of God. Fletcher wrote, "In the Gospel sense of the Word, no man hath the Spirit till he is convinced of sin. for not believing in Jesus: Joh: 14:8 and till the conviction hath passed from his head to his heart—Then of a truth he hath received the Spirit of Bondage unto fear. Rom. 8:15."[111] Those who have the Spirit of Bondage must wait until the Spirit is manifested as "a Spirit of Adoption & love."[112] Scripture clearly reveals that the unconverted are sinful and dead; thus unbelievers cannot have the Spirit of life in them.

---

that his experience was comparable to the disciples of John and longed for the baptism of the Spirit as CW described in the account of Hannah Richardson (JF→CW, 24 November 1771).

108. Vickers, "Charles Wesley and the Revival of the Doctrine of," 285.
109. Newport, *Sermons of Charles Wesley*, 221.
110. Fletcher-Darby, 95.
111. Ibid., 96.
112. Ibid., 97.

Fletcher connected the continual presence of the Spirit with being born of the Spirit: "[I]f all men <u>have always the Spirit</u>, they are all <u>born again of the Spirit</u> contrary to what our Lord says: Joh: 3:7. <u>Ye must be born again</u>."[113] Fletcher linked the baptism of fire with regeneration: "[I]f Mrs. Darby is right, they are all regenerate, they have all the baptism of fire, for <u>they have always the Spirit in them</u>."[114] The day of Pentecost was the initiation of the baptism of fire or the baptism of the Spirit. Thus Fletcher wrote, "Our Lord himself (who knew what is in man) would not allow that his Apostles had always the Holy Spirit in them before the day of Pentecost. Now said he to them before his Decease, <u>he dwelleth with you,</u> but then <u>he shall be in you</u>. Joh: 14:17. Now <u>he dwelleth with you</u> as a Guest, then <u>he shall be in You</u> as the soul of your soul, as an inseparable guide and Director."[115] Mrs. Darby taught, according to Fletcher, that all humans always have the Spirit. Fletcher opposed this teaching because it undermined the doctrine of regeneration and its concurrent experience of being baptized with the Spirit. In his thought, only regenerate believers have the constant presence of the Spirit.

ALTERATIONS UNDER WESLEY'S COUNSEL

Benson's Treatise on the Baptism of the Holy Spirit

During the late 1760s and early 1770s, Benson and Fletcher tended toward a radical view of Christian perfection, and Benson re-evaluated his spiritual state in that light. Wesley was concerned about Benson's critical self-evaluation and admonished Benson on 28 December 1770 not to cast away his confidence: "You are a child of God; you are justified freely through the redemption which is in Christ Jesus. Your sins are forgiven!" Unaware of Benson's imminent departure, Wesley further admonished him to confirm the faith of the students who had attained "remission of sins" and to encourage them to expect "a second change, whereby they shall be saved from all sin and perfected in love." Wesley added, "If they like to call this 'receiving the Holy Ghost,' they may: only the phrase in that sense is not scriptural and not quite proper; for they all 'received the Holy Ghost' when they were justified. God then 'sent forth the Spirit of His Son into their hearts, crying Abba, Father.'"[116] Wesley had received word of Shirley's tendency to dismiss

---

113. Ibid., 99.
114. Ibid., 99–100.
115. Ibid., 103.
116 LJW, 5:215.

the doctrine of Christian perfection.[117] On the other hand, certain students, under the influence of Benson and Fletcher, aspired for the experience of receiving the Spirit, infuriating Shirley.

While headmaster of the College, Benson wrote a treatise on the subject of the "baptism of the Holy Ghost."[118] The treatise is no longer extant.[119] However, Fraser summarizes several elements of Benson's treatise that can be identified: first, although the assumed title of the work was apparently "The Baptism with the Holy Ghost" the principal subject matter was Christian perfection though the term may not have been used expressly. Secondly, Benson was not a cessationist; he believed that the prophecy of Joel that Peter quoted was pertinent for the subsequent eras of the Church. Thirdly, "he may have maintained that the Christian could receive discernible and multiple Spirit-baptisms." Fourthly, "they [Benson and Fletcher] seem to have taught that the believer could receive a Spirit-baptism after justification." Fifthly, they taught that baptism with the Holy Spirit was linked to full assurance of faith.[120]

In his dissertation, Fraser reports the discovery of a fragment written in Wesley's handwriting where Wesley remarked on another document, presumably the aforementioned treatise. Wesley's notes shed light on the particular points of disagreement with Benson's theology. Below is a transcript of Fraser's copy.

> p. 9 Q? If Cornelius then rec^d any more
> than ye <u>Xtian Faith</u> of a Babe?
> p. 10 Q? If any more than y^s [this?] is implied
> in J° [John] 14.15 &c.
> p. 15 Is not an assurance of God['s] favour
> ye fruit of "receiving the H. Ghost"? i.e. in
> ye first degree?
> ib. "In <u>any one</u> of these Xtian Dispensations."
> Q? In any more than one?
> p. 16 N° &. This sentiment, I think, is
> utterly new. I never yet baptized a real
> Penitent w[h] ° was not then baptized with

---

117. Cf. LJW, 5:222.

118. Fletcher made reference to Benson's treatise with the words: "what you had wrote upon the baptism of the Holy Ghost" (JF→JB, 22 March [1771]).

119. Unsuccessful attempts have been made to find the treatise (Dayton, *Theological Roots of Pentecostalism*, 49; and Fraser, "Strains in the Understanding of Christian," 361). Fletcher asked Benson to send him a copy (JF→JB, 23 November 1771).

120. Fraser "Strains in the Understanding of Christian," 364–69.

yᵉ H. Ghost. See our Catechism <u>One Bapt'm</u>
includes yᵉ Outward Sign & yᵉ Inw[ar] ᵈ Grace.
The Quakers only speak otherwise in
order to set aside Water Baptism.
p. 19 I allow all yᵗ [that] is said in ye latter end of ye
page. But let us confine yᵉ term <u>New Birth</u>
to its one Scriptural meaning.
p. 23 "Ought to be distinguished." Epexo [Greek]
p. 24 Every <u>Penitent</u> is then baptized w[i] ᵗ
yᵉ H. G. i.e. received ri[ghteousnes] ˢ & pe[ace] & <u>jo</u>[joy]
in yᵉ HG.

I have proved it over and over.
I do not think yᵉ Doctrine of ye three
fold Dispensation requires one word
to be said about Water baptism. It
may be built on a less disputable Foundation.

p. 20 Q. Is this a parallel case?
<u>Birth</u>[.]
21. Of this? Still I scruple yᵉ term
23. Have ye recᵈ ye H. G. He does not use
yᵉ term <u>Birth</u> here.
24. <u>Ye shall be baptᵈ with yᵉ H. Ghost</u>"—
i.e. shall receive him as ye have not yet done.
25. St. Paul certainly means yᵗ [that]
to Xtians there is but <u>One Baptism</u>
or Outw[ar]ᵈ sign of yᵉ New Birth.
29. I doubt if yᵉ <u>Expression</u> be worth so
much dispute; it <u>seldom</u> occurs in yᵉ Bible.
33. Were it needful, I sh[oul] ᵈ make
many Queries here. But tis lis de verbis.1

Still I doubt, whether we need ˢᵉᵗ [???]
about Water Baptism. I doubt if yᵉ word
<u>Baptism</u> is ever used (unless 2ᶜᵉ or 3ce
metaphorically) for any but Water Ba[ptis]m.
And we can sufficiently prove our
whole Doctrine, without laying any
stress on those metaphorical Expressions.
38. It will never quit[?] (could it be done)
to confute our Church Catechism.
The thing I object to all along, is the
laying so much stress on yᵉ e metapho[-]

rical expression, "Baptize with the H. Ghost."[121]

Wesley's comments reveal several concerns over the theology reflected in Benson's treatise. First, Wesley held that all persons who receive the Spirit have a measure of divine assurance. Wesley feared that the theology of treatise would denigrate the faith of babes in Christ. Secondly, Wesley objected to what he felt was an artificial distinction between Spirit-baptism and water baptism. In his opinion, any penitent who received the outward sign of water baptism received at the same time the inward grace of Spirit-baptism.[122] Thirdly, Wesley objected to the overemphasis of the metaphorical expression, "baptism with the Spirit."

"Ours is An Improvement to His"

Fletcher did occasionally differ with Wesley or posited his own thought as an improvement to Wesley's. On 23 November 1771, Fletcher acknowledged that certain aspects of his thought were an addition to Wesley's. "I have begun my tract, I shall bring in <u>our</u> doctrine,[123] and hope so to tell the truth ~~as to propose~~ without opposing Mr. J. W.s system. ~~And~~ His and ours are one; ~~ours only as clearer:~~ he holds the truth, only <u>ours</u> is an improvement to <u>his</u>. I once beg'd you would give me a copy of what you wrote upon it. Now is the time to repeat that request: ~~grant~~ send it me with additions if you can, as soon as possible."[124] What precisely were these doctrinal distinctions between Wesley and Fletcher?

Christian Perfection

As previously discussed, Fletcher amalgamated Charles Wesley's distinctions between the Spirit dwelling with the pre-Pentecost disciples and the Spirit's indwelling the post-Pentecost disciples with John Wesley's doctrine of Christian perfection. Writing to Charles on 24 November 1771, Fletcher regarded the amalgamation as an improvement on John's theology: "He

---

121. Ibid., 490–92.

122. Wesley did not consistently hold that all adults were automatically regenerated at baptism (Holland, *Baptism in Early Methodism*, 47).

123. The proximity of thought may not be as close as he presumed, Walter Churchey wrote to Benson: "Let Him [Fletcher] phrases till He enjoys it's Meaning (in our sense! . . .)" (William Churchey→JB, 30 April 1771).

124. JF→JB, 23 November 1771. Benson apparently returned the manuscript without comment (JF→JB, 10 December 1771).

holds the truth, but this will be an ~~addition to it~~ improvement upon it, if I am not mistaken."[125]

On 14 August 1774, John Fletcher addressed further the issue of differences between himself and John Wesley.

> The difference consists, (if there is any) in my thinking, that those who were justified as Christians, and baptized and sealed with the Holy Ghost on the day of pentecost, and were made of one heart and mind, or were perfected in one &C. were in the state of christian perfection, or under the dispensation of the Holy Ghost: At least in the infancy of it. And that (genuine Christian faith <u>of Assurance</u> as contradistinguished from the faith of ~~the~~ babes, or carnal believers a faith this ~~such a~~ which the apostles had before the day of pentecost) introduces us into <u>perfect christianity</u>, or the full kingdom of God, which we must ~~gro~~ learn to stand in & to be established on.[126]

Wesley acknowledged to Fletcher on 22 March 1775 differences on the doctrine of Christian perfection: "It seems our views of Christian Perfection are a little different, though not opposite. It is certain every babe in Christ has received the Holy Ghost, and the Spirit witnesses with his spirit that he is a child of God. But he has not obtained Christian Perfection. Perhaps you have not considered St. John's threefold distinction of Christian believers: little children, young men, and fathers. All these received the Holy Ghost; but only the fathers were perfected in love."[127]

Wesley's observation was made after numerous corrections to portions of Fletcher's treatise on Christian perfection, i.e., *Last Check*, by both Wesley brothers.[128] John had approved of the work "in general" prior to Charles' corrections; on 21 May 1775, Fletcher wrote to Charles,

> I throw myself at your feet to put my manuscript upon Perfection, into your hands, and I implore your corrections for Christ's sake, and for the sake of truth and souls. I give you <u>carte blanche to add, or lop off; but to none but you</u>. Your brother saw it as he went to Ireland, and I believe approved of it in general: I hope you see it improved, as I have made many alterations, I trust, for the better. I have not skill to make my book <u>shorter</u> and <u>full</u>.

---

125. JF→CW, 24 November [1771].
126. JF→CW, 14 August [1774].
127. LJW, 6:146.
128. As early as 6 February 1773, Fletcher submitted the treatise on Christian perfection to John Wesley for correction (Tyerman, *Life and Times of the Rev.*, 3:149).

The Dispensation of the Spirit

God has given you the gift to be sententious: my ~~outcome~~ way is the reverse of yours, correct it.[129]

Later on 8 August 1775, Fletcher wrote to Charles: "I have sent to ~~your~~ him [John Wesley] the four addresses which conclude my Essay on perfection. So he has seen the whole, except the section against Martin's book."[130] However, on 18 August 1775, John Wesley wrote, "I have now received all your papers, and here and there made some small corrections."[131] Further, he conceded, "I do not perceive that you have granted too much, or that there is any difference between us. The Address to the Perfect I approve of most, and think it will have a good effect."[132] The above commendation may apply to the *Last Check* or more specifically to its four addresses and not to the entire body of Fletcher's writings. In fact, there were differences between their views on babes in Christ.

Babes in Christ

During the early 1770s, Fletcher's and Benson's views were in general closely aligned. Wesley was aware of the proximity of their views and recognized that one of the differences was the doctrine of assurance for babes in Christ. On 9 March 1771, he expressed to Benson his concerns over theological matters, admonishing him to read the Conference minutes. "Likewise think whether you can abstain from speaking of Universal Salvation and Mr. Fletcher's late discovery. The Methodists in general could not bear this. It would create huge debate and confusion. I wish you would read over that sermon in the first volume on the Spirit of Bondage and of Adoption. Invenio te corde simplicem, as the Count speaks, sed turbatis ideis. (I find thee simple in heart, but troubled in ideas)."[133]

The above letter led Benson to suppose that his beliefs disqualified him from close association with Methodism. Wesley replied to Benson's 16 March letter affirming that "Providence calls" Benson to association with the Methodists. He addressed some doctrinal issues: "A babe in Christ (of whom I know thousands) has the witness sometimes. A young man (in St. John's sense) has it continually. I believe one that is perfected in love, or filled with the Holy Ghost, may be properly termed a father. This we must

---

129. JF→CW, 21 May 1775.
130. JF→CW, 8 August 1775.
131. LJW, 6:174.
132. Ibid., 6:175.
133. Ibid., 6:228.

press both babes and young men to aspire after—yea, to expect. And why not now? I wish you would give another reading to the Plain Account of Christian Perfection."[134]

On 22 March 1771, Fletcher reported to Benson his discomfort in ministry at the College and his resignation as president to Lady Huntingdon. In the postscript, Fletcher addressed his perspective on the doctrinal issues between himself and Wesley: "Now with respect to Mr. W- letter to you, I would have you ~~ask leave to pray for~~ preach the seal of the Spirit the witness of the Spirit, or as he properly calls it the Spirit of Adoption: None can have it (for a constancy) but the baptiz'd; that you know, whether he assent to it or not. Besides you may preach faith—faith in an indwelling Christ faith in the promise of an . . ."[135] At this point, one can only surmise what Wesley meant precisely by "Fletcher's late discovery."[136] Wesley was concerned that Fletcher was denigrating the faith of babes in Christ[137] and wanted him to acknowledge that babes in Christ have a measure of the Spirit.

Fletcher made some concessions to Wesley's position in his *Essay on Truth* (1774): "This truth, 'Messiah is come in the flesh,' superadded to the Jewish gospel, has enlarged the hearts of all the disciples of John, or the 'babes in Christ.'"[138] In Fletcher's view, "babes in Christ" have an objective knowledge of Christ that is superior to that of Jews under the previous dispensation who believed that "The Messiah will come to point out clearly the way of salvation."[139] The objective faith of the Jews is an anticipatory faith in the coming Messiah—a hope of deliverance. However, the faith of "babes in Christ" exceeds the faith of the Jews because it no longer anticipates the Messiah, but is faith in an antecedent event. The faith of the "babes in Christ" is inferior to the faith of the adult Christians because the latter have subjectively appropriated the privileges of the superior dispensation:

---

134. Ibid., 5:229.

135. The original letter is fragmented, and the remainder is missing [JF→JB, 22 March [1771].

136. Editor John Telford indicated that Fletcher's late discovery "was his doctrine of 'Receiving the Holy Ghost.' . . . Wesley held that it was improper to separate the work of sanctification from justification, and that all who were justified had received the Holy Spirit." [LJW, 5:228].

137. On 23 November 1771, Fletcher recounted Benson's frustrated attempts to receive "the Baptism" and then asserted, "[Y]ou have been diverted again in London, and now temptations return to shew you the need of that full assurance which nothing can give but the Baptism, nothing can keep but the indwelling God" (JF→JF, 23 November 1771).

138. Fl-W1856, 4:36–37.

139. Fl-W1856, 4:36.

> And these truths, "Christ died for my sins, and rose again for my justification: he is ascended up on high: He has received the gift of the Spirit for men—for me. I believe on him by the power of that Spirit. He dwells in my heart by faith. He is in me the hope of glory. The promise of the Father is fulfilled: the kingdom of God, righteousness, peace, and joy in the Holy Ghost, is come with power;" these richer truths, I say, superadded to those which are essential to the inferior dispensations, tincture the hearts of all adult Christians.[140]

What is significant here is the use of personal pronouns, signifying the personal appropriation of objective truth.

Again in *An Equal Check to Parisaism & Antinomianism Continued* or *The First Part of the Scripture Scales* (1774), Fletcher discussed the second class of worshippers, which is comprised of "devote Jews" or "babes in Christ" who are compared to disciples of John or disciples of Christ before the day of Pentecost.[141] They are characterized as being "comparatively carnal" and are contrasted with "those holy souls" who are "fully possessed of Christ's Spirit, deserve to be called 'Christians,' in the full sense of the word."[142] There was continuity between the objective, extrinsic revelation of the babes in Christ and adult Christians. However, there was a discontinuity in the appropriation of the revelation. In part, the difficulty for the babes in Christ who live in the post-Pentecost era and have access to the full revelation of God in Christ is the inhibited ability to understand spiritual things: as Fletcher wrote in *La Grâce et Nature*: "Carnal and worldly man understands spiritual and heavenly things only with great difficulty."[143] Spiritual regeneration enables one to understand spiritual things. In the Pauline language of 1 Corinthians 3, Fletcher described the state of babes in Christ who consume milk. However, "strong meat belongeth to them that are of full age, even those who, by reason of use, have their spiritual sense exercised to discern both good and evil,' truth and error, as quickly and as surely as our bodily sense distinguish bitter from sweet, and light from darkness. Truth is spiritual light; too much of it might dazzle the weak eyes of our understanding."[144] As was seen previously, spiritual regeneration is

---

140. Fl-W1856, 4:37.

141. Fl-W1856, 4:288.

142. Ibid.

143. "L'Homme charnel, et mondain, ne comprend les choses spirituelles et célestes qu'avec beaucoup de difficulté" (Fletcher-Grâce, xxviii).

144. Fl-W1856, 4:33–34; 9:19.

an epistemological event and is a privilege for those under the dispensation of the Spirit.

Thus, Fletcher, in writing the *Essay on Truth* (1774), clarified his views on babes in Christ and allowed for measures of the Spirit.[145] Wesley held that babes in Christ have the witness of the Spirit sometimes; Fletcher did not disagree, but insisted that only the Spirit-baptized have the constant witness of the Spirit. Wesley wrote that when one is justified, one receives the Spirit. However, Fletcher insisted that while babes in Christ have a measure of the Spirit, such a measure is not the full measure available for the believers under the dispensation of the Spirit.

Benson identified himself and the Trevecka students as "almost" Christians who had experienced remission of their sins, but had not yet received the Spirit in the NT sense. Both Fletcher and Benson furthermore classified themselves and the students as John's disciples or pre-Pentecost disciples who again had not received the Spirit. Wesley was not pleased. Wesley felt that Fletcher and Benson had fallen into the error of acknowledging "that he is not a believer who has any sin remaining in him."[146] Both Fletcher and Benson felt that their faith fell short of the NT norm whereas Wesley felt that they were denigrating the first work of grace.[147] True their faith was weak, but they denigrated their state too much. Wesley wanted them to acknowledge that babes in Christ receive the Spirit and have at least a measure of assurance and that such babes should aspire for Christian perfection. Babes in Christ should be encouraged to expect Christian perfection, moving from faith to faith. In his comments on Benson's treatise, Wesley was not opposed to the dispensational scheme, but felt only that it should not be founded on

---

145. Fl-W1856, 4:116.

146. LJW, 5:252. L. Wood argues that Wesley was concerned that Benson and Fletcher had fallen into the error of Count Zinzendorf and furthermore that "Benson did not consider himself a believer if he did not have the full assurance of his entire sanctification" (*Meaning of Pentecost in Early Methodism*, 39). However, it is obvious from the December 1770 letter that Benson did not question his status as a fully sanctified believer, but his status as a believer.

147 L. Wood concludes from John Wesley's letter to Mary Bishop the following, "It shows that Wesley believed that Benson and Fletcher were saying that every justified believer was also entirely sanctified" (*Meaning of Pentecost in Early Methodism*, 44). However, Benson's undated letter, in particular, gives clear evidence that he believed in the doctrine of sanctification, but felt that he had not obtained it. Wood furthermore ignores the portion of Fletcher's letter cited by Tyerman, which states "that a day of Pentecost would make them what they did not appear to me to be as yet—Christians and preachers" (Tyerman, *Wesley's Designated Succesor*, 181); Wood cites only that Fletcher was anticipating a "day of Pentecost" (L. Wood, *Meaning of Pentecost in Early Methodism*, 21).

a distinction between water baptism and Spirit-baptism.[148] Wesley thought that the phrase "baptism with the Spirit," was overused.

Fletcher maintained a high view of the Christian life. Pentecost ensured the full benefits of the Christian life, and only those who had been baptized with the Spirit had a constant witness of the Spirit, the Spirit of Adoption. Genuine Christian faith, differentiated from the faith of babes or carnal Christians, is the only valid Christian faith, and it ushers believers into the kingdom of God. In Fletcher's thought, babes in Christ have a valid objective, Christian faith, but an invalid subjective, Christian faith. They were justified, but were not fully regenerate; their subjective experience was similar to the pious Jews and possessed intermittently the Spirit. Justification was a privilege available under the Jewish dispensation—a position that was perhaps produced as Fletcher encountered antinomianism.

Despite Fletcher's occasional disagreement with Wesley, Fletcher sought Wesley's approval of his publications.[149] Wesley approved Fletcher's publications both in private and in public forums.[150]

Wesley approved of Fletcher's doctrine of dispensations and eventually, asked Fletcher to serve as his successor as the leader of Methodism.[151] On 1 June 1776, Wesley wrote Fletcher requesting that he join him in route or at Conference. He indicated his approval of Fletcher's classification of babes in Christ as almost Christians: "The generality of believers in our Church (yea, and in the Church of Corinth, Ephesus, and the rest, even in the Apostolic age) are certainly no more than babes in Christ; not young men, and much less fathers. But we have some, and we should certainly pray and expect that our Pentecost may fully come."[152]

Benson Modified His Views

Throughout the 1770s, Joseph Benson's views on the baptism of the Spirit and the doctrine of dispensations were developing. Wesley and Fletcher made conflicting assessments of Benson's spiritual state. Wesley wrote on 28 December 1770, "You are a child of God; you are justified freely through

---

148 L. Wood holds that Wesley did not like the doctrine of dispensations (*Meaning of Pentecost in Early Methodism*, 37). However, this is not what Wesley said in the fragment. Wesley did not like the foundation upon which it was built, i.e., the division between water baptism and Spirit baptism.

149. JF→JB, 12 February 1772.

150 LJW, 6:137.

151. Ibid., 5:274; 6:10; 6:33.

152. Ibid., 6:221.

the redemption which is in Christ Jesus. Your sins are forgiven!"[153] On 12 February 1772, Fletcher encouraged Benson to continue the soul-searching and his pursuit for the "great promise" of the Father: "Keep up Jewish till you have Christian faith."[154]

On 10 September 1773, Wesley admonished Benson to "keep to the plain, old Methodist doctrine." He added, "At Trevecca you were a little warped from this; but it was a right-hand error."[155] On 8 January 1774, Wesley wrote to Benson, "I am glad you 'press all believers' to aspire after the full liberty of the children of God. They must not give up their faith in order to do this; herein you formerly seemed to be in some mistake. Let them go on from faith to faith—from weak faith to that strong faith which not only conquers but casts out sin. Meantime it is certain many call themselves believers who do not even conquer sin, who are strangers to the whole inward kingdom of God and void of the whole fruit of the Spirit."[156] Benson eventually modified his early position, which was largely in agreement with Fletcher, in the early 1770s to disagree with him on certain points later in the decade. The letters that reveal this modification were exchanged with no less than Fletcher's future wife, Mary Bosanquet.

Their discussion centered on a manuscript written by John Fletcher that Bosanquet had sent to Benson. Benson expressed his concerns over Fletcher's doctrine of dispensations and its effect on the doctrine of assurance.[157] Fletcher's doctrine of dispensations would cause those under the dispensation of the Spirit who had not yet experienced all the privileges of that dispensation to rest in the privileges of inferior dispensations. This was true because Fletcher taught a measure of assurance was available to those under the inferior dispensations: Benson wrote, "We cannot rest in the low attainmts of a jew much less in the lower grace of the Heathen & yet be (as he [Fletcher] says) accepted as the children of God according to our dispensation."[158] On the other hand, the emphasis on the figurative language of the baptism of the Spirit would have "a tendency to puzle & perplex the minds of those who have been ~~thought~~ accustomed to hear (from the pulpit

---

153. Ibid., 5:214.

154. JF→JB, 12 February 1772. According to M. Olson, the Conference Minutes of 13 May 1746 raise the question about the type of faith the pre-Calvary disciples had and resolve that it is a Jewish faith ("Roots of John Wesley's Servant Theology," 123).

155 LJW, 6:40.

156. Ibid., 6:65.

157. Though undated, it is docketed to 1778 according to internal evidence: "This was seven years ago after I had left Oxford & begun to travel as a prr [preacher]" (JB→MBF [1778]).

158. Ibid.

& press) ~~to~~ a different kind of language."¹⁵⁹ Such language would "tend to raise the expectations of earnest faithful souls too high & of consequences when after long striving their expectations are not answd. ~~it~~ will strip them of all their confidence plunge them into doubts & despondency if not into infidelity & Sin."¹⁶⁰ Benson based his conclusions on his own experience: "I know the time when my expectations were too high & extraordinary."¹⁶¹ Miss Bosanquet, while expressing admiration for her future husband, responded to Benson's analysis, sharing his concerns for the implications of Fletcher's theology of dispensations.

After Fletcher's return from convalescence in Switzerland, Benson wrote him to renew their friendship but distanced himself from their earlier theology. He recounted that they had spent hours together in prayer for the baptism of the Holy Spirit and acknowledged that previously he had "formed too <u>gross</u> an idea of the gift of the Holy Ghost & expected something too <u>marvelous</u> & <u>extraordinary</u> & 2d As I did not do sufficient honour to <u>faith</u> nor cast myself with a proper confidence on the unbounded love of God."¹⁶²

In assessing Benson's later theology, Fraser writes, "Benson's published writings contain no evidence of Spirit-baptism terminology, including his <u>Two Sermons on Sanctification</u>."¹⁶³ The doctrinal split from a high view of Spirit-baptism must have been complete prior to Benson's first publication in 1782.

THE PRIVILEGES BELONGING TO THE DISPENSATION OF THE SPIRIT¹⁶⁴

In his sermon, *Justification by Faith* (1746), Wesley described the doctrines of justification and sanctification as follows: "The one [justification] implies what God *does for us* through His Son; the other [sanctification] implies

---

159. Ibid.

160. Ibid.

161. Ibid. Benson did not entirely abandon pneumatological language; as late as 1777, Benson wrote of his own experience, "About six years ago, when at Oxford, my convictions, desire, &c. were the same that they are now; and then, as now, I longed for the baptism of the Holy Ghost" [Macdonald, *Memoirs of the Rev.*, 52].

162. JB→JF, 12 June 1781.

163. Fraser, "Strains in the Understanding of Christian," 362.

164. Fletcher-Dispensations. Fletcher used this concept of "degrees of grace belonging" to a given dispensation.

what he *works in us* by His Spirit."[165] When Fletcher reified this distinction between justification and sanctification in his theology of history, the result was the dispensations of the Son and of the Spirit.[166] The distinction arose in two polemical contexts. First, Fletcher made a distinction between water baptism and Spirit-baptism in his controversy with the Quaker Abiah Darby. Second, the dispensational scheme, particularly making a distinction between the last two dispensations, arose during the Calvinistic controversy. In his polemic against antinomianism, Fletcher sought to distinguish between the work of the Son and that of the Spirit. The Calvinists argued for finished salvation, which was based upon their doctrine of predestination. While Fletcher accepted the idea of a finished atonement,[167] he rebutted the doctrine of finished salvation with his argument for personal history. If salvation is finished, history is sapped of its meaning. "If our justification is finished, there is no need of believing in order to be justified. If our sanctification is finished, there is no need of mortifying one sin, praying for one grace, taking up one cross, parting with either right eye or right hand, in order to perfect holiness."[168] Furthermore, Fletcher argued that based on the involvement of the third Person of the Trinity in history, salvation was not complete. The ongoing redemptive activity of the Spirit in the world is a testimony to the unfinished character of salvation. "And should we not, even in speaking of redemption, imitate the judicious Calvinists of the last century, who carefully distinguished between redemption by the price of Jesus' blood, and redemption by the power of his Spirit? 'The former,' said they, 'as finished upon the cross but the latter is not so much as begun in thousands; even in all that are unborn or unconverted.'"[169] Thus, Fletcher, against the fatalistic view of his opponents, reasserted the role of human response to the redemptive activity of the Trinity. Salvation is conditioned upon the responsiveness of individuals to receive and appropriate the grace of God. Grace is an accommodation to the condition of fallen humanity, supplying the ability to conform to divine expectations and implies an eschatological dimension of future divine judgment.[170]

165. BiCentWJW, 1:187.
166. Cf. O'Brien, "Trinitarian Revisioning of the Wesleyan," 34.
167. Fl-W1856, 2:366.
168. Fl-W1856, 2:364.
169. Fl-W1856, 2:367.
170. Fl-W1856, 2:257.

Spiritual and Internal Character of the Privileges

In *Spiritual Manifestation of the Son of God* (1767), Fletcher developed his doctrine of revelation in his polemic against Sandemanianism, a rationalistic form of Christianity that envisioned mere assent to Christian truth. However, Fletcher did not deny the noetic quality of revelation. Wiggins observes, "Fletcher's understanding of nature gives clues to his view of revelation. Since revelation produces saving knowledge, that is, it is of a strongly noetic quality, and since the spiritual senses are the antennae by which revelation is perceived, it is clear that the meaning of revelation is a self-disclosing act of God, the experience of which results in religious knowledge which is always saving."[171] In this section, the topic of spiritual revelation will be discussed because it is directly related to the dispensation of the Spirit.

Fletcher distinguished between the external manifestations and the spiritual manifestations of Christ. The earlier dispensations had direct manifestations as in Moses' day, but the manifestations of the Christian dispensation are superior to those of the dispensation of Moses because they are spiritual.[172] The manifestations of the bodily presence of Christ certainly ceased with his ascension, but the spiritual manifestations have not.[173]

Fletcher's emphasis upon the dispensation of the Spirit called the rationalist to move past the cognitive content of the first two dispensations to experience the fullness of the Godhead. Often he quoted Romans 14:17 in addressing the full-orbed reign of the Spirit: "The kingdom of God is righteousness, peace and joy in the Holy Ghost." For Fletcher, this is the dispensation of the Spirit: it is love ruling and reigning in the heart.

As stated previously, the source of the experimental knowledge of the Redeemer is not found within human capabilities, but in divine grace. Regeneration is the activity of the Spirit that recreates and gives life to the one who responds to the preventing grace of God. The key response for the inward manifestation is humility: Zaccheus experienced both an inward and an outward manifestation because "he came down from the pinnacle of proud nature, as well as from the sycamore-tree."[174]

Pentecost is a major turning point in salvation history because it made the new birth a common experience and the prerequisite for participation in the kingdom. The same was true for Wesley as Wilfred H. Blevins observes,

---

171. Wiggins, "Pattern of John Fletcher's Theology," 219.
172. Fl-W1856, 9:45–46.
173. Fl-W1856, 9:51–52.
174. Fl-W1856, 9:49.

"For Wesley, spiritual sight is only possible when the Holy Spirit opens and enlightens our 'spiritual sensorium.'"[175] Spiritual regeneration is essential for participation in the full kingdom of God, but it is not the only manifestation of the Spirit. Fletcher taught three degrees of the manifestation of the Spirit: In the age of the Father, the Spirit strove with human beings in the antediluvian era. "Some have 'the spirit of bondage unto fear,'" which is a divinely given consciousness that they have not yet the full redemption. Others have "the Spirit of adoption," which is participation in the full kingdom of God.[176] Evangelical regeneration is the divide between the dispensation of the Son and of the Spirit.

The divide is illustrated by the contrast between the characteristics of the worshippers under the dispensation of the Son and those under the Spirit. The obedience that characterized the former is rendered to "our Creator and our external Redeemer"[177] whereas the obedience which characterized the latter was yielded to God "as our inward Redeemer and sanctifying Comforter."[178] This seems to be a pastoral accommodation on Fletcher's part. Fletcher recognized, as a faithful son of the Church of England, the validity of the baptismal rite of the church and the validity of the faith of his baptized parishioners, but recognized the rite as an external one. While he recognized the validity of their faith, he longed for them to internalize the truths of Christianity.

In discussing the sacrament of baptism, Fletcher employed the language of "antitype" and "archetype." Clearly water baptism is the antitype of which Spirit-baptism is the archetype.

> "The invisible things of God," says St. Paul, "are understood by the things that are made," or visible; but who considers the profound truth couched under his words? Certainly not those heathens who worship the *material*, instead of the *immaterial* Sun: nor those Jews who are regardless of the circumcision of the heart, and rest satisfied with an external circumcision: nor those Papists who pay Divine honours to a bit of typical bread which their fancy has turned into the identical body of our Lord: nor yet those Protestants who, being unmindful of the baptism of the Spirit, exert themselves only in sprinkling infants with, or dipping adults in material water: for they all equally forget that the letter of natural and typical things alone profiteth little, or nothing comparatively; and that it killeth, when it is opposed to

---

175. Bevins, "Pneumatology in John Wesley's Theological Method," 107.
176. Fl-W1856, 2:441.
177. Fletcher-Dispensations, 10.
178. Ibid., 11.

The Dispensation of the Spirit

the Spirit, and made to supersede the invisible and heavenly archetypes, which visible and earthly things shadow out; or when it causes us to set aside the precious antitypes which typical things point unto.[179]

Baptism of the Spirit is the reality; water baptism is the symbol of that reality. Baptism of the Spirit ushers one into participation in the full kingdom of God and enables one to benefit from all of its privileges.

The nature of the privileges of believers under the dispensation of the Spirit is spiritual and internal. The spirit and temper of the worshipers under the dispensation of the Spirit differ from those of worshipers under the dispensation of the Son who are "unsettled" and "in part spiritual, and in part carnal" and share both "in the severity of the law, and in the sweetness of the gospel."[180] All believers under the dispensation of the Spirit "are made free from the law of sin and death."[181] The Holy Spirit engraves the words of Jesus, spoken principally on the Sermon on the Mount, on the hearts of the believers under the dispensation of the Spirit. The inscription of the law occurred on the day of Pentecost.[182] Under the dispensation of the Spirit, believers are truly spiritual:

> They ~~have the can~~ approach the throne of grace rather with the humble familiarity and chearful love of sons, ~~rather~~ with the ~~chilling~~ uncomfortable fear ~~and uncomfortable~~ of servants and the chilling dread of ~~servants and~~ slaves. Gratitude, love and joy are the ~~spring~~ overflowing springs of their tempers and actions: The love of God being shed abroad in their hearts, they walk in ~~the light of holiness~~ love as God manifest in the flesh also walked: The love of Christ constrains them to give and forgive as God gives and forgives: They bear with others as God bears with them.[183]

Born of the Spirit

As stated above, Fletcher quoted the collects from Quinquagesima Sunday or Shrove Sunday and the collect for purity as examples of prayers for those who want to be born again of the Spirit or "to stand fast in the grace of

179. Fl-W1856, 4:31.
180. Ibid., 31.
181. Ibid., 19.
182. Ibid., 21.
183. Ibid., 31.

spiritual regeneration."[184] Both these sorts of prayers are comprehensively summed up in the daily absolution:

> He (God) pardoneth and absolveth all them that truly repent, and unfeignedly believe his holy gospel. Wherefore let us beseech him to grant us true repentance (the only true mark that we are really born again of water) and his Holy Spirit (the only true mark that we are really born again of the Spirit) that those things may please him which we do at this present, and that the rest of our life hereafter may be pure and holy, &c so that at the last we may come to his eternal joy thro' Jesus Christ our Lord.[185]

Thus, the grace of spiritual regeneration was associated with the birth of the Spirit whereas Fletcher associated "born again of water" with penitential grace and an external religious experience. The inferior birth was associated with the dispensation of the Son whereas the fuller birth of the Spirit was associated with the dispensation of the Spirit. The two births were essential for one to enjoy the greatest privileges of the Christian dispensation: "[H]e must be born again of water and of the Spirit, he must first have he must have not only the initial righteousness, peace and joy sealed to believers by a baptism of water before the day of Pentecost; but also the perfective righteousness, peace and joy sealed to believers by a baptism of the Spirit on that memorable day."[186]

Thus, Fletcher distinguished between those who were born of God "in the lower sense of the word" and those who were born of God in the full sense of the word.[187] The former are sealed to the covenant of peculiarity by water baptism; the latter are sealed to their covenant of peculiarity by the baptism of the Holy Spirit.[188] In *An Essay on Truth* (1774), Fletcher insisted that believers under the OT had a measure of the Spirit's influence, but "they were not fully baptized."[189] Old Testament believers experienced a visitation of the Spirit, but not the indwelling of the Spirit. Fletcher cited Wesley's notes on Acts 8:15 as proof of his position, noting that the Samaritan be-

---

184. Fletcher-Loose.

185. Ibid. The original uses brackets that have been replaced with parentheses. Heitzenrater points out that Wesley made this distinction as early as January 1739 ("Great Expectations," 74). Fletcher wrote, "Do not say, 'I was born again in baptism'" (Fl-W1856, 8:384).

186. Fletcher-Dispensations, 31.

187. Fletcher-New, 71; [Wood, "Essay on the Doctrine of the New Birth," 44].

188. Fletcher-Dispensations., 3.

189. Fl-W1856, 4:116.

lievers received water baptism in the name of the Lord Jesus, but had not received the Holy Spirit. Receiving the Spirit is synonymous with the term, baptism of the Holy Ghost, among others.[190]

Fletcher quoted at length from Wesley's sermon, *The Great Privilege of those that are Born of God* (1748), in which Wesley describes the experience of those who are born of the Spirit.[191] Fletcher quoted favorably from Wesley who extolled the qualities of those who are "born of God" after which phrase, Fletcher interpolated the parenthetical comment "according to the dispensation of the Spirit."[192] Fletcher's particular concern was to respect the faith of those who are not yet born of the Spirit, but have a measure of faith. Fletcher argued that Wesley allowed "a birth, and a sonship, inferior" to the birth of the Spirit.[193] However, the term, born of the Spirit, "suits none but complete Christians."[194]

When Wesley distinguished the privileges of Christians from those available to OT believers, Fletcher further distinguished the latter's privileges from the believers under "the preparatory dispensation of the gospel." Below is the passage from Wesley's sermon on *Christian Perfection* (1741) with Fletcher's interpolations in brackets:

> Those who have duly considered these things must allow, that the privileges of Christians are in no wise to be measured by what the Old Testament records concerning those who were under the Jewish dispensation" [nor by what the New Testament records concerning those, who are under the preparatory dispensation of the gospel, which is sealed by water baptism] "seeing the fullness of time is now come, the Holy Ghost is now given; the great salvation of God is brought unto men, by the" [spiritual as well as external] "revelation of Jesus Christ.[195]

The fact that Fletcher interpolates "the preparatory dispensation of the gospel" proves that he wanted to make a distinction between the experiences

---

190. Fletcher-New, 72; L. Wood, ed., "'Essay on the Doctrine of the New Birth,'" 45. Wood assumes that this is a difference between Fletcher and Wesley: "Perhaps Wesley was assuming a distinction between 'receiving the Spirit' and being 'filled with the Spirit,' whereas Fletcher did not" (L. Wood, "Exegetical-Theological Reflections on the Baptism," 59).

191. Fletcher erroneously attributes his citation to Wesley's sermon on John 3:8, *Marks of the New Birth* (1748) (Fletcher-New, 73; Wood, ed., "'Essay on the Doctrine of the New Birth,'" 45).

192. Fletcher-New, 45.

193. Ibid., 46.

194. Ibid.

195. BiCentWJW, 2:111.

of the believers under the Jewish dispensation and the pre-Pentecostal disciples. The same interpolation evinces his desire to heighten the contrast between the privileges of the pre-Pentecost disciples and those of the post-Pentecost disciples. Fletcher recognized the validity of the faith of believers whose faith paralleled that of the pre-Pentecost disciples. He wrote, "Hence it follows, that, so sure as this great Vindication of Christian perfection allows, ~~that~~ that there are <u>imperfect</u>, as well as <u>perfect</u> ~~believers~~ Christians, he allows also, that there are believers, who [tho' born of God according to the <u>preparatory</u> gospel dispensation, which is sealed by ~~a bap~~ water baptism] are not yet <u>born of God</u> according to the <u>perfective</u> gospel-dispensation, which was opened ~~by the~~ on the day of Pentecost."[196] In an unpublished treatise on the categorization of believers in the hymns, Fletcher introduced a list of Scriptures, "which display the Promise of the Father—the promise to baptize believers with the Holy Ghost that they may be born again of the Spirit."[197] Clearly in Fletcher's thought there is a distinction between one who is born of water and one who is born of the Spirit.

Indwelling Spirit

Above, Charles Wesley's trinitarian hymns were the source for a distinction that Fletcher made between the Spirit as Monitor and the Spirit as Comforter. In the dispensation of the Son, worshippers experienced the Spirit dwelling with them, and under the subsequent dispensation, they experienced the Spirit indwelling them. It is this latter characteristic that will now be examined.

Previously, the doctrine of the spiritual manifestation of the Son of God was analyzed. The extrinsic knowledge of God, the historical revelation, and doctrinal truths must be internalized by the Holy Spirit. Knight writes, "It is through the Holy Spirit that the work of God in Christ is carried on in individuals and in all of history. However, Fletcher maintained that the internal or saving knowledge of God comes only by the Holy Spirit."[198] The Holy Spirit is the Agent of saving knowledge and relationships. What David Rainey affirms of Wesley's theology can be said of Fletcher's thought: "It was the Spirit that brought humanity into a genuine encounter with the triune God. This meant for Wesley, that the work of the Spirit was perceptible which would then generate God's grace into a person's life through

---

196. Fletcher-New, 80; Wood, ed., "'Essay on the Doctrine of the New Birth,'" 47.
197. J. Fletcher, Hymn I, Fletcher-Tooth, JRULM, MAM Fl. 18.
198. J. Knight, "John William Fletcher and the Early Methodist," 249.

faith."[199] This was central to Fletcher's thought: the indwelling presence of the Triune God was made possible by the agency of the Holy Spirit.

Early Methodists emphasized the experimental and spiritual revelation of the Trinity. Kenneth Collins asserted that Wesley assessed the experience of Methodists by this standard:

> For Wesley the truth of the distinct person of Trinity is known in an active salvific process that occurs in the lives of some believers. In fact, Wesley was so impressed with Marquis de Renty's claim that he bore about him "an experimental verity, and a plenitude of the presence of the ever blessed Trinity," that he used this observation as a kind of standard by which he assessed the experience of the Methodists. Thus, while Wesley was preaching in Bristol in 1786, he observed one who could say with Monsieur de Renty, "I bear with me and experimental verity, and a plenitude of the presence of the ever-blessed Trinity."[200]

Such an experimental verification of the Trinity characterized a select few of those who were perfect in love. One who had such an experience was William Perronet, a close friend of John Fletcher: "[He] 'was led at first to Jesus the Mediator . . . Afterward he had communion with the Father, next with the Spirit, and then with the whole Trinity.'"[201]

Fletcher employed frequently quoted Romans 14:17 "For the kingdom of God is not meat and drink; but righteousness, and peace, and joy in the Holy Ghost." For him, the internalization of righteousness, peace, and joy is the epitome of the kingdom of God. Fletcher quoted often a phrase from Charles Wesley: "Perfection is nothing but the unshaken kingdom of God peace righteousness & joy in the H.G. [Holy Ghost] or by the baptism of the H.G."[202] The inward kingdom of God was made possible by the indwelling Spirit.

Witness of the Spirit or Full Assurance

One of the issues that arose frequently in correspondence prior to and immediately following Benson's dismissal from Trevecka College was the doctrine of the witness of the Spirit or full assurance. Fletcher's doctrine of

---

199. Rainey, "John Wesley's Doctrine of Salvation in Relation," 115.
200. Collins, *Theology of John Wesley*, 147.
201. Ibid.
202 JF→CW, 16 January 1773, Cf. JF→CW, 14 August [1774].

the witness of the Spirit came under scrutiny from Wesley. As with other doctrines, his was considerably nuanced. Fletcher differentiated between the faith of full assurance and other degrees of assurance.

Fletcher developed his doctrine of assurance in the *Essay on Truth* (1774) where an explicit faith in Christ was not essential to a measure of assurance.[203] Each dispensation afforded the worshippers at least a measure of comfort,[204] but the degree of comfort differed with each dispensation or each degree of faith and upon the "peculiar operation of God."[205] In the manuscript, *Essay on the Doctrine of Dispensations*, Fletcher distinguished three degrees of assurance: "If a ~~sincere~~ Penitent hopes God (as God of mercy) ~~will~~ ~~forgive him his sin~~ be gracious to him, he is ~~but~~ a weak believer under the Father's dispensation. If he trusts that God for Christ's sake ~~for~~ is now reconciled to him, he is advanced to the Son's economy, and if the Spirit of truth and love bears witness with his spirit that he is a now a child of God, he is a spiritual man."[206] In Fletcher's thought, there is a direct link between the operation of the Spirit and the measure of assurance as well as with the measure of the faith of the believer.[207] Worshippers under inferior dispensations do not always have assurance due to the measure of divine operations.[208] Disciples of John or babes in Christ who have experienced the Spirit in a lesser degree have an inferior degree of assurance than the normative Christian experience. Believers under the dispensation of the Spirit have the "witness in themselves."[209] In *Portrait* (1779), Fletcher linked the dispensation of the Spirit with the Spirit of adoption.[210] Fletcher made clear the connection between the Christian dispensation and Christian assurance: "[U]ndoubtedly assurance is inseparably connected with the faith of the Christian dispensation, which was not fully opened till Christ opened his glorious baptism on the day of pentecost, and till his spiritual kingdom was set up with power in the hearts of his people. Nobody therefore can truly believe, according to this dispensation, without being immediately conscious both of the forgiveness of sins, and of peace and joy in the Holy

---

203. Fl-W1856, 4:107.
204. Fl-W1856, 4:98.
205. Fl-W1856, 4:108.
206. Fletcher-Dispensations, 95.
207. Fl-W1856, 4:116–17.
208. Fl-W1856, 3:331–32.
209. Fl-W1856, 4:101.
210. Fletcher-Portrait, 2:211.

Ghost."²¹¹ Those who do not have such assurance either were never believers according to the Christian dispensation or they have fallen from grace.²¹²

How did Wesley respond to Fletcher's doctrine of the Holy Spirit given his concerns that he expressed in his correspondence? In the abridged edition of *The First Part of an Equal Check*, which Wesley himself published, Wesley indicated the passages with a "*," which he considered to be most useful. One of the paragraphs that Wesley highlighted was a passage in which Fletcher linked Pentecost with the doctrine of Christian assurance.²¹³

Baptism with the Spirit

One of the issues that has preoccupied neo-Wesleyan theologians in recent years has been whether or not Wesley and Fletcher equated the doctrine of baptism of the Spirit with the doctrine of entire sanctification.²¹⁴ Many conclude that Fletcher has equated the two doctrines, identifying baptism of the Spirit with entire sanctification, an experience subsequent to conversion or regeneration.²¹⁵ W. T. Purkiser describes four positions on the way that Spirit-baptism relates to present-day Christian experience. While Purkiser does not classify correctly Fletcher's position, he does provide a category that enables the present author to describe more accurately Fletcher's position.²¹⁶ Fletcher taught that Spirit-baptism embraces the "entire scope of individual Christian experience, initially in regeneration but not fully accomplished until there is a cleansing of the moral nature."²¹⁷

In the *Last Check* (1775), Fletcher does not equate Christian perfection or full sanctification with baptism of the Spirit;²¹⁸ his position is much more nuanced. Fletcher refused to flatten the experiences of the early disciples to one commonality: Luke's phrase, "great grace was upon them all" (Acts 4:33), "does not necessarily mean, that they were all equally strong in

211. Fl-W1856, 3:331–32.
212. Fl-W1856, 4:101.
213. Fletcher-EC1, v–vi.
214. L. Wood is an example of this position; he argues that Fletcher holds to an equation of the Pentecostal dispensation with Christian perfection (*Pentecostal Grace*, 180).
215. Purkiser, *Exploring Christian Holiness*, 109–10.
216. The present writer is indebted to Reasoner for this insight (*Wesleyan Theology of Holiness for the Twenty-First Century* (forthcoming), 390).
217. Purkiser, *Exploring Christian Holiness*, 109. Greathouse writes, "For Wesley as for Fletcher, the baptism with the Holy Spirit embraces the total work of the Spirit in the heart" (*Exploring Christian Holiness*. 244).
218. Fl-W1856, 6:165.

grace."[219] The term "baptism with the Spirit" can apply to various experiences: e.g., either justification or sanctification.[220] While the believers on the day of Pentecost took "an extraordinary turn together in the Canaan of perfect love," they were not all perfected in love as the incident with Ananias and Sapphira clearly demonstrates.[221] Fletcher cautioned the interpreters of the Acts accounts not to restrict the experiences to Christian perfection: "[I]n this case, the account which St. Luke gives of the primitive believers ought to be taken with some restriction: thus, while many of them were perfect in love, many might have the imperfection of their love only covered over by a land-flood of 'peace and joy in believing.'"[222]

The day of Pentecost demonstrated the objective power of the Spirit to transform the human heart, a power that would be subjectively appropriated when the believers "shall *fully embrace* the promise of full sanctification."[223] Baptism with the Spirit in Fletcher's thought is a designation for the operation of the Holy Spirit that effects a transformation of the human heart.[224] The "ardour of the faith" of the believer as well as the quality of the truth embraced determines the degree of divine transformation that is experienced.[225]

Thus, there is in Fletcher's thought a distinction between the objective bestowal of the Spirit at Pentecost and the subjective appropriation of it. The foundation for the distinction, which Fletcher made between the objective

---

219. Fl-W1856, 6:166.

220. Fl-W1856, 6:165.

221. Fl-W1856, 6:166–67.

222. Fl-W1856, 6:166.

223. Fl-W1856, 6:167; emphasis added.

224. Fletcher addressed the second category of his congregants (normally seekers) in the following words: "Ye that are straiten'd, for want of liberty, new birth the good Spirit. bless God, beg for more of this blessed eagerness—Look to Jesus baptiz'd with blood, & baptizing with ye holy Ghost." [JF→sermon Luke 12.50]. Fletcher wrote, "II. The words belong to every follower of Xt.
1. A baptism of tears or sorrow, repentance.
2. A baptism of divine blood & living water.
3. The baptism of the holy Ghost & fire.
Matt. 3. The stands one among you whom ye know not.
4. The baptism of contempt, afflictions, grave.
We are to be straitend till this fiery baptism is accomplish'd, because
1. It is to wash our sins, it is the substance of baptism which John administers.
2. It is to burn our corruptions, refine our souls
3. It is to melt our hearts & fill them with holy love.
4. The servant is not above his master" (JF→sermon, Luke 12.50).

225. Fl-W1856, 6:167.

The Dispensation of the Spirit

"power" and the subjective "faith," is the divine-human synergism that is basic to his theological system.[226]

The ultimate goal of Spirit baptism is Christian perfection. However, in Fletcher's thought, the phrase "baptism of the Spirit" cannot be equated explicitly with Christian perfection because, in part, it is an operation of the Spirit whose fulfillment hinges upon the faith of the human being. To do so would confuse the end with the means. The term centers on the agency of the Spirit. Fletcher's position was more nuanced than many neo-Wesleyans acknowledge; Fletcher used the phrase, "completely baptized with the Holy Ghost."[227] To be "completely baptized with the Holy Ghost" indicates the experience of entire sanctification whereas justification indicates an experience that is less than being *completely* baptized with the Spirit.

Much of the fracas over the doctrine of baptism of the Spirit in recent years has pitted Wesley's position on the subject against Fletcher's position. Wesley recognized the term "baptism with the Spirit" as a metaphor; in the fragment containing his observations on Benson's treatise, he asserted, "And we can sufficiently prove our whole Doctrine, without laying any stress on those metaphorical Expressions."[228] In his sermon *Of the Church* (1786), Wesley commented on Ephesians 4:5: "Some indeed have been inclined to interpret this in a figurative sense, as if it referred to that baptism of the Holy Ghost which the apostles received at the day of Pentecost, and which in a lower degree is given to all believers. But it is a stated rule in interpreting Scripture never to depart from the plain, literal sense, unless it implies an absurdity. And beside, if we thus understood it, it would be a needless repetition, as being included in, 'There is one spirit.'"[229] In this citation, Wesley made it clear that he held to higher and lower degrees of the Spirit: the reception of the Spirit at Pentecost and the lower degree of reception of the Spirit given to all believers; he nevertheless remained wary of using the term in the figurative sense (at least in this passage) and/or of the Quakers and pentecostalists "who had either rejected sacramental baptism or had claimed that 'the baptism of the Spirit superseded it.'"[230] Wesley maintained his focus on the goal of the Christian life, and rejected, at least at the writing of his comments on Benson's treatise, the term "baptism with the Spirit" as a figurative term that was without significant theological content. Fletcher

---

226. Cf. Fl-W1856, 3:185.
227. Fl-W1856, 2:442.
228. Fraser, "Strains in the Understanding of Christian," 490–92.
229. BiCentWJW, 3:49–50.
230. Ibid., 3:49–50n22.

on the other hand, viewed baptism with the Spirit as a means to the end, perfect love. The Agent of true spiritual transformation was the Holy Spirit.

If the doctrine of baptism with the Spirit has specific theological content in Fletcher's thought, the content centers on the *telos* of the doctrine, i.e., perfect love, which safeguards the idea of maturation in the Christian life. The multiplicity of the various degrees is prominent in Fletcher's thought and attests to the perfecting activity of the Holy Spirit throughout salvation history. While the Holy Spirit is the agent of transformation, the power of the Spirit is not without content but is power to transform the believer into the likeness of Christ. The Holy Spirit is the Agent of the "real participation" in Christ. In a sermon on Isaiah 9:6, Fletcher wrote,

> There he must feel the nail that piercd his every limb, he must be fastend not have power to Stir, & there bleed out all its strength—& not only so but he must give up the Ghost and feel the power of His death then being burid with Christ by the baptism of the holy Ghost Thou must Farther experience the power of his Resurrection—thy Soul must be filld with Light love & power the Spirit of the living God must ~~agai~~ come into thee thou must partake of a more excellent life—& then the Child that is born Shall be grown up unto the measure of the stature of the fulness of Xt.[231]

The Holy Spirit has been active throughout the history of humankind: "[T]he Holy Ghost, by which the souls of the faithful are divinely regenerated, is the same Spirit that primarily *moved upon the face of the waters.*"[232] Fletcher made a distinction between water baptism and Spirit baptism as was noted previously. This distinction was partially an historical issue. Fletcher argued that Wesley held the doctrine of the full Christian regeneration rests on the full or Pentecostal dispensation of the Spirit.[233] Citing Wesley's sermon on *Christian Perfection* and specifically his explanation of John 7:38, Fletcher argued that the Holy Spirit was not given "in ~~the~~ his sanctifying graces" until after Jesus was glorified.[234] True spiritual transformation was unavailable in the preceding eras of history because the sanctifying graces of the Spirit were not operable until after the completion of Christ's earthly ministry. The outpouring of the Spirit is the summation of history and retains an eschatological dimension. Fletcher is confident that Pentecost is the dawn of the new age or the dawn of the kingdom of God—its characteristic

---

231. JF→sermon, Isaiah 9.6 b.
232. Fletcher-Portrait, 2:167.
233. Fletcher-New, 77; L. Wood, "'Essay on the Doctrine of the New Birth' by," 46.
234. Ibid.

sign is the baptism of the Spirit. The dispensation of the Spirit serves to perfect the dispensations of the Father and Son;[235] the gospel is perfected in the dispensation of the Holy Spirit.[236]

Christian Perfection

In the *Third Check*, Fletcher argued that final salvation is conditioned upon the obedience of the believer to divine law. Final justification is reserved for "those who bear fruit unto perfection, according to one or another of the divine dispensations."[237] The basis for judgment is not equivalent for all persons, but is accommodated to the measure of grace and knowledge of the dispensation of the worshipper. While perfection is demanded in all dispensations, the same measure of perfection is not demanded of all individuals regardless of dispensation. Fletcher conceived of different degrees of perfection that correspond with the various dispensations of divine grace. In the *Last Check*, the degrees of perfection are as follows: gentile's perfection, the Jew's perfection, the perfection of infant Christianity, the perfection of adult, perfect Christianity, the perfection of disembodied spirits, and the complete perfection of glorified saints.[238]

The believers under these various dispensations must employ the means of grace bestowed in order to attain the measure of perfection demanded under their respective dispensation. Achieving the perfection of a particular dispensation is to arrive at its fullness: "The doctrine of Christian perfection is entirely founded on the privileges of the Christian dispensation in its fullness."[239] How did Fletcher distinguish the fullness of the dispensation of the Spirit from inferior dispensations?

In his 7 March 1778 letter to Mary Bosanquet, Fletcher, writing from Marseille, responded to accusations that there was material difference between his own doctrine of Christian perfection and that of Wesley's.

> A word to the important contents. [I cannot] be answerable for what the person you mention thinks [of] Mr. Wesley or me, or our sentiments. Nothing is more [common] than to see people drawing inferences from [premises] which are partly false and partly true. I can [only answer] for myself, and for what I esteem to be [the truth. If you ask] me what I think to be truth with

235. Fletcher-Portrait, 2:167.
236. Ibid., 2:212.
237. Fl-W1856, 2:434.
238. Fl-W1856, 4:462–64.
239. Fl-W1856, 4:114.

respect to [Christian] perfection, I reply, that my sentiments are exprosed to the world in my Essay on Xn Perfection—and in my Essay on truth, where I lay the stress of the promise and doctrine, on the great promise of the Father and on the Christian fulness of the Spirit. This I have done more particularly in a treatise on the birth of the Spirit, which treatise is not yet published. I do not rest the doctrine of Xn perfection on the absence of sin that is the perfection of a dove, or a lamb—nor [on] the loving of God with all one's power, for I believe th[at] all perfect gentiles and jews have done so: but on the fulness of that superior, nobler, warmer, and more pow[er]ful love, which the apostle calls the love of the Spirit, or the love of God shed abroad by the Holy Ghost given unto the christian believers, who (since the day of Pentecost) go on to the perfection of the christian dispensation. The pious jews, and the believing disciples of John wh were children of God under their dispensation, and consequently they had the Spirit of God—the spirit of adoption but not according to the fulness pentecostal fulness of the Christian Church. They had love, but not the first love of the primitive church, a more fervent and purer love this, which perfects in one all who drink of it, and do not not leave it. You will find my views of this matter in Mr. W's sermons on Chr. Perf. and on Th Scriptural Christianity: with this difference that I would distinguish more exactly between the believers baptized with the pentecostal power of the Holy Ghost, and the believer who (like the apostles after our Lord's ascension) were is not yet fill'd with that power.[240]

Fletcher acknowledged that he had developed his mentor's theology; specifically Fletcher held to more precise contrast between the pre-Pentecost disciples and the post-Pentecost disciples than did Wesley. As W. Brian Fletcher pointed out that John Fletcher held, quoting Wesley in his support, that the promises that were enjoyed by the Jews in a measure were not fully realized until the Christian dispensation and the outpouring of the Holy Spirit.[241]

In the OT, Pentecost commemorated the giving of the law from Mount Sinai on the fiftieth day after the nation of Israel left Egypt. Fletcher recognized that in Acts, Pentecost was the re-inscription of the law on the hearts of believers. In the *Essay on the Doctrine of Dispensations*, Fletcher

---

240. JF→MBF, 7 March 1778. Due to the fragmentation of the original certain words are added in brackets from Tyerman's transcription (Tyerman, *Wesley's Designated Successor*, 411).

241. W. B. Fletcher, "Christian Perfection in Wesley and Fletcher with," 78.

introduced three editions of the law—one under each dispensation. He identified this edition of the law as the "most spiritual edition of the moral law."[242] Whereas the first edition of the law was written on tables of stone and the second written on "the drum of the ears of Christ disciples," the third edition of the law under the dispensation of the Spirit was spiritual. It was written on the hearts of believers: "The Spirit of this law, together with power to keep it, was first given to the 120 Disciples of Christ assembled at Jerusalem in an upper room."[243] Fletcher emphasized that the Spirit "the God of love began to dwell in all believers thus baptized: Love, the fulfilling of the law overflow'd their souls."[244] The indwelling Holy Spirit enlightens the spiritual senses, filling the heart of the believers with love and enables them to fulfill the law of love.

Fletcher identified Pentecost with true Christianity and held that spiritual regeneration (as opposed to ritualistic or partial regeneration) makes one a true Christian. Does regeneration, which makes one a true Christian, constitute Christian perfection or is Christian perfection a result of growth or subsequent baptisms of the Spirit following an initiatory Christian experience? In *Discours sur la Régénération*, Fletcher clearly distinguished between justification and sanctification as two separate operations of the Spirit. The latter term is defined broadly as the progressive restoration of the image of God. The Holy Spirit operates upon the subject, a justified sinner, bringing about a progressive restoration of the image of God until the believer is filled with the fullness of God or with the love of God. To attain to the fullness of God or to be filled with the love of God is to experience "Régénération complette."[245] Complete regeneration is the result of the process of sanctification and is not to be identified with the initiatory experience, evangelical regeneration. Evangelical regeneration, the initiatory experience in the Christian life, constitutes one a Christian, but it is distinct from what follows, i.e., complete regeneration.

The various degrees of regeneration have one goal: the perfection of the believer in love. The goal and advanced privileges of the believers under the dispensation of the Spirit is perfect love:

> [B]efore we can rank among perfect Christians, we must receive so much of the truth and Spirit of Christ by faith, as to have the pure love of God and man shed abroad in our hearts by the Holy Ghost given unto us, and to be filled with the meek and lowly mind which was in Christ. And if one outpouring of the Spirit,

---

242. Fletcher-Dispensations, 19.
243. Ibid., 21.
244. Ibid., 25.
245. Fletcher-Discours, 35.

one bright manifestation of the sanctifying truth, so empties us of self, as to fill us with the mind of Christ, and with pure love, we are undoubtedly Christians, in the full sense of the word.[246]

The apex of Christian experience was defined as perfect love—"the love of God is shed abroad in our hearts by the Holy Ghost which is given unto us" (Romans 5:5).

True Christian

An important emphasis in Wesley's theology was upon primitive Christianity or genuine Christianity. Richard P. Heitzenrater discusses Wesley's developing views about genuine Christianity and his views on the "two orders of Christians," which was developed in his sermon *The More Excellent Way* (1787). The two orders included first those Christians who respected the externals of the Christian faith (i.e., avoiding sin, doing good works, and attending the ordinances of God); the second order of Christians included those who were faithful not only externally, but were faithful also internally to Christ.[247] Heitzenrater concludes that mature Wesley had a growing appreciation for the almost Christian states, e.g., faith of a servant and viewed more positively those in the first category of Christians as nominal Christians whereas previously he had labeled them "half-Christians."[248] In a late sermon (1786), *On Divine Providence*, Wesley posited three concentric circles of divine providence of human beings. The outer circle included "the whole race of mankind;" the next smaller circle included those "that are called Christians;" the innermost circle contained "only the real Christians."[249] God is more particularly concerned for those within the inner circles than for those in the outer circle, but cares for them nevertheless. Heitzenrater notes that Wesley's depreciation of the pre-Christian states "begins to disappear in later years" as Wesley developed greater pastoral sensitivity and theological acumen.[250] This may have been due, in part, to Fletcher's influence and his pastoral accommodation in recognizing the validity of the faith of the almost Christians. While Fletcher recognized the faith of the almost Christians as valid, he did not recognize it as true Christian experience.

---

246. Fl-W1856, 6:168.
247. BiCentWJW, 2:265.
248. Heitzenrater, "Great Expectations," 87.
249. BiCentWJW, 2:542–43.
250. Heitzenrater, "Great Expectations," 87.

According to John Knight, Fletcher held that "one becomes a Christian in the dispensation of the Son, as the disciples of Jesus; and a 'true' Christian with full assurance (perfection) in the dispensation of the Holy Spirit, as the disciples at Pentecost."[251] However, both Fletcher and Wesley held that one becomes a true Christian at Pentecost.[252] Indeed, Fletcher asserted that the mark of the true Christian is being filled with the Spirit. One's identity as a Christian hinges upon receiving the promise of the Father: "St. Peter unreservedly offers it to the truly penitent (Acts ii.38); and St. Paul every where declares, that it is the common privilege of Christians to *be filled with the Spirit* (Eph. v.18; 1 Cor. vi.19). Nay, he even intimates, that the name of *christian* should be refused to those who have not received the promise of the Father (Rom. viii.9)."[253] Fletcher's theology does not accord with Holiness scholars who assert the pre-Pentecost apostles were "real Christians" who were entirely sanctified on the day of Pentecost. Consistent with Wesley's theology, Fletcher's doctrine of dispensations viewed the pre-Pentecost disciples as almost (or imperfect) Christians whose faith was preparatory to the full Christian dispensation.[254] True Christian faith "is one in its great object, 'God manifest in the flesh:' one in its great promise, 'the promise of the Father,' or 'the kingdom in the Holy Ghost:' one in its new commandment, brotherly, universal love, that perfects believers in one, and makes them partakers of so great salvation."[255] Genuine Christianity is linked to the dispensation of the Spirit. However, human beings must pass through

---

251. J. Knight, "John William Fletcher and the Early Methodist," 28.

252. J. Knight writes, "Wesley agreed that one becomes a 'true' Christian, as the disciples at Pentecost; but that there is yet a higher stage of the Christian life, namely Christian perfection" (ibid., 28). However, Heitzenrater does not agree: "The implication is that the latter, being born again in the higher sense, is the genuine Christian" (Heitzenrater, "Great Expectations," 74).

253. Fletcher-Portrait, 2:181.

254. J. Wesley commented on Acts 1:5, "*Ye shall be baptized with the Holy Ghost—* And so are all true believers, to the end of the world" (*Explanatory Notes upon the New Testament*, in loco). On June 16, 1747, Wesley discussed the following question with other ministers: "Q. 4. But do you not know that the Apostles themselves had it not till after the day of Pentecost?" The following reply was given: "A. The Apostles themselves had not the proper Christian faith till after the day of Pentecost" (WJW, 8:291).

255. Fl-W1856, 4:92–93. In another place, Fletcher wrote, "Will you become true Christians, the members of the Lord Jesus, the temples of the Holy Ghost?" [Fl-W1856, 8:362]. In his sermon on 2 Corinthians 5:17, Fletcher insists that in order to be a true Christian, one must be regenerated "by being truly born again, not of water only, but of the Spirit of Christ" (Fl-W1856, 8:364). He wrote, "[R]egeneration is absolutely necessary in order to be a true Christian" (Fl-W1856, 8:364).

TRUE CHRISTIANITY

three states before becoming true Christians: an unawakened or "natural man," "penitent man," and finally a "true believer."[256]

Summary

Many of Fletcher's interpreters have concluded that Fletcher diverged from the theology of early Methodism. However, this chapter has traced the development of Fletcher's theology as an amalgamation of certain strains of the theologies of the Wesley brothers. Furthermore, Fletcher reified John Wesley's distinction between the doctrines of justification "what God *does for us* through His Son" and sanctification "what he *works in us* by His Spirit." The doctrine of justification resonates with the dispensation of the Son, which is analogous to the experience of the "almost" Christian, and the doctrine of sanctification (including evangelical regeneration) resonates with the dispensation of the Spirit, which is analogous to the experience of the "altogether" Christian. The reification provided an overall structure for Fletcher's theological system within which were a great variety of human experiences of God.

This chapter and the preceding one question implicitly the Wesleyan-holiness paradigm that has been used to interpret Fletcher's thought. The categories of that tradition are too narrow to conceptualize the scope of Fletcher's soteriology and pneumatology. Fletcher recognized the validity of many experiences and nuanced his soteriology accordingly providing for many degrees of salvation; however not all experiences of God were valid *Christian* experience. Valid Christian experience was described best by the Apostle Paul as "the love of God" that "is shed abroad in our hearts by the Holy Ghost which is given unto us" (Romans 5:5). Despite the variety of experiences, Fletcher attempted to retain the *telos* of soteriology as Christian perfection, which provided unity to his theological system.[257]

---

256. Fl-W1856, 8:339–40.

257. Indeed, as David R. Wilson points out the focus of Fletcher's entire ministry "was building . . . a more faithful version of Anglicanism, ergo, primitive Christianity" (Wilson, "Church and Chapel," 163). Cf. ibid., 189, 229.

Conclusion

ALTHOUGH JOHN FLETCHER HAS been called the "Arminian of the Arminians,"[1] one of the key doctrines of his theological system was the doctrine of accommodation, which is largely viewed as a foundational doctrine of the Calvinistic system.[2] Central to this doctrine is the God of love who, knowing human limitations and the noetic effects of sin, acts in accordance with them in order to communicate effectively. Theologians who have studied Fletcher's writings have acknowledged that the doctrine of dispensations provides a structure to Fletcher's theology; however, they have failed to recognize that the doctrine of accommodation is the principal foundation for Fletcher's doctrine of dispensations.

PRACTICAL IMPLICATIONS

The doctrine of accommodation is not merely theoretical, but has, in Fletcher's thought, some significant implications for Christian ministry. As God accommodated divine revelation to the fallen human condition in order to communicate effectively to human beings, Christian ministers who participate in the redemptive activity of God must accommodate their ministry to their hearers in order to communicate the gospel effectively. This is the fundamental dialectic of Fletcher's theological system and of his functional synergism: divine condescending grace and human perfecting faith.[3] Fletcher's theology may be summarized as follows: God has, through history, accommodated divine revelation to the limitations of finite human capacity and calls Christian ministers to accommodate themselves to their hearers (congregants) in order for them to appropriate the Christian message.

1. D. S. Schaff, "Fletcher, John William," 332.
2. In Calvinism, divine accommodation is made only to the elect.
3. Fl-W1856, 5:101.

The practical implications of the doctrine of accommodation were made explicit in his writings. In *The Portrait of St. Paul* (1779), which provides a theology of ministry, Fletcher wrote, "Hence, it is necessary, that the faithful minister should acquaint himself with the different conditions and capacities of his hearers, *if he would happily accommodate spiritual things to spiritual men*. Without this knowledge, he will, under every dispensation, run the hazard of refusing to advanced christians the solid nourishment they need, and of presenting to the natural man that celestial manna which his very soul abhors."[4] Fletcher insisted that "the true minister studies the different dispensations in order to qualify himself for the discharge of every part of his duty" and identified four categories of people in light of their spiritual development. The minister must have not only an understanding of the various states, but "an experimental knowledge" of them without which "a minister can no more lead sinners to evangelical perfection, than an illiterate peasant can communicate sufficient intelligence to his rustic companions to pass an examination for the highest degree in a university."[5] He wrote that the true minister "easily distinguishes the mixed multitude of his hearers into a variety of classes."

Fletcher made application of his theology of dispensations in his sermons. He insisted that preachers must make clear the distinctions between the three states of faith: "He, who preaches the Gospel, without tracing out the lines which separate the three dispensations of grace, may be said to exhibit a sundial, upon which the hours are unmarked, and from which little else but confusion if not dangerous mistakes, can be expected to flow."[6] Fletcher made clear these distinctions in his sermons. This conclusion evaluates Fletcher's sermon notes in order to gain insight into his pastoral practice and ministry and will endeavour to provide a more complete picture of Fletcher's doctrine of dispensations through the fundamental doctrine of accommodation.

CHARACTERISTICS OF THE SERMONS[7]

One rather distinct feature of Fletcher's sermon notes is the amount of space that Fletcher dedicated to application of his messages to his hearers, which appear frequently in the conclusion of his sermons.[8] For example, Fletcher

---

4. Fletcher-Portrait, 2:156; emphasis added.
5. Ibid., 2:153.
6. Ibid., 2:207.
7. Wilson analyzes the sermons at length ("Church and Chapel," Appendix 1, 285ff.).
8. An example is found in the sermon, "The Nature of Regeneration" (Fl-W1883, 4:138).

devoted much space to application in his sermon on John 1:12, which was preached at Smisby; the application portion of his sermon notes consumes exactly one half of the space dedicated to the entire sermon.[9]

Another unique feature of the sermons is the way that Fletcher categorized his parishioners according to their spiritual development or stages of faith. Nearly sixty percent of the extant sermons, contain some type of categorization, normally in the conclusion in which the sermon notes indicate an address is made to the persons in each of these categories.[10] The categories emerge from his morphology of conversion, which, as is stated above, is analogous to his doctrine of dispensations.

CATEGORIES OF CONGREGANTS IN FLETCHER'S SERMONS

Fletcher employed many different categories for his hearers. However the predominant pattern that emerges is sinners, awakened sinners, and believers. In a sermon on 1 Corinthians 2:14, which appears in the *Works*, Fletcher noted three states in his morphology of conversion:

> There are then three states through which all the children of Adam must pass before they can be real Christians. That of an unawakened or "natural man," who neither loves nor fears God: that of a penitent man, or returning sinner, who, being awakened into a real concern for his salvation, fears God, and the threatenings of his law, and dreads death with its consequences: and, thirdly, that of a man "under grace," or a true believer, who loves God above all persons and things, and rejoices in the expiation and pardon of his sins, which he has now received in Christ by a living faith.[11]

Fletcher reflected Wesley's understanding of the Methodist *ordo salutis* in his writings,[12] but made pastoral application by crafting addresses to parishioners in each of the three stages of spiritual development in the conclusions of his sermons.

---

9. JF→sermon, John 1.12 a. Cf. JF→sermon, 2 Peter 3.14 in which Fletcher dedicates more than half of his written notes to application.

10. Out of all the 321 sermons, 130 do not have any categorization of the hearers. In addition, there are a number of sermons whose entire structure is dedicated to the categorization of parishioners.

11. Fl-W1856, 8:340.

12. Fletcher's use of the above categories reflects an understanding of J. Wesley's doctrine of the order of salvation and of the degrees of faith (BiCentWJW, 1:248).

AN ANALYSIS OF THE CATEGORIES

In order to analyze the various categories adequately, they have been labeled as follows: sinners = A; awakened sinners = B; believers = C. In the table below, the most frequently used synonyms are shown; the numbers indicate the number of times the synonym appears.

Category A: "Sinners"	Category B: "Seekers"	Category C: "Believers"
Variations: sinners (38), careless sinners (22), ungodly (17), self-righteous (12), unconverted sinners (10), Pharisees (10), unbelievers (9), worldlings (7), natural man (4), unawakened (4), foolish virgins (4), wicked (3), open sinners (3), stouthearted (2), publicans and harlots (2), openly impenitent (2), deceivers (2, with false repentance), infidels (3), despisers of Christ's doctrine (2), moralists (2), professors (2)	Variations: mourners (56), seeking souls (13), penitent (7), convinced (6), awakened (5), willing (5, but unable), poor (3), guilty (3), wounded (2)	Variations: believers (68), Christians (12), children of God (5), godly (4), weak Christians (4), blessed/happy souls (2), born again (2), converted (2), saints (2), wise virgins (2)

In the table below, the number of occurrences of addresses to the categories and their synonyms are indicated.[13]

	Category A	Category B	Category C
Normal labels	sinners	awakened sinners	believers
Number of sermons that contain addresses	159	125	129
Total number of addresses to each category	224	136	130

13. Occasionally, Fletcher employs other categories of congregants that do not appear to fit the above categories. These appear sixty-eight times in the sermon notes; forty-nine of the sixty-eight times are occurrences of an address to backsliders.

Conclusion

The normal pattern is ABC with addresses to sinners, to awakened sinners, and to believers. This pattern occurs approximately 50 times in the sermons. Another pattern is AB: addresses to sinners and to awakened sinners, which appears 10 times. The third pattern that will be mentioned is ABDC: an address to sinners, awakened sinners, backsliders, and believers; this materializes 10 times in the sermons. In the discussion below, the three categories, sinners, seekers, and believers, mentioned above will be treated in greater detail below.

Sinners

Variety of Terms:

The category that Fletcher used most frequently was "sinners" and its synonyms. Often Fletcher added adjectives, employed synonyms or made adaptations, providing a great deal of variety within the designation. In the sermon on Acts 5, Fletcher adds the following adjectives and gives a more specific application for each: "lost sinners," "guilty sinners," "weak sinners," and "stubborn sinners."[14] Fletcher often adapted the categories to the biblical passage from which his sermon is drawn or used clear biblical imagery: ye worldly syrians, those who are of Ahab's mind, you who don't flee or permit others to do so, you that groan in Egypt, ye publicans and harlots, ye outward Pharisees, ye citizens of Sodom, ye foolish virgins, those who are like Festus are neither (i.e., almost or altogether Christians), etc.

Observations on the Condition of the Hearers:

The condition of those in category A is described clearly. They are in bondage to sin; however, their prison is of their own making. Their lack of foresight, their unconcern and indifference toward their own sinful condition causes a lack of good judgment regarding their response to divine overtures of grace. The hearers in this category are labeled as careless or foolish. At times, Fletcher characterized them as troubled or miserable because they were apparently conscious of their sin, but normally he described them as oblivious to their condition; they lacked consciousness of their own condition when the plight of their sin was so evident.

In his sermon on John 1:12, Fletcher classified those who had received Christian baptism under the category of sinners: "1. 1. <u>Sinner</u>. You are one

---

14. JF→sermon, Acts 5.42.

TRUE CHRISTIANITY

of <u>his own</u>. You are his <u>creature</u> by <u>Creation</u>—his <u>brother</u> by your human nature—his <u>Servant</u> by Baptism—his <u>follower</u> by Profession—his <u>Spouse</u> by name Xn."[15] Though members of his parish may have been recipients of the ordinances of the Church, this did not guarantee their standing before God.

The Nature of the Address

In a sermon on Luke 15:7, Fletcher summarized the nature of his address to sinners: "The unawakend Sinner for example ~~the lost wild sheep~~ must be continualy pursued with the threatnings of the law till he awakes ~~stops~~ he must hear Cursed is he that does not persevere in doing all the things that are writ in the book of the law."[16] Because Fletcher perceived the parishioners in this category to be unconcerned and indifferent, his address to this group of people assumes a hortatory tone. In a sermon on 2 Peter 3:14, Fletcher addressed the ungodly "How will you stand in that day You tremble at a Storm, what will you do when all the elements shall melt & pass away. If even the earth must be burnt up because it hath been a stage of Sin O what fire will seize upon the wicked! what wrath!"[17]

Seekers

The next category of congregants is the category of seekers. A variety of synonyms are employed for this category.

Variety of Terms:

The most frequently employed designation is "mourners," which is used 55 times. Other designations include: ye that are awakened, ye that tremble at Gods word, ye humbled ones, downcast professors, you that will be the Lord's people; dejected; seekers of true repentance, unconverted that receive the word, John's disciples, wandering, heavy-laden sinners, etc.

---

15. JF→sermon, John 1.12 a.
16. JF→sermon, Luke 15.7.
17. JF→sermon, 2 Peter 3.14.

Conclusion

OBSERVATIONS ON THE CONDITION OF THE HEARERS:

The greatest distinction between category A and category B is the attitude of the hearers. Those in category A are sinners, but are not yet convinced or convicted of their sins. The hearers in category B are also sinners, but are different from category A because they are convinced of their sins and are weary of them, but do not have the power to overcome sin. In a sermon on Romans 7:24, Fletcher described awakened sinners at length. The eyes of their understanding are opened to the judgment of God and to the fact that God rewards all persons according to their works and words. In addition, they understand the meaning of the law of God and their own sinful condition in the light of the demands of the law. Their attitude is described as downcast, dejected, or wounded as any thought of their goodness is dispelled by a recognition of their true standing before God. They fear the impending judgment of God, but they are unable to free themselves from the bondage of sin.[18]

THE NATURE OF THE ADDRESS:

In the sermon on Luke 15:7, Fletcher wrote of the content of the address to the seekers: "[T]he repenting Sinner the returning sheep should hear not[h]ing but tender invitations to embrace ~~to lay hold~~ Gods Mercy and to lay hold of the promises of the Gospel by faith in a dying saviour."[19] The tone of the address to category B differs from the tone of the address to category A: Fletcher encouraged the mourners in his congregation to believe and to appropriate the promise of salvation proffered to them. In a sermon on Matthew 14:26-27, Fletcher wrote, "<u>Mourners.</u>—Toil yet. It not all vain till Jesus comes.—He is here.—you fear, & cry to Him.—Hear Him encouraging you.—Venture with Peter.—It is I. be not afraid."[20] Consistently, Fletcher encouraged this group to believe in Christ; the lack of faith in Christ was the primary burden of his addresses to them.

Believers

The next category of congregants is believers. A variety of terms is used to describe these congregants.

18. JF→sermon, Romans 7.24.
19. JF→sermon, Luke 15.7.
20. JF→sermon, Matthew 14.26-27.

TRUE CHRISTIANITY

Variety of Terms:

The category C hearers are most commonly called believers. Other designations for this category include, brothers of Jesus, healed souls, righteous, those who build on the Cornerstone, suffering believers, those who like Paul are altogether Christians, saved, sanctified, etc.

Observations:

The hearers in category C differ from the hearers in category B. The latter do not have assurance whereas the believers in category C have repented and have assurance of salvation. They have a filial relationship with God and are described as righteous. In one of Fletcher's printed sermons on 1 Corinthians 2:14, he describes the state of a true Christian as "a state of peace, joy, love and holiness" but clarifies that in order to attain such a state, "he must go through a course of fear, anxiety, and repentance."[21] The seeking state is compared to the "spirit of bondage" and the "true Christian" state is compared to the "Spirit of adoption."[22] Thus, assurance of salvation is one of the important characteristics that distinguishes the believers from the mourners in category B.

Conversion opens the eye of faith so that believers can behold the grace and mercy of God. In an unpublished sermon on Romans 7:24, Fletcher described the transformation that is wrought in the believer:

> Heavenly healing light now breaks in upon his soul. He looks on him whom he had pierced, and God who out of darkness commanded light to shine, shineth in his heart. He sees the light of the glorious love of God in the face of J.C. He has a divine evidence of things not seen by sense even of the deep things of God more particularly of the love of God of his pardoning love to him that believes ~~savingly~~ in Jesus: Over power'd with the Sight his whole soul cries out with believing Thomas My Lord and my God, for he sees all his iniquities layd on him who bare them in his own body on the tree: he beholds the Lamb of God taking away his sins, and sees his soul washd in the blood of the everlasting covenant. Here end at once the Guilt and the power of Sin for knowing and feeling that hence forth he is a member of Christ he experiences immediatly le power of his resurrection he passes from death unto life and can now say I am crucified with Christ, Nevertheless I live yet not I but Christ

---

21. Fl-W1856, 8:339.
22. Ibid.

lives in me, and the life which I now live, I live by faith in the Son of God who loved <u>me</u> and gave himself for <u>me</u> His heaviness is turned into joy: His bondage is ended for his heart standeth fast believing in the Lord, His fears of the Devil of Death and hell are vanishd: How could he fear knowing that he that has the kees of hell and death is on his side and has sealed him for the day of the redemption by giving him the earnest of his spirit—And where the spirit of the Lord is there is liberty liberty not only from guilt and fear but from the power of sin, from that heaviest of all yokes that basest of all bondage, Sin no longer reigns in his mortal body as St. Paul expresses it but being now made free from sin he is become the Servant of righteousness, for in the moment he receives power over sin he receives also power to do God's works which he never had before being not justified and having not receiv'd the spirit of Christ . . . Thus having peace with God thro' our L.J.C. rejoicing in hope of the glory of God and having power over ~~all~~ sin over every evil temper and word & work he is a living witness of the Glorious liberty of the Sons of God All his former sins are blotted out for he is freely justified by grace By living faith he is one with Christ as Christ is one with his father ~~so that~~ For ~~he~~ as he dyed with him by true repentance so he is risen from the dead with him.[23]

According to the above description, believers have attained normative Christian experience, as Fletcher viewed it, and were clearly regenerated.

THE NATURE OF THE ADDRESS:

The nature of the addresses to sinners was principally hortatory, and the addresses to mourners encouraged them to trust Christ for salvation. The message to believers is principally irenic and affirming, but often Fletcher warned them to be on their guard. In the following sample application from his sermon on John 3:7, Fletcher warns the believers against drawing back, challenges them to spiritual growth, encourages them to perseverance and to good works: "To all those who are born again. 1. Do not draw back from the light as Esau did. 2. Eat. Grow unto Christ in all things. to the measure of 3. Use the life given as well as keep it. 4. Help others into life, & live as born of God."[24]

---

23. JF→sermon Romans 7.24.
24. JF→sermon, John 14.7 b.

TRUE CHRISTIANITY

THE MINISTER AND THE PRACTICE OF ACCOMMODATION

It must be noted that the accommodation that Fletcher advocated did not alter the message of the Word of God.[25] In one place, Fletcher cautioned against over accommodating: "Special care is, however, to be taken that this charitable condescension may never betray the interests of truth and virtue."[26]

However, Fletcher recognized that divine accommodation must be played out over time; for him, accommodation was progressive. It began with inferior knowledge and progressed to increasing superior knowledge. "To require of spiritual infants any high and important acts of faith in Jesus Christ, or in the Holy Spirit, before they are taught to entertain just notions of the Supreme Being, would be equally unreasonable, as for a man to pretend, that it is possible to make a good geometrician of an ignorant peasant, by instructing him to repeat the terms of Euclid's last propositions, without ever bringing him to a true understanding of the first."[27] Thus, knowledge is progressive, and experimental knowledge of believers is contingent upon the divine, cognitive revelation. The minister's responsibility is to lead parishioners in an ever-increasing spiritual development until they reach Christian perfection by dispensing truth in appropriate measures as a physician appropriately dispenses medicine.[28]

Thus, in order to minister effectively, ministers need to have an understanding of the three stages of faith; the dispensations of grace become a subject of preaching and application to the congregation.[29] In a sermon on Luke 15:7, Fletcher assumed that pastors who know best their congregations are best suited to make application of the stages of faith to parishioners: "A The ministers of the Gospel who desires to divide the word of God aright and to give to everyone in due season the portion that is proper for him finds theimselfves often at a loss especially if he is called to preach to a congregation unknown to him: Every congregation is made up of three sorts or classes of people."[30] More appropriate applications could be made by a pastor who knows the members of the parish than a visiting preacher or

25. He would have agreed with Wesley who also cautioned against over accommodating (BiCentWJW, 4:250).

26. Fl-W1856, 6:294.

27. Fletcher-Portrait, 2:282–83.

28. Ibid., 2:165.

29. Ibid., 2:137. Fletcher signaled to the congregation his intention to conclude with application to different categories of persons (JF→sermon, Luke 15.7).

30. JF→sermon, Luke 15.7.

an itinerant preacher.³¹ Each person in each category of parishioners should receive instruction in every sermon: "Now all these should find Some spiritual food for their souls in every sermon."³²

The accommodation of the minister to parishioners extends not only to preaching, but also to every aspect of ministerial practice.³³ The source of the willingness to accommodate lies in the love of the pastor for the people: "Hence the charitable pastor cannot act otherwise than with a holy condescension toward all men, and especially toward the ignorant and poor, with whom the ministers of the present age will scarcely deign to converse."³⁴

In addition to the minister's responsibility, Fletcher admonished the stronger believers in his congregation to consider their responsibility toward the weaker members of the parish. Not only are ministers to accommodate others, but the members of the parish must do so as well. Fletcher pointed out that all saints have not experienced the same spiritual growth, and after noting the marks of the weak, some words of encouragement for them and some of their duties, Fletcher closed his discourse with some admonitions of the "duties incumbent on the strong towards them [i.e., the spiritually weak]."³⁵ These admonitions are as follows:

1. Those who are strong ought to bear with the infirmities of ye weak.
2. They ought to look more upon the good than the evil.
3. In things indifferent let them deny themselves & please the weak, 1 Cor. 8.13.
4. Support the weak—be patient toward all. 1 Th: V.14. Es: 35.3.
5. Take heed that ye offend not one of these little ones. it were better.

---

31. Such understanding was perhaps behind Fletcher's refusal to itinerate with Wesley.

32. JF→sermon, Luke 15.7. While all persons should be addressed in every sermon, Mary Fletcher insisted that an address made to persons in a higher category of spiritual development may not be understood by persons in a lower category: "It must be observed this sermon is addrest to sincere penitents—careless sinners have nothing to do with it nor will they understand the language. but sincere penitents fervent of the Light of a Brighter faith Frequently condemn themselves as having no work of God upon them; for that reason they are here invited to cast themselves just as they are on the Savior" (M. Fletcher, Notes on a sermon, Fletcher-Tooth, JRULM, 36, 6).

33. Wilson argues that Fletcher's church extension strategy was an attempt to "establish church religion as the religion of the people" and "to take the church to the people, rather than just trying to get people to the church" (Wilson, "Church and Chapel," 122, 130). Such is an example of the doctrine of accommodation applied to practical ministry in light of the established Church's failure to accommodate (ibid., 124).

34. Fl-W1856, 6:293.

35. JF→sermon, Ephesians 3.8 a.

6. To suit all things to the Capacity of the weak. 1 Cor: 3.2.
7. To strengthen them by words & examples.
8. To cast a Mantle on the Infirmities of the weak. l.[ove] covereth a m[ultitude] The mantle of Wisdom—compassion—forgetfulness.
9. To sympathize with the weak. Xt. bears the lambs.
10. To honor the weak. as partakers of the same grace.[36]

Furthermore, in *The Portrait of St. Paul*, Fletcher pointed out that one of the advantages of the doctrine of dispensations is the ability to act redemptively toward other believers: "By the light of this doctrine, true worshippers, of every different class, may be taught to acknowledge and esteem one another, according to their different degrees of faith."[37]

The doctrine of accommodation was central to both Fletcher's dogmatic theology and his theology of ministry. God who accommodated divine revelation to the frailties of the human condition exemplifies for Christian ministers the way to dispense appropriately the grace of God. Foundational to both divine revelation and Christian ministry is love. Love, the reigning attribute of the divine nature, must be the reigning characteristic of the minister's life and ministry. Like early Methodists and especially his close friend, Charles Wesley who proclaimed "thy name and thy nature is love,"[38] Fletcher extolled the love of God; for him, the doctrine of the love of God became the *terminus a quo* of his theological system. John William Fletcher who was resolved, as John Wesley noted, to be "altogether a Christian"[39] emphasized perfect love as the *telos* of the Christian life and as the goal of God's salvific activity in history—altogether Christianity from an altogether Christian.

---

36. JF→sermon, Ephesians 3.8 a.
37. Fletcher-Portrait, 207.
38. BiCentWJW, 7:250–52.
39. Ibid., 21:481.

Bibliography

Abbey, C. J., and J. H. Overton. *The English Church in the Eighteenth Century*. London: Longmans, Green, 1885.
Actes du colloque de Nyons, 1735–1850. Archives Cantonales Vaudoises, Lausanne, Bdb pp. 648–53.
Adams, Charles. "Walking with God: Mrs. Mary Fletcher." *Ladies Repository* 22/9 (1863) 513–17.
Adams, J. W. "By What Means Can Methodism Be Made More Aggressive?." *Zion's Herald* 71/9 (1893): 67.
Adams, Miss. "Letter to John Fletcher. 8 March 1782." The Fletcher-Tooth Collection, The John Rylands University Library, The University of Manchester, MAM Fl. 37/1.
Agnew, Milton S. "Baptized with the Spirit." *Wesleyan Theological Journal* 14/2 (1979) 7–14.
Alden, Joseph. "The First Battle-Field." *Christian Advocate* 58/8 (1883) 119.
Alibion. "Notes from England." *Christian Advocate* 54/16 (1879) 249.
———. "Regular Correspondence." *Christian Advocate* 58/2 (1883) 20.
Allen, Margaret. *Fletcher of Madeley*. 1905. Reprint, Allegheny, PA: Allegheny Wesleyan Methodist Connection, 1974.
Allen, R. W. "Christian Experiences In Its Varied Phases And States." *Zion's Herald* 55/38 (1878) 298.
Allison, C. FitzSimons. *The Rise of Moralism: The Proclamation of the Gospel from Hooker to Baxter*. Wilton, CT: Morehouse-Barlow, 1966.
Amiel, Henri-Frédéric, and August Bouvier. *L'enseignement supérieur à Genève depuis la fondation de l'académie, le 5 juin 1559 jusqu'à l'inauguration de l'université, le 26 octobre 1876, facultés et chaires-professeurs et redacteurs-étudiants*. Geneva: Rambox & Schuchardt, 1878.
Anderson, John Corbet. *Shropshire: Its Early History and Antiquities, Comprising a Description of the Important British and Roman Remains in that County: its Saxon and Danish Reminiscences; The Domesday Survey of Shropshire: And the History of its Forests, Towns, Manors, Abbeys, Churches, Castles, and Great Baronial Houses*. London: Willis & Sotheran, 1864.
Anderson, William K., editor. *Methodism*. Nashville: Methodist Publishing House, 1947.
Anonyme. *A Letter to the Rev. Mr. Fletcher of Madeley on the Differences Subsisting Between Him and the Hon. and Rev. Mr. Shirley*. Bath: Gye, 1772.

Bibliography

———. ["Review of Robert Cox's Life of John Fletcher, Vicar of Madeley"]. *Christian Observer, Conducted by Members of the Established Church* 22/4 (1822) 193–205.

———. "Rues de chez nous." *Journal de Nyon* 57/52 (1949) n.p.

———. *Vie de M. de la Fléchère, de Nyon: Pasteur de Madeley, dans le Shropshire en Angleterre, accompagnée d'une lettre inédite et de notes, Traduit de l'anglais.* Lausanne: Hignou Aîné, 1826.

———. *Vie de M. de la Fléchère, de Nyon: Pasteur de Madeley, dans le Shropshire en Angleterre, accompagnée d'une lettre inédite et de notes, Traduit de l'anglais.* Jersey: Marston, 1845.

Anonymous. "American Controversy." *The Monthly Review, Or Literary Journal* 54 (1776) n.p.

———. "Atonement as Taught by Wesley, Fletcher, Clarke, and Watson, in Their Sermons and Other Theological Writings." *The Methodist Quarterly Review* 7 (1847) 414–33.

———. "The Birthplace of the Rev. John Fletcher." *The Christian Miscellany*, second series 4 (1858) 321–23.

———. "Chateau at Nyon." *The Youth Instructor and Guardian* 11/3 (1847) 97–101.

———. *Christian Biography: Life of the Rev. J. W. Fletcher, Vicar of Madeley Abridged from the Narrative of Rev. J. Wesley, the Biographical Notes of the Rev. W. Gilpin, and His "Life" by Rev. J. Benson with Extracts from Rev. R. Cox.* [London]: Religious Tract Society, n.d.

———. "The Conversion of John Fletcher." *Christian Advocate* 68/6 (1893) 87.

———. "Dr. William Dodd." *Episcopal Recorder* 25/47 (1848) 188.

———. "The Early Experience of Mrs. Fletcher." *Christian Advocate* 68/11 (1893) 167.

———. "Fletcher in the Pulpit." *Christian Advocate and Journal* 38/4 (1863): 313.

———. "Fletcher of Madeley Compared with Brainerd." *Zion's Herald* 9/9 (1838) 36.

———. "Fletcher's Checks." *The Methodist Magazine* 11/11 (1828) 413–20.

———. "John Fletcher and the Quakers of Madeley." *Proceedings of the Wesley Historical Society* 9/3 (1913) 66–68.

———. *A Letter to the Rev. Mr. Fletcher, of Madeley, on the Differences Subsisting Between Him and the Hon. and Rev. Mr. Shirley.* Bath: Gye, 1772.

———. "Letters of John Fletcher." *Wesley Historical Society, West Midlands Branch* 1/5 (1967) 43–44.

———. "Madeley Church." *The Youth Instructor and Guardian* 11/5 (1847) 193–98.

———. *A Madeley Meander.* Madeley, UK: St. Michael's Parish Church, 2005.

———. "Methodist Sermon Register of the Eighteenth Century." *Proceedings of the Wesley Historical Society* 9/8 (1914) 191–94.

———. "Mrs. Fletcher and Dr. Dodd." *Wesleyan Methodist Magazine* (1879) 768–71.

———. "Obituary [Account of Mrs. Fletcher's Death]." *The Methodist Magazine* 39 (1816) 80.

———. "The Old Church at Madeley: John Fletcher's Ministry There." *Christian Miscellany, and Family Visitor* 5 (1859) 33–35, 75–77, 141, 142, 174–75.

———. "On Reading the Checks and Other Polemical Works of Mr. Fletcher." *The Arminian Magazine* 2 (1779) 47.

———. *The Parish of St. Michael's Church and Early Methodism.* Madeley, UK: St. Michael's Parish Church. 2005.

———. "Prayer for the Recovery of the Rev. J. Fletcher." *The Local Preacher's Magazine and Mutual-Aid Association Reporter for the Year 1852* 2 (1852) 112–13.

———. "Religious Communications." *Christian Observer, Conducted by Members of the Established Church* 22/244 (1822) 193.

———. *Respect Paid to Merit; or a Just Character of the Late Reverend John Fletcher*. Madeley: n.p., 1785.

———. Review of *Holiness Unto the Lord, Illustrated in the Character and Life of Miss Bosanquet, of Leytonstone, Afterwards Mrs. Fletcher of Madeley, Compiled Chiefly from Her Journal* by the Rev. Stephen Cox. *Sword and Trowel* (1876) 430–32.

———. Review of *The Life of the Rev. John William De La Flechere* by Joseph Benson. *Christian Observer* 4/6 (1805) 349–61.

———. Review of *The Life of the Rev. John William de la Flechere, Compiled from the Narratives of the Rev. Mr. Wesley; the Biographical Notes of the Rev. Mr. Gilpin; from His Own Letters; and Other Authentic Documents, Many of Which Were Never Before Published* by Joseph Benson. *Eclectic Review* 1 (1805) 407–12.

———. Review of *Wesley's Designated Successor*, by L. Tyerman. *Wesleyan-Methodist Magazine* (1883) 74–77.

———. Review of *Wesley's Designated Successor: The Life, Letters, and Labours of the Rev. John William Fletcher, Vicar of Madeley, Shropshire*, by Rev. L. Tyerman. *London Quarterly Review* 60 (1883) 136–64.

———. "The Rev. John Fletcher and His Excellent Wife." *Local Preacher's Magazine* 1 (1853) 172–173.

———. "The Rev. John Fletcher and the Rev. C. Simeon." *Christian Miscellany and Family Visitor* 3 (1848) 326.

———. "Select List of Books Recently Published, Chiefly Religious." *Methodist Magazine* 48 (1825) 539–41.

———. *Spiritual Letters by Several Eminent Christians*. Chester: Read & Huxley, 1767.

———. *A Tribute to the Memory of the Rev. John Fletcher, Late Vicar of Madeley, Shropshire by an Old Friend*. London: Frys & Couchman, 1786.

———. "Vicar of Madeley and the Duellist." *Christian Register* 1/5 (1822) 305–306.

Archinard, Charles. *Histoire de l'Eglise du Canton de Vaud Depuis Son Origine Jusqu'aux Temps Actuels*. Lausanne: Blanc, 1862.

Armstrong, Brian G. "Amyraut (Amyraldus) Moïse (1596–1664)." In *Encyclopedia Of The Reformed Faith*, edited by Donald K. McKim, 6. Edinburgh: Saint Andrew, 1992.

———. *Calvin and the Amyraut Heresy: Protestant Scholasticism and Humanism in Seventeenth-Century France*. Eugene, OR: Wipf & Stock, 1969.

Arnett, William M. "Current Theological Emphases in the American Holiness Tradition." *Mennonite Quarterly Review* 35/2 (1961) 120–29.

———. "The Role of the Holy Spirit in Entire Sanctification in the Writings of John Wesley." *Wesleyan Theological Journal* 14/2 (1979) 15–30.

Augustine. *The Enchiridion: or On Faith, Hope and Love*. In *Augustine: On the Holy Trinity, Doctrinal Treatises, Moral Treatises*, vol. 3 of *Nicene and Post-Nicene Fathers, First Series*, edited by Philip Schaff, 237–76. Peabody, MA: Hendrickson, 2004.

Aukema Cieslukowski, Corrie M., and Elmer M. Colyer. "Wesley's Trinitarian Ordo Salutis." *Reformation and Revival Journal* 14/4 (2005) 105–31.

B., J. "The Church on the Hill: Recollections of the Rev. Walter Sellon." *The Wesleyan-Methodist Magazine* 2 (1856) 35–42, 133–40, 231–39, 332–40.

Bibliography

B., S. W. "Fletcher of Madeley." *The Monthly Religious Magazine and Independent Journal* 24/5 (1860) 328–36.

Baker, Frank. "Doctrines in the Discipline: A Study of the Forgotten Theological Presuppositions of American Methodism." *Duke Divinity School Review* 31 (1966) 39–55.

———. "The Early Experience of Fletcher of Madeley." *Proceedings of the Wesley Historical Society* 33/2 (1961) 25–29.

———. "John Fletcher, Methodist Clergyman." *London Quarterly and Holborn Review* 185 (1960) 291–98.

———. "John Fletcher's Sermon Notes." *Proceedings of the Wesley Historical Society* 28/2 (1951) 30–33.

———. "John Wesley on Christian Perfection." *Proceedings of the Wesley Historical Society* 34/3 (1963) 53–57.

Ball, John. *A treatise of the covenant of grace wherein the graduall breakings out of gospel grace from Adam to Christ are clearly discovered, the differences betwixt the Old and New Testament are laid open, divers errours of Arminians and others are confuted, the nature of uprightnesse, and the way of Christ in bringing the soul into communion with himself.are solidly handled.* London: Miller, 1645.

Balzer, Cary. "John Wesley's Developing Soteriology and the Influence of the Caroline Divines." PhD thesis, University of Manchester, 2005.

Bangs, Carl. *Arminius: A Study in the Dutch Reformation.* Grand Rapids: Asbury, 1985.

Barker, Esther T. *Lady Huntingdon, Whitefield, and the Wesleys.* Maryville, TN: Barker, 1984.

Barton, Benard. "Poetry: John William Fletcher, Written After Reading His Life." *The Wesleyan-Methodist Magazine* 52 (1829) 71.

Bassett, Paul M., and William M. Greathouse. *Exploring Christian Holiness.* Vol. 2, *The Historical Development.* Kansas City: Beacon Hill, 1985.

Baugh, G. C., et al., editors. "Madeley: Churches." In *A History of the County of Shropshire*, edited by G. C. Baugh et al., 11:59–66. London: Victoria County History, 1985. Online: http://www.british-history.ac.uk/report.asp?compid=18071.

Baxter, Richard. *The Reformed Pastor.* Edited by William Brown. Abridged ed. Carlisle, PA: Banner of Truth Trust, 2005.

Baynes, H. S. "The Excursions of the Rev. J. W. Fletcher to Scenes of the Persecution of the Huguenots in the South of France, and to Italy and Switzerland." *The Wesleyan-Methodist Magazine* (1881) 103–8.

Bays, Mamie. "John William Fletcher, the St. John of Methodist Theology." In *The Theologians of Methodism: Theses by Members of the Senior Class in the Biblical Department of Vanderbilt University*, 46–53. [1895]. Reprint, Salem, OH: Schmul, 1992.

Bear, James E. "Dispensationalism and the Covenant of Grace." *Union Seminary Review* 49/4 (1938) 285–307.

Bebbington, David W. *Evangelicalism in Modern Britain: A History from the 1730s to the 1980s.* London: Routledge, 1989.

Beddows. "John William Fletcher." *Notes and Queries* 12/6 (1920) 25.

Benson, Joseph. *The Holy Bible Containing the Old and New Testaments According to the Present Authorized Version with Notes Critical and Explanatory and Practical.* 6th ed. London: Mason, 1815.

———. Letter to [John Wesley]. 15 October 1785. The Papers of Joseph Benson, The John Rylands University Library, The University of Manchester, PLP 7/8/13.

———. Letter to John Fletcher. 1772/1773. Joseph Benson Papers, The John Rylands University Library, The University of Manchester, PLP 7/7/2.

———. Letter to John Fletcher. 12 June 1781. The Papers of Joseph Benson, The John Rylands University Library, The University of Manchester, PLP 7/8/9.

———. Letter to John Wesley. n.d. The Papers of Joseph Benson, The John Rylands University Library, The University of Manchester, PLP 7/12/8.

———. Letter to Mary Bosanquet. [1778]. The Frank Baker Collection, Duke University, Box 3, Folio 4 (J. Benson).

———. Letter to Mary Fletcher. 5 August 1788. The Papers of Joseph Benson, The John Rylands University Library, The University of Manchester, PLP 7/8/18.

———. *The Life of the Rev. John W. de la Fléchère compiled from the Narrative of Rev. Mr. Wesley; the Biographical Notes of Rev. Mr. Gilpin; from His Own Letters, and Other Authentic Documents, Many of Which Were Never Before Published*. 11th ed. London: Mason, 1835.

———. *The Life of the Rev. John W. de la Fléchère compiled from the Narrative of Rev. Mr. Wesley; the Biographical Notes of Rev. Mr. Gilpin; from His Own Letters, and Other Authentic Documents, Many of Which Were Never Before Published*. 1855. Reprint, Salem, OH: Allegheny, 1984.

Berg, Daniel N. "The Theological Context of American Wesleyanism." *Wesleyan Theological Journal* 20/1 (1985) 45–60.

Berger, Teresa. *Theology in Hymns? A Study of the Relationship of Doxology and Theology According to A Collection of Hymns for the Use of the People Called Methodists (1780)*. Translated by Timothy E. Kimbrough. Nashville: Kingswood, 1995.

Berridge, John. *The Christian World Unmasked. Pray Come and Peek*. London: Dilly, 1773.

———. *The Whole Works of the Rev. John Berridge, A.M., Late Fellow of Clare-Hall, Cambridge, Vicar of Everton, Bedfordshire, and Chaplain to the Earl of Buchan, With a Memoir of His Life*. Edited by Richard Whittingham. London: Palmer, 1864.

Bevins, Winfield H. "A Pentecostal Appropriation of the Wesleyan Quadrilateral." *Journal of Pentecostal Theology* 14/2 (2006) 229–46.

———. "A Pentecostal Appropriation of the Wesleyan Quadrilateral." The Pneuma Foundation: Resources for the Spirit-Empowered Ministry. Online: http://www.pneumafoundation.org/article.jsp?article=/article_0060.xml.

———. "Pneumatology in John Wesley's Theological Method." *Asbury Theological Journal* 58/2 (2003) 101–13.

Bible, Ken. "The Wesleys' Hymns on Full Redemption and Pentecost: A Brief Comparison." *Wesleyan Theological Journal* 17/2 (1982) 79–87.

Bicknell, E. J., and H. J. Carpenter. *A Theological Introduction to the Thirty-Nine Articles*. 2nd ed. London: Longmans, Green, 1925.

Bolton, Samuel. *The trve bovnds of Christian freedome. Or a treatise wherein the rights of the law are vindicated, the liberties of grace maintained, and severall late opinions against the law are examined and confuted. Whereunto is annexed a discourse of the learned John Camerons, touching the three-fold covenant of God with man, faithfully translated*. London: Kemb, 1656.

Borgeaud, Charles. *Histoire de l'Université de Gene8ve. L'Académie de Calvin 1559–1798*. Geneva: Libraires de l'Université, 1900.

Bibliography

Bourchenin, Daniel. *Études sur les Académies Protestantes en France au XVIe et au XVIIe Siècles*. 1882. Reprint, Geneva: Slatkine, 1969.

Bouvier, A. *La faculté de théologie de Genève: Documents pour servir à l'histoire de l'Académie de Genève*. Vol. 1 of Archive d'Etat de Genève.

Bowmer, John C. "The Relations Between the Society of Friends and Early Methodism." *London Quarterly and Holborn Review* 175 (1950) 148–53 and 222–27.

Boyle, G. D. *Richard Baxter*. London: Hodder & Stoughton, 1883.

Brain, Miss. Letter to John Fletcher. [21 January 1768–1770?]. The Fletcher-Tooth Collection, The John Rylands University Library, The University of Manchester, MAM Fl. 1/13/7.

———. Letter to John Fletcher. 22 February [1768–70]. The Fletcher-Tooth Collection, The John Rylands University Library, The University of Manchester, MAM Fl. 1/13.

———. Letter to John Fletcher. 12 May 1768. The Fletcher-Tooth Collection, The John Rylands University Library, The University of Manchester, MAM Fl. 1/13/1.

———. Letter to John Fletcher. 3 October 1769. The Fletcher-Tooth Collection, The John Rylands University Library, The University of Manchester, MAM Fl. 1/13/2.

———. Letter to John Fletcher. 6 January 1770. The Fletcher-Tooth Collection, The John Rylands University Library, The University of Manchester, MAM Fl. 1/13/3.

———. Letter to John Fletcher. 20 February 1770. The Fletcher-Tooth Collection, The John Rylands University Library, The University of Manchester, MAM Fl. 1/13/5.

———. Letter to John Fletcher. 29 July 1770. The Fletcher-Tooth Collection, The John Rylands University Library, The University of Manchester, MAM Fl. 1/13/4.

———. Letter to John Fletcher. 14 October 1770. The Fletcher-Tooth Collection, The John Rylands University Library, The University of Manchester, MAM Fl. 1/13/6.

Bramwell, William. *A Short Account of the Life and Death of Ann Cutler Commonly Known by the Name Praying Nanny Who Was a Principal Instrument in the Beginnings of the Late Revival of the Work of God in Lancashire, Yorkshire. With an Account of Elizabeth Dickinson's Two Wonderful Trances and an Excellent Letter from the Rev. Mr. J. Fletcher*. Leeds: n.p., 1798.

Bremer, Francis J. "Puritanism." In *The Encyclopedia of Religion*, 2:103: New York, Macmillan, 1967.

Bretherton, F. F. "Fletcher Memorials at Cliff College." *Proceedings of the Wesley Historical Society* 21/8 (1938) 194–97.

———. "John and Mary Fletcher: Valuable Manuscripts Found at Cliff." *The Cliff Witness* (1939) n.p.

———. "Letter of Mrs. Mary Fletcher to Rev. George Lowe." *Proceedings of the Wesley Historical Society* 20/3 (1935) 56.

———. "Letters to Henry Brooke of Dublin." *Proceedings of the Wesley Historical Society* 20/2 (1935) 33–36.

———. "Mrs. Fletcher's Class Paper." *Proceedings of the Wesley Historical Society* 21/8 (1938) 197–98.

———. "Two Wesley Letters to the Countess of Huntingdon." *Proceedings of the Wesley Historical Society* 27/1 (1949) 2–4.

[Bretherton, F. F.]. "A Society of Ministers of the Gospel in the Church of England Is Proposed to be Established Under the Following Rules and Regulations." *Proceedings of the Wesley Historical Society* 22/3 (1939) 52–57.

Bibliography

Brettell, Jeremiah. "Memoir of the Rev. Jeremiah Brettell." *Wesleyan Methodist Magazine* 9 (1830) 649–60, 721–30.

Bridel, L., and P.S. Bridel. "Nécrologie: J.G. de la Fléchère." *Le Conservateur Suisse, ou Recueil Complet des Étrennes Helvétiennes* 8 (1817) 359–60.

Brigden, T. E. "Mrs. Fletcher of Madeley and the Old Tythe Barn." *Proceedings of the Wesley Historical Society* 17/4 (1929) 77–78.

Bright, John. *The Authority of the Old Testament*. 1967. Reprint, Grand Rapids: Baker, 1975.

Brinton, Crane. "Enlightenment." In *The Encyclopedia of Philosophy*, edited by Paul Edwards, 2:519–25. London: Collier-Macmillan, 1967.

Brooke, Henry. Letter to John Fletcher. November [1783]. The Fletcher-Tooth Collection, The John Rylands University Library, The University of Manchester, MAM Fl. 1/16/2.

———. Letter to John Fletcher. [1784]. The Fletcher-Tooth Collection, The John Rylands University Library, The University of Manchester, MAM Fl. 1/15.

———. Letter to John Fletcher. [1785]. The Fletcher-Tooth Collection, The John Rylands University Library, The University of Manchester, MAM Fl. 1/16/2.

Brooke, Henry, and John Wesley. *The History of Henry, Earl of Moreland*. London: Paramore, 1781.

Brown, W. Adams. "Covenant Theology." In *Encyclopedia of Religion and Ethics*, edited by James Hastings, 4:216–224: Edinburgh: T. & T. Clark, 1994.

Brown-Lawson, Albert. *John Wesley and the Anglican Evangelicals of the Eighteenth Century: A Study in Cooperation and Separation with Special Reference to the Calvinistic Controversies*. Edinburgh: Pentland, 1994.

Bruce, F. F. *History of the Bible in English from the Earliest Versions*. 3rd ed. New York: Oxford University Press, 1978.

Bryant, Barry Edward. "John Wesley's Doctrine of Sin." PhD thesis, King's College, University of London, 1992.

Budé, Eugène de. *Vie de Jacob Vernet, Théologian Genevois, 1698–1789*. Lausanne: Bridel, 1893.

———. *Vie de J.-A. Turrettini: Théologian Genevois, 1671–1737*. Lausanne: Bridel, 1880.

Bunyan, John, and John Wesley. "An Extract from 'A Prospect of Divine Providence.'" In *A Christian Library: Consisting of Extracts from and Abridgments of the Choicest Pieces of Practical Divinity Which Have Been Written in the English Tongue*. 22:361–478. London: Kershaw, 1825.

Burder, Samuel. "Mrs. Mary Fletcher." In *Memoirs of Eminently Pious Women of the British Empire*, 3:365–412. London: Ogle & Duncan, 1823.

Burns, Jabez. *Life of Mrs. Fletcher With a Brief Sketch of Her Beloved Husband, John Fletcher of Madeley to Which is Annexed Several of Their Letters*. London: Smith, 1843.

Burrowes, W. Letter to John and Mary Fletcher. 10 April 1784. The Fletcher-Tooth Collection, The John Rylands University Library, The University of Manchester, MAM Fl. 1/2/32.

"Butler, Joseph." In *The Encyclopedia Britannica*, 11th ed., 4:885. New York: Encyclopedia Britannica.

Butler, Joseph. *The Analogy of Religion, to the Constitution and Course of Nature. To Which Are Added Two Brief Dissertations: I. On Personal Identity. II. On the Nature of Virtue*. Edited by Howard Malcom. 17th ed. Philadelphia: Lippincott, 1873.

Bibliography

C., J. E. "Providential Agency—Reply to 'J. W. S.'" *The Quarterly Review of the Methodist Episcopal Church, South* 3/4 (1849) 333–63.

Cadman, S. P. "Fletcher's Church." *Zion's Herald* 87/21 (1909) 642.

Caldwell, Merritt. "Theory of Temptation: Art. III, Fifth Article of the Methodist Quarterly Review for July, 1824." *The Methodist Quarterly Review* 25 (1843) 377–401.

Calvin, John. *Calvin's Commentaries*. 22 vols. Edinburgh: Calvin Translation Society; Repr., Grand Rapids: Baker Books, 2005.

———. *Institutes of the Christian Religion*. Edited by John T. McNeill. Translated by Ford Lewis Battles. 2 vols. Library of Christian Classics 20–21. Philadelphia: Westminster, 1960.

Campbell, Gordon. "Milton, John (1608–1674)." In *Oxford Dictionary of National Biography*, edited by H. C. G. Matthew and Brian Harrison. Oxford: Oxford University Press, 2004. Online: http://www.oxforddnb.com/view/article/18800.

Campbell, Ted A. "John Wesley and Conyers Middleton on Divine Intervention in History." *Church History* 55/1 (1986) 39–49.

Cannon, William R. "Methodism in a Philosophy of History." *Methodist History* 12 (1974) 27–43.

Carden, Allen. *Puritan Christianity in America: Religion and Life in Seventeenth-Century Massachusetts*. Grand Rapids: Baker, 1990.

Carey, Patrick W., and Joseph T. Lienhard, editors. *Biographical Dictionary of Christian Theologians*. Peabody, MA: Hendrickson, 2000.

Carter, Grayson. Review of *Reluctant Saint? A Theological Biography of Fletcher of Madeley*, by Patrick Strieff. *Anglican and Episcopal History* 71/4 (2002) 576–78.

Carthy, Clayton. Letter to John Fletcher. n.d. The Fletcher-Tooth Collection, The John Rylands University Library, The University of Manchester, MAM Fl. 2/1/5.

Cartledge, Mark J., and David Miles, editors. *Covenant Theology: Contemporary Approaches*. Carlisle, UK: Paternoster, 2001.

Casino, T. C. "Revelation." In *Dictionary of Mission Theology: Evangelical Foundations*, edited by John Corrie, 339–344. Nottingham, England: InterVarsity, 2007.

Caswell, James. "Thomas Hill, Esq. of Tern-Hill, Salop, and the Rev. John Fletcher." *The Wesleyan-Methodist Magazine* 23 (1844) 541.

Cell, George Croft. *The Rediscovery of John Wesley*. London: University Press of America, 1935.

Cellerier, J. E. *L'Académie de Genève esquisse d'une histoire abridgée de cette académie pendant les trois premières périodes de son existence (1559–1798)*. Paris: Meyrueis, 1855.

Certificate of appointment as Chaplin to Lord Buchan. 7 December 1767. The Fletcher-Tooth Collection, The John Rylands University Library, The University of Manchester, MAM P4d11.

Certificate of institution as Vicar of Madeley. 7 October 1760. The Fletcher-Tooth Collection, The John Rylands University Library, The University of Manchester, MAM P4d9.

Certificate of ordination as a deacon. 6 March 1757. The Fletcher-Tooth Collection, The John Rylands University Library, The University of Manchester, MAM P4d1.

Certificate of ordination as a priest. 13 March 1757. The Fletcher-Tooth Collection, The John Rylands University Library, The University of Manchester, MAM P4d2.

Bibliography

Certificate of presentation to the vicarage. 4 October 1760. The Fletcher-Tooth Collection, The John Rylands University Library, The University of Manchester, MAM P4d5.
Certificate of subscription to Thirty-nine Articles. 7 October 1760. The Fletcher-Tooth Collection, The John Rylands University Library, The University of Manchester, MAM P4d7.
Certificate on conforming to the liturgy on presentation to the curacy of Madeley. 14 March 1757. The Fletcher-Tooth Collection, The John Rylands University Library, The University of Manchester, MAM P4d3.
Certificate on conforming to the liturgy. 7 October 1760. The Fletcher-Tooth Collection, The John Rylands University Library, The University of Manchester, MAM P4d8.
Certificate upon reading prayers in conformity to the Liturgy and public assent to the 39 Articles. 1 December 1760. The Fletcher-Tooth Collection, The John Rylands University Library, The University of Manchester, MAM P4d10.
Chambre, R. Letter to John Fletcher. 21 January 1775. Shropshire Archives, 2280/3/14/15.
Chandler, D. R. "Toward the Americanizing of Methodism." *Methodist History* 8 (1974) 3–16.
Chiles, Robert. *Theological Transitions in American Methodism 1790–1935*. Nashville: Abingdon, 1965.
Church of England. *The Constitutions and Canons Ecclesiastical (Made in the Year 1603, and Amended in the Year 1865) To Which Are Added the Thirty-Nine Articles of the Church of England*. London: SPCK, 1900.
———. *Sermons, or Homilies, Appointed to be Read in Churches. To Which Are Added, The Articles of Religion; The Constitutions and Canons Ecclesiastical; Indexes to Subjects, Scriptures, and Names; and a Collation of Principal Editions*. 1853. Reprint, Lewes, UK: Focus Christian Ministries Trust, 1986.
Church, Leslie F. "Fletcher of Madeley: An Interesting Manuscript." *London Quarterly and Holborn Review* 176 (1951) 97–101.
Churchey, Walter. Letter to John Fletcher. 14 January 1771. The John Rylands University Library, The University of Manchester, S.L., 5:217, T.S.C.
———. Letter to Joseph Benson. n.d. [1755/6]. Wesley Family Collection, The John Rylands University Library, The University of Manchester, 1/19.
———. Letter to Joseph Benson. 30 April 1771. Emory University, ALS, 3 p.
———. Letter to Joseph Benson. n.d. [1795/6]. Early Preachers Collection, The John Rylands University Library, The University of Manchester, 1/19.
Churchhill, Caroline. "Birthplace of Mary Fletcher." *The Christian Miscellany and Family Visitor* 21 (1875) 97–99.
Clergy of the Church of England Database. "Hatton, Thomas (1758–1807)." Online: http://www.theclergydatabase.org.uk/jsp/persons/index.jsp.
Clifford, Alan C. *Amyraut Affirmed or "Owenism, a Caricature of Calvinism," A Reply to Ian Hamilton's "Amyraldianism": Is It Modified Calvinism?* Norwich: Charenton, 2004.
———. *Atonement and Justification: English Evangelical Theology 1640–1790, An Evaluation*. Oxford: Clarendon, 1990.
———. *Calvinus: Authentic Calvinism, A Clarification*. Norwich: Charenton, 1996.

Bibliography

Coke, Thomas. Letter to John Fletcher. 28 August 1775. The Papers of the Dr Thomas Coke, The John Rylands University Library, The University of Manchester, PLP 28/3/1.

———. Letter to John Fletcher. 6 January 1784. The Papers of the Dr Thomas Coke, The John Rylands University Library, The University of Manchester, PLP 28/5/16.

Collins, Kenneth J. *John Wesley: A Theological Journey*. Nashville: Abingdon, 2003.

———. "The New Creation as a Multivalent Theme in John Wesley's Theology." *Wesleyan Theological Journal* 37/2 (2002) 77–102.

———. "Reconfiguration of Power: Basic Trajectory of John Wesley's Practical Theology." *Wesleyan Theological Journal* 33/1 (1998) 164–84.

———. *The Scripture Way of Salvation: The Heart of John Wesley's Theology*. Nashville: Abingdon, 1997.

———. "The State of Wesley Studies in North America: A Theological Journey." *Wesleyan Theological Journal* 44/2 (2009) 7–38.

———. *The Theology of John Wesley: Holy Love and the Shape of Grace*. Nashville: Abingdon, 2007.

———. "Wesley's Platonic Conception of the Moral Law." *Wesleyan Theological Journal* 21/1–2 (1986) 116–28.

Cooke, Bernard. *Power and the Spirit of God: Toward an Experienced-Based Pneumatology*. Oxford: Oxford University Press, 2004.

Coomer, Duncan. "The Influence of Puritanism and Dissent on Methodism." *The London Quarterly and Holborn Review* 175 (1950) 346–50.

Cooper, Thomas. "Memoir of the Late Rev. Thomas Cooper." *The Wesleyan-Methodist Magazine* 14 (1835) 81–92.

Coppedge, Allan. "Entire Sanctification in Early American Methodism: 1812–1835." *Wesleyan Theological Journal* 13 (1978) 34–50.

———. *The God Who Is Triune: Revisioning the Christian Doctrine of God*. Downers Grove, IL: InterVarsity, 2007.

———. *John Wesley in Theological Debate*. Wilmore, Kent: Wesley Heritage, 1987.

Cornwall, Robert D. "Bull, George (1634–1710)." In *Oxford Dictionary of National Biography*, edited by H. C. G. Matthew and Brian Harrison. Oxford: Oxford University Press, 2004. Online: http://www.oxforddnb.com/view/article/3903.

Coulton, Barbara. "Tern Hall and the Hill Family 1700–1775." *Transactions of the Shropshire Archaeological Society* 66 (1989) 97–105.

———. "Tutor to the Hills: The Early Career of John Fletcher." *Proceedings of the Wesley Historical Society* 47, 3 (October 1989): 94–103.

Cox, Robert. *The Life of the Rev. John William Fletcher, Vicar of Madeley*. 2nd ed. London: Butterworth & Son, 1825.

———. *The Life of the Rev. John William Fletcher, Vicar of Madeley*. 1st American ed. Philadelphia: George & Byington, 1836.

Cragg, Gerald R. *Reason and Authority in the Eighteenth Century*. Cambridge: Cambridge University Press, 1964.

Cranage, A. Letter to John Fletcher. 7 September 1774. The Fletcher-Tooth Collection, The John Rylands University Library, The University of Manchester, MAM Fl. 2/1/26.

Cranage, D. H. S. "Madeley." In *An Architectural Account of the Churches of Shropshire*, 205–6. Wellington, UK: Hobson, 1912.

Bibliography

[Crane, Thomas], and John Wesley. "A Prospect of Divine Providence." In *A Christian Library: Consisting of Extracts from and Abridgments of the Choicest Pieces of Practical Divinity Which Have Been Written in the English Tongue*. 22:359–478. London: Cordeux, 1825.
Crawford, Nathan, editor. *The Continuing Relevance of Wesleyan Theology: Essays in Honor of Laurence W. Wood*. Foreword by Stanley Hauerwas. Eugene, OR: Pickwick, 2011.
Crinsoz de Bionens, Théodore. *Abrège de l'Essai sur les prophéties de Daniel, qui regardent les derniers tems*. Lausanne: Hignou, 1799.
———. *Apologie de Mr De Bionens, contre un écrit intitulé: 'Défense de la dissertation de Mr Turretin sur les Article Fondamentaux de la Religion, etc*. Yverdon: Genath, 1727.
———. *Essai sur l'apocalypse, avec des éclaircissements sur les prophéties de Daniel qui regardent les derniers tems*. [Yverdon]: [Genath], 1729.
———. *Lettre de Mr. T. C. à un ami. ou Examen de quelques endroits de la Dissertation de Monsieur Jean-Alphonse Turrettin sur les Articles fundamentaux de la Religion*. n.p.: n.d.
[Crinsoz de Bionnens, Théodore]. Transcribed copy of "Eclaircissement sur les prophètes de Daniel qui regardent ces derniers temp." The Fletcher-Tooth Collection, The John Rylands University Library, The University of Manchester, MAM Fl. 19/5.
[———]. Transcribed copy of "Les Proverbes de Salomon." The Fletcher-Tooth Collection, The John Rylands University Library, The University of Manchester, MAM Fl. 19/8.
"Crisp, Tobias." In *Cyclopedia of Biblical, Theological, and Ecclesiastical Literature*, edited by John M'Clintock and James Strong, 2:566: New York: Harper, 1889.
Crow, Earl P. "Wesley and Antinomianism." *The Duke Divinity School Review* 31/1 (1966) 10–19.
Crutchfield, Larry V. "Ages and Dispensations in the Ante-Nicene Fathers." In *Vital Prophetic Issues: Examining Promises and Problems in Eschatology*, 44–59. Vital Issues Series 5. Grand Rapids: Kregel Resources, 1995.
———. "Rudiments of Dispensationalism in the Ante-Nicene Period." *Bibliotheca Sacra* 144 (1987) 254–76; 377–99.
Cubie, David L. "John Wesley's Concept of Perfect Love: A Motif Analysis." Ph D diss., Boston University Graduate School, 1965.
———. "Perfection in Wesley and Fletcher: Inaugural or Teleological?" *Wesleyan Theological Journal* 11 (1976) 22–37.
Cudworth, Ralph. *The True Intellectual System of the Universe: The First Part; Wherein All the Reason and Philosophy of Atheism is Confuted, With a Discourse Concerning the True Notion of the Lord's Supper*. Vol. 1. 2nd ed. London: Walthoe et al., 1743.
Cudworth, William. *Nature and Grace: Or, Some Essential Differences Between the Sentimeuts of the Natural and Spiritual Man, in Things Pertaining to Everlasting Salvation*. Salop: Cotton & Eddowes, 1763.
Cunliffe, Christopher. "Butler, Joseph (1692–1752)." In *Oxford Dictionary of National Biography*, edited by H. C. G. Matthew and Brian Harrison. Oxford: Oxford University Press, 2004. Online: http://www.oxforddnb.com/view/article/18800.
Da., H. editor. "Turrettini." In *Dictionnaire d'Histoire et de Géographie Ecclesiastiques*, edited by Alfred Baudrillart, 6:714. Paris: Librarie Letouzey et Ané, 1938.

Bibliography

Dallimore, Arnold A. *George Whitefield: The Life and Times of the Great Evangelist of the Eighteenth-Century Revival*. 2 vols. London: Banner of Truth Trust, 1970.

Darby, Abiah. "Extracts from the Diary of Abiah Darby." *Journal of the Friends Historical Society* 10/2 (1913) 79–92.

———. "Further Extracts from the Diary of Abiah Darby." *Journal of the Friends Historical Society* 10/4 (1913) 295.

———. Letter to John Fletcher. 22 June 1784. The Fletcher-Tooth Correspondence, The John Rylands University Library, The University of Manchester, MAM Fl 2/7/1–4.

———. Letter to John Fletcher. 22 September 1761. Labouchere Collection, Ironbridge Gorge Museum Library and Archives, MJAB.

———. Letter to John Fletcher. 19 August 1762. Labouchere Collection, Ironbridge Gorge Museum Library and Archives, MJAB.

Dardier, Charles. "Ostervald (Jean-Frédéric)." In *Encyclopédie des sciences religieuses*, edited by Frédéric Lichtenberger, 4:98–104: Paris, Sandoz et Fischbacher, 1878.

Davenport, Thomas. Letter to John Fletcher. 15 June 1781. The Fletcher-Tooth Collection, The John Rylands University Library, The University of Manchester, MAM Fl. 2/7/5.

Davies, William R. "John Fletcher of Madeley as Theologian." PhD thesis, University of Manchester, 1965.

———. "John Fletcher's Georgian Ordinations and Madeley Curacy." *Proceedings of the Wesley Historical Society* 36/5 (1968) 139–42.

———. Review of *Reluctant Saint? A Theological Biography of Fletcher of Madeley* by Patrick Streiff. *Epworth Review* 29/2 (2002) 95–96.

Dayton, Donald W. "The Doctrine of the Baptism of the Holy Spirit: Its Emergence and Significance." *Wesleyan Theological Journal* 13 (1978) 114–26.

———. "A Final Round with Larry Wood." *Pneuma* 28/2 (2006) 265–70.

———. "John Fletcher as John Wesley's Vindicator and Designated Successor? A Response to Laurence W. Wood." *Pneuma* 26/2 (2004) 355–61.

———. "Rejoinder to Larry Wood." *Pneuma* 27/2 (2005) 367–75.

———. *Theological Roots of Pentecostalism*. 1987. Reprint, Peabody, MA: Hendrickson, 2000.

———. "Wesleyan Tug-of-War on Pentecostal Link." *Christianity Today* 23 (1978) 43.

Deasley, Alex R. G. "Entire Sanctification and the Baptism with the Holy Spirit: Perspectives on the Biblical View of the Relationship." *Wesleyan Theological Society* 14/1 (1979) 27–44.

Deschner, John. *Wesley's Christology: An Interpretation*. Dallas: Southern Methodist University Press, 1960.

"Description of the Monuments Erected in the City-Road Chapel, London." *Methodist Magazine* 6 (1823) 431–35.

Dieter, Melvin E. "The Development of Nineteenth-Century Holiness Theology." *Wesleyan Theological Journal* 20/1 (1985) 61–77.

Ditchfield, G. M. Review of *Reluctant Saint? A Theological Biography of Fletcher of Madeley* by Patrick Streiff. *English Historical Review* 118/476 (2003) 523–25.

Downey, Edward A. *The Knowledge of God in Calvin's Theology*. Exp. ed. Grand Rapids: Eerdmans, 1994.

"Dr. William Dodd." *Episcopal Recorder* 25/47 (1848) 188.

"Dr. William Dodd." *The Rural Repository Devoted to Polite Literature* 1/1 (1848) 20.

Dublin Society. Letter to John and Mary Fletcher. October 1783. The Fletcher-Tooth Collection, The John Rylands University Library, The University of Manchester, MAM Fl. 2/7/10.

DuBose, Horace Mellard. "John Fletcher and Matrimony." *Methodist Review Quarterly* 65/4 (1916) 780–82.

Duncan, J. Ligon. "Irenaeus of Lyon: A True Radical Orthodox Theologian." *Reformation 21: The Online Magazine of the Alliance of Confessing Evangelicals*. Online: http://www.reformation21.org/Past_Issues/2006_Issues_1_16_/2006_Issues_1_16_Articles/Irenaeus/25 (site removed).

Dunn, Lewis Romaine. "Wesley's Designated Successor." *The Methodist Quarterly Review* 66 (1884) 205–26.

Dunn, Samuel. "Bust of Wesley." *The Christian Miscellany, and Family Visitor* 2 (1848) 230.

Dunning, H. Ray. *Grace, Faith, and Holiness: A Wesleyan Systematic Theology*. Kansas City: Beacon Hill, 1988.

E. "Johann Fletscher's Pfarrer Zu Madely; nach der von J. Benson. mit ciner Vorre." *Western Christian Advocate* 7/33 (1840) 130.

Eby, Patrick A. "John and Charles Wesley's Use of John Milton: Trinity and Heresy." *Methodist History* 44/2 (2006) 115–24.

"Editor's Visit to Madeley." *Wesley Banner and Revival Record* 2 (1850) 314–15.

Edwards, David L. *Christian England*. Vol. 2, *From the Reformation to the 18th Century*. Grand Rapids: Eerdmans, 1983.

Edwards, Jonathan. *A History of the Work of Redemption. Containing, The Outlines of a Body of Divinity, In a Method Entirely New*. London: Bukland & Keith, 1774.

———. *Sermons and Discourses, 1739–1742*. Edited by Harry S. Stout and Nathan O. Hatch. The Works of Jonathan Edwards 22. New Haven: Yale University Press, 2003.

Edwards, Joseph. Letter to John Fletcher. 28 December 1774. The Fletcher-Tooth Collection, The John Rylands University Library, The University of Manchester, MAM Fl. 2/14/1.

Edwards, Maldwyn L. "John Fletcher and 1966." *Bulletin of the Wesley Historical Society: West Midlands Branch* 1/4 (1966) 35–36.

———. "A Saint in Israel." In *My Dear Sister: The Story of John Wesley and the Women in His Life*. Manchester: Penwork, [1980].

Ehlert, Arnold D. *A Bibliographic History of Dispensationalism*. Grand Rapids: Baker, 1965.

Emerson, Everett H. "Calvin and Covenant Theology." *Church History* 25/2 (1956) 136–44.

English, John C. "The Cambridge Platonists in Wesley's 'Christian Library.'" *Proceedings of the Wesley Historical Society* 36 (1968) 161–68.

Entwisle, Joseph. "The Testimony of Mr. Fletcher to the Doctrine of Christ's Eternal Sonship." *Methodist Magazine* 41 (1818) 97–107.

Etheridge, J. W. The Life of John William Fletcher. The Fletcher-Tooth Collection, The John Rylands University Library, The University of Manchester, MAR 218 EQ4.

Falletti, N. Charles. *Jacob Vernet, théologien genevois. 1698–1789*. Geneva: 1885.

Felleman, Laura. "John Wesley's Natural Philosophy: A Survey of Several Misconceptions." *Methodist History* 44/3 (2006) 170–76.

Bibliography

Ferguson, Everett. "The Covenant Idea in the Second Century." In *Texts and Testaments: Critical Essays on the Bible and Early Church Fathers*, edited by W. Eugene March, 135-62. San Antonio: Trinity University Press, 1980.

Ferguson, Robert Lynn. "Early Methodist Piety and Polemics, A Study of the Life of John Fletcher, Vicar of Madeley." MA thesis, Southern Methodist University, 1956.

Ferguson, Sinclair B. *John Owen on the Christian Life*. Carlisle, PA: Banner of Truth Trust, 1987.

Field, Clive Douglas. *John William Fletcher (1729-1785), Vicar of Madeley, A Methodist Bicentenary: Catalogue of an Exhibition Held in the John Rylands University Library of Manchester*. John Rylands University Library of Manchester, Summer 1985.

Fielding, B. F. "Letter from John Fletcher to Miss Loxdale." *Proceedings of the Wesley Historical Society* 9/6 (1914) 139.

Finney, Gale Wayne. "The Baptism of the Holy Spirit in Early Methodism." Term paper presented to the Church History Department in partial fulfillment of the requirements for the course GHI 371, Modern European Church History, Cincinnati Bible Seminary, April, 1993. 27 pages.

Fletcher, John. *An Address To Such As Enquire*. London: Conference Office, 1807.

———. "Advocate and Journal [Fragment of a Sermon on Luke 22.44]." *Christian Advocate and Journal* 1/48 (1827) 189.

———. *American Patriotism Farther Confronted with Reason, Scripture, and the Constitution: Being Observations on the Dangerous Politicks Taught by the Rev. Mr. Evans, M.A. and the Rev. Dr. Price with a Scriptural Plea for the Revolted Colonies*. Shrewsbury, UK: Eddowes, 1776.

———. An Answer to the Objections and Queries of Mrs. Darby in her Dispute with me John Fletcher Vicar of Madeley On Thursday the 22d Nov.br 1764. To which are added some Remarks upon what she calls a faithful Declaration of that Dispute, by Way of Appendix. The Fletcher-Tooth Collection, The John Rylands University Library, The University of Manchester, 31 (Item E).

———. *An Answer to the Rev. Mr. Toplady's "Vindication of the decrees," &c.* London: n.p., 1776.

———. *An Appeal to Matter of Fact and Common Sense, or A Rational Demonstration of Man's Corrupt and Lost Estate*. Bristol: Pine, 1772.

———. *An Appeal to Matter of Fact and Common Sense. Or A Rational Demonstration of Man's Corrupt and Lost Estate*. Bristol: n.p., 1783.

———. Baptism of John and Christ. The Fletcher-Tooth Collection, The John Rylands University Library, The University of Manchester, MAM Fl. 21/11.

———. *Beauties of Fletcher*. New York: Lane & Sandford, 1853.

———. *The Bible and the Sword, or, The Appointment of the General Fast Vindicated in an Address to the Common People, Concerning the Propriety of Repressing Obstinate Licentiousness With the Sword, and of Fasting When theSword Is Drawn for That Purpose*. London: Hawes, 1776.

———. Catechism. Arthur Skevington Wood Archive Library, Cliff College, A/1/04.

———. "A Charimeter or A Scriptural Method of Trying the Spirits and Knowing the Proposition of Our Faith." Edited by Laurence W. Wood. *Asbury Theological Journal* 53/1 (1998) 83-90.

———. Check to Socinianism and Arianism. The Fletcher-Tooth Collection, The John Rylands University Library, The University of Manchester, MAM Fl. 17.

Bibliography

———. *Christ Manifested, Or, The Manifestations of the Son of God*. Edited by David R. Smith. Philadelphia: Christian Literature Crusade, 1969.

———. *The Christian Experience of Mrs. S****** (As Dictated by Herself) Written by the Rev. Mr. John Fletcher, Late Vicar of Madeley, in Shropshire to Which Are Added Extracts from Two Letters by the Same Divine, Relative to the Doctrine of Christian Holiness*. London: Hawes, 1785.

———. *Christian Letters*. London: Hawes, 1779.

———. *Christian Perfection*. Edited by T. Rutherford. Blackburn: Hemingway & Nuttall, 1797.

———. Commonplace Book. Arthur Skevington Wood Archive Library, Cliff College, A/1/11 (a).

———. Commonplace Book, c. 1752–1754. Arthur Skevington Wood Archive Library, Cliff College, A/1/07.

———. Commonplace book of French sermon notes. Arthur Skevington Wood Archive Library, Cliff College, A/1/15.

———. Copy of a Sermon on [Matthew 11.28]. Shropshire Archives, 2280/16/81.

———. Covenant with God. 24 August 1754. The Fletcher-Tooth Collection, The John Rylands Library, The University of Manchester, MAM P4d15.

———. "A Dialogue Between a Minister and One of His Parishioners: On Man's Depravity and Danger in His Natural State." *Methodist Magazine* 25 (1802) 32–37, 64–71, 112–18, 163–67, 210–15, 252–58.

———. *Discours Sur la Régénération*. London: 1759.

———. *The Doctrines of Grace and Justice Equally Essential to the Pure Gospel: With Some Remarks on the Mischievous Divisions Caused Among Christians by Parting Those Doctrines. Being an Introduction to a Plan of Reconciliation Between the Defenders of the Doctrines of Partial Grace, Commonly Called Calvinists' and the Defenders of the Doctrines of Impartial Justice, Commonly Called Arminians*. London: Moore, 1778.

———. Draft letter to [Monsieur du Luc]. The Fletcher-Tooth Collection, The John Rylands University Library, The University of Manchester, MAM F. 19.

———. *A Dreadful Phenomenon Described and Improved: Being a Particular Account of the Sudden Stoppage of the River Severn, and of the Terrible Desolation that Happened at the Birches Between Coalbrook-Dale and Buildwas Bridge in Shropshire on Thursday Morning, May the 27th, 1773 and the Substance of a Sermon Preached the Next Day, on the Ruins, to a Vast Concourse of Spectators*. 2nd ed. Bristol: Pine, 1774.

———. *Essai sur la Paix de 1783 dédié à l'Archevêque de Paris par un pasteur Anglican*. London: Hindmarsh, 1784.

———. "An Essay on the Doctrine of the New Birth." Edited by Laurence W. Wood. *Asbury Theological Journal* 53/1 (1998) 35–56.

———. Essay on the New Birth. The Fletcher-Tooth Collection, The John Rylands University Library, The University of Manchester, 21/12.

———. "An Essay to Doctor Priestly on the Trinity." Edited by Laurence W. Wood. *Asbury Theological Journal* 53/1 (1998) 79–81.

———. *An Essay Upon the Peace of 1783. Dedicated to the Archbishop of Paris*. Translated by J. Gilpin. London: Hindmarsh, 1785.

———. *The Fictitious and the Genuine Creed: Being "A Creed for Arminians," Composed by Richard Hill, Esq; to Which is Opposed A Creed for Those Who Believe that Christ

Bibliography

———. *Tasted Death for Every Man. By the Author of the Checks to Antinomianism.* The Second Edition. London: Hawes, 1775.

———. *The First Part of an Equal Check to Pharisaism and Antinomianism.* Shrewsbury: Eddowes, 1774.

———. *The First Part of an Equal Check to Pharisaism and Antinomianism.* Edited by John Wesley. 2nd ed. Bristol: Pine, 1774.

———. Fragment from Socinianism Unscriptural or A Rational Vindication of the Catholic Faith. The Frank Baker Collection, Duke University, Box 4, Folio 9.

———. "General Observations on the Redemption of Mankind by Jesus Christ." Translated by Miles Martindale. *Arminian Magazine* 18 (1795) 339–44; 381–85.

———. *La Grâce et la Nature, Poème.* 2nd ed. London: Hindmarsh, 1785.

———. *An Interesting Extract from Fletcher's Essay on Truth Essay on Truth.* Burlington, NJ: Ustick, 1807.

———. "Introduction" to "La Grâce et la Nature." The Fletcher-Tooth Collection, The John Rylands University Library, The University of Manchester, MAM Fl. 19/7.

———. Inward Witness of the Spirit. The Fletcher-Tooth Collection, The John Rylands University Library, The University of Manchester, 17/1.

———. "The Language of the Father's Dispensation." Edited by Laurence W. Wood. *Asbury Theological Journal* 53/1 (1998) 65–78.

———. *The Last Check to Antinomianism: A Polemical Essay on the Twin Doctrines of Christian Imperfection and a Death Purgatory.* London: Hawes, 1775.

———. "Letter CCCLXII [From the Rev. Mr. Fletcher to the Rev. Messrs. John and Charles Wesley]." *Arminian Magazine* 11 (1788) 384–86.

———. "Letter CXV [From the Rev. Mr. Fletcher to Miss F-, and Miss R-]." *Arminian Magazine* 3 (1780) 277–78.

———. "Letter CXV [From the Rev. Mr. Fletcher to the Rev. Mr. Wesley, Asking Advice Concerning His Entry into Holy Orders]." *Arminian Magazine* 3 (1780) 46–48.

———. "Letter DCIX [From the Rev. Mr. Fletcher to James Ireland, Esq.]." *Arminian Magazine* 15 (1792) 609–10.

———. "Letter DCX [From the Rev. Mr. Fletcher to James Ireland, Esq.]." *Arminian Magazine* 15 (1792) 610–12.

———. "Letter DCXII [From the Rev. Mr. Fletcher to Mr. William Wase]." *Arminian Magazine* 15 (1792) 665–66.

———. "Letter DCXIII [From the Rev. Mr. Fletcher to the Rev. Mr. Greaves]." *Arminian Magazine* 15 (1792) 667–69.

———. "Letter DLIII [From the Rev. Mr. Fletcher to C.B.]." *Arminian Magazine* 14 (1791) 48–49.

———. "Letter DLXXXI [From the Rev. Mr. F. to Miss H.]." *Arminian Magazine* 15 (1792) 48–49.

———. "Letter DXCVIII [From the Rev. Mr. F. to C.B.]." *Arminian Magazine* 15 (1792) 497–500.

———. "Letter LIII [From the Rev. Mr. Fletcher to C.B.]." *Methodist Magazine* 2 (1798) 234.

———. Letter to "Sir" [Lord Gower]. n.d. The Fletcher-Tooth Collection, The John Rylands University Library, The University of Manchester, MAM Fl. 17.19.

———. Letter to [Charles Wesley]. 9 February 1760. The Fletcher-Tooth Collection, The John Rylands University Library, The University of Manchester, MAM Fl. 36/5.

Bibliography

———. Letter to [Claude Bosanquet]. [22 September 1781]. The Fletcher-Tooth Collection, The John Rylands University Library, The University of Manchester, MAM Fl. 36/4.

———. Letter to [Claude Bosanquet]. [22 September 1781]. The Fletcher-Tooth Collection, The John Rylands University Library, The University of Manchester, MAM Fl. 36/4.

———. Letter to [John Wesley]. 17 October 1773. The Fletcher-Tooth Collection, The John Rylands University Library, The University of Manchester, MAM Fl. 36/1.

———. Letter to [Lady Mary's sister]. n.d. The Fletcher-Tooth Collection, The John Rylands University Library, The University of Manchester, MAM Fl. 36/5.

———. Letter to Abiah Darby. 22 November 1764. The Fletcher-Tooth Collection, The John Rylands University Library, The University of Manchester, MAM Fl. 20 and MAM Fl. 31 (Item E).

———. Letter to Alexander Benjamin Greaves. 31 May 1781. The Fletcher-Tooth Collection, The John Rylands University Library, The University of Manchester, MAM Fl. 18/3.

———. Letter to Anonymous. 28 February 1762. Wesley Center, Oxford, Westminster Institute of Education, Oxford Brookes University, Fletcher Papers.

———. Letter to Bishop Beauclerk (Testimonial for Greaves). 22 March 1777. The Fletcher-Tooth Collection, The John Rylands University Library, The University of Manchester, MAM Fl. 36/2/6.

———. Letter to Bishop Beauclerk. 22 March 1777. The Fletcher-Tooth Collection, The John Rylands University Library, The University of Manchester, MAM Fl. 36/2/6.

———. Letter to Charles Perronet. 7 September 1772. The Frank Baker Collection, Duke University, Box 4, Folio 9 (J.W. Fletcher Papers).

———. Letter to Charles Wesley. 16 August 1758. The New Room, 2001/179.

———. Letter to Charles Wesley. 26 September 1760. Wesley's Chapel, City Road, London, LDWMM 2000/7969.

———. Letter to Charles Wesley. [8 May 1760]. The New Room, 2001/136.

———. Letter to Charles Wesley. 27 April 1761. The Fletcher-Tooth Collection, The John Rylands University Library, The University of Manchester, Fl. Vol. 1:13.

———. Letter to Charles Wesley. 19 July 1762. The Fletcher-Tooth Collection, The John Rylands University Library, The University of Manchester, MAM Fl. 36/5.

———. Letter to Charles Wesley. 26 December 1763. The Fletcher-Tooth Collection, The John Rylands University Library, The University of Manchester, MAM Fl. 36/1.

———. Letter to Charles Wesley. 20 May [1769]. The United Library, Garrett Evangelical Divinity School, William Colbert Coll., 48.

———. Letter to Charles Wesley. 26 May 1771. The Frank Baker Collection, Duke University, Box 8 (Wesley Family Papers).

———. Letter to Charles Wesley. 13 October 1771. The Robert W. Woodruff Library of Advanced Studies, Special Collections Department, Emory University, J. Wesley Coll., 1734–1864, AL.

———. Letter to Charles Wesley. 5 July 1772. The Fletcher-Tooth Collection, The John Rylands University Library, The University of Manchester, MAM Fl. 36/1.

———. Letter to Charles Wesley. 20 April 1773. The Fletcher-Tooth Collection, The John Rylands University Library, The University of Manchester, Fl. Vol. 1:87.

Bibliography

———. Letter to Charles Wesley. 20 February 1774. The Fletcher-Tooth Collection, The John Rylands University Library, The University of Manchester, MAM Fl. 36/1.

———. Letter to Charles Wesley. 2 July 1775. The New Room, 2001/180.

———. Letter to Charles Wesley. 15 September 1776. The Fletcher-Tooth Collection, The John Rylands University Library, The University of Manchester, MAM Fl. 36/1.

———. Letter to Charles Wesley. 11 May 1776. The Fletcher-Tooth Collection, The John Rylands University Library, The University of Manchester, Fl. Vol. 1:53.

———. Letter to Charles Wesley. 19 December 1782. John and Mary Fletcher Papers, GCAH, Drew University, 1306.5.3.01.

———. Letter to Countess of Huntingdon. 26 September 1760. Wesley's Chapel, City Road, London, LDWMM 2000/7969.

———. Letter to Dr. Turner. 28 May 1777. The Frank Baker Collection, Duke University, unnumbered box, folio 7.

———. Letter to George Whitefield. 3 July 1767. The Fletcher-Tooth Collection, The John Rylands University Library, The University of Manchester, MAM Fl. 36/1.

———. Letter to Henri-Louis de La Fléchère. 11 May 1755. The Fletcher-Tooth Collection, The John Rylands University Library, The University of Manchester, MAM Fl. 31 (Item J, booklet, 13–62).

———. Letter to Henri-Louis de La Fléchère. 24 February 1756. The Fletcher-Tooth Collection, The John Rylands University Library, The University of Manchester, MAM Fl. 31 (Item J, booklet, 62 ff.).

———. Letter to Henry Brooke. 6 September 1772. The Fletcher-Tooth Collection, The John Rylands University Library, The University of Manchester, MAM Fl. 36/5.

———. Letter to Henry Burder. 12 July [1781?]. The Fletcher-Tooth Collection, The John Rylands University Library, The University of Manchester, MAM Fl. 36/4.

———. Letter to Jacques de la Fléchère. 7 mars 1752. The Fletcher-Tooth Collection, The John Rylands University Library, The University of Manchester, MAM Fl. 31 (Item J, booklet, 1ff.).

———. Letter to Jacques de la Fléchère. December 1752. The Fletcher-Tooth Collection, The John Rylands University Library, The University of Manchester, MAM Fl. 31 (Item J, booklet, 8ff.).

———. Letter to Jacques de la Fléchère. 7 mars 1752. The Fletcher-Tooth Collection, The John Rylands University Library, The University of Manchester, 31.

———. Letter to James Ireland. c. September 1781. The Fletcher-Tooth Collection, The John Rylands University Library, The University of Manchester, MAM Fl. 36/3.

———. Letter to John Wesley. 27 October 1760. Department of Special Collections, Davidson Library, University of California, Santa Barbara, Isaac Foot Collection, Mss 33.

———. Letter to John Wesley. 27 October 1760. Isaac Foot Collection, Mss 33, Department of Special Collections, Davidson Library, University of California, Santa Barbara.

———. Letter to John Wesley. 17 February 1765. The Fletcher-Tooth Collection, The John Rylands University Library, The University of Manchester, MAM Fl. 36/1.

———. Letter to John Wesley. 18 March [1771]. Lamplough Collection, The John Rylands University Library, The University of Manchester, II J. 10.

―――. Letter to John Wesley. 20 February 1771. The Fletcher-Tooth Collection, The John Rylands University Library, The University of Manchester, Fl. Vol. 1:46.

―――. Letter to John Wesley. 13 February 1772. The Fletcher-Tooth Collection, The John Rylands University Library, The University of Manchester, MAM Fl. 36/1.

―――. Letter to John Wesley. 17 February 1778. The Fletcher-Tooth Collection, The John Rylands University Library, The University of Manchester, MAM Fl. 19.

―――. Letter to John Wesley. August/September 1781. The Fletcher-Tooth Collection, The John Rylands University Library, The University of Manchester, MAM Fl. 36/4.

―――. Letter to Joseph Benson. [July 1770]. The Frank Baker Collection, Duke University, Box 3, Folio 4 (J. Benson).

―――. Letter to Joseph Benson. 7 January 1771. The Frank Baker Collection, Duke University, Box 3, Folio 4 (J. Benson).

―――. Letter to Joseph Benson. 10 January 1771. The Frank Baker Collection, Duke University, Box 3, Folio 4 (J. Benson).

―――. Letter to Joseph Benson. 22 March 1771. The Frank Baker Collection, Duke University, Box 3, Folio 4 (J. Benson).

―――. Letter to Joseph Benson. 23 November 1771. The Frank Baker Collection, Duke University, Box 3, Folio 4 (J. Benson).

―――. Letter to Joseph Benson. 10 December 1771. The Frank Baker Collection, Duke University, Box 3, Folio 4 (J. Benson).

―――. Letter to Joseph Benson. 12 February 1772. The Frank Baker Collection, Duke University, Box 3, Folio 4 (J. Benson).

―――. Letter to Joseph Benson. 20 March 1774. The Frank Baker Collection, Duke University, Box 3, Folio 4 (J. Benson).

―――. Letter to Joseph Benson. 2 May 1775. The Frank Baker Collection, Duke University, Box 3, Folio 4 (J. Benson).

―――. Letter to Joseph Benson. 12 July 1775. The Frank Baker Collection, Duke University, Box 3, Folio 4 (J. Benson).

―――. Letter to Joseph Benson. 24 July [1775]. The Frank Baker Collection, Duke University, Box 3, Folio 4 (J. Benson).

―――. Letter to Joseph Benson. 20 July 1781. The Frank Baker Collection, Duke University, Box 3, Folio 4 (J. Benson).

―――. Letter to Joseph Benson. 22 July 1783. The Frank Baker Collection, Duke University, Box 3, Folio 4 (J. Benson).

―――. Letter to Lady Huntingdon and Students of Trevecka College. [Nov. 1770]. Westminster College, Cheshunt Foundation Archives, A3/3/25.

―――. Letter to Lady Huntingdon. 10 November 1768. Westminster College, Cheshunt Foundation Archives, F/1/1449.

―――. Letter to Lady Huntingdon. 15 November 1768. Westminster College, Cheshunt Foundation Archives, F/1/1449.

―――. Letter to Lady Huntingdon. 12 April 1769. Westminster College, Cheshunt Foundation Archives, F/1/1464.

―――. Letter to Lady Huntingdon. 27 May 1769. Westminster College, Cheshunt Foundation Archives, F/1/1467.

―――. Letter to Lady Huntingdon. 10 February 1769. Westminster College, Cheshunt Foundation, F/1/1457.

Bibliography

———. Letter to Lady Huntingdon. Autumn 1770. Westminster College, Cheshunt Foundation Archives, A3/3/25.

———. Letter to Lady Huntingdon. 7 March 1771. Westminster College, Cheshunt Foundation Archives, E4/7/1.

———. Letter to Lady Huntingdon. Saturday morning [9 March 1771]. Westminster College, Cheshunt Foundation Archives, E4/7/2.

———. Letter to Lady Huntingdon. 10 October 1777. Westminster College, Cheshunt Foundation Archives, A1/13/12.

———. Letter to Lady Huntingdon. 28 May 1777. Westminster College, Cheshunt Foundation, A1/13/11.

———. Letter to Lord Darmouth. 19 September 1774. Darmouth Manuscripts, Staffordshire Record Office, Box 2.

———. Letter to Lord Darmouth. 19 June 1783. Darmouth Manuscripts, Staffordshire Record Office, Box 2.

———. Letter to Mary Bosanquet Fletcher. 20 October 1777. The Fletcher-Tooth Collection, The John Rylands University Library, The University of Manchester, MAM Fl. 36/2.

———. Letter to Mary Bosanquet Fletcher. 7 March 1778. The Fletcher-Tooth Collection, The John Rylands University Library, The University of Manchester, MAM Fl. 36/2.

———. Letter to Mary Bosanquet Fletcher. 12 February 1779. The Fletcher-Tooth Collection, The John Rylands University Library, The University of Manchester, MAR, 223A.

———. Letter to Mary Bosanquet Fletcher. 1 May 1781. The Fletcher-Tooth Collection, The John Rylands University Library, The University of Manchester, MAM Fl. 36/2.

———. Letter to Mary Bosanquet Fletcher. 2 September 1781. The Fletcher-Tooth Collection, The John Rylands University Library, The University of Manchester, MAM Fl. 36/3.

———. Letter to Mary Bosanquet Fletcher. 6 September 1781. The Fletcher-Tooth Collection, The John Rylands University Library, The University of Manchester, MAM Fl. 36/3.

———. Letter to Mary Bosanquet Fletcher. 10 September 1781. The Fletcher-Tooth Collection, The John Rylands University Library, The University of Manchester, MAM Fl. 36/3.

———. Letter to Mary Bosanquet Fletcher. 11/12 September 1781. The Fletcher-Tooth Collection, The John Rylands University Library, The University of Manchester, MAM Fl. 36/3.

———. Letter to Mary Bosanquet Fletcher. 19 September 1781. The Fletcher-Tooth Collection, The John Rylands University Library, The University of Manchester, MAM Fl. 36/3.

———. Letter to Mary Bosanquet Fletcher. 22 September 1781. The Fletcher-Tooth Collection, The John Rylands University Library, The University of Manchester, MAM Fl. 36/3.

———. Letter to Mary Bosanquet Fletcher. [19 October 1782]. The Fletcher-Tooth Collection, The John Rylands University Library, The University of Manchester, MAM Fl. 36/4.

———. Letter to Mary Bosanquet Fletcher. 21 October 1783. The Fletcher-Tooth Collection, The John Rylands University Library, The University of Manchester, MAM Fl. 36/3.

———. Letter to Mary Bosanquet. 7 March 1778. The Fletcher-Tooth Collection, The John Rylands University Library, The University of Manchester, 36/2.

———. Letter to Masters and Students of Lady Huntingdon's College. 23 July 1770. The Frank Baker Collection, Duke University, Box 4, Folio 9 (J. Benson).

———. Letter to Messrs. Hare, Terry Fox, and Good at Hull and Messrs. Preston, Simpson and Ramsden at York. October 1776. The Fletcher-Tooth Collection, The John Rylands University Library, The University of Manchester, MAM Fl. 18.

———. Letter to Miss Hatton. 5 March 1764. Sidney Lawson Collection, The John Rylands University Library, The University of Manchester, 97.

———. Letter to Miss Hatton. 28 March [1766?]. The Fletcher-Tooth Collection, The John Rylands University Library, The University of Manchester, MAM Fl. 36/5.

———. Letter to Miss Locksdale. 17 March 1782. Wesley's Chapel, City Road, London, LDWMM 2001/8215.

———. Letter to Miss Loxdale. 22 June 1781. The Fletcher-Tooth Collection, The John Rylands University Library, The University of Manchester, MAM Fl. 36/3.

———. Letter to Miss Perronet. 4 September 1781. The Fletcher-Tooth Collection, The John Rylands University Library, The University of Manchester, MAM Fl. 36/3.

———. Letter to Mons. Bridel (3). n.d. The Fletcher-Tooth Collection, The John Rylands University Library, The University of Manchester, MAM Fl. 18/4/1.

———. Letter to Mons. Bridel (4). n.d. The Fletcher-Tooth Collection, The John Rylands University Library, The University of Manchester, MAM Fl. 18/4/1.

———. Letter to Mons. Bridel (5). n.d. The Fletcher-Tooth Collection, The John Rylands University Library, The University of Manchester, MAM Fl. 18/4/1.

———. Letter to Mons. Bridel (6). n.d. The Fletcher-Tooth Collection, The John Rylands University Library, The University of Manchester, MAM Fl. 18/4/1.

———. Letter to Monsieur de Luc. 19 December 1782. The Fletcher-Tooth Collection, The John Rylands University Library, The University of Manchester, MAM Fl. 19.

———. Letter to Mr. Powers. 20 June 1778. The Upper Room Chapel and Museum, The General Board of Discipleship of the United Methodist Church, L/209.

———. Letter to Mr. Wase. 16 October 1766. Shropshire Archives, 2280/16/1.

———. Letter to Mr. Wase. 11 February 1779. The Fletcher-Tooth Collection, The John Rylands University Library, The University of Manchester, MAM Fl. 36/2.

———. Letter to Mr. William Perronet. 9 November 1779. Shropshire Archives, 2280/16/1.2.

———. Letter to Mrs. Dolier. [November 1783]. The Fletcher-Tooth Collection, The John Rylands University Library, The University of Manchester, MAM Fl. 36/5.

———. Letter to Mrs. Ford. 23 February 1777. The Robert W. Woodruff Library of Advanced Studies, Special Collections Department, Emory University, J. Wesley Coll., 1734–1864.

———. Letter to Mrs. Goodwin. [after 1781]. Shropshire Archives, 2280/16/2.

———. Letter to Mrs. Leighton. 30 April 1768. The Frank Baker Collection, Duke University, Box 5, Folio 3 (Leighton Correspondence).

———. Letter to Mrs. Leighton. 19 November 1768. The Frank Baker Collection, Duke University, Box 5, Folio 3 (Leighton Correspondence).

Bibliography

———. Letter to Peter Maber. 7 May 1776. Lovely Lane Museum, Commission on Archives and History, Baltimore-Washington Conference, United Methodist Church.

———. Letter to Rev. Beale. 15 October 1771. The Upper Room Chapel and Museum, The General Board of Discipleship of the United Methodist Church, L/68.

———. Letter to Rev. Beale. 14 November 1771. The Upper Room Chapel and Museum, The General Board of Discipleship of the United Methodist Church, L/69.

———. Letter to Rev. Mr. Lewis. 3 February 1762. The Fletcher-Tooth Collection, The John Rylands University Library, The University of Manchester, MAM Fl. 18/18.

———. Letter to Rev. Mr. Prothero. 25 July 1761. John and Mary Fletcher Papers, The Methodist Collections, Drew University.

———. Letter to Rev. Mr. Prothero. 3 February 1762. The Fletcher-Tooth Collection, The John Rylands University Library, The University of Manchester, MAW Fl. 31.

———. Letter to Rev. Peard Dickenson. 29 March 1785. Wesley's Chapel, City Road, London, LDWMM 2000/7971.

———. Letter to Rev. Vincent and Miss Perronet. 2 December 1777. The Frank Baker Collection, Duke University, Box 6 (Perronet Family).

———. Letter to Rev. Vincent Perronet. 8 February 1779. The Fletcher-Tooth Collection, The John Rylands University Library, The University of Manchester, MAM Fl. 36/1.

———. Letter to Rev. Vincent Perronet. 4 September 1781. The Fletcher-Tooth Collection, The John Rylands University Library, The University of Manchester, MAM Fl. 36/3.

———. Letter to Sarah Ryan. 5 September 1759. The Fletcher-Tooth Collection, The John Rylands University Library, The University of Manchester, MAM Fl. 36/1.

———. Letter to Sir [Claude Bosanquet]. [22 September 1781]. The Fletcher-Tooth Collection, The John Rylands University Library, The University of Manchester, MAM Fl. 36/4.

———. Letter to Societies in and about Madeley. 1778. The Fletcher-Tooth Collection, The John Rylands University Library, The University of Manchester, MAM Fl. 18/4.

———. Letter to Thomas Slaughter. May 1762. The Fletcher-Tooth Collection, The John Rylands University Library, The University of Manchester, MAM Fl. 17/19.

———. Letter to unidentified. 17 October 1773. The Fletcher-Tooth Collection, The John Rylands University Library, The University of Manchester, MAM Fl. 36/5.

———. Letter to unknown ["Dear Madam"]. n.d. The Fletcher-Tooth Collection, The John Rylands University Library, The University of Manchester, MAM Fl. 36.

———. Letter to V.C. 12 February 1779. The Fletcher-Tooth Collection, The John Rylands University Library, The University of Manchester, MAW PLP 41/26/6.

———. Letter to William Perronet. 2 June 1778. The Frank Baker Collection, Duke University, Perronet Family Scrapbook, 39.

———. Letter to William Perronet. 18 November 1779. Wesley's Chapel, City Road, London, LDWMM 2000/7967.

———. Letter to William Perronet. 31 December 1780. The Frank Baker Collection, Duke University, Box 6, Perronet Family Scrapbook, 37.

———. Letter to William Perronet. 14 January 1781. The Fletcher-Tooth Collection, The John Rylands University Library, The University of Manchester, MAM Fl. 36/2.

———. Letter to William Smith. [24 November 1783]. The Fletcher-Tooth Collection, The John Rylands University Library, The University of Manchester, MAM Fl. 15.
———. "Letter XCVII [From the Rev. Mr. Fletcher to the Rev. Mr. Wesley]." *Arminian Magazine* 3 (1780) 99–101.
———. *Letters of John Fletcher*. Edited by Edward Cook. Stoke-on-Trent: Harvey Christian, 1999.
———. *Logica Genevensis Continued, or, The Second Part of the Fifth Check to Antinomianism*. The Second Edition. Bristol: Pine, 1774.
———. *Logica Genevensis: or, A Fourth Check to Antinomianism, in Which St. James's Pure Religion is Defended Against the Charges, and Established upon the Concession, of Mr. Richard and Rowland Hill in a Series of Letters to Those Gentlemen, by the Vindicator of the Minutes*. Bristol: Pine, 1772.
———. Loose Hints on the Spirit. The Fletcher-Tooth Collection, The John Rylands Library, The University of Manchester, MAM Fl 17.1.
———. *La Louange, Poème Moral et Sacré, Tiré du Psaume CXLVII*. Nyon: n.p., 1781.
———. Manifestation of Christ. The Fletcher-Tooth Collection, The John Rylands Library, The University of Manchester, MAM Fl 21/12.
———. Manifestation of Christ. The Fletcher-Tooth Collection, The John Rylands Library, The University of Manchester, MAM Fl 17/1.
———. Manifestation of X. The Fletcher-Tooth Collection, The John Rylands Library, The University of Manchester, MAM Fl 20.17.
———. A Manuscript extract of Bishop Latimer's sermons. Arthur Skevington Wood Archive Library, Cliff College, A/1/06.
———. A Moral and Evangelical Catechism for the use of Sunday Schools. The Fletcher-Tooth Collection, The John Rylands University Library, The University of Manchester, 17/9.
———. "Mr. Fletcher on Prophecies." *Arminian Magazine* 16 (1793) 370–76, 409–16.
———. "Mr. Fletcher's Letters." *Arminian Magazine* 17 (1794) 102–5, 219–20, 319–23, 381–86, 489–92, 541–45.
———. "Mr. Fletcher's Letters." *Arminian Magazine* 18 (1795) 48–52, 102–5, 149–55, 205–8, 256–61, 302–7, 361–65, 409–12, 456–61, 513–18, 612–17.
———. "Mr. Fletcher's Letters." *Arminian Magazine* 19 (1796) 43–48, 96–100, 145–52, 192–98, 246–51, 286–91, 342–47.
———. "Mr. Fletcher's Pastoral Letters." *Arminian Magazine* 16 (1793) 106–9.
———. "Mr. Fletcher's Pastoral Letters." *Arminian Magazine* 17 (1794) 42–46.
———. *The Nature and Rules of a Religious Society: Submitted to the Consideration of the Serious Inhabitants of the Parish of Madeley*. Edited by Melvill Horne. Madeley: Edmunds, 1788.
———. Nature et Grace. The Fletcher-Tooth Collection, The John Rylands University Library, The University of Manchester, 19/4.
———. *The New Birth*. Bristol: Lancaster & Edwards, 1794.
———. Notes on Gospel Chronology. The Fletcher-Tooth Collection, The John Rylands University Library, The University of Manchester, 17/1.
———. "On Internal Religion." *Arminian Magazine* 15 (1792) 604–6.
———. "A Pastoral Letter from Rev. Mr. Fletcher to the Parishioners of Madeley." *Arminian Magazine* 16 (1793) 484–86, 551–53.
———. "Pastoral Letters from the Rev. Mr. Fletcher." *Arminian Magazine* 16 (1793) 659–63.

Bibliography

———. "Pastoral Letters from the Rev. Mr. Fletcher." *Arminian Magazine* 16 (1793) 596–99.

———. *The Penitent Thief: or, A Narrative of Two Women Fearing God, Who Visited in Prison a Highway-man, Executed at Stafford, April the 3d, 1773 With a Letter to a Condemned Malefactor: and A Penitential Office, for Either a True Churchman, or a Dying Criminal, Entirely Extracted from the Scriptures and the Established Liturgy.* 2nd ed. London: Hawes, 1773.

———. Pocketbook of Sermons "June 1764." Arthur Skevington Wood Archive Library, Cliff College, A/1/08.

———. Pocketbook of Sermons (vol. 1). The Fletcher-Tooth Collection, The John Rylands University Library, The University of Manchester. MAM Fl. 20.14.

———. Pocketbook of Sermons (vol. 2). The Fletcher-Tooth Collection, The John Rylands University Library, The University of Manchester. MAM Fl. 20.14.

———. Pocketbook of Sermons (vol. 3). The Fletcher-Tooth Collection, The John Rylands University Library, The University of Manchester. MAM Fl. 20.14.

———. Pocketbook of Sermons (vol. 4). The Fletcher-Tooth Collection, The John Rylands University Library, The University of Manchester. MAM Fl. 20.14.

———. Pocketbook of Sermons (vol. 5). The Fletcher-Tooth Collection, The John Rylands University Library, The University of Manchester. MAM Fl. 20.14.

———. Pocketbook of Sermons (vol. 6). The Fletcher-Tooth Collection, The John Rylands University Library, The University of Manchester. MAM Fl. 20.14.

———. Pocketbook of Sermons (vol. 7). The Fletcher-Tooth Collection, The John Rylands University Library, The University of Manchester. MAM Fl. 20.14.

———. Pocketbook of Sermons. Arthur Skevington Wood Archive Library, Cliff College, A/1/11 (b).

———. Pocketbook of Sermons. The Fletcher-Tooth Collection, The John Rylands University Library, The University of Manchester. MAM Fl. 31 (Item I).

———. Pocketbook of Sermons. The Frank Baker Collection, Duke University, Box 4, Folio 9 (J. W. Fletcher).

———. A Pocketbook "Spiritual Extracts." The Fletcher-Tooth Collection, The John Rylands University Library, The University of Manchester, 20/11.

———. Pocketbook of Transcribed Sermons by Sarah Lawrence. The Fletcher-Tooth Collection, The John Rylands University Library, The University of Manchester, MAM Fl. 19 (vol. 1).

———. *The Portrait of St. Paul: or, The True Model for Christians and Pastors. Translated from a French Manuscript of the Late Rev. John William de la Flechere, Vicar of Madeley, to which is Added, some Account of the Author, by the Rev. Joshua Gilpin, Vicar of Rockwardine, in the County of Salop.* Joshua Gilpin, trans. 2 vols. Shrewsbury: Eddowes, 1790.

———. A Proposal for an union among Gospel Ministers. April 19, 1764. Arthur Skevington Wood Archive Library, Cliff College, A/1/01 (a).

———. A Proposal for an union among Gospel Ministers. April 19, 1764. Arthur Skevington Wood Archive Library, Cliff College, A/1/01 (b).

———. Pulpit Preparations or Brief Sketches of Sermons by the Late Rev. John Fletcher, Vicar of Madeley: Written for His Own Use Carefully Transcribed by J. Gill. The Fletcher-Tooth Collection, The John Rylands University Library, The University of Manchester, MAM Fl. 31 (Item G).

Bibliography

———. *A Race for Eternal Life: Being an Extract from "The Heavenly Footman," A Sermon on 1 Corinth. ix.24. Written by the Author of The Pilgrim's Progress.* London: Hawes, 1777.

———. *The Reconciliation or, An Easy Method to Unite the Professing People of God, by Placing the Doctrines of Grace and Justice in Such Light, as to Make the Candid Arminians Bible-Calvinists, and the Candid Calvinists, Bible-Arminians.* London: Hawes, 1777.

———. *A Reply to the Principal Arguments by Which the Calvinists and the Fatalists Support the Doctrine of Absolute Necessity Being Remarks on the Rev. Mr. Toplady's "Scheme of Christian and Philosophical Necessity."* London: Hawes, 1777.

———. A Scriptural Vindication First Letter: The Occasion and Design of These Letters. The Fletcher-Tooth Collection, The John Rylands University Library, The University of Manchester, 17/21.

———. *A Second Check to Antinomianism, Occasioned by A Late Narrative, in Three Letters, to the Hon. and Rev. Author by the Vindicator of the Rev. Mr. Wesley's Minutes.* London: New-Chapel, [1771].

———. Second Part Containing Answers to the Objections Made in This Essay. The Fletcher-Tooth Collection, The John Rylands University Library, The University of Manchester, MAM Fl. 18/9.

———. "Second Part Containing Answers to the Objections Made to This Essay." Edited by Laurence W. Wood. *Asbury Theological Journal* 53/1 (1998) 57–64.

———. "A Sermon by the Rev. J. Fletcher, Preached at Madeley at an Early Period of His Ministry [on Deut. 32.9]." *Methodist Magazine* 4 (1821) 174–83.

———. Sermon on "Fasting." The Fletcher-Tooth Collection, The John Rylands University Library, The University of Manchester, MAM Fl. 31 (Item H).

———. Sermon on "God with us." The Fletcher-Tooth Collection, The John Rylands University Library, The University of Manchester, MAM Fl. 20/17.

———. Sermon on "Occasion Exhortation." The Fletcher-Tooth Collection, The John Rylands University Library, The University of Manchester, MAM Fl. 19.

———. Sermon on "Prerequisites." The Fletcher-Tooth Collection, The John Rylands University Library, The University of Manchester, MAM Fl. 17/3.

———. Sermon on "Thomas Lydia new Creature." The Fletcher-Tooth Collection, The John Rylands University Library, The University of Manchester, MAM Fl. 20/17.

———. Sermon on [2 Corinthians 8.1–7]. The Fletcher-Tooth Collection, The John Rylands University Library, The University of Manchester, MAM Fl. 20/17.

———. Sermon on [To the Gospel Feast]. Shropshire Archives, 2280/16/81.

———. Sermon on 1 Corinthians 16.22. John Fletcher's Sermon Notes, GCAH, Drew University, 1306.5.3:2/A.

———. "A Sermon [on 1 Cor. 5.17]." *Methodist Magazine* 4 (1821) 161–165, 201–205.

———. Sermon on 1 Corinthians 6.19–20. The Fletcher-Tooth Collection, The John Rylands University Library, The University of Manchester, MAM Fl. 17.2.

———. Sermon on 1 John 1.7. The Fletcher-Tooth Collection, The John Rylands University Library, The University of Manchester, MAM Fl. 20/5.

———. Sermon on 2 Corinthians 5.14. The Fletcher-Tooth Collection, The John Rylands University Library, The University of Manchester, MAM Fl. 20/17.

———. Sermon on Acts 26.28. The Fletcher-Tooth Collection, The John Rylands University Library, The University of Manchester, MAM Fl. 20.17.

Bibliography

———. Sermon on Acts 3.19. The Fletcher-Tooth Collection, The John Rylands University Library, The University of Manchester, MAM Fl. 19.

———. Sermon on Daniel 3.11. Shropshire Archives, 2280/16/78.

———. Sermon on Exodus 3.14. The Fletcher-Tooth Collection, The John Rylands University Library, The University of Manchester, MAM Fl. 20/17.

———. "A Sermon [on Ezek. 2.7]." *Methodist Magazine* 4 (1821) 321–325.

———. Sermon on Ezekiel 13.10-11. Shropshire Archives, 2280/16/68.

———. Sermon on Ezekiel 33.7-9. The Fletcher-Tooth Collection, The John Rylands University Library, The University of Manchester, MAM Fl. 31 (Item F).

———. Sermon on Galatians 6.15. The Fletcher-Tooth Collection, The John Rylands University Library, The University of Manchester, MAM Fl. 19/10.

———. Sermon on Genesis 1:26 (b). The Fletcher-Tooth Collection, The John Rylands University Library, The University of Manchester, MAM Fl. 20/17.

———. Sermon on Genesis 45.1. The Fletcher-Tooth Collection, The John Rylands University Library, The University of Manchester, MAM Fl. 20/17.

———. Sermon on Haggai 2.7. The Fletcher-Tooth Collection, The John Rylands University Library, The University of Manchester, MAM Fl. 20/17.

———. Sermon on Hebrews 13.1. The Fletcher-Tooth Collection, The John Rylands University Library, The University of Manchester, MAM Fl. 20/17.

———. Sermon on John 1.12 (b). The Fletcher-Tooth Collection, The John Rylands University Library, The University of Manchester, MAM Fl. 20/17.

———. Sermon on John 1.29. John Fletcher's Sermon Notes, GCAH, Drew University, 1306.5.5:2/A.

———. Sermon on John 14.6. The Fletcher-Tooth Collection, The John Rylands University Library, The University of Manchester, MAM Fl. 20.17.

———. "A Sermon [on John 3.3]." *Methodist Magazine* 4 (1821) 241–245, 281–287.

———. Sermon on John 3.13-15. John Fletcher's Sermon Notes, GCAH, Drew University, 1306.5.3:2/A.

———. Sermon on John 3.14-15. The Fletcher-Tooth Collection, The John Rylands University Library, The University of Manchester, MAM Fl. 20/17.

———. Sermon on John 3.30. John Fletcher's Sermon Notes, GCAH, Drew University, 1306.5.3:2/A.

———. "A Sermon [on John 6.66-68]." *Methodist Magazine* 4 (1821) 401–406, 441–448.

———. Sermon on Luke 22.44. Shropshire Archives, 2280/16/79.

———. Sermon on Matthew 11.12. Shropshire Archives, 2280/16/80.

———. Sermon on Matthew 11.28. John Fletcher's Sermon Notes, GCAH, Drew University, 1305.5.3.2.

———. Sermon on Matthew 25.46. The Fletcher-Tooth Collection, The John Rylands University Library, The University of Manchester, MAM Fl. 20/17.

———. Sermon on Matthew 25.6. Shropshire Archives, 2280/16/70.

———. Sermon on Matthew 6.10 (a). The Fletcher-Tooth Collection, The John Rylands University Library, The University of Manchester, MAM Fl. 20/17.

———. Sermon on Matthew 6.10 (b). The Fletcher-Tooth Collection, The John Rylands University Library, The University of Manchester, MAM Fl. 20/17.

———. Sermon on Matthew 6.11. The Fletcher-Tooth Collection, The John Rylands University Library, The University of Manchester, MAM Fl. 20/17.

———. Sermon on Matthew 6.12. The Fletcher-Tooth Collection, The John Rylands University Library, The University of Manchester, MAM Fl. 20/17.

———. Sermon on Matthew 6.13 (a). The Fletcher-Tooth Collection, The John Rylands University Library, The University of Manchester, MAM Fl. 20/17.

———. Sermon on Matthew 6.13 (b). The Fletcher-Tooth Collection, The John Rylands University Library, The University of Manchester, MAM Fl. 20/17.

———. Sermon on Matthew 6.33 (b). The Fletcher-Tooth Collection, The John Rylands University Library, The University of Manchester, MAM Fl. 20/17.

———. Sermon on Matthew 6.33 (c). The Fletcher-Tooth Collection, The John Rylands University Library, The University of Manchester, MAM Fl. 20/17.

———. Sermon on Matthew 6.9 (a). The Fletcher-Tooth Collection, The John Rylands University Library, The University of Manchester, MAM Fl. 20/17.

———. Sermon on Matthew 6.9 (b). The Fletcher-Tooth Collection, The John Rylands University Library, The University of Manchester, MAM Fl. 20/17.

———. Sermon on Matthew 7.13-14. The Fletcher-Tooth Collection, The John Rylands University Library, The University of Manchester, MAM Fl. 20/17.

———. Sermon on Numbers 23.10. The Fletcher-Tooth Collection, The John Rylands University Library, The University of Manchester, MAM Fl. 36/7.

———. Sermon on Philippians 1.21. The Fletcher-Tooth Collection, The John Rylands University Library, The University of Manchester, MAM Fl. 19/2.

———. Sermon on Philippians 3.18-20. Shropshire Archives, 2280/16/68.

———. Sermon on Philippians 3.8. The Fletcher-Tooth Collection, The John Rylands University Library, The University of Manchester, MAM Fl. 20/17.

———. Sermon on Proverbs 3.17. Shropshire Archives, 2280/16/69.

———. Sermon on Psalm 39. The Fletcher-Tooth Collection, The John Rylands University Library, The University of Manchester, MAM Fl. 20/17.

———. Sermon on Psalm 80.19. Shropshire Archives, 2280/16/69.

———. Sermon on Psalm 94.19. The Fletcher-Tooth Collection, The John Rylands University Library, The University of Manchester, MAM Fl. 20/17.

———. Sermon on Revelation 3.15-16. Shropshire Archives, 2280/16/77.

———. Sermon on Romans 13.12-14. The Fletcher-Tooth Collection, The John Rylands University Library, The University of Manchester, MAM Fl. 17.19.

———. Sermon on Romans 14.8. Shropshire Archives, 2280/16/70.

———. Sermon, "1. Why we must love God." The United Library, Garrett Evangelical Divinity School, William Colbert Coll., 26.

———. Sermon, "Thomas. Lydia [New Creatures]." The United Library, Garrett Evangelical Divinity School, William Colbert Coll., 26.

———. Sermon, 1 Corinthians 3.2. Arthur Skevington Wood Archive Library, Cliff College, A/1/02.

———. Sermon, 1 Kings 18.21. Wesley College, Bristol, D6/1/p. 242.

———. Sermon, 2 Samuel 12.7. Arthur Skevington Wood Archive Library, Cliff College, A/1/02.

———. Sermon, Ecclesiastes 11.9. Wesley College, Bristol, D6/1/p. 242 (e).

———. Sermon, Isaiah 27.13. Wesley College, Bristol, D6/3/1 p. 73.

———. Sermon, Jeremiah 23.5. Wesley College, Bristol, D6/1/242 (c).

———. Sermon, John 1.12. The United Library, Garrett Evangelical Divinity School, William Colbert Coll., 26.

———. Sermon, John 1.29. Wesley College, Bristol, D6/1/p. 242 (a).

Bibliography

———. Sermon, John 20.25. Wesley College, Bristol, D6/1/p. 242 (b).
———. Sermon, John 6.44. Wesley College, Bristol, D6/1/p. 242 (d).
———. Sermon, John 9.30. Wesley College, Bristol, D6/1/p. 242 (e).
———. Sermon, Luke 15.7. Arthur Skevington Wood Archive Library, Cliff College, A/1/02.
———. Sermon, Luke 18.8. Wesley College, Bristol, D6/3/1 p. 73.
———. Sermon, Matthew 22.39. The United Library, Garrett Evangelical Divinity School, William Colbert Coll., 26.
———. Sermon, Matthew 5.20. Arthur Skevington Wood Archive Library, Cliff College, A/1/02.
———. Sermon, Matthew 5.43. Wesley College, Bristol, D2/14.
———. Sermon, Romans 2.4–5. Arthur Skevington Wood Archive Library, Cliff College, A/1/02.
———. Sermon, Romans 7.24. Arthur Skevington Wood Archive Library, Cliff College, A/1/02.
———. *Sermons*. 2nd ed. Paris, 1853.
———. *Six Letters of the Late Rev. John Fletcher, Vicar of Madeley, in Shropshire*. Bath: Hazard, 1788.
———. *Six Letters on the Spiritual Manifestation of the Son of God*. Edited by Melvill Horne. Leeds: n.p., 1791.
———. "Six Letters on the Spiritual Manifestation of the Son of God." *Arminian Magazine* 16 (1793) 45–53, 88–94, 147–53, 203–8, 260–68, 313–21.
———. A Society of Ministers of the Gospel, in the Church of England, is proposed to be established, under the following Rules & Regulations. 1765. Arthur Skevington Wood Archive Library, Cliff College, A/1/24.
———. *Socinianism Unscriptural; or, The Prophets and Apostles Vindicated From the Charge of Holding the Doctrine of Christ's Mere Humanity; Being the Second Part of a Vindication of His Divinity*. Edited by J. Benson. 2nd ed. Birmingham: Jones, 1791.
———. *Some Genuine Letters of the Late Rev. Mr. Fletcher, Vicar of Madeley, Shropshire to Which is Added, His Heads of Self-Examination*. Dublin: Dugdale, 1788.
———. Theorems. Arthur Skevington Wood Archive Library, Cliff College, A/1/05.
———. *A Third Check to Antinomianism in a Letter to the Author of Pietas Oxoniensis by the Vindicator of the Rev. Mr. Wesley's Minutes*. 2nd ed. London: Hawes, 1775.
———. *Thirteen Original Letters Written by the Late Rev. John Fletcher, Vicar of Madeley, Shropshire. To Which Are Added His Heads of Self-Examination*. Bath: Campbell & Gainsborough, 1791.
———. "Thoughts on Fanaticism." Translated by Miles Martindale. *Arminian Magazine* 18 (1795) 536–42.
———. *Three National Grievances: The Increase of Taxation: And the Continual Rise of the Poor's Rates: with the Causes and Remedies of These Evils: Humbly Submitted to the Consideration of the Legislature: in a letter to the Righ Honorable Lord Cavendish. Chancellor of the Exchequer, and One of the Lords of the Treasury*. London: n.p., 1783.
———. "The Three Principles." *Arminian Magazine* 19 (1795) 17–19.
———. Transcribed letter to Henri-Louis de la Fléchère. 11 mai 1755. The Fletcher-Tooth Collection, The John Rylands University Library, The University of Manchester, 31 (Item J).

Bibliography

———. Unidentified manuscript containing in part arguments for two baptisms. The Fletcher-Tooth Collection, The John Rylands University Library, The University of Manchester, MAM Fl. 18/13.

———. *A Vindication of the Rev. Mr. Wesley's "Calm Address to our American Colonies" in Three Letters to Mr. Caleb Evans*. 3rd ed. London: Hawes, 1776.

———. *A Vindication of the Rev. Mr. Wesley's Last Minutes: Occasioned by a Circular, Printed Letter, Inviting Such Principal Persons, Both Clergy and Laity, as well as of the Dissenters of the Established Church, who Disapprove of Those Minutes, to Oppose Them in a Body, as a Dreadful Heresy: and Designed to Remove Prejudice, Check Rashness, Defend the Character of an Eminent Minister of Christ, Prevent Some Important Scriptural Truths from Being Hastily Branded as Heretical, and Stem the Torrent of Antinomianism in Five Letters to the Hon. and Rev. Author of The Circular Letter, by a Lover of Quietness and Liberty of Conscience*. 4th ed. London: Hawes, 1775.

———. "The Wicked Described and Warned [on Ezek. 33.7-9]." *Methodist Magazine* 5 (1822) 321–26, 361–66.

———. *The Works of the Reverend John Fletcher*. 4 vols. New York: Phillips & Hunt, 1883.

———. *The Works of the Reverend John Fletcher*. 9 vols. London: Edwards, 1806–1810.

———. *The Works of the Reverend John Fletcher*. 9 vols. London: Wesleyan Conference Office, 1856–1860.

———. *The Works of the Reverend John Fletcher*. 9 vols. London: Wesleyan Conference Office, 1877.

———. *Zelotes and Honestus Reconciled: or, An Equal Check to Pharisaism and Antinomianism Continued: Being the First Part of the Scripture Scales to Weigh the Gold of Gospel Truth - To Balance a Multitude of Opposite Scriptures - To Prove the Gospel Marriage of Free-Grace and Free-Will, and Restore Primitive Harmony of the Gospel of the Day. With a Preface, Containing Some Strictures upon the Three Letters of Richard Hill, Esq; Which Have Lately Been Published*. 2nd ed. London: Hawes.

[Fletcher, John]. *The Furious Butcher Humbled, A True and Remarkable Story as Related by the Late Rev. Mr. Fletcher, Vicar of Madeley, in Shropshire*. London: A. Paris, [1800?].

Fletcher, John, and Joseph Benson. *A Rational Vindication of the Catholic Faith, Being the First Part of a Vindication of Christ's Divinity, Inscribed to the Reverend Dr. Priestly*. London: New-Chapel, 1790.

Fletcher, John, and J. C. B. Campbell. *Prophecies of Remarkable Events Now Taking Place in Europe. By the Late Rev. John Fletcher, in a Letter to the Late Rev. John Wesley, A. M. Dated London, Nov. 20, 1755. To Which are Prefixed a Sketch of the Author's Life, and an Account of a Benevolent Society in Bath Entitled 'The Poor Stranger's and Sick Man's Friend.' Published for the Benefit of the Said Society*. Bath: Campbell, 1793.

Fletcher, John, and Samuel Dunn. *Selections from the Works of the Rev. John Fletcher, Vicar of Madeley: Systematically Arranged With a Life of the Author*. London: Mason, 1837.

Fletcher, John, and Mary Bosanquet Fletcher. Commonplace book. Arthur Skevington Wood Archive Library, Cliff College, A/1/09.

Bibliography

———. Letter to George Gibbons. 3 June 1785. The Frank Baker Collection, Duke University, Box 4, Folio 9 (J.W. Fletcher).

———. Letter to Lady Mary Fitzgerald. 19 July 1785. The Fletcher-Tooth Collection, The John Rylands University Library, The University of Manchester, MAM Fl. 17/22.

———. Letter to the Dublin Society. 21 October 1783. The Fletcher-Tooth Collection, The John Rylands University Library, The University of Manchester, MAM Fl. 36/4.

Fletcher, John, and Aaron Merritt Hills. *Honour the Holy: Sermons*. N.p.: n.p., 1961.

Fletcher, John, and Melvill Horne. *Posthumous Pieces of the Late Rev. John Fletcher: Containing His Pastoral and Familiar Epistles, Together with Six Letters on the Manifestation of Christ*. London: Mason, 1833.

———. *Posthumous Pieces of the Late Rev. John William de la Flechere*. Madeley: Edmunds, 1791.

Fletcher, John, and J. Kingston. *Fletcher's Appeal to Matter of Fact and Common Sense, or, A Rational Demonstration of Man's Corrupt and Lost Estate with the Address to Earnest Seekers for Salvation and an Appendix from the Nineteenth London Edition to Which is now Added The Life of the Venerable Author, Compiled for this Work from the Most Authentic Sources*. Edited by J. Kingston. Baltimore: Robinson, 1814.

Fletcher, Mary Bosanquet. "Account of M. Matthews of Madeley." *Methodist Magazine* 23 (1800) 219–23.

———. *An Aunt's Advice to a Niece: Also Some Account of a Correspondence with the Late Rev. Dr. Dodd, During His Imprisonment*. Leeds: Bowling, 1780.

———. *Jesus, Altogether Lovely: or A Letter to Some of the Single Women in the Methodist Society*. Bristol: n.p., 1766.

———. "Letter from Mrs. Fletcher to the Rev. J. Wesley." *Arminian Magazine* 13 (1790) 390–391.

———. Letter to John Fletcher. 1 September 1781. The Fletcher-Tooth Collection, The John Rylands University Library, The University of Manchester, MAM Fl. 37/6.

———. Letter to John Fletcher. 2 October 1781. The Fletcher-Tooth Collection, The John Rylands University Library, The University of Manchester, MAM Fl. 37/6.

———. Letter to Joseph Benson. 6 July 1779. The Frank Baker Collection, Duke University, Box 3, Folio 4 (J. Benson).

———. *A Letter to Mons. H. L. De la Fléchère, Assessor Ballival of Nyon, in the Canton of Berne, Switzerland, on the Death of His Brother, the Reverend John William De la Fléchère, Twenty-five Years Vicar of Madeley, Shropshire*. London: Hindmarsh, 1786.

———. *A Letter to the Rev. Mr. Wesley, By a Gentlewoman*. London: n.p., 1764.

———. *A Letter to the Rev. Mr. Wesley on the Death of the Rev. Mr. Fletcher, Vicar of Madeley in Shropshire*. Madeley: Edmunds, [1785].

———. *A Letter to the Rev. Mr. Wesley on the Death of the Rev. Mr. Fletcher, Vicar of Madeley in Shropshire*. Falmouth: Elliot, [1786].

———. *A Letter Written to Elizabeth A——ws, On Her Removal from England*. Leeds-Bridge: Bowling, 1770.

———. Notes on a sermon. The Fletcher-Tooth Collection, The John Rylands University Library, The University of Manchester, 36/6.

———. Sermon, Isaiah 61. Arthur Skevington Wood Archive Library, Cliff College, A/1/03.

———. The Test of a New Creature Being Questions of Examination for the Spiritually Minded. September 1758. The Fletcher-Tooth Correspondence, The John Rylands University Library, The University of Manchester, MAM Fl. 36/6.

———. "Watchwords: Names of Christ." *Asbury Theological Journal* 61/2 (2006) 13–94.

Fletcher, Mary Bosanquet, and Joseph Entwisle. *A Legacy to the People of Madeley*. London: Cordeaux, 1819.

Fletcher, W. Brian. "Christian Perfection in Wesley and Fletcher with Implications for Today." PhD thesis, University of Edinburgh, 1997.

Fletcher Volume. The Fletcher-Tooth Collection, The John Rylands University Library, The University of Manchester, MAM Fl.

Flick, Stephen Allen. "John William Fletcher: The Portrait of a Christian Pastor." Chamberlain Holiness Lectures, Wesley Biblical Seminary, Jackson, Mississippi, cassette tape, 1995.

———. "John William Fletcher, Vicar of Madeley: A Pastoral Theology." PhD diss., Drew University, 1994.

Foras, Cte. E-Amedee de. *Armorial et nobiliaire de l'ancien duché de Savoie*. 2nd ed. Grenoble: Allier, 1878.

Forsaith, Peter Stuart. "Charles Wesley and John Fletcher." In *Charles Wesley: Life, Literature and Legacy*, edited by Kenneth G. C. Newport and Ted A. Campbell, 109–23. London: Epworth, 2007.

———. "The Correspondence of the Revd. John W. Fletcher: letters to the Revd Charles Wesley, considered in the context of the Evangelical Revival." PhD diss., Oxford Brookes University, 2003.

———. "'A Dearer Country' the Frenchness of the Rev. Jean de la Fléchère of Madeley, a Methodist Church of England Vicar." In *From Strangers to Citizens: The Integration of Immigrant Communities in Britain, Ireland and Colonial America, 1550–1750*, edited by Randolph Vigne and Charles Littleton, 519–526. Brighton: Sussex Academic, 2001.

———. "A Dreadful Phenomenon at the Birches." Paper presented at the Ecclesiastical History Society Conference, 2008.

———. *The Eagle and the Dove: John Fletcher, Vicar of Madeley: Towards a New Assessment*. Bristol: Forsaith, 1979.

———. "An Eighteenth Century Worcester Association." In *Wesley Historical Society, West Midlands Branch, "Silver Jubilee Miscellany 1965–1990*," 44–51. Warwick: Wesley Historical Society, West Midlands Branch, 1990.

———. "John Fletcher: A Failure in His Parish." TD (Fletcher Collection, Ironbridge Gorge Museum Trust, Ironbridge, Telford, England) (July 13, 1985).

———. *John Fletcher: Vicar of Madeley*. People Called Methodist 3. Petersborough: Foundery, 1994.

———. "John Wesley and John Fletcher." *Bulletin of the Wesley Historical Society, Shropshire Branch* (2004) 1–17.

———. "'Mon tres cher Ami.'" *Proceedings of the Charles Wesley Historical Society* 4 (1997) 53–67.

———. "Portraits of John Fletcher of Madeley and Their Artists." *Proceedings of the Wesley Historical Society* 47/5 (1990) 187–201.

———. Review of *Reluctant Saint? A Theological Biography of Fletcher of Madeley* by Patrick Streiff. *Expository Times* 113/6 (2002) 214.

Bibliography

———. "A Swiss Among the French Churches: Fletcher of Madeley." *Wesley Historical Society London and South East Branch Journal* 67 (2003) 15–27.

———. "Wesley's Designated Successor." *Proceedings of the Wesley Historical Society* 42/3 (1979) 69–74.

———, editor. *Unexampled Labours: Letters to the Revd John Fletcher to Leaders in the Evangelical Revival*. Introduction by Peter S. Forsaith, additional notes by Kenneth Loyer. Petersborough: Epworth, 2008.

Fraser, M. Robert. "Strains in the Understanding of Christian Perfection in Early British Methodism." PhD diss., Vanderbilt University, 1985.

Frazier, J. Russell. "The Doctrine of Dispensations in the Thought of John William Fletcher (1729–1785)." PhD thesis, University of Manchester, 2011.

———. "John Wesley's Covenantal and Dispensational View of Salvation History." *Wesley and Methodist Studies* 1/1 (2009) 33–54.

———. Review of *Unexampled Labours: Letters of the Revd John Fletcher to Leaders in the Evangelical Revival* by Peter S. Forsaith, ed. *Wesleyan Theological Journal* 44/1 (2009) 260–63.

Fuhrman, Eldon Ralph. "The Concept of Grace in the Theology of John Wesley." PhD diss., State University of Iowa, 1963.

———. "The Contribution of John Fletcher to Wesleyan-Arminian Theology." MA thesis, Biblical Seminary, New York, 1957.

———. *John Fletcher: Saint of the Eighteenth Century*. Typescript manuscript, n.d.

Fujimoto, Mitsuru Samuel. "John Wesley's Doctrine of Good Works." PhD diss., Drew University, 1986.

Gaberel, Jean Pierre. *Histoire de l'Eglise de Genève depuis le commencement de la réformation jusqu'à nos jours*. Geneva: Cherbulieuz, 1855.

———. "Vernet (Jacob)." In *Encyclopédie des sciences religieuses*, edited by Frédéric Lichtenberger, 4:321–25. Paris, Sandoz et Fischbacher, 1878.

———. *Voltaire et les Genevois*. Geneva: Cherbulieuz, 1856.

Galliers, B. J. N. "Shirley, Walter." In *The Encyclopedia of World Methodism*, edited by Nolan B. Harmon, 2:2146. Nashville: United Methodist Publishing House, 1974.

Gargett, Graham. *Jacob Vernet, Geneva, and the Philosophes*. Studies in Voltaire and the Eighteenth Century 321. Oxford: Voltaire Fondation, 1994.

Garner, Lawrence. *Churches of Shropshire*. Shrewsbury, UK: Shropshire, 1994.

Geisendorf, Paul F. *L'Université de Genève 1559–1959, Quatre siècles d'histoire*. Geneva: Jullien, 1959.

Gentry, Peter W. "Editorial." *Flame* 4/51 (1985) 12–14.

———. "On the Fletcher Trail." *Flame* 4/51 (1985) 2.

Gertz, Steven. "Potential Successor and Successful Wife." *Christian History* 20/1 (2001) 2–3.

Gibson, Edgar C. S. *The Thirty-Nine Articles of the Church of England Explained with an Introduction*. 3rd ed. London: Methuen, 1902.

Gill, Thomas E. *The Life of Mrs. Fletcher*. London: Simpkin & Marshall, 1845.

Gilpin, Joshua. "The Character of the Rev. Mr. Fletcher." *Arminian Magazine* 15 (1792) 643–51; 16 (1793) 3–7, 57–62, 113–19, 169–75, 225–30, 281–84, 337–41, 393–95, 449–55, 505–11, 551–56, 617–21.

Goldhawk, Norman P. "Fletcher of Madeley [review of Streiff's Jean Guillaume de la Fléchère]." *Expository Times* 98/6 (1987) 186–87.

Bibliography

Gonzalez, Justo L. *A History of Christian Thought*. Vol. 1, *From the Beginnings to the Council of Chalcedon*. Nashville: Abingdon, 1970.

———. *The Story of Christianity*. Vol. 2, *The Reformation to the Present Day*. San Francisco: HarperSanFrancisco, 1985.

Gornie, P. Douglass. "Rev. John W. Fletcher, A.M." Chap. in *The Lives of Eminent Methodist Ministers Concerning Biographical Sketches, Incidents, Anecdotes, Records of Travel, Reflections, etc.* Auburn: Derby & Miller, 1853.

Greathouse, William M. "John Wesley's View of the Last Things." In *The Second Coming: A Wesleyan Approach to the Doctrine of the Last Things*, edited by H. Ray Dunning, 139–160. Kansas City: Beacon Hill, 1995.

Green, John. *Decency of Behaviour at the Table of the Lord Vindicated in a Letter to a Person Unknown*. London: n.p., 1770.

———. *Grace and Truth Vindicated, or the Way to Heaven Manifested, From Scripture and Experience*. London: Cock & James, 1752.

Gregory, Benjamin. "John Fletcher, the Controversialist." *City Road Magazine* 2 (1872) 351–56.

———. "John Fletcher, the Saint." *City Road Magazine* 2 (1872) 312–18.

———. "John Fletcher, the Theologian." *City Road Magazine* 2 (1872) 32–37, 72–79, 177–83, 221–28, 260–66.

Gregory, Jeremy. "The Long Eighteenth Century." In *The Cambridge Companion to John Wesley*, edited by Randy Maddox and Jason E. Vickers, 13–39. Cambridge: Cambridge University Press, 2010.

Grenz, Stanley J., and E. Olson Roger. *Twentieth-Century Theology: God and the World in a Transitional Age*. Downers Grove, IL: InterVarsity, 1992.

Grider, J. Kenneth. "Evaluation of Timothy Smith's Interpretation of Wesley." *Wesleyan Theological Journal* 15/2 (1980) 64–69.

———. "Spirit-Baptism the Means of Sanctification: A Response to the Lyon View." *Wesleyan Theological Journal* 14/2 (1979) 31–50.

Gunter, W. Stephen. *The Limits of "Love Divine": John Wesley's Response to Antinomianism and Enthusiasm*. Nashville: Kingswood, 1989.

Hall, Robert. "Fletcher and Brainerd Compared." *Christian Advocate and Journal* 22/36 (1847) 144.

Haller, William. *The Rise of Puritanism, Or, The Way to the New Jerusalem as Set Forth in Pulpit and Press from Thomas Cartwright to John Lilburne and John Milton, 1570–1643*. Philadelphia: University of Pennsylvania Press, 1984.

Hammond, Geordan, and S. Forsaith Peter, editors. *Religion, Gender, and Industry: Exploring Church and Methodism in a Local Setting*. Eugene, OR: Pickwick, 2011.

Harding, Alan. *The Countess of Huntingdon's Connexion: A Sect in Action in Eighteenth-Century England*. Oxford Theological Monographs. Oxford: Oxford University Press, 2003.

Hawkin, E. "Wesley and Toplady." *Proceedings of the Wesley Historical Society* 8 (1912) 11–14.

Heitzenrater, Richard P. *The Elusive Mr. Wesley: John Wesley His Own Biographer*. 2 vols. Nashville: Abingdon, 1984.

———. "Great Expectations: Aldersgate and the Evidences of Genuine Christianity." In *Aldersgate Reconsidered*, edited by Randy L. Maddox, 49–91. Nashville: Kingswood, 1990.

Bibliography

———. *Mirror and Memory: Reflections on Early Methodism.* Nashville: Abingdon, 1989.
———. *Wesley and the People Called Methodists.* Nashville: Abingdon, 1995.
Henry, Matthew. *Matthew Henry's Commentary on the Whole Bible.* 6 vols. McLean, VA: MacDonald, n.d.
Henshaw, J. Letter to John Fletcher. 24 September 1762. The Fletcher-Tooth Collection, The John Rylands University Library, The University of Manchester, MAM Fl. 3/8.
Herklots, Hugh G. C. Review of *Shropshire Saint: A Study in the Ministry and Spirituality of Fletcher of Madeley* by George Lawton. *Church Quarterly Review* 163 (1962) 108–109.
Hervey, James. *Theron and Aspasio: Or, A Series of Dialogues and Letters, Upon the Most Important and Interesting Subjects.* 3 vols. London: Rivington, 1755.
Heyer, Henri. *L'Eglise de Genève: 1555–1909, Esquisse historique de son organisation suive de ses divers constitutions de la liste de ses pasteurs et professeurs et d'une table biographique.* Geneva: Jullien, 1909.
Hiebert, Paul G., and Eloise Hiebert Meneses. *Incarnational Ministry: Planting Churches in Band, Tribal, Peasant, and Urban Societies.* Grand Rapids: Baker, 1995.
Hill, Richard. *A Conversation Between Richard Hill, Esq., the Rev. Mr. Madan, and Father Walsh, Superior of a Convent of Benedictine Monks at Paris, Held at the Same Convent, July 13, 1771, in the Presence of Thomas Powis, Esq., and Others, Relative to Some Doctrinal Minutes Advanced by the Rev. Mr. John Wesley and Others, at a Conference Held in London, August 7, 1770, To Which Are Added Some Remarks by the Editor.* London: Dilly, 1771.
———. *The Finishing Stroke: Containing Some Strictures on the Rev. Mr. Fletcher's Pamphlet, Entitled, Logica Genevensis, or, A Fourth Check to Antinomianism.* London: Dilly, 1773.
———. *Five Letters to the Reverend Mr. Fletcher, Relative to his Vindication of the Minutes of the Reverend Mr. John Wesley, Intended Chiefly for the Comfort of Mourning Backsliders, and Such as May Have Been Distressed and Perplexed by Reading Mr. Wesley's Minutes, or the Vindication of Them.* second edition. London: Dilly, 1772.
———. *Friendly Remarks Occasioned by the Spirit and Doctrines Contained in the Rev. Mr. Fletcher's Vindication, and More Particularly in His Second Check to Antinomianism to Which is Added a Postscript Occasioned by His Third Check to Antinomianism in a Letter to the Author.* N.p.: n.p., 1772.
———. Letter to John Fletcher. 31 July 1773. Wesley Family Letters, The John Rylands University Library, The University of Manchester, Wesley Family II, 97.
———. Letter to John Fletcher. 20 August 1773. Early Preachers Collection, The John Rylands University Library, The University of Manchester, DDPr 1/93.
———. Letter to John Fletcher. 16 December 1784. The Fletcher-Tooth Collection, The John Rylands University Library, The University of Manchester, MAM Fl. 3/8.
———. *A Review of all the Doctrines Taught by the Rev. Mr. John Wesley; Containing, A Full and Particular Answer to a Book Entitled, "A Second Check to Antinomianism." In Six Letters to the Author of that Book. Wherein the Doctrines of a Twofold Justification, Free Will, Man's Merit, Sinless Perfection, Finished Salvation, and Real Antinomianism, Are Particularly Discussed; and The Puritan Divines Vindicated from the Charges Brought Against Them of Holding Mr. Wesley's Doctrines.* London: Dilly, 1772.

———. *Some Remarks on a Pamphlet Entitled, A Third Check to Antinomianism by the Author of Pietas Oxoniensis*. London: Dilly, 1772.

———. *Three Letters written by Richard Hill, Esq. to the to the Reverend J. Fletcher, Vicar of Madeley. In the Year 1773. Setting Forth Mr. Hill's Reasons for declining any further Controversy relative to Mr. Wesley's Principles*. Shrewsbury: Wood.

Hindmarsh, D. B. "The Olney Autobiographers; English Conversion Narrative in the Mid-Eighteenth Century." *Journal of Ecclesiastical History* 49/1 (1998) 61–84.

Hindmarsh, Robert. Letter to John Fletcher. 25 November [1783]. The Fletcher-Tooth Collection, The John Rylands University Library, The University of Manchester, MAM Fl. 3/8.

———. Letter to John Fletcher. 1 September 1784. The Fletcher-Tooth Collection, The John Rylands University Library, The University of Manchester, MAM Fl. 3/8.

"The History of St. Michael's Church in Madeley." BBC Shropshire. Faith. Online: www.bbc.co.uk/shropshire/content/articles/2005/03/14/madeley_church_feature.shtml.

Hodson, James H. "John Fletcher's Covenant with God." *Experience* (1914) 57–61.

Hodson, John. *A Widow Indeed, A Sermon Occasioned by the Lamented Death of Mrs. Fletcher, Widow of the Late Rev. John Fletcher, Vicar of Madeley, Preached at Broseley and Coalbrookdale, on Sunday, Jan. 7, 1816*. Wednesbury: Booth, 1816.

Holland, Bernard G. *Baptism in Early Methodism*. London: Epworth, 1970.

Hollenweger, Walter J. "Pentecostalism: Article Research Centers, Bibliographies and Selected Literature." European Pentecostal Charismatic Research Association. Online: http://www.epcra.ch/articles_pdf/Pentecostalisms.PDF.

Holy, Thomas. Letter to [John Fletcher]. 14 December 1784. The Fletcher-Tooth Collection, The John Rylands University Library, The University of Manchester, MAM Fl. 3/8.

Hoon, Paul W. "The Soteriology of John Wesley." PhD thesis, Edinburg University, 1936.

Hopkins, Wilfred Morley. *Fletcher of Madeley, A Lecture*. King's Lynn: Matsell & Targett, 1898.

Hosman, Glenn Burt. "The Problem of Church and State in the Thought of John Wesley as Reflecting His Understanding of Providence and His View of History." PhD diss., Drew University, 1970.

Hull, James E. "The Controversy Between John Wesley and the Countess of Huntingdon." PhD thesis, Edinburgh University, 1959.

Hunsberger, George R. "Accommodation." In *Evangelical Dictionary of World Missions*, edited by A. Scott Moreau, 31–32. Grand Rapids: Baker, 2000.

Hutton, Sarah. "Smith, John (1618–1652)." In *Oxford Dictionary of National Biography*, edited by H. C. G. Matthew and Brian Harrison. Oxford: Oxford University Press, 2004. Online: http://www.oxforddnb.com/view/article/25838.

Impeta, Christoffel Nicholaas. *De Leer der Heiliging en Volmaking bij Wesley en Fletcher*. Leiden: Mulder, [1913].

Ireland, James. Letter to John Fletcher. 25 May 1781. The Fletcher-Tooth Collection, The John Rylands University Library, The University of Manchester, MAM Fl. 19.3.

———. Letter to John and Mary Fletcher. [1783?]. The Fletcher-Tooth Collection, The John Rylands University Library, The University of Manchester, MAM Fl. 4/1/4.

Irenaeus. *Against Heresies*. Edited by Alexander Roberts and James Donaldson. In *Ante-Nicene Fathers*. 1:309–567. Peabody, MA: Hendrickson, 2004.

Bibliography

———. *Demonstration of Apostolic Preaching*. Translated by J. Armitage Robinson. New York: Macmillan, 1920.

Jeffrey, David Lyle. Review of *Reluctant Saint? A Theological Biography of Fletcher of Madeley* by Patrick Streiff. *Perspectives in Religious Studies* 28/2 (2001) 135–39.

"John Fletcher." In *The Oxford Dictionary of the Christian Church*, edited by F. L. Cross, 509. London: Oxford University Press, 1957

Jones, Marsh Wilkinson. "Pulpit, Periodical, and Pen: Joseph Benson and Methodist Influence in the Victorian Prelude." PhD thesis, University of Illinois at Urbana-Champaign, 1995.

Jones, Scott J. *John Wesley's Conception and Use of Scripture*. Nashville: Kingswood, 1995.

Jones, William. *The Catholic Doctrine of a Trinity: Proved by Above an Hundred Short and Clear Arguments, expressed in the Terms of Holy Scriptures, With a Few Reflections, Occasionally Interspersed Upon Some of the Arian Writers, Particularly Dr. S. Clarke; To Which Is Also Prefixed a Discourse to the Reader on the Necessity of Faith in the True God, and Upon Diversity of Opinion*. Oxford: Parker, 1756.

Keck, Leander. *Paul and His Letters*. Proclamation Commentaries. Philadelphia: Fortress, 1979.

Keeble, N. H. *Richard Baxter: Puritan Man of Letters*. Oxford: Clarendon, 1982.

Keefer, Luke L. "Characteristics of Wesley's Arminianism." *Wesleyan Theological Society* 22/1 (1987) 88–100.

———. "John Wesley and English Arminianism." *Evangelical Journal* 4/1 (1986) 15–28.

Kellett, Norman Lawrence. "John Wesley and the Restoration of the Doctrine of the Holy Spirit to the Church of England in the 18th Century." PhD diss., Brandeis University, 1975.

Kinghorn, Kenneth Cain. "Faith and Works: A Study in the Theology of John Fletcher." PhD diss., Emory University, 1965.

———. "Fletcher, John William." In *The Encyclopedia of World Methodism*, edited by Noland B. Harmon, 1:852. Nashville: United Methodist Publishing House, 1974.

Kirk, John. "John Fletcher." *The Christian Miscellany and Family Visitor* 11 (1865) 3–7.

Klauber, Martin I. "Between Calvinist and Philosophe: Jacob Vernet's Theological Dilemma." *Westminster Theological Journal* 63 (2001) 377–92.

———. *Between Reformed Scholasticism And Pan-Protestantism: Jean Alphonse Turretin (1671–1737) And Enlightened Orthodoxy At The Academy Of Geneva*. London: Associated University Press, 1994.

———. "Continuity and Discontinuity in Post-Reformation Reformed Theology: An Evaluation of the Muller Thesis." *Journal of Evangelical Theology* 33/4 (1990) 467–75.

———. "The Drive toward Protestant Union in Early Eighteenth-Century Geneva: Jean-Alphonse Turrettini on the "Fundamental Articles" of the Faith." *Church History* 61/3 (1992) 334–49.

———. "The Eclipse of Reformed Scholasticism in Eighteenth-Century: Natural Theology from Jean-Alphonse Turretin to Jacob Vernet." In *The Identity of Geneva: The Christian Commonwealth, 1564–1864*, edited by Martin I. Klauber and John B. Roney, 129–42. London: Greenwood, 1998.

———. "The Helvetic Formula Consensus (1675): An Introduction and Translation." *Trinity Journal* 11/1 (1990) 103–23.

Bibliography

———. "Jean-Alphonse Turrettini (1671–1737) on Natural Theology: The Triumph of Reason over Revelation at the Academy of Geneva." *Scottish Journal of Theology* 47/3 (1994) 301–25.

———. "Jean-Alphonse Turrettini and the Abrogation of the Formula Consensus in Geneva." Tacoma, WA: Microform, 1990. 28 pages.

———. "Reason, Revelation, and Cartesianism: Louis Tronchin and Enlightened Orthodoxy in Late Seventeenth-Century Geneva." *Church History* 59/3 (1990) 326–39.

———. "Theological Transitions in Geneva from Jean-Alphonse Turretin to Jacob Vernet." Paper presented at the American Society of Church History conference, Atlanta, GA, January 4–7, 1996. 21 pages.

Klauber, Martin I., and John B. Roney, editors. *The Identity of Geneva: The Christian Commonwealth, 1564–1864*. London: Greenwood, 1998.

Klauber, Martin I., and Glenn S. Sunshine. "Jean-Alphonse Turrettini on Biblical Accomodation: Calvinist or Socinian?" *Calvin Theological Journal* 21/1 (1990) 7–27.

Knickerbocker, Waldo Emerson. "Doctrinal Sources and Guidelines in Early Methodism: Fletcher of Madeley as a Case Study." *Methodist History* 14 (1975) 186–202.

———. "The Doctrine of Authority in the Theology of John Fletcher." PhD diss., Emory University, 1972.

Knight, Helen C. *Lady Huntington and Her Friends, or The Revival of the Work of God in the Days of Wesley, Whitefield, Romaine, Venn, and Others in the Last Century*. New York: American Tract Society, 1853.

Knight III, Henry H. *The Presence of God in the Christian Life: John Wesley and the Means of Grace*. Pietist and Wesleyan Studies 3. London: Scarecrow, 1992.

Knight, John Allan. "Aspects of Wesley's Theology After 1770." *Methodist History* 4/3 (1968) 33–42.

———. *The Holiness Pilgrimage: Reflections on the Life of Holiness*. Kansas City: Beacon Hill, 1973.

———. "John Fletcher's Influence on the Development of Wesleyan Theology in America." *Wesleyan Theological Journal* 13 (1978) 13–33.

———. "John William Fletcher and the Early Methodist Tradition." PhD diss., Vanderbilt University, 1966.

Knowles, G. W. S. "John William Fletcher (1729–1785)." *Wesley Historical Society, North Lancashire Branch* 42 (2005) 9–24.

Kudo, Hiroo. "John Fletcher's Concept of Christian Holiness with Particular Reference to the Doctrine of the Baptism of the Holy Spirit." MA thesis, Nazarene Theological College, 1997.

Kwon, Tae Hyoung. "John Wesley's Doctrine of Prevenient Grace: Its Impact on Contemporary Missiological Dialogue." PhD diss., Temple University, 1996.

L., M. "Ostervald." In *Dictionnaire d'Histoire et de Géographie Ecclegsiastiques*, edited by Alfred Baudrillart, 5:208. Paris: Librarie Letouzey et Ané, 1938.

La Fléchère, Henri-Louis de. Letter to John Fletcher. October 1784. The Fletcher-Tooth Collection, The John Rylands University Library, The University of Manchester, MAM Fl. 42/1.

La Fléchère, de. Nyon XIVe à XXe. Archives Cantonales Vaudoises. Lausanne: Campiche 282.

Bibliography

Lane, A. N. S. "Accommodation." In *New Dictionary of Theology*, edited by Sinclair B. Ferguson and David F. Wright, 3. Leicester: InterVarsity, 1988.

Lane, William Craig. *Reasonable Faith: Christian Truth and Apologetics*. Rev. ed. Wheaton, IL: Crossway, 1994.

Langford, Thomas A. *Practical Divinity: Theology in the Wesleyan Tradition*. 2 vols. Rev. ed. Nashville: Abingdon, 1983.

Larrabee, William Clark. "Fletcher's Last Hours." *The Ladies' Repository* 11/5 (1851) 93.

[Law, William]. *Pensées sur la nature et le dessin du christianisme*. [Translated by John Fletcher]. London: Strahan, 1761.

Lawton, George. "Abiah Darby—Holy Woman, Militant Egotist—Had 'Close Work of It for Above Three Hours.'" *Shropshire Magazine*, May 1952, 23–24.

———. "John Fletcher's Incumbency at Madeley." *London Quarterly and Holborn Review* 181 (1956) 281–87.

———. "John Fletcher's Pulpit Prayers." *Proceedings of the Wesley Historical Society* 30, 1 (1955) 2–6.

———. "Madeley in the Eighteenth Century." *London Quarterly and Holborn Review* 181 (1956) 142–48.

———. *Shropshire Saint: A Study in the Ministry and Spirituality of Fletcher of Madeley*. Wesley Historical Lecture 26. London: Epworth, 1960.

———. *Within the Rock of Ages: The Life and Work of Augustus Montague Toplady*. Cambridge: Clarke, [1983].

Lee, Grace Lawless. *The Story of the Bosanquets*. Canterbury: Phillimore and Co., Ltd., 1966.

Lelièvre, Matthieu. "Fletcher (John William)." In *Encyclopédie des sciences religieuses*, edited by Frédéric Lichtenberger, 4:773–75. Paris: Sandoz et Fischbacher, 1878.

———. *John Wesley: sa vie et son œuvre*. 7th ed. Nîmes, France: Évangéliques Méthodistes, 1992.

———. *La théologie de Wesley*. Nîmes, France: Évangéliques Méthodistes, 1990.

Lenton, John. "Mary Fletcher and her adopted daughters: Women Preachers at Madeley 1782–1843." *Bulletin of the Wesley Historical Society, Shropshire Branch* 9 (2008) 3–13.

[Lenton, John]. "James Glazebrook—A Protégé of John Fletcher (and His Double!)." *Bulletin of the Wesley Historical Society Shropshire Branch*, Wesley Historical Society, Shropshire Branch. n.d.

Letter to Mrs. King. Wesley's Chapel, City Road, London. 17 March 1782. LDWMM 2000/8214.

Leysall, Katherine Eleanor. Letter to John Fletcher. 11 July 1776. The Fletcher-Tooth Collection, The John Rylands University Library, The University of Manchester, MAM Fl. 4/8/2.

License to preach upon being appointed to the curacy of Madeley. 14 March 1757. The Fletcher-Tooth Collection, The John Rylands University Library, The University of Manchester, MAM P4d4.

Lindsey, Leroy E. "Checks to Antinomianism." In *Beacon Dictionary of Theology*, edited by W. T. Purkiser, Richard Taylor, and Willard H. Taylor, 100–101. Kansas City: Beacon Hill, 1977.

Lindström, Harald. *Wesley and Sanctification: A Study in the Doctrine of Salvation*. Nashville: Abingdon.

Bibliography

Lloyd, A. M. "The Story of John Fletcher, Saintly 18th Century Vicar of Madeley." *Shropshire Magazine*, May 1955, 17–19.

Lloyd, Arthur. "Fletcher of London." *Wesley Historical Society, London and Home Counties Branch* 28 (1983) 5–10.

———. "Fletcher of London II." *Wesley Historical Society, London and Home Counties Branch* 29 (1984) 11–16.

Lloyd, David. A Reminiscence of the Rev John Fletcher by the Rev David Lloyd. Herefordshire Council, BH28/1/50.

Lloyd, Gareth. "The Methodist Archives and Research Center at the John Rylands University Library of Manchester." In *The Global Impact of the Wesleyan Traditions and the Related Movements*, edited by Charles Yrigoyen, 285–92. Lanham, MD: Scarecrow, 2002.

Lockhart, Wilfred C. "The Evangelical Revival as Reflected in the Life and Times of John William de la Fléchère 1729–1785." PhD thesis, University of Edinburg, 1936.

———. *John Fletcher, Evangelist*. Wesley Bicentenary Manuals 11. London: Epworth, 1939.

Lodahl, Michael. *God of Nature and of Grace: Reading the World in a Wesleyan Way.* Nashville: Abingdon, 2003.

Loder, Allan Thomas. "An Examination of the Classical Pentecostal Doctrine of the Baptism in the Holy Spirit in Light of the Pentecostal Position on the Sources of Theology." Bibliothèque nationale du Canada, 2000. Online: http://www.collectionscanada.ca/obj/s4/f2/dsk2/ftp01/MQ46226.pdf.

Long, Elmer. "Pentecost." *Arminian Magazine* 1/1 (1980) 1.

Lord, Alex. "Fletcher of Madeley." *Church and People* (1957) 157–60.

———. "Fletcher of Madeley." *English Churchman and St. James Chronicle* 5955 (1957) 97.

———. "Fletcher of Madeley." *Hereford Diocesan Messenger* 49/2 (1957) 7–8.

———. "Fletcher of Madeley: Bi-Centenary of His Ordination Observed on Ash Wednesday." *Life of Faith* (1957) 161–62.

———. The Induction of the Methodist Vicar of Madeley, TD. Shropshire Archives.

Lord Erskine, Earl of Buchan. Letter to John Fletcher. 10 December 1767. The Fletcher-Tooth Collection, The John Rylands University Library, The University of Manchester, MAM Fl. 2/14/7.

Loyer, Kenneth M. "'Adoring the Holy Trinity in Unity': John Fletcher's Doxological Trinitarianism." Paper presented at Religion, Gender, and Industry: Exploring Church and Methodism in a Local Setting, Shropshire, England, 16–18 June 2009. 23 pages.

Lyon, Robert W. "Baptism and Spirit Baptism in the New Testament." *Wesleyan Theological Journal* 14/1 (1979) 14–44.

MacDonald, Frederic William. *Fletcher of Madeley*. Men Worth Remembering. London: Hodder & Stoughton, 1885.

MacDonald, James. *Memoirs of the Rev. Joseph Benson*. New York: Methodist Episcopal Church, 1823.

MacMillan, Ken. "John Wesley and the Enlightened Historians." *Methodist History* 38/3 (2000) 121–32.

Maddox, Randy L. "Respected Founder/Neglected Guide." *Methodist History* 37 (1999) 71–88.

Bibliography

———. *Responsible Grace: John Wesley's Practical Theology*. Nashville: Kingswood, 1994.

———. "Responsible Grace: The Systematic Perspective of Wesleyan Theology." *Wesleyan Theological Journal* 19/2 (1998) 7–22.

———. "Wesley's Understanding of Christian Perfection: In What Sense Pentecostal?" *Wesleyan Theological Journal* 34/2 (1999) 78–110.

Maddox, Randy, and Laurence W. Wood. "Point/Counterpoint: 'Baptism of the Spirit' Language." *Wesleyan Theological Journal* 36/1 (2001) 256–58.

Mandate for induction as Vicar of Madeley. 7 October 1760. The Fletcher-Tooth Collection, The John Rylands University Library, The University of Manchester, MAM P4d6.

Marrat, Jabez. *John Fletcher: Saint and Scholar*. London: Kelly, 1901.

———. *The Vicar of Madeley, John Fletcher, A Biographical Study*. London: Kelley, 1902.

Martin, Hugh. *Puritanism and Richard Baxter*. London: SCM, 1954.

Martin, Sidney. "John Fletcher: Saint Exemplary." *Flame* 4/51 (1985) 6–8.

Maser, Frederick E. "A Revealing Letter from Joseph Pilmore." *Methodist History* 10/3 (1972) 54–58.

Mason, Matthew W. "The Significance of the Systematic and Polemical Function of Union with Christ in John Owen's Contribution to the Seventeenth Century Debates Concerning Eternal Justification." MTh thesis, Oak Hill College, 2005.

Matlock, Paul Russell. *The Four Justifications in Fletcher's Theology*. Salem, OH: Schmul, 1980.

Matthews, Rex Dale. "'Reason and Revelation Joined': A Study in the Theology of John Wesley." PhD diss., Harvard University, 1986.

Mattke, Robert A. "The Baptism of the Holy Spirit as Related to the Work of Entire Sanctification." *Wesleyan Theological Journal* 5/1 (1970) 22–32.

———. "John Fletcher's Involvement in the Antinomian Controversy of 1770–1776." MA thesis, School of Religion in the Graduate College of the State University of Iowa, 1965.

———. "John Fletcher's Methodology in the Antinomian Controversy of 1770–76." *Wesleyan Theological Journal* 3/1 (1968) 38–47.

———. "John Fletcher's Methodology in the Antinomian Controversy of 1770–76." Revival Theology Resources. Online: http://twtministries.com/articles/1_cal_arm/fletcher/fletcher35.html.

May, George Lacey. "Fletcher of Madeley." *Theology: A Monthly Journal of Historic Christianity* 1/1 (1920) 18–28.

Maycock, Joseph. "The Fletcher-Toplady Controversy." *London Quarterly and Holborn Review* 191 (1966) 227–35.

McDonald, H. D. *Ideas of Revelation: An Historical Study, A.D. 1700 to A.D. 1860*. Vol. 1 of *Theories of Revelation: An Historical Study, 1700–1960*. 1 vol. ed. 1959. Reprint, Grand Rapids: Baker, 1979.

McDonnell, Kilian. "A Trinitarian Theology of the Holy Spirit?" *Theological Studies* 46/2 (1985) 191–227.

McGonigle, Herbert. "Architects of Wesleyan Theology." *Nazarene Preacher* (1972) 14–16, 45–46.

———. "John Fletcher's Influence on Wesleyan Theology." *Flame* 4/51 (1985) 3–5.

———. *John Wesley's Arminian Theology: An Introduction*. 2nd ed. Occasional Paper 3. Lutterworth, UK: Wesley Fellowship, 2005.

Bibliography

———. "Pneumatological Nomenclature in Early Methodism." *Wesleyan Theological Journal* 8 (1973) 61–72.

———. *Sufficient Saving Grace: John Wesley's Evangelical Arminianism.* Carlisle: Paternoster, 2001.

McGowan, A. T. B. *The Federal Theology of Thomas Boston.* Rutherford Studies in Historical Theology. Edinburgh: Paternoster, 2002.

McGrath, Alister E. *Christian Theology: An Introduction.* 3rd ed. Oxford: Blackwell, 2001.

———. *A Scientific Theology.* Vol. 1, *Nature.* Grand Rapids: Eerdmans, 2003.

McKim, Donald K. "The Puritan View of History, or Providence Without and Within." *Evangelical Quarterly* 70/4 (1980) 215–37.

McPherson, Joseph D. "The Acts of the Spirit, Part 1, Pentecost: A Special Day." *Arminian* 25/2 (2007) 3–6.

———. "Early Methodist Teaching on Water and Spirit Baptism." *Arminian* 22/2 (2004) 1–5.

———. Review of *The Meaning of Pentecost in Early Methodism* by Laurence W. Wood. *Arminian* 21/2 (2003) 9–11.

Milburn, G.E. "Early Methodism and the Huguenots." *Proceedings of the Wesley Historical Society* 45/3 (1985) 69–79.

Milton, John. *The Doctrine and Discipline of Divorce, in Two Books: also the Judgement of Martin Bucer; Tetrachordon; and an Abridgement of Colasterion.* London: Sherwood, Neely, & Johne, 1820.

———. *The Poetical Works of John Milton: Reprinted from the Best Editions with Biographical Notice, etc.* New York: Hurst, n.d.

"Ministerial Heroism." *Methodist Magazine* 5 (1822) 382–84.

Mitchell, T. Crichton. "Response to Dr. Timothy Smith on the Wesley's Hymns." *Wesleyan Theological Journal* 16/2 (1981) 48–57.

Møller, Jens G. "The Beginnings of Puritan Covenant Theology." *Journal of Ecclesiastical History* 14/1 (1963) 46–67.

Monk, Robert C. *John Wesley: His Puritan Heritage.* Nashville: Abingdon, 1966.

Montet, Albert de. "LA FLECHERE (Jean-Jacques de)." In *Dictionnaire Biographique des Genevois et des Vaudois, qui se sont distingués dans leur pays ou à l'egtrangère*, 2:436–37: Paris: Barre & Dayez, 1878

Moore, Henry. *The Life of Mrs. Mary Fletcher Consort and Relict of the Rev. John Fletcher Compiled from Her Journal and Other Interesting Documents.* New York: Paul, 1818.

———. *The Life of Mrs. Mary Fletcher: Consort and Relict of the Rev. John Fletcher, Vicar of Madeley, Salop.* 1848. Reprint, Salem, OH: Schmul, 1997.

Moorman, John R. H. *A History of the Church in England.* Harrisburg, PA: Morehouse, 1994.

Morgan, Irvonwy. *The Nonconformity of Richard Baxter.* London: Epworth, 1946.

Mottos which were displayed on Fletcher's study walls. The Fletcher-Tooth Collection, The John Rylands University Library, The University of Manchester, MAM P4d12.

Muller, Richard A. *Christ and the Decree: Christology and Predestination from Calvin to Perkins.* Grand Rapids: Baker, 1988.

———. *Dictionary of Latin and Greek Theological Terms: Drawn Principally from Protestant Scholastic Theology.* Grand Rapids: Baker Academic, 1985.

Bibliography

———. "Perkins' A Golden Chaine: Predestinarian System or Schematized Ordo salutis?" *Sixteenth Century Journal* 91 (1978) 68–81.

———. *Post-Reformation Reformed Dogmatics*. Vol. 1, *Prolegomena to Theology*. Grand Rapids: Baker, 1987.

———. "Predestination and Christology in Sixteenth Century Reformed Theology." PhD diss., Duke University, 1976.

Murlin, John. *A Letter to Richard Hill, Esquire: Containing Some Remarks on that Gentleman's Five Letters to the Rev. J. Fletcher*. London: Pr. William Pine, 1775.

Murray, John. *The Covenant of Grace: A Biblico-Theological Study*. London: Tyndale House, 1977.

Nash, Ronald H. *The Meaning of History*. Nashville: Broadman & Holman, 1998.

"Nature, n." In *The American Heritage Dictionary of the English Language*. 4th ed. Houghton Mifflin, 2006

Neff, Blake J. "John Wesley and John Fletcher on Entire Sanctification: A Metaphoric Cluster Analysis." PhD diss., Bowling Green State University, 1982.

Nelson, J. Robert. "Live and Let Live. and Die When You Must." *Perkins Journal* 39/1 (1986) 1–9.

Newton, John A. Review of *Reluctant Saint? A Theological Biography of Fletcher of Madeley* by Patrick Streiff. *Theology* 106/829 (2003) 65–66.

Newport, Kenneth G. C. "Charles Wesley's Interpretation of Some Biblical Prophecies According to a Previously Unpublished Letter Dated 25 April 1754." *Bulletin of the John Rylands University Library of Manchester* 77/2 (1995) 31–52.

———. "Premillennialism in the Early Writings of Charles Wesley." *Wesleyan Theological Journal* 32/1 (1997) 85–106.

———. *The Sermons of Charles Wesley: A Critical Edition, with Introduction and Notes*. New York: Oxford University Press, 2001.

Niebuhr, Reinhold. *Faith and History: A Comparison of Christian and Modern Views of History*. London: Nisbet, 1949.

Nippert, Ludwig. *Leben und Wirken des ehwüdigen Johannes Fletcher*. Bremen: Tractahauses, 1887.

Noble, T. A. "East and West in the Theology of John Wesley." *Bulletin of the John Rylands Library* 85/2–3 (2003) 359–72.

———. "Our Knowledge of God according to John Calvin." *Evangelical Quarterly* 54/1 (1982) 2–13.

Noms des Enfans qui ont Eté baptisés dans lEglise de Nyon présque depuis le comencement de Septemb.' de l'année 1729 et Enregistrés Par moy Isaac François Monod mnre de lad Eglise. Archives Cantonales Vaudoises, Lausanne, Eb 91/4 p. 1.

[Norris, William Herbert]. ["A friend of Sabbath-Schools"]. *The Life of Rev. John Fletcher: abridged from authentic sources*. New York: Lane & Scott, 1850.

Nuelsen, John Louis. *Jean Guillaume de la Fléchère, John William Fletcher, des erste schweizerische Methodist: Ein Gedenkblatt zu seinem zweihundertsten Geburstag, 12 September 1729*. Zürich: Vereinsbuchhandlug, 1929.

Nuttall, Geoffrey. Review of *Jean Guillaume de la Flechere (John William Fletcher), 1729–1785: Ein Beitrag zur Geschichte Des Methodismus* by Patrick Phillip Streiff. *Journal of Theological Studies* 37/2 (1986) 647–49.

———. *Richard Baxter*. Edinburgh: Nelson & Sons, 1965.

———. *The Significance of Trevecca College, 1768–91*. London: Epworth, 1969.

Bibliography

"Obituary [Mrs. Mary Fletcher]." *Methodist Magazine* 39 (1816) 80.

O'Brien, Glen Ashley. "A Trinitarian Revisioning of the Wesleyan Doctrine of Perfection." MA thesis, Asbury Theological Seminary, 1998.

O'Donovan, Oliver. *On the Thirty-Nine Articles: A Conversation with Tudor Christianity.* Exeter: Paternoster, 1986.

Okely, Francis. Letter to John Fletcher. 22 May 1776. The Fletcher-Tooth Collection, The John Rylands University Library, The University of Manchester, MAM Fl. 5/11.

Oliver, Robert W. Review of *Letters of John Fletcher* by Edward Cook., ed. *The Banner of Truth* 442 (2000) 29.

Olivers, Thomas. *The Defense of the Rev. John Wesley, In Answer to the Several Personal Reference.* London: n.p., 1774.

———. *A Full Refutation of the Doctrine of Unconditional Perseverance in a Discourse of Hebrews, Chapter 2, Verse 3.* London: Hawes, n.d.

———. Letter to John Fletcher. 16 July 1765. Arthur Skevington Wood Archive, Cliff College, A/1/20.

———. Letter to John Fletcher. [1776?]. The John Rylands University Library, The University of Manchester, PLP 80/23/2.

———. *A Letter to the Rev. Mr. Toplady Occasioned by His Late Letter to the Rev. Mr. Wesley.* London: Cave, 1771.

———. *A Rod for the Reviler: Or a Full Answer to the Mr. Rowland Hill's Letter, Entitled Imposture Detected, and the Dead Vindicated.* London: Fry, 1777.

———. *A Scourge to Calumny In Two Parts Inscribed to Richard Hill, Esq. Pt. the First, Demonstrating the Absurdity of That Gentleman's Farrago. Pt. the Second. Containing a Full Answer to All That is Material in His Farrago Double-Distilled.* London: Hawes, 1774.

Olson, Bessie Goldie. *John Fletcher: The Great Saint.* Des Moines, IA: Boone, [1944].

Olson, Mark. "The Roots of John Wesley's Servant Theology." *Wesleyan Theological Journal* 44/2 (2009) 120–41.

O'Malley, J. Steven. "Pietistic Influence on John Wesley: Wesley and Gerhard Tersteegen." *Wesleyan Theological Journal* 31/2 (1996) 48–70.

———. Review of *Jean Guillaume de la Flechere (John William Fletcher), 1729–1785: Ein Beitrag zur Geschichte Des Methodismus* by Patrick Phillip Streiff. *Church History* 55/4 (1986) 539–41.

O'Neal, Ernest E. "John Fletcher's Conception of Christian Perfection." BD thesis, Duke University, 1940.

Osborn, George, editor. *The Poetical Works of John and Charles Wesley: Reprinted from the Originals, with the Last Corrections of the Authors; Together, with the Poems of Charles Wesley Not Before Published.* 13 vols. London: Wesleyan-Methodist Conference Office, 1869.

Oswalt, John N. "John Wesley and the Old Testament Concept of the Holy Spirit." *Religion in Life* 48 (1979) 283–92.

Outler, Albert C. "A Focus on the Holy Spirit and Spirituality in John Wesley." *Quarterly Review* 8 (1988) 3–18.

———. "Theodosius' Horse: Reflections on the Predicament of the Church Historian." *Church History* 34 (1965) 253.

———. *The Wesleyan Theological Heritage: Essays of Albert C. Outler.* Edited by Thomas C. Oden and Leicester R. Longden. Grand Rapids: Zondervan, 1991.

Bibliography

Owen, John. *The Works of John Owen.* Edited by William H. Goold. Vol. 16 vols. London: Banner of Truth Trust, 1966.

Packer, James Innell. *A Quest for Godliness: The Puritan Vision of the Christian Life.* Wheaton, IL: Crossway, 1990.

―――. *The Redemption and Restoration of Man in the Thought of Richard Baxter: A Study in Puritan Theology.* Vancouver, BC: Regent College, 2003.

Parlby, William. "The First Methodist Martyr: William Seward. His Grave at Cusop, 1702–1740." *Proceedings of the Wesley Historical Society* 17/8 (1930) 187–91.

―――. "The Rev. John Fletcher, Vicar of Madeley: His Induction at Hereford." *Proceedings of the Wesley Historical Society* 7 (1909–1910) 56–58.

Parnham, David. "The Humbling of 'High Presumption': Tobias Crisp Dismantles the Puritan Ordo Salutis." *The Journal of Ecclesiastical History* 56/1 (2005) 50–74.

Pasquarello, Mike. "Sermon: 'On the Trinity', John Wesley: Homiletic Theologian." *Asbury Journal* 61/1 (2006) 97–108.

Percy, Lord Eustace. *John Knox.* London: Hodder & Stoughton, 1937.

Perkins, William. *A golden chaine, or The description of theologie containing the order of the causes of saluation and damnation, according to Gods woord. A view of the order wherof, is to be seene in the table annexed. Written in Latine by William Perkins, and translated by an other. Hereunto is adioyned the order which M. Theodore Beza vsed in comforting troubled consciences.* London: Alde, 1592.

―――. *The Works of that Famous and VVorthy Minister of Chrst in the Vniuersitie of Cambridge, Mr. William Perkins. The First Volume: Newly corrected according to his owne Copies. With Distinct Chapters, and contents of euery Booke, and two Tables of the whole: one, of the matter and questions, the other of choice places of Scripture.* London: Legatt, 1612.

Petty, John. "Reflections on a Visit to Mr. Fletcher's Tomb." *Primitive Methodist Magazine* (1846) 47–52.

[Phelps, E. E.]. *Great Lives and Their Lessons: Fletcher of Madeley: Or. The Power of a Holy Life.* London: McIntosh, [1870].

Philagathos. *The Tears of Piety: An Elegy on the Much Lamented Death of the Rev. John Fletcher, Late Vicar of Madeley in Shropshire, Who Died August 14th, 1785, By Way of Condolence to His Afflicted Widow, and Bereaved Flock.* Bristol: Hazard, 1785.

Piercy, Richard. *Fidelity Smiling in Death: Some Elegiac Thoughts, Occasioned by the Death of the Rev. John Fletcher, Late Vicar of Madeley.* London: Simmons, 1785.

Podmore, C. J. "Ingham, Benjamin (1712–1772)." In *Oxford Dictionary of National Biography,* edited by H. C. G. Matthew and Brian Harrison. Oxford: Oxford University Press, 2004. Online: http://www.oxforddnb.com/view/article/14389.

Pope, William Burt. *A Compendium of Christian Theology.* 3 vols. 2nd ed. New York: Phillips & Hunt, n.d.

Preston, Henry. Letter to John Fletcher. 13 January 1783. The Fletcher-Tooth Collection, The John Rylands University Library, The University of Manchester, MAM Fl. 5/11/12.

Price, James Matthew. "H. Orton Wiley—Dominant Images from the Life of a Holiness Educator." *Wesleyan Theological Journal* 39/2 (2004) 182–95.

―――. "The Influence of Personalism on the Theology and Education of H. Orton Wiley." *Wesleyan Theological Journal* 41/2 (2006) 142–60.

Prideaux, Sela M. "John Fletcher, Saintly Vicar of Madeley—The Mecca of Methodism." *Shropshire Magazine,* October 1973, 16–17.

Bibliography

Purkiser, W. T. *Exploring Christian Holiness*. Vol. 1, *The Biblical Foundations*. Kansas City: Beacon Hill, 1983.
Purkiser, W. T., Richard Taylor, and Willard H. Taylor. *God, Man, and Salvation: A Biblical Theology*. Kansas City: Beacon Hill, 1977.
Quantrille, Wilma Jean. "The Triune God in the Hymns of Charles Wesley." PhD diss., Drew University, 1989.
R., M. "La Fléchère." In *Dictionnaire Historique et Bibliographique de la Suisse*, edited by Victor Attinger, 4:428. Piaget, France: Administration du Dictionnaire Historique et Biographique de la Suisse, 1928.
Rack, Henry D. "Early Methodist Visions of the Trinity." *Proceedings of the Wesley Historical Society* 46 (1987) 38–44, 57–69.
———. "John Wesley and the Enlightenment." Lecture delivered at Nazarene Theological College, Manchester, England, 2005.
———. *Reasonable Enthusiast: John Wesley and the Rise of Methodism*. London: Epworth, 1989.
Rainey, David. "John Wesley's Doctrine of Salvation in Relation to His Doctrine of God." PhD thesis, King's College, University of London, 2006.
Ramsay, Chevalier (Andrew Michael). *The Philosophical Principles of Natural and Revealed Religion Unfolded in Geometrical Order*. Glasgow: Foulis, 1748.
Randall, John. *The History of Madeley*. Madeley: Salop, 1880.
———. *The History of Madeley*. [Shrewsbury]: Salop County Library, [1975].
———. *A Short but Comprehensive Sketch of the Lives and Usefulness of the Rev. John W. and Mary Fletcher, With Interesting Statistics Showing the Religious Aspects of Madeley Then and Now, the Increase of Population and the Growth of Religious and Educational Means and Appliances*. Madeley: Randall, n.d.
Rattenbury, J. Ernest. *The Evangelical Doctrines of Charles Wesley's Hymns*. London: Epworth, 1941.
Reasoner, Victor Paul. "The American Holiness Movement's Paradigm Shift Concerning Pentecost." *Wesleyan Theological Journal* 21/2 (1996) 132–46.
———. *The Hope of a Christian World: Wesleyan Eschatology and Cultural Transformation*. Unpublished paper, Evangelical Theological Society, Washington, DC, 15 November 2006. 15 pages typewritten.
———. *The Hope of the Gospel: An Introduction to Wesleyan Eschatology*. Evansville, IN: Fundamental Wesleyan, 1999.
———. "John Fletcher Revisited." *Arminian* 16/2 (1998) 9–11.
———. *A Wesleyan Theology of Holiness for the Twenty-First Century*. forthcoming.
Recueil de Généalogies Vaudoises publié par la société vaudoise de Généal.; tome 1er Sixième Fascicule, Index des noms cités dans les cinq premier fascicules du Tome 1er. Lausanne, Georges Bridel et Cie Editeurs. 1923
Rees, D. A. "Platonism and the Platonic Tradition." In *The Encyclopedia of Philosophy*, edited by Paul Edwards, 6:333–41. London: Collier-Macmillian, 1967.
Rees, Paul S. *The Valiant Vicar of Madeley*. University Park, Iowa: Fletcher, [1937].
Registre de la Classe de Morges dès l'an 1780. Archives Cantonales Vaudoises, Lausanne, B db 5, p. 23.
Registre des lettres de Classe envoyées à leur Excellences. Archives Cantonales Vaudoises, Lausanne, B db 9, 31–34.

Bibliography

Rice, H. A. L. "Portuguese Captain Became a Great Shropshire Vicar, Jean de la Flechere—The Rev. John Fletcher of Madeley." *Shropshire Magazine*, December 26 and 29, 1950.

Rigg, James H. "John Fletcher's Letter to John Wesley." *Methodist Recorder and General Church Chronicle*, January 13, 1898, 10–11.

———. "A Remarkable Letter to Wesley from His 'Designated Successor.'" *Methodist Recorder and General Church Chronicle*, January 6, 1898, 10–11.

Roberts, Griffith T. "The Trevecka Manuscripts." *Proceedings of the Wesley Historical Society* 27 (1950) 178–80.

Rogers, Hester Ann. *The Life of Faith Exemplified or, Extracts from the Journal of Mrs. Hester Ann Rogers*. New York: Carlton & Porter, 1861.

———. *Spiritual Letters: Calculated to Illustrate and Enforce Holiness of Heart and Life*. Dublin: Napper, 1822.

Roney, John B. "Introduction." In *The Identity of Geneva: The Christian Commonwealth, 1564–1864*, edited by Martin I. Klauber and John B. Roney, 1–20. London: Greenwood, 1998.

Rose, E. Alan. "Ingham, Benjamin." In *Dictionary of Evangelical Biography, 1730–1860*, edited by Donald M. Lewis, 1:590–91: Peabody, MA: Hendrickson, 2004.

Royal Commission on the Historical Monuments of England. *Nonconformist Chapels and Meeting-houses: Shropshire and Staffordshire*. London: HMSO, 1986.

Rudd, Katherine, and Dorthea Johnson. Letter to John and Mary Fletcher. 19 November 1784. The Fletcher-Tooth Collection, The John Rylands University Library, The University of Manchester, MAM Fl. 4/5A/1.

Ruffet, Louis. *J. G. de la Fléchère: Esquisse Biographique*. Toulouse: Société des livres religieux, 1862.

Runyon, Theodore. *The New Creation: John Wesley's Theology for Today*. Nashville: Abingdon, 1998.

Rutherford, Samuel. *The covenant of life opened, or, A treatise of the covenant of grace containing something of the nature of the covenant of works, the sovereignty of God, the extent of the death of Christ. the covenant of grace. of surety or redemption between the*. Edinburgh: Anderson, 1655.

Ryle, John Charles. *The Christian Leaders of the Last Century, or England a Hundred Years Ago*. London: Nelson, 1870.

Saint Michael's Parish, "The Parish of St. Michael's Church and Early Methodism.," A paper prepared by the St. Michael's Parish to propagate an historical understanding of the parish. Received 7/16/2005 from the Rev. Henry Morris, Vicar of Madeley.

Saladin, J.L. *Mémoire histoirique sur la vie et les ouvrages de Mr. J. Vernet, ministre de l'Eglise de Genève accompané de l'invocation aux Muses de Montesquieu et de plusieurs lettre de J.-J. Rousseau et Voltaire qui n'ont pas encore été publiée*. Paris: Chez Desray, 1795.

Salon, T. M. "John Fletcher: Paradigm for the Global Impact of Wesleyanism." In *The Global Impact of the Wesleyan Traditions and the Related Movements*, edited by Charles Yrigoyen, 245–58. Lanham, MD: Scarecrow, 2002.

Sandeman, Robert. *Letters on Theron and Aspasio. Addressed to the Author. In Two Volumes*. 2 vols. 2nd ed. Edinburgh: Sands, Donaldson, Murray, and Cochran, 1759.

Sangster, W.E. *The Path to Perfection*. Nashville: Abingdon-Cokesbury, 1943.

Bibliography

Schaff, D. S. "Fletcher, John William (Fletcher of Madeley)." In *The New Schaff-Herzog Encyclopedia of Religious Knowledge*, edited by Samuel Macauley Jackson, 4:331–32. New York: Funk & Wagnalls, 1909.
Schaff, Philip, and David S. Schaff, editors. *The Creeds of Christendom: With a History and Critical Notes.* Vol. 1, *The History of Creeds.* 6th ed. Grand Rapids: Baker, 1983.
———. *The Creeds of Christendom: With a History and Critical Notes.* Vol. 3, *The Evangelical Protestant Creeds.* 6th ed. Grand Rapids: Baker, 1983.
Schlenther, Boyd Stanley, and Eryn Mant White. *Calendar of the Trevecka Letters.* Aberystwtth: National Library of Wales, 2003.
———. *Queen of the Methodists: The Countess of Huntingdon and the Eighteenth-Century Crisis of Faith and Society.* Durham, UK: Durham Academic, 1997.
Schlimm, Matthew R. "Defending the Old Testament's Worth: John Wesley's Reaction to the Rebirth of Marcionism." *Wesleyan Theological Journal* 42/2 (2007) 28–51.
Schmidt, Darren. "The Pattern of Revival: John Wesley's Vision of 'Iniquity' and 'Godliness' in Church History." In *Revival and Resurgence in Church History: Papers Read at the 2006 Summer Meeting and the 2007 Winter Meeting of the Ecclesiastical History Society*, edited by Kate Cooper and Jeremy Gregory, 142–53. Studies in Church History 44. Woodbridge, UK: Boydell Press for the Ecclesiastical History Society, 2008.
Schmul, Harold E. "John Fletcher and the Baptismal Flame." *God's Revivalist and Bible Advocate* 118/4 (2006) 8.
Scott, Abraham. "A Biographical Sketch of the Author [John Fletcher]." In *The Works of the Rev. John Fletcher With a Life by the Rev. Abraham Scott*, new ed., 1:i–xxxvi. London: Allman, 1840.
Scott, David. "Radical Images in John Wesley's "Thoughts Upon Slavery." *Wesleyan Theological Journal* 43/2 (2008) 87–100.
Seaborn, Joseph W. "Wesley's Views on the Uses of History." *Wesleyan Theological Journal* 21/1–2 (1986) 129–36.
Seed, Thomas Alexander. *John and Mary Fletcher: Typical Methodist Saints.* Library of Methodist Saints. London: Kelly, [1906].
"Select List of Books Recently Published, Chiefly Religious." *Wesleyan Methodist Magazine* (1830) 257–58.
Sellon, Walter. *An Answer to Aspasio Vindicated in Eleven Letters.* London: Cave, 1761.
———. *Arguments Against the Doctrine of General Redemption Considered.* London: Cave, 1761.
———. *The Church of England Vindicated from the Charge of Calvinism.* London: Cave, 1771.
Senex. "Mrs. Fletcher and Dr. Dodd." *Wesleyan Methodist Magazine* (1879) 768–71.
Seymour, Aaron Cropley Hobart. *The Life and Times of Selina, Countess of Huntingdon.* Vol. 2/1–2. 1840. Reprint, Elibron Classics, 2003.
———. Transcribed copy of Twenty-Five Letters from the Rev. John Fletcher, Vicar of Madeley Shropshire to the Right Honorable the Countess of Huntingdon with Copious Notes, Biographical and Explanatory. Countess of Huntingdon Connexion Archives, Rayleigh.
———, editor. Letters from the Rev. John Fletcher, Vicar of Madeley Shropshire to the Right Honorable the Countess of Huntingdon with Copious Notes, Biographical and Explanatory. The Fletcher-Tooth Collection, The John Rylands University Library, The University of Manchester.

Bibliography

Shelton, R. Larry. "A Covenant Context for Wesleyan Ethics." In *Holiness as a Root of Morality: Essays on Wesleyan Ethics in Honor of Lane A. Scott*, edited by John S. Park, John Sungmin, and Lane A. Scott, 209–44. Lewiston, NY: Mellen, 2006.

Shimizu, Mitsuo. "Epistemology in the Thought of John Wesley." PhD diss., Drew University, 1980.

Shipley, David Clark. "Development of Theology in American Methodism in the Nineteenth Century." *London Quarterly and Holborn Review* 184 (1959) 249–64.

———. "Methodist Arminianism in the Theology of John Fletcher." PhD diss., Yale University, 1942.

———. "Methodist Ministry in the Eighteenth Century." *Perkins School of Theology Journal* 13/1 (1959) 5–13.

———. "Wesley and Some Calvinistic Controversies." *Drew Gateway* 25/4 (1955) 195–210.

Shirley, Walter. *A Narrative of the Principle Circumstances Relative to the Rev. Mr. Wesley's Conference, Held in Bristol, August the 6th, 1771, at Which the Rev. Mr. Shirley, and Others Were Present With the Declaration Then Agreed to by Mr. Wesley and Fifty-three of the Preachers in Connexion With Him in a Letter to a Friend.* Bath: Gye, 1771.

"Short Reviews and Notices of Book, 24." *Methodist Quarterly Review* 31/1 (1849) 504.

Sigler, Matt, and Lester Ruth. "Charles Wesley and the Power of Poetic Theology." *Asbury Herald* 117/2 (2007) 12–14.

Sigston, James. *Memoir of the Life and Ministry of William Bramwell, Lately an Itinerant Methodist Preacher; With Extracts From His Interesting and Extensive Correspondence.* New York: Phillips & Hunt, 1891.

Skinner, Raymond Frank. "Jean Guillaume de la Flechere: A Remarkable Vicar of Madeley." *Shropshire Magazine*, November 1983, 34–36.

———. *Nonconformity in Shropshire: A Study in the Rise and Progress of Baptist, Congregational, Presbyterian Quaker and Methodist Societies, 1662–1816.* Shrewsbury: Wilding & Son, 1964.

Slaatte, Howard Alexander. *The Arminian Arm of Theology: The Theologies of John Fletcher, First Methodist Theologian, and His Precursor, James Arminius.* Washington, DC University Press of America, 1977.

Slaughter, Thomas. Letter to John Fletcher. [1762]. The Fletcher-Tooth Collection, The John Rylands University Library, The University of Manchester, MAM Fl. 6/1/14.

Slaughter, [Thomas]. Letter to John Fletcher. 21 September 1762. The Fletcher-Tooth Collection, The John Rylands University Library, The University of Manchester, MAM Fl. 6/10/13.

Smith, David Rushworth. *John Fletcher: An Upholder of Holiness.* Braughing, UK: Rushworth, 1972.

Smith, Larry D. "John Fletcher: The Work of the Holy Spirit in Sanctification." Paper presented at School of the Prophets, Interchurch Holiness Convention, Salem, OH, n.d. 11 pages.

Smith, Oswald J. *Fletcher of Madeley.* Chicago: World Wide Christian Couriers, 1929.

Smith, Oswald J., editor. *The Lives of Brainerd and Fletcher.* Rev. ed. London: Marshall, Morgan & Scott, 1965.

Smith, Timothy L. "The Doctrine of the Sanctifying Spirit in John Wesley and John Fletcher." *Preacher's Magazine* 55/1 (1979) 16–17, 55–60.

———. "A Historical and Contemporary Appraisal of Wesley Theology." In *A Contemporary Wesleyan Theology*, edited by Charles W. Carter, 77–101. Grand Rapids: Asbury, 1983.

———. "The Holiness People and the Doctrine of the Holy Spirit." *Quarterly Review* 8/2 (1988) 49–70.

———. "The Holy Spirit in the Hymns of the Wesleys." *Wesleyan Theological Journal* 16/2 (1981) 20–47.

———. "How John Fletcher Became the Theologian of Wesleyan Perfectionism, 1770–1776." *Wesleyan Theological Journal* 15/1 (1980) 68–87.

———. "Notes on the Exegesis of John Wesley's Explanatory Notes Upon the New Testament." *Wesleyan Theological Journal* 16/1 (1981) 107–13.

———. *Revivalism and Social Reform: American Protestantism on the Eve of the Civil War*. Gloucester, MA: Smith, 1976.

Snyder, Howard A. "Charles Wesley's Hymn and Prayer to the Trinity." *Asbury Journal* 61/1 (2006) 109–12.

———. "The Church as Holy and Charismatic." *Wesleyan Theological Journal* 15/2 (1980) 7–32.

Société Vaudoise de Généologie, La. *Recueil de Généalogies Vaudoises*. Lausanne: Bridel & Cie, 1923.

Sommer, Carl Ernst. "John William Fletcher (1729–1785) Mann der Mitte: Prolegomena zu seinem Verstandnis." In *Basileia: Walter Freytag zum 60 Geburstag*, edited by Jan Hermelink and Hans Jochen Margull, 437–53. Stuttgart: Evang. Missionsverlag, 1959.

Sorkin, David. "Geneva's 'Enlightened Orthodoxy': The Middle Way of Jacob Vernet (1698–1789)." *Church History* 74/2 (2005) 286–305.

Stamp, John S. "Memoir of the Rev. Charles Atmore, Compiled from Various Documents." *Wesleyan-Methodist Magazine* 1 (1845) 1–18.

———. "Memoir of the Rev. John Crosse, A. M., Late Vicar of Bradford, Yorkshire." *Wesleyan-Methodist Magazine* 23 (1844) 89.

Stanley, Susie C. *Holy Boldness: Women Preacher's Autobiographies and the Sanctified Self*. Knoxville: University of Tennessee Press, 2002.

Staples, Rob L. "The Current Wesleyan Debate on the Baptism of the Holy Spirit." Unpublished paper, Kansas City, 1979.

———. "Things Shakable and Things Unshakeable in Holiness Theology." Boise, ID, The Edwin Crawford Lecture, Northwest Nazarene University. February 9, 2007. 9 pages.

Starkey, Lycurgus M. "The Holy Spirit and the Wesleyan Witness." *Religion in Life* 49 (1980) 72–80.

Steele, Daniel. *A Defense of Christian Perfection, Or A Criticism of Dr. James Mudge's "Growth in Holiness Toward Christian Perfection."* Salem, OH: Schmul, 1984.

———. *Love Enthroned*. Salem, OH: Schmul, [1977].

Stehle, Henri. *Le Collège de Genève, 1559–1959, Mélanges historiques et Littéraires*. Geneva: Jullien, 1959.

Stelling-Michaud, S., editor. *Le Livre du Rector de l'Académie de Genève (1550–1878)*. Geneva: Droz, 1959.

Stevens, Abel. *The History of the Religious Movement of the Eighteenth Century Called Methodism Considered in its Different Denominational Forms, and Its Relations to*

Bibliography

British and American Protestantism. Vol. 1, *From the Origin of Methodism to the Death of Whitefield*. 29th ed. New York: Carlton & Lanahan, 1858.

Stevenson, George John. "John Fletcher, of Madeley." In *Methodist Worthies: Character Sketches of Methodist Preachers of Several Denominations, With a Historical Sketch of Each Connexion*, 1:128–41. London: Jack, 1884.

Streiff, Patrick Phillip. "Fletcher, John William." In *Dictionary of Evangelical Biography, 1730–1860*, edited by Donald M. Lewis, 1:393–94: Peabody, MA: Hendrickson, 2004.

———. "Fletcher, John William (bap. 1729, d. 1785)." In *Oxford Dictionary of National Biography*, edited by H. C. G. Matthew and Brian Harrison. Oxford: Oxford University Press, 2004. Online: http://www.oxforddnb.com/view/article/9733.

———. "Jean Guillaume de la Fléchère, John William Fletcher, 1729–1785." ThD thesis, Bern University, 1983

———. *Reluctant Saint? A Theological Biography of Fletcher of Madeley*. Translated by G. W. S. Knowles. Petersbourough: Epworth, 2001.

Stroup, Thomas B. "Review: Accommodation." Review of *God, Man, and Satan*, by Roland Mushat Frye. *South Atlantic Bulletin* 27/4 (1962) 10.

Suter. "An Account of Mary Wales, of Coalpit-bank, Near Wellington, Shropshire." *Arminian Magazine* 16 (1793) 528–32.

[T?]. Letter to John Fletcher. 17 June 1777. The Fletcher-Tooth Collection, The John Rylands University Library, The University of Manchester, MAM Fl. 17/1.

Taft, Zechariah. *Biographical Sketches of the Lives and Public Ministry of Various Holy Women Whose Eminent Usefulness and Successful Labours in the Church of Christ, Have Entitled Them to Be Enrolled Among the Great Benefactors of Mankind: In Them Are Included Several Letters from the Rev. Wesley Never Before Published*. Lodon: Kershaw & Baynes, 1825.

Taylor, Willard H. "The Baptism with the Holy Spirit: Promise, Grace or Judgment?" *Wesleyan Theological Society* 12/1 (1977) 16–25.

Telford, John. *Two West-end Chapels: or, Sketches of London Methodism from Wesley's Day (1740–1886)*. London: Wesleyan Methodist Book-Room, 1886.

Thackeray, Veronica. "John Fletcher and an American Connection." *Shropshire Magazine*, September 1984, 36–37.

Thomas, Emyr. *Coalbrookdale and the Darbys: The Story of the World's First Industrial Dynasty*. York, England: Sessions Book Trust, 1999.

Thomas, Evan. *An Elegiac Tribute to the Memory of the Rev. John Fletcher, Late Vicar of Madeley, Shropshire, Who Died Sunday August 14th, 1785, in the Fifty-Sixth Year of His Age*. Shrewsbury, England: Wood, 1785.

Thompson, Claude H. "John Fletcher, First Theologian of Methodism." *Emory University Quarterly* 16/4 (1960) 239–50.

Thornton, J. Letter to John Fletcher. 30 July 1776. The Fletcher-Tooth Collection, The John Rylands University Library, The University of Manchester, MAM Fl. 7/4.

Thorsen, Donald A. D. "The Wesleyan Impulse in Teaching." *Asbury Journal* 63/2 (2008) 49–58.

———. *The Wesleyan Quadrilateral: Scripture, Tradition, Reason and Experience as Model of Evangelical Theology*. Nappanee, IN: Asbury, 1990.

Tilbury, Charity. Letter to John Fletcher. 18 June 1768. The Fletcher-Tooth Collection, The John Rylands University Library, The University of Manchester, MAM Fl. 7/1.

Bibliography

———. Letter to John Fletcher. 3 November 1768. The Fletcher-Tooth Collection, The John Rylands University Library, The University of Manchester, MAM Fl. 7/1/13.
Tilbury, Charles. Letter to John Fletcher. 16 August 1766. The Fletcher-Tooth Collection, The John Rylands University Library, The University of Manchester, MAM Fl. 7/1/11.
Tooth, Mary. "Obituary: Account of Mrs. Fletcher's Death to the Rev. Joseph Benson." *Methodist Magazine* 39 (1816) 179–82.
———. "Obituary, Further Account of Mrs. Fletcher's Death." *Methodist Magazine* 39 (1816) 157–59.
Toplady, Augustus. *The Works of Augustus Toplady, B.A., Late Vicar of Broad Hembury, Devon*. New ed. Harrisonburg, VA: Sprinkle, 1987.
Tranter, William. "Methodism in Madeley." *Wesleyan-Methodist Magazine* 16 (1837) 900–903.
Treffry, Richard. *Memoirs of the Rev. Joseph Benson*. London: Mason, 1840.
Trinder, Barrie. "Darby, Abraham (1750–1789)." In *Oxford Dictionary of National Biography*, edited by H. C. G. Matthew and Brian Harrison. Oxford: Oxford University Press, 2004. Online: http://www.oxforddnb.com/view/article/7139.
———. *The Darbys of Coalbrookdale*. 1974; 1981; Reprint, Chichester, UK: Phillimore, 1991.
———. *A History of Shropshire*. The Darwen County History Series. Chichester, UK: Phillimore, 1983.
———. *The Industrial Revolution in Shropshire*. Chichester, UK: Phillimore, 1973.
———. *The Industrial Revolution in Shropshire*. 3rd ed. Chichester: Phillimore, 2000.
———. *John Fletcher: Vicar of Madeley during the Industrial Revolution*. Museum Guide 6.01. Telford: Ironbridge Gorge Museum Trust, n.d.
Truesdale, Al. "Reification of the Experience of Entire Sanctification in the American Holiness Movement." *Wesleyan Theological Journal* 31/2 (1996) 95–119.
Tucker, Maria. Letter to John Fletcher. 9 September 1773. The Fletcher-Tooth Collection, The John Rylands University Library, The University of Manchester, MAM Fl. 7/1/25.
Turner, George Allen. "The Baptism of the Holy Spirit in the Wesleyan Tradition." *Wesleyan Theological Journal* 14/1 (1978) 60–76.
Turner, Henry. "Mr. Fletcher's Preaching." *Wesleyan-Methodist Magazine* 52 (1829) 527–28.
Turner, Max. "Trinitarian Pneumatology in the New Testament? Towards an Explanation of the Worship of Jesus." *Asbury Theological Journal* 57–58/1–2 (2002–2003) 167–86.
Turretin, Jean-Alphonse. *Défense de la Dissertation de Mons. Turrettin sur les articles fondamentaux de la Religion, Contre une brochure intitulée: Lettre de M. T. cC., c'est-à-dire, de Mons. Théodore Crinsoz, qu'on appelle Mons. de Bionens, etc.* Geneva: Fabri & Barillot, 1727.
———. *Nubes Testium Pro Moderato et Pacifico de Rebus Theologicis Judicio, et Instituenda Inter Protestantes Concordia. Praemissa Est Brevis & Pacifica de Articulis Fundamentalibus Disquisitio*. Geneva: Fabri & Burrillo, 1719.
"Turrettini." In *Dictionnaire d'Histoire et de Géographie Ecclesiastiques*, 14:714–15. Paris: Touzey & Ané, 1738
Tuttle, Robert G. Review of *Pentecostal Grace*, by Laurence W. Wood. *TSF Bulletin* 6 (1982) 21.

Bibliography

Tyerman, Luke. *The Life and Times of the Rev. John Wesley, M.A., Founder of the Methodists*. 3 vols. New York: Harper & Bros., 1872.

———. *The Life of the Rev. George Whitefield*. 2 vols. New York: Randolph, 1877.

———. *Wesley's Designated Successor: The Life, Letters, and Literary Labours of the Rev. John William Fletcher, Vicar of Madeley, Shropshire*. London: Hodder & Stoughton, 1882.

Tyson, John R. *Charles Wesley on Sanctification: A Biographical and Theological Study*. Salem, OH: Schmul, 1992.

Tyson, John R., and Boyd S. Schlenther. *In the Midst of Early Methodism: Lady Huntingdon and Her Correspondence*. Lanham, MD: Scarecrow, 2006.

Valton, John. Letter to John Fletcher. 24 November 1784. The Fletcher-Tooth Collection, The John Rylands University Library, The University of Manchester, MAM Fl. 7/6.

Van Asselt, Willem J. *The Federal Theology of Johannes Cocceius (1603–1669)*. Translated by Raymond A. Blacketer. Leiden: Brill, 2001.

Van der Meer, T. "Accommodation." In *Dictionary of Mission Theology: Evangelical Foundations*, edited by John Corrie, 1–2. Nottingham, England: InterVarsity, 2007.

Van Stam, Frans Pieter. *The Controversy over the Theology of Saumur, 1635–1650: Disrupting Debates among the Huguenots in Complicated Circumstances*. Amsterdam: APA-Holland University Press, 1988.

Veritas. "To the Editor of the Methodist Magazine." *Methodist Magazine* 25 (1802) 572–73.

Vernet, Jacob. *Instruction chrétienne*. 5 vols. Neuveville: 1751–1754.

———. *Instruction chrétienne, divisée en cinq volumes; seconde édition, retouchée par l'auteur & augmentée de quelques pièces*. 5 vols. Geneva: 1756.

———. *Traité de la vérité de la religion chrétienne, tiré du latin de M. J.-Alphonse Turretin, professeur en théologie et en histoire ecclésiastique à Genève*. 7 vols. Geneva: 1730–1788.

Vickers, Jason E. "Albert Outler and the Future of Wesleyan Theology: Retrospect and Prospect." *Wesleyan Theological Society* 43/2 (2008) 56–67.

———. "'And We the Life of God Shall Know': Incarnation and the Trinity in Charles Wesley's Hymns." *Anglican Theological Review* 90/2 (2008) 329–44.

———. "Charles Wesley and the Revival of the Doctrine of the Trinity: A Methodist Contribution to Modern Theology." In *Charles Wesley: Life, Literature and Legacy*, edited by Kenneth G. C. Newport and Ted A. Campbell, 278–98. Peterborough, England: Epworth, 2007.

———. "Charles Wesley's Doctrine of the Holy Spirit: A Vital Resource for the Renewal of Methodism." *Asbury Journal* 61/1 (2006) 47–60.

Vuilleumier, Henri. *Histoire de l'Eglise Réformée du Pays de Vaud Sous le Régime Bernois*. Vol. 2, *L'Orthodoxie Confessionnelle*. Lausanne: Concorde, 1929.

———. *Histoire de l'Eglise Réformée du Pays de Vaud Sous le Régime Bernois*. Vol. 3, *Le Refuge Le Piétisme L'Orthodoxie Libérale*. Lausanne: Concorde, 1933.

———. *Histoire de l'Eglise Réformée du Pays de Vaud Sous le Régime Bernois*. Vol. 4, *Le Déclin du Régime Bernois*. Lausanne: Concorde, 1933.

———. "Quand et Comment la Formule Consensus a-t-elle été définitivement abrogée?" *Revue Théologie et de Philosophie* 12 (1879) 471–78.

———. "Théodore Crinsoz de Bionnens et Son Interprétation Prophétique de l'Ecriture." *Revue de Théologie et de Philosophe* 20 (1887) 113–35, 294–319, 481–504.

Bibliography

Wainwright, Geoffrey. "The Trinitarian Hermeneutic of John Wesley." In *Reading the Bible in Wesleyan Ways: Some Constructive Proposals*, edited by Barry L. Callen and Richard P. Thompson, 17–37. Kansas City: Beacon Hill, 2004.

———. "Trinitarian Theology and Wesleyan Holiness." In *Orthodox and Wesleyan Spirituality*, edited by Steven T. Kimbrough, 59–80. Crestwood, NY: St. Vladimir's Seminary Press, 2002.

Walker, James B. *A Philosophy of the Plan of Salvation*. Chautauqua ed. Cincinnati: Hitchcock & Walden, n.d.

Walls, Jerry L. "The Free Will Defense, Calvinism, Wesley, and the Goodness of God." *Christian Scholars Review* 13/1 (1984) 19–33.

Warter, Thomas. Letter to John Fletcher. 27 November 1784. The Fletcher-Tooth Collection, The John Rylands University Library, The University of Manchester, MAM Fl. 7/12.

———. Letter to John Fletcher. 15 January 1785. The Fletcher-Tooth Collection, The John Rylands University Library, The University of Manchester, MAM Fl. 7/12.

Welch, Edwin. "John Fletcher and the Trevecka College Revival." *Proceedings of the Wesley Historical Society* 51/2 (1997) 25–30.

———. *Spiritual Pilgrim: A Reassessment of the Life of Countess of Huntingdon*. Cardiff: University of Wales Press, 1995.

Welch, Edwin, and Peter J. Lineham. "Ingham, Lady Margaret." *Dictionary of Evangelical Biography, 1730–1860*, edited by Donald M. Lewis, 1:591. Peabody, MA: Hendrickson, 2004.

Wendel, Francois. *Calvin: Origins and development of His Religious Thought*. Translated by Philip Mairet. Durham, NC: Labyrinth, 1963.

Wesley, Charles. *Hymns on the Trinity*. Bristol: Pine, 1767; Reprint, Madison, NJ: Charles Wesley Society, 1998.

———. *The Journal of Charles Wesley*. 2 vols. London: Mason, 1849; Reprint, Kansas City: Beacon Hill, 1980.

———. Letter to an unidentified correspondent. 25 April 1754. The Charles Wesley Papers, The John Rylands Library, The University of Manchester, DDCW 1/51.

———. Letter to John and Mary Fletcher. 13 February 1782. The Robert W. Woodruff Library of Advanced Studies, Special Collections Department, Emory University, JW Family Papers OBVt p. 36.

———. Letter to John and Mary Fletcher. 13 March 1784. The Robert W. Woodruff Library of Advanced Studies, Special Collections Department, Emory University, J. Wesley Coll., ALS, p. 3.

———. Letter to John and Mary Fletcher. 21 June 1785. The Charles Wesley Papers The John Rylands University Library, The University of Manchester, DDCW 1/75.

———. Letter to John Fletcher. 22 February 1772. Wesley's Chapel, City Road, London, LDWMM 2000/7978.

———. Letter to John Fletcher. 12 September 1776. The Charles Wesley Papers, The John Rylands University Library, The University of Manchester, DDCW 1/66.

———. Letter to John Fletcher. 11/13 October 1783. The Charles Wesley Papers, The John Rylands University Library, The University of Manchester, DDCW 1/74.

———. "Original Hymn of the Rev. Charles Wesley, for the Rev. John Fletcher, June 30th, 1776." *Wesleyan-Methodist Magazine* 3/14 (1835) 576.

———. *Sermon, prêché devant l'Université d'Oxford: traduit d'Anglois*. Translated by [John Fletcher]. London: Strahan, 1761.

Bibliography

———. *A Short Account of the Death of Mrs. Hannah Richardson*. 7th ed. London: Foundery, 1754.

Wesley, Charles, and John Wesley. *Whitsunday Hymns*. Edited by Randy Maddox. Bristol: Farley, 1746. Online: http://divinity.duke.edu/sites/default/files/documents/cswt/37_Whitsunday_Hymns_%281746%29.pdf.

Wesley, John. *The Bicentennial Edition of the Works of John Wesley*. 35 vols. Edited by Frank Baker and Richard P. Heitzenrater. Nashville: Abingdon, 1984–.

———. *A Compend of Wesley's Theology*. Edited by Robert W. Burtner and Robert E. Chiles. Nashville: Abingdon, 1954.

———. *A Concise Ecclesiastical History: From the Birth of Christ to the Beginning of the Present Century*. 4 vols. London: Paramore, 1781.

———. *A Concise History of England, From the Earliest Times, to the Death of George II*. 4 vols. London: Hawes, 1776.

———. *Explanatory Notes upon the New Testament*. London: Epworth, 1950; Reprint, Naperville, IL: Allenson, 1966.

———. *The Journal of Rev. John Wesley*. Edited by Nehemiah Curnock. 8 vols. London: Epworth, 1909–1916.

———. Letter to John Fletcher. 28 February 1766. The John Rylands University Library, The University of Manchester, S.L., 5:3, Wesley Letter File.

———. Letter to John Fletcher. 27 February 1771. J. Benson Collection, Duke University.

———. Letter to John Fletcher. 16 January 1771. The John Rylands University Library, The University of Manchester, S.L., 5:217, T.S.C.

———. Letter to John Fletcher. 21 July 1773. The John Rylands University Library, The University of Manchester, S.L. 6:33, Wesley Letter File.

———. Letter to John Fletcher. 1 October 1773. The John Rylands University Library, The University of Manchester, Lamplough Coll.

———. Letter to John Fletcher. 24 November 1781. The John Rylands University Library, The University of Manchester, DDWes 5/62.

———. Letter to John Fletcher. 2 April 1785. The John Rylands University Library, The University of Manchester, S.L. 7:214, Wesley Letter File.

———. *The Letters of the Rev. John Wesley*. Edited by John Telford. 8 vols. London: Epworth, 1931.

———. "The Life and Death of the Rev. John Fletcher." *Arminian Magazine* 2 (1790) 36–47, 75–84, 131–41, 183–91, 135–244, 287–96, 340–48, 391–400, 443–53, 495–504, 547–54.

———. *Le Salut par la Foi, Traduit de l'Anglois*. Translated by John Fletcher. London: Strahan, 1759.

———. *A Sermon Preached on the Death of the Rev. John Fletcher, Vicar of Madeley, Shropshire*. London: Stebbins, 1797.

———. *A Short Account of the Life and Death of the Rev. John Fletcher*. London: Paramore, 1786.

———. *A Treatise on Justification: Extracted from Mr. John Goodwin With a Preface, Wherein All That is Material, in Letters Just Published, Under the Name of the Rev. Mr. Hervey, is Answered*. Bristol: Pine, 1765.

———. *The Works of John Wesley, Complete and Unabridged*. 14 vols. London: Wesleyan Methodist Book Room, 1872; Reprint, Grand Rapids: Baker, 1991.

———. *The Journal of Rev. John Wesley*. Edited by Nehemiah Curnock. 8 vols. London: Epworth, 1909–1916.

White, Charles Edwin. "Phoebe Palmer and the Development of Pentecostal Pneumatology." *Wesleyan Theological Journal* 23/1–2 (1988) 198–212.

Wiggins, James B. "The Embattled Saint: Aspects of the Life and Work of John Fletcher." *Wesleyan Quarterly Review* 2/4 (1965) 221–23.

———. "The Embattled Saint: Aspects of the Life and Work of John Fletcher." *Wesleyan Quarterly Review* 3/3 (1966) 153–221.

———. *The Embattled Saint: Aspects of the Life and Work of John Fletcher*. Wesleyan Studies 2. Macon, GA: Wesleyan College, 1966.

———. "John Fletcher: Wesley's Designated Successor." *Wesleyan Quarterly Review* 2/4 (1965) 212–23.

———. "The Pattern of John Fletcher's Theology: As Developed in His Poetic, Pastoral, and Polemical Writings." PhD diss., Drew University, 1963.

Wiley, H. Orton. *Christian Theology*. 3 vols. Kansas City: Beacon Hill, 1940.

Williams, Anne. "Gracious Accommodations: Herbert's "Love III." Review of *Love III* by George Herbert. *Modern Philology* 82/1 (1984) 13–22.

Williams, Bernard. "Descartes, René." In *Encyclopedia of Religion*, edited by Vergilius Ferm, 2:350. New York: Philosophical Library, 1945.

Williamson, Barry. "The Spilsbury Portrait of John Fletcher." *Proceedings of the Wesley Historical Society* 47/2 (1989) 44–49.

Wilson, David Robert. "Church and Chapel: Parish Ministry and Methodism in Madeley, c.1760–1785, with Special Reference to the Ministry of John Fletcher." PhD thesis, University of Manchester, 2010.

Withrow, W. H. "John Fletcher and Mary Bosanquet." In *Makers of Methodism*, 165–94. New York: Eaton & Mains, 1898.

Wood, Arthur Skevington. "The Eighteenth Century Methodist Revival Reconsidered." *Evangelical Quarterly* 53 (1981) 130–48.

———. "Revelation and Reason Tape 3: Fletcher and Priestly." Didsbury Lectures, Nazarene Theological College, Manchester, England, 1986. Cassette tape.

———. *Revelation and Reason: Wesleyan Responses to Eighteenth-Century Rationalism*. Nuneaton: Wesley Fellowship, 1992.

Wood, Laurence W. "The Biblical Sources of John Fletcher's Pentecostal Theology." *Wesleyan Theological Journal* 42/2 (2007) 98–113.

———. [John Fletcher.] "An Essay on the Doctrine of the New Birth." *Asbury Theological Journal* 53/1 (1998) 35–56.

———. "Exegetical-Theological Reflections on the Baptism with the Holy Spirit." *Wesleyan Theological Journal* 14/2 (1979) 51–63.

———. "Historiographical Criticisms of Randy Maddox's Response." *Wesleyan Theological Journal* 34/2 (1999) 111–35.

———. "John Fletcher and the Rediscovery of Pentecost in Methodism." *The Asbury Theological Journal* 53/1 (1998) 7–34.

———. "John Fletcher as the Theologian of American Methodism and Mary Bosanquet Fletcher as Its Model Devotional Writer." Paper presented at Religion, Gender, and Industry: Exploring Church and Methodism in a Local Setting conference, Shropshire, England, 16–18 June 2009. 14 pages.

———. "John Fletcher of Madeley, John Wesley's Designated Successor and 'Equal Partner.'" http://www.lcoggt.org/Fletcher/X_john_fletcher_rediscovered.htm.

Bibliography

———. "John Fletcher Revisited." Online: http://home.insightbb.com/~larrywood/index.html (site discontinued).

———. "John Fletcher's Influence on John Wesley." *Bulletin of the John Rylands University Library of Manchester* 85/2–3 (2003) 387–404.

———. "John Fletcher's Influence on John Wesley." Lecture delivered at Nazarene Theological College, Manchester, England, 2005. 15 pages.

———. *The Meaning of Pentecost in Early Methodism: Rediscovering John Fletcher as John Wesley's Vindicator and Designated Successor*. Pietist and Wesleyan Series 15. Oxford: Scarecrow, 2002.

———. "The Need for a Contextual Interpretation of John Wesley's Sermons." *Wesleyan Theological Journal* 45/1 (2010) 259–67.

———. "The Origin, Development, and Consistency of John Wesley's Theology of Holiness." *Wesleyan Theological Journal* 43/2 (2008) 33–55.

———. *Pentecostal Grace*. Grand Rapids: Asbury, 1980.

———. "Pentecostal Sanctification in Wesley and Early Methodism." *Wesleyan Theological Journal* 34/1 (1999) 24–63.

———. "Pentecostal Sanctification in Wesley and Early Methodism." *Pneuma* 21/2 (1999) 251–87.

———. "Pentecost and the Wesleyan Doctrine of Full Sanctification." Online: http://home.insightbb.com/~larrywood/index2.html (site discontinued).

———. *Theology as History and Hermeneutics: A Post-critical Conversation with Contemporary Theology*. Lexington: Emeth, 2005.

———. "Third Wave of the Spirit and the Pentecostalization of American Christianity: A Wesleyan Critique." *Wesleyan Theological Journal* 31/1 (1996) 110–40.

———. "Thoughts upon the Wesleyan Doctrine of Entire Sanctification with Special Reference to Some Similarities with the Roman Catholic Doctrine of Confirmation." *Wesleyan Theological Journal* 15 (1980) 88–99.

———. *Truly Ourselves, Truly the Spirit's: Reflections on Life in the Spirit*. Grand Rapids: Asbury, 1989.

Worman, J. H. "Moulin, Pierre du." In *Cyclopaedia of Biblical, Theological, and Ecclesiastical Literature*, prepared by John M'Clintock and James Strong, 6:700–701. New York: Harper, 1888.

Wright, Thomas. Letter to John Fletcher. 24 February 1774. The Fletcher-Tooth Collection, The John Rylands University Library, The University of Manchester, MAM Fl. 7/18.

W. T. "To the Editor of the Methodist Magazine, Verses to the Memory of Mary Fletcher." *Methodist Magazine* 44 (1821) 240.

Wynkoop, Mildred Bangs. *Foundations of Wesleyan-Arminian Theology*. Kansas City: Beacon Hill, 1967.

———. "Theological Roots of the Wesleyan Understanding of the Holy Spirit." *Wesleyan Theological Journal* 14/1 (1979) 77–98.

———. *A Theology of Love: The Dynamic of Wesleyanism*. Kansas City: Beacon Hill, 1972.

Yong, Amos. "The Spirit, Christian Practices, and the Religions: Theology of Religions in Pentecostal and Pneumatological Perspective." *Asbury Journal* 62/2 (2007) 5–31.

Subjects and Names

Aberystwyth, xvi
Académie de Genève 1, 12, 15, 19, 19n, 20. *See also*, Université de Genève
Académie de Saumur, 14, 15
Accommodation, doctrine of. *See* God, accommodation; Fletcher's theology, accommodation, doctrine of
Adversus Haereses, 11, 92n
Agnew, Milton S., 3n
Allison, C. FitzSimons, 24, 24n
Amyraut, Moïse, 13–14, 14n, 18, 27, 27n
Amyrauldianism, 18, 27
analogy, 38–40, 78, 81, 115
Analogy of Religion, 39, 39n, 40n
An Earnest Appeal to Men of Reason and Religion, 66
Anglicanism. *See* Church of England; Fletcher's theology; Anglican theology
Antinomianism, 1, 25, 26–28, 31, 34, 87, 120, 122
a posteriori, 14
a priori, 14
Aquinas, Thomas, 47, 50, 112
Arianism, 21, 22
Archives d'Etat de Genève, xv
Archives Cantonales Vaudoises, Etat de Vaud, xv
Archives Communales de Nyon, xvi
Arminianism, xii, 1, 5, 12, 18, 21, 25, 27, 95
  Dutch Arminianism, 5, 102
  Methodist Arminianism, 5
Armstrong, Brian, 13, 14, 14n
Asbury Theological Journal (or *Asbury Journal*), 7n
Asbury Theological Seminary, xvi
Atlanta, Georgia, xvi
atonement, 13, 26, 27, 32, 100, 125, 159. *See also* Fletcher's theology, atonement.
Attingham Park, xvi
Augustine, 12, 12n, 18, 67, 88, 94, 101, 146,
Aukema Cieslukowski, Corrie M., 90, 90n,
authority, 35, 38, 123. *See also* Fletcher's theology, authority
Authur Skevington Wood Archive, xv, 154n

Balzer, Cary, 24n
Baltimore, Maryland, xvi
baptism, 42. *See also* Fletcher's theology, baptism.
Baptism of the Holy Spirit, 4, 180–183
Baxter, Richard, 13n, 26–28, 122, 168
Bebbington, David, 37, 37n
Bengel, Johann Albrecht, 92n
Benson, Joseph, xviii, xxi, 4, 6 (as biographer), 31n, 45, 45n, 72n, 155, 163–70, 175, 180–91, 199, 203
Bentley, Richard, 35
Berne, 20
Berridge, John, 54, 54n, 137
Beveridge, William, 24

279

Subjects and Names

Bible. *See* Scripture; Fletcher's theology, Scripture
Bishop, Mary, 188n
Bionnes, Théodore Crinsoz de, 9n, 20
Bosanquet, Claude, 12n, 19, 19n
Bosanquet, Mary. *See* Fletcher, Mary (née Bosanquet)
Boyle Lecture, 35
Breckon, 168n
Bretell, Jeremiah, 48n
Bridwell Library, xvi
Bristol, xv, 199
British Library, xv
Brown, W. Adams, 10n, 11n, 25n
Buildwas, 46
Bull, George, 24
Bunyan, John, 122
Butler, Joseph, 38–40

Calvin, John, 12–13, 16, 16n, 18, 21, 77
Calvinism, xii, 1, 2, 5, 7, 12, 13, 14, 18, 20, 21, 22, 24, 27, 28, 51, 53, 54, 55, 62, 64, 70, 74, 81, 93, 94, 100, 104, 107, 108, 115, 121, 131, 134, 167, 168,170, 210. *See also* Fletcher's theology, Calvinism
  divine fiat, xii, 70, 77, 92
  effective call, 54, 115
  finished salvation, xii, 46, 81, 82, 83, 93, 94, 95, 121, 134, 170, 192
  hyper-Calvinism, xii, 25, 26, 28, 33,121, 122, 138
  limited atonement, 104–5, 106n, 141
  perseverance, 169
Cambridge Platonists, 36, 37, 40,44, 44n, 91n, 97
Campbell, Gordon, 29n
Cameron, John, 13, 13n, 27, 27n
Cannon, William, 80, 80n, 95n
Caroline divines, 24
Carrim, Rhonda, xvi
Cartesian, 14, 15, 16, 18
catechism, 15, 182
categorization (of believers), 32, 33, 60, 99, 198, 213, 213n. *See also* Fletcher's theology, categorization

Catholicism. *See* Roman Catholicism
Chambers, Rowland, 23, 23n
Charismatic movement, 2, 3
Charles II, 29
Cheshunt Foundation Archives, xv
Chillingworth, William, 24
Christianity, 5, 10, 15, 18, 32, 33, 35, 36, 39, 40, 41, 44, 39, 41, 101, 121, 205. *See also* Fletcher's theology, Christianity
Christianity as Old as Creation, 36, 39
Christology, 11, 12, 17, 26, 40, 56, 77, 90, 121. *See also* Fletcher's theology, Christ
Church, xi, 6, 10n, 12, 20, 30, 35, 36, 37, 38, 64, 71, 74, (Eastern and Western) 88, 89, 94, 97, 116, 120, 121, 124, 143, 146, 160, 165, 175, 181, 189, 206, 221n. *See also* Fletcher's theology, Church
Church of England, xi, 1, 6, 10, 18, 23–25, 30, 33–34, 48, 64, 65, 71n, 93, 102, 103, 110, 122, 143, 146, 152, 155, 182, 194, 210n, 216. *See also* Fletcher's theology, Anglican theology
Cliff College, xv, 154
Clifford, Alan C., 27n, 28, 28n
Coalbrook-Dale, 46, 143
Cocceius, John, 18, 25, 59–60, 81n, 92n
Collins, Kenneth, xvi, 66n, 67, 67n, 75n, 82n, 89–90, 107n, 135, 135n, 137n, 139n, 141, 141n, 146n, 199, 199n
Colyer, Elmer M., 90
condescension, 16, 17, 17n, 66, 91, 92, 108, 211, 220, 221. *See also* God, accommodation; Fletcher's theology, accommodation, doctrine of
Confessio Fidei Gallicana, 21
Confessio Helvetica Posterior, 21
conscience, 16, 20, 52, 67, 102, 102n
continental theology, 5, 9, 13, 15, 33

conversion, 3, 31, 32, 114, 163, 168. *See also* Fletcher's theology, conversion
cosmology, 41
Countess of Huntingdon Connexion Archives, xvi
covenant theology, 10–13, 25–26, 27, 30, 32, 33, 59–63, 78n, 113, 115, 116, 128, 129, 59–63. *See also* Fletcher's theology, covenants
Cox, Robert, xviii, 6
Cragg, Gerald R., 35, 35n, 36, 37n, 38, 38n, 39n, 40, 40n, 49n
Cranmer, Thomas, 24
creation, xi, 11, 27, 28, 38, 40, 44, 45, 47, 49, 51. *See also* Fletcher's theology, creation
creeds, 10–11, 19–21, 22, 23, 54, 115, 143
Crisp, Tobias, 18, 26, 26n, 28, 122, 152
Cruickshank, Joanna, xvi
Cudworth, Ralph, 53n, 91n
Cullmann, Oscar, 92n
Cunningham, John, xvi

Dallas, Texas, xvi
D'Alembert, Jean-Baptiste le Rond, 22
Darby, Abiah, xix, 142n, 143–44, 166, 166n, 175, 179–80, 192
Darby, Abraham II, 143
Davenant, John, 24
Davies, William Ryes, 5, 5n, 20n, 76, 76n, 84n, 101n
Dayton, Donald, 3, 3n, 4, 5, 181n
decree (decretal theology), 14, 25, 33, 93, 95
degree, 17, 32
Demonstration of Apostolic Preaching, xvii, 11
Deasley, Alex R. G., 3n
Decency of Behaviour at the Table of the Lord, 31n
dialectical thought, xiii, 16, 16n, 18, 60
dichotomizing, 26, 81
Discourse of the Faith and Hope of the Gospel, 64
Discourse on Mental Errors, 85
deism, 35, 36, 39, 72, 123

dispensations, 11, 12, 13, 32, 33, 79. *See also* Fletcher's theology, dispensations
dissent, 64
divorce, 29
dogmatism, 36, 222
Downey, Edward A. Jr., 76, 77, 77n
Drew University, xvi
Duarte, Eugénio, xvii
Duke University, xv
Du Luc, Jean-André 41, 42, 42n
Dunham, 23
Durham, North Carolina, xv
Dunning, H. Ray, xvi, 68n, 70n, 88, 88n

Early Church Fathers, 10–12
Ebonitism, 91
Edwards, David L., 37
election, 21, 31, 62
Elwall, Edward, 91
England, xi, 1, 19, 20, 21, 22, 23, 29, 37, 40, 41, 116
English, John C., 44
English language, 7, 91n, 170
Enlightenment, 9, 14, 15, 18, 19, 35, 36, 37, 51, 123
enthusiasm, 36, 36n, 72
Emerson, Everett H., 25
Emory University, xvi
empiricism, 2, 66, 72
Epicurus, 46
epistemology, 15, 39, 40, 50, 51, 53, 56, 57, 67, 69, 72, 188. *See also* Fletcher's theology, epistemology
eschatology, 28, 74, 192, 204, 74. *See also* Fletcher's theology, eschatology
evangelical, xi, 1, 30, 37, 44n, 53, 69, 73, 97, 104, 109, 110, 111, 126, 134, 136, 137, 138, 139, 139, 148, 150, 156, 157, 168, 170, 175, 194, 207, 210, 212
Evanston, Illinois, xvi
existential, 17, 51, 58, 62, 63, 71–73, 82, 84, 111, 129, 176. *See also* Fletcher's theology, existential

281

Subjects and Names

experience, 31, 98

faith. *See* sola fide
federal theology. *See* covenant theology
Ferguson, Everett, 11, 11n
Ferguson, Robert Lynn, 9n, 13n
Five Letters to the Reverend Mr. Fletcher, 83, 83n, 105n, 131n
Flavel, John, 26, 85, 122, 138
Fléchère, Henri-Louis de la, 22, 22n
Fletcher, John William, xi
   academy, 1, 12, 15, 19, 20, 22
   A Dialogue Between a Minister and One of His Parishioners, 48
   A Dreadful Phenomenon Described and Improved, 46
   An Appeal to Matter of Fact and Common Sense, 24, 47, 57, 72, 101, 107, 173
   A Race for Eternal Life, 122, 122n
   biographers, xi, 1n, 5, 6, 9, 165, 168n
   birth, 1, 12
   Checks to Antinomianism, 1, 26n, 28, 51, 29, 121, 125, 155, 160
   controversy, xii, 1, 7, 28, 53–57, 69, 74, 92, 96, 104, 120, 121, 122, 125, 127, 128, 130, 134, 143–47, 156n, 168, 192
   convalescence, 22, 23, 191
   conversion, 1, 23
   curacy, 23
   death, 1, 2
   Discours Sur la Régénération, 54n, 67n, 153, 170–173, 174, 175n, 207, 207n
   England, xi, 1, 20, 22, 23, 40
   Essay on Truth, 56, 85, 110, 150, 174, 186, 188, 196, 200, 206
   Equal Check, 10, 21, 30, 75, 125, 155, 187, 201
   Essai sur la Paix do 1783, 41
   experience, 68, 72, 79, 82, 87, 89, 98, 101, 110, 114–15, 117, 145, 147, 149, 151, 152, 153, 154, 156, 158, 163, 165, 167, 168, 168n, 173, 175–78, 179, 180, 181, 188, 189, 190, 191, 191n, 193, 196, 197, 199, 200, 201, 202, 203, 204, 207, 208, 210, 219, 221
   family, 19
   Fourth Check, 53, 81
   Geneva. *See* Geneva
   influence, xi, 1
   La Grâce et la Nature, viii, xiii, 40, 41, 42, 87, 90, 161
   La Louange, 40
   La Nature & le Dessin du Christianisme, 153
   Last Check, 33n, 86, 184, 185, 201, 205
   Madeley parish, xi, 1, 6, 23, 30, 46, 48, 101, 122, 125, 143, 155, 156, 216, 220, 221
   military, 19, 20
   methodism (connection to), 1, 9, 23, 24, 30–33. *See also* methodist/Methodist.
   ordination, 1, 19, 20, 22, 23
   parishioners, xiii, 48, 101, 122, 125, 143, 155, 156, 156n, 157, 166, 175, 194, 202n, 211, 213–22
   piety, xi, 2, 9, 9n, 42, 59, 87, 92, 113n
   The Reconciliation, 129
   Réveille toi, toi qui dors, 153
   Salut par la Foi, 153
   sermon, xii, 7, 8, 46, 47–48, 63, 67, 102, 104, 104n, 107n, 109, 109n, 113, 125–35, 155, 155n, 156, 156n, 174, 202n, 204, 204n, 209, 212–22
   Six Letters on the Spiritual Manifestation of the Son of God, 7, 63–66, 72
   studies, 19, 33
   successor to Wesley, 2, 124, 189
   Swiss origins, xi, 2, 7, 9, 12, 13, 21, 23, 40, 191
   The Doctrines of Grace and Justice, 74
   The Portrait of Saint Paul, 7, 21, 51, 200, 212, 222
   The Scripture Scales, 96, 97, 124, 187
   Third Check, 83, 121, 150, 205
   vicar, xi, 1, 6, 23, 30, 123, 143, 155–56, 157, 194, 208, 216, 220–221

Subjects and Names

vindicator, 121
voyages, 23
Fletcher's theology, xi, 41
   accommodation, doctrine of, xii, xiii, 12, 18, 33, 50, 60, 61, 76–82, 90, 92, 98, 99, 100, 104, 105, 108, 109, 113, 117, 118, 124, 129, 132, 133, 134–40, 156, 167, 192, 205, 208, 210n, 211, 212, 220, 221, 222. See also *condescension*
   adoption, 91
   Anabaptist, 145, 146
   analogy, 43, 44, 45–50, 52, 59, 63, 70, 96, 210, 213
   Anglican theology, 6, 10, 18, 23–25, 33, 65, 71n, 93, 102, 110, 143, 145, 146–47, 155, 174, 175, 182, 194, 195, 210n
   antinomianism, 25, 26–28, 34, 87, 96, 100, 112, 113, 120, 121–23, 124, 125, 128, 131, 138, 155, 159, 189, 192
   anthropology. See Fletcher's theology, humanity
   Arminianism, 5, 12, 13, 20, 21, 31, 74, 75, 95, 115, 116, 118, 122, 211
   atonement, 22, 49, 58, 62, 65, 72, 81, 100, 101, 104–5, 107, 108, 110, 113, 128, 134–40, 156, 163, 218, 219
   authority, 71, 71n, 98
   assurance, 118, 150–52, 184, 188, 190, 191, 200, 201, 218
      full assurance, 181, 186n, 188n, 199–201
   baptism, 74, 142–49, 152, 152n, 155, 156, 156n, 165, 166, 166n, 167, 174, 175, 182, 189, 189n, 194, 195, 196, 197, 198, 204, 215, 216
   Calvinism, 20, 21, 30, 31, 33, 51, 52, 53, 55, 62, 70, 74, 75, 92, 94, 100, 115, 118, 122, 125, 131, 138, 192, 211
   categorization (of believers), 189, 202n, 212–22
      awakened sinners, 213–22

      believers, 213–22
   catholicism, 170
   Church, 30, 71n, 88, 116, 143, 189, 206, 216, 221n
   Christ, 3, 52, 56, 58, 65, 72, 81, 85, 86, 87, 93, 106, 108–9, 112, 113, 119, 127, 132, 134, 135–36, 139, 140–153, 156, 160, 162, 171, 173, 193, 194, 204, 209n, 217, 218, 220, 221n
      ascension, 81, 140, 154, 160, 187, 193, 207
      death 171, 187, 204, 218
      incarnation, 91, 108, 140
      King, 148
      light, 108–9
      Mediator, 199
      Priest, 148
      resurrection, 81, 91, 171, 187, 218
   Christian perfection, xii, 2, 3, 4, 7, 28, 33, 63, 72, 86–87, 100, 128, 132, 151n, 163, 164, 167n, 168, 169, 169n, 180, 181, 183–85, 186, 188, 197, 198, 201, 201n, 202, 203, 204, 205–8, 209n, 210, 212, 220. See also Fletcher's theology, perfection
   Christianity, xiii, 86n, 87, 96, 101, 109, 120, 150, 160, 162, 165, 166, 167, 173, 179, 193, 194, 206, 208–10, 222
      almost/altogether Christian, xiii, 165n, 166, 175, 179, 188, 189, 197, 207, 208–10, 213, 215, 218, 222
      covenant of, 120, 130
      dispensation of, 92, 109, 142, 146, 155, 160, 162, 175n, 184, 213, 205, 261,
      genuine Christianity, 101, 166, 175, 184, 189, 208–10
      nominal Christianity, 33, 101, 154, 155–56, 208
      perfect/imperfect Christianity, xiii, 86, 87, 155–56, 173, 175n, 180, 181, 184, 205, 207, 209
      primitive Christianity, 144, 167, 170, 208, 210n

283

Subjects and Names

comprehensive, 73–76
condemnation, 33, 78n, 107n, 114, 118, 137, 140, 161
condescending. *See* Fletcher's theology, accommodation, doctrine of
conversion, 3, 114, 156n, 168, 169,170, 174, 175, 175n, 201, (morphology of) 213, 218
covenants, 5, 33, 59–63, 78, 103, 126–34, 163
covenant of works/grace, 5, 60, 113, 126–34, 135, 138
covenant of peculiarity, 115–18, 142, 196
creation, 59, 91, 101, 194, 216
damnation, 52, 62, 74, 103, 113, 116, 124
degree, 11, 29–30, 33, 33n, 49, 50, 63, 63n, 67, 74, 82–86, 90, 92, 95, 97, 107, 108, 109, 110, 117, 126–27, 136, 147, 150, 165, 204
degrees of assurance, 117–18, 150–152, 200
degrees of faith, 11, 84, 92, 95, 107, 110, 111–12, 140, 154, 190, 200, 202, 213n, 222
degrees of grace, 32, 110, 126–27, 191n, 126–27, 191n
degrees of justification, 83
degrees of knowledge, 63, 136, 127
degrees of light, 83
degrees of obedience, 136, 148
degrees of perfection, 38, 83, 86, 86n, 205
degrees of regeneration, 147–49, 174, 175, 207
degrees of salvation, 126n, 210
degrees of sin, 83
degrees of the manifestation of the Spirit, 83, 193, 194, 203
degrees of truth, 83–85, 97
deism, 21, 36, 72
dispensations, xii, xiii, 5, 6, 7, 8, 9, 10, 11, 17n, 24, 40, 49, 50, 51, 53, 57, 58–98, 75, 76, 77, 78, 79, 81, 86, 88–93, 95, 97, 108, 112, 113, 114, 117, 119, 128–31, 135, 136, 138, 140, 141, 142, 149, 150, 154, 158, 161, 162, 165, 166, 174, 182, 189, 190, 191n, 200, 205, 209, 211, 212
babes in Christ, 32, 183, 184, 185–89, 200
Biblical basis, 9
creeds, 10–11, 24
continuity, 109
definition, 62, 63
dispensation of Abraham, 92, 110
dispensation of Christianity, 75, 85, 87, 92, 94, 99, 100, 105, 109, 110, 111, 127, 130, 138, 140, 141, 145, 146, 148, 159, 161, 164, 166, 181, 187, 190, 193, 196, 198, 200, 209. *See also* Fletcher's theology, Christianity
dispensation of the Father, 5, 61, 78, 79, 83,92, 99–119, 138, 148, 149, 158, 159, 194, 200, 205
dispensation of the Son, xiii, 5, 61, 78, 79, 84, 92, 119, 120–157, 157, 159, 161, 162, 163, 192, 194
dispensation of the Spirit, xiii, 5, 61, 78, 79, 84, 92, 100, 147, 149, 150, 158–210
Gentilism, 33, 47, 49, 51, 51n, 61, 63, 85, 86, 87, 115, 116, 130, 142, 205, 206
hermeneutical tool, 30
heathen, 22, 32, 33, 52n, 53n, 61, 76, 79, 85, 87, 92, 94, 99–115, 117, 117, 128, 136, 141, 150, 155, 159, 167,190, 194
influence of, 29
influence upon, 9
inferior and higher, 11, 30, 33, 51, 73, 79, 83, 87, 97, 114, 123, 127, 141, 142, 147, 150, 152, 152n, 153, 159, 161, 162, 163, 186, 187, 190, 197, 200, 205, 221n
John the Baptist, 61, 87, 88, 91, 92, 141–47, 150, 151, 151n, 154, 165, 170,179n, 186, 187, 188, 200, 206, 216
Judaism, 49, 61, 63, 68, 75, 85, 87, 92, 94, 99, 105, 109, 110, 111,

115–18, 123, 130, 138, 151, 151n, 154, 159, 164, 166, 167, 167n, 186, 189, 190, 194, 197, 198, 205
Mosaic dispensation, 68, 123, 137–40, 159, 159n, 161, 162, 193
novelty, 30
seal, 101, 142, 144, 145, 151, 156, 176, 178, 184, 186, 196
Trinitarian, 11, 63, 149, 158, 159, 161, 198
unity, 30, 86, 109
dialectical thought, xiii, 5–6, 16, 18, 25, 30, 33, 48, 49, 56, 57, 60, 74, 75, 76, 95, 96, 124, 211
ecumenical appeal of, xi
Early Church, 10–12. *See also* Church.
election (or reprobation), 6, 30, 49, 62, 94, 115–17
entire sanctification, xiii, 3, 4, 163, 188n, 201, 203
epistemology, 67, 72
eschatology, 74, 86, 192, 204
ethic, 81, 123, 172
existential, 17, 72, 77
ex opera operato, 146
faith, 5, 10, 11, 22, 48, 51, 53, 56, 58, 72, 75, 77, 79, 80, 84, 85, 93, 110, 111, 115, 121, 125, 139, 140, 145–46, 149, 150, 154, 156, 158, 159, 162, 164, 166, 173, 179, 180, 184, 186, 187, 188, 189, 190, 194, 197, 202, 203, 208, 209, 209n, 211, 218, 219
faith history. *See* Fletcher's theology, ordo salutis
free will, 4, 5, 10, 68, 69, 70, 71, 95, 107, 116, 124
French, 7, 41
God, 41, 48, 117
  attributes, 42, 43, 90n, 132, 222
  Comforter, 69, 126
  Creator (as), xiii, 41, 44, 47, 49, 50, 51, 52, 53, 56, 57, 60, 62, 69, 78, 79, 83, 126, 132, 134, 140, 194
  Father, 12, 199. *See also* Fletcher's theology, dispensations, dispensation of the Father
  holy-love of, xii, 75, 116, 117
  holiness, 75, 78, 121
  justice, 47, 48, 49, 74, 111, 117, 147
  knowledge, 51, 52, 53, 57
  love, 43, 52, 55, 57, 62, 76, 77, 99, 100–101, 104, 106, 116, 118, 127, 191, 195, 207, 211, 218, 222
  mercy, 48, 49, 74, 101, 117, 148, 217, 218
  partiality/impartial, 30, 49, 94, 115–17, 131
  perfections, 86
  Preserver, 126, 134
  providence, 29, 32, 32n, 39, 40, 45, 46, 47, 48 49, 51, 52, 55, 56, 59, 74, 75, 80, 94, 101, 208
  Redeemer, xiii, 44, 51, 53, 57, 60, 61, 62, 66, 69, 78, 79, 82, 83, 126, 132, 133, 134, 140, 162, 192, 193, 194
  Sanctifier, 40, 78, 79, 83, 84, 133
  sovereignty, 5, 46, 49, 74, 115–16
  transcendence, 43, 43n, 76, 94
  wisdom, 50, 55
  will, 80, 165
  wrath, 80, 48, 118, 216
good works, 24, 42, 55, 84, 93, 97, 112–14, 120, 122n, 126, 127, 139, 219
gospel, 85, 96, 105, 106, 113, 205, 211
grace, xiii, 30, 41, 48, 49, 50, 51, 52, 54, 54n, 56, 57, 61, 66, 68, 70, 71, 74, 80, 81, 91, 101, 105, 106, 107, 112, 113, 117, 118, 123, 124, 126, 128, 129, 131, 132, 133, 134, 144, 146, 148, 174, 192, 213, 215, 218, 222
free grace, 4, 10, 71, 107, 124
gospel grace, 69, 79, 86, 113, 126, 134
grace and justice, 5, 74, 75, 76, 111, 113, 124
grace and nature, xiii, 8, 35–57, 62, 70, 71, 101

instantaneous work, 82, 83, 83n
original grace, 69, 126, 134
prevenient grace, 47, 48, 52, 53, 55, 57, 69–72, 80, 90, 107, 108, 112, 113, 135, 171, 171n, 193
proportionate grace, 62, 115–17
regenerating grace, 47, 48, 52, 55, 57, 68, 72, 145, 145n, 156
work of, 176, 188
hermeneutic, 5, 30, 44, 80, 81, 83, 88, 96–98
history, of, xi, xii, 8, 51, 53, 58, 74, 78, 81, 85
holiness, 24, 33, 91, 218
Holy Spirit, xiii, 2, 3, 7, 60, 64n, 71, 88–89, 151, 152–53, 154, 158, 160, 162, 163, 167, 167n, 168, 172, 176–80, 187, 192, 193, 194, 195, 198, 199, 201, 201n, 203, 204, 206, 208, 210, 220
baptism with the Spirit, 1, 2–3, 4, 7, 7, 142–49, 156, 156n, 157, 160, 162, 164, 165, 166, 166n, 167, 168, 169, 169n, 171, 171n, 173, 174, 175n, 180–183, 184, 185, 186n, 188, 189, 189n, 190, 191, 191n, 194, 195, 196, 197, 197n, 198, 199, 200, 201–5, 206, 207, 208–9, 209n
born of the Spirit, 1, 145, 146, 146n, 147, 151, 151n, 173, 174, 180, 182, 195–98, 206
Comforter, 152, 153, 178, 179, 194, 198
indwelling Spirit, 175–80, 183, 186n, 196, 198–99
Monitor, 152–53, 198
omnipotence, 179
Spirit of adoption/bondage, 151n, 152, 153, 179, 185, 186, 189, 194, 200, 206, 218
Witness, 158, 186, 188, 189, 199–201
humanity, xii, xiii, 49, 50, 53, 60, 61, 67, 71, 75, 76, 80, 82, 99, 101, 102, 107
human finitude, 60, 76, 90, 108, 211, 222

image of God, 58, 59, 63, 102n, 161, 207
influence of, 1–6, 12
influence upon, xi, 5, 8, 9, 26n, 28, 40
integrated system of, xii, 80, 86, 124, 211
interpreters of, xiii, 1–6, 161, 167n, 201
irenic spirit of, xi, 74. *See also* Fletcher's theology as reconciling
judgment, 113–14, 117, 205, 217
justification, 28, 45, 46, 67, 83, 84, 90, 91, 112–14, 131, 149, 150, 156, 171, 172, 175, 180, 181, 186n, 187, 188, 189, 191, 192, 202, 203, 207, 210, 219
final justification, 97, 113, 128, 207
general justification, 55, 106–8, 127
kingdom of God, 33, 60, 161, 166, 166n, 170, 174, 175n, 187, 190, 193, 194, 195, 199
knowledge of God, 65, 73, 87, 89, 140, 161, 173
law, 28, 46, 52n, 121, 123, 131, 132, 133, 134–40, 147–49, 195, 205, 206, 207, 213, 217
law of innocence, 129
law of faith/law of liberty, 135
moral law, 135–39, 148, 152, 207
love, 84, 87, 139, 148, 173, 202n, 206, 207, 210
macro. *See* Fletcher's theology, ordo temporum
manuscripts, 7, 125–27, 158, 198
merit, 112–14, 127, 159
meritum de condigno, 112, 127
meritum de congruo, 112, 127
micro. *See* Fletcher's theology, ordo salutis
miracles, 73
morals, 80, 87, 172
mysticism, 9, 46, 52n, 97
nature, xiii, 43, 45, 47, 48, 49, 50–52, 56, 62, 70, 106, 107
noetic order, 78, 82, 114, 193, 211

Subjects and Names

modification to Wesley's theology, 2, 3, 4, 70, 183–91, 206
obedience, 52, 61, 72, 74, 78, 80, 112–14, 118, 125, 127, 134, 136, 138, 139, 148, 150, 156, 205
ordo temporum (objective view of history), xii, xiii, 8, 59–63, 82, 86, 93, 95, 100, 109, 110, 114, 129, 130, 147, 158, 159, 162, 175n
ordo salutis (order of salvation), xii, xiii, 8, 59–63, 82, 85, 86, 88, 89–90, 92, 93, 95, 99, 100, 109, 110, 114, 117, 129, 147, 159, 162, 175n, 213
originality, 5
paedobaptists, 146
Pentecost, 32, 61, 141, 149, 150, 151, 151n, 153–54, 159–61, 163, 166, 167–70, 173, 174, 175, 175n, 176, 177, 178, 180, 183, 184, 187, 188, 188n, 189, 193, 195, 196, 198, 200, 201, 201n, 202, 203, 204, 206, 207, 209, 209n
perfection, xiii, 33, 83, 86–87, 134, 135, 136, 137, 140, 148, 150, 160, 165n, 167, 169, 176, 185, 199, 205, 206, 207, 211, 212. *See also* Christian perfection
perfect love, 163, 184, 185, 199, 202, 204, 207, 208, 209, 222
pietism, 9n, 59, 92
Platonism, 43n, 44, 97
Pneumatology. *See* Fletcher's theology, Holy Spirit
polemical, xiii, 1, 24, 28, 39, 64, 73, 92, 93, 94–96, 99, 99n, 100, 113, 120, 122, 143, 192, 193
practical theology, xii, 6, 7, 8, 211, 212, 221n, 222
predestination, 20, 75, 99, 168
Protestantism, 19, 116, 120, 194
reason, 44, 67, 71–72, 109, 171
reconciling, as, xii, 5. *See also* Fletcher's theology, irenic spirit of
regeneration, xiii, 53, 55, 66, 67–69, 72, 91, 94, 115, 141, 145–46, 147, 149, 152, 156, 157, 161, 170–175, 175n, 180, 182, 187, 189, 193, 194, 196, 201, 202n, 204, 207, 209n, 210, 219
repentance, 48, 115, 146, 165, 174, 196, 202n, 216, 218
revelation, doctrine of, xii, 8, 30, 40, 50, 51, 52, 52n, 57, 58, 59, 60, 62, 63, 65, 71, 72, 73, 77, 81, 82, 87, 90, 97, 104, 108–9, 129, 132, 140, 187, 193, 220, 222
progressive revelation. *See* Fletcher's theology, salvation history, progress
righteousness, 84, 99n, 100, 128, 142, 146, 146n, 182, 187, 196, 199, 218, 219
salvation, xiii, 2, 22, 30, 34, 46, 50, 55, 56, 57, 59, 62, 63, 68, 73–82, 86, 91, 94, 99, 100, 104, 106, 107, 126, 133, 134, 141, 144, 145–46, 158, 163, 170, 190, 192, 210, 213
conditions, 111–15, 117, 144, 145–46
pardon of sin, 149, 151, 164, 167, 171, 172, 180, 188, 190, 200, 218
salvation history, 29, 30, 46, 50, 51, 52, 52n, 57, 58, 61, 62, 63, 68, 78, 79–82, 85, 88, 89, 94, 95, 99, 100, 104, 106, 109, 112–14, 116, 123–25, 128, 129, 130, 131, 132, 133, 140, 141, 160, 192, 193, 204, 222
progress, 59, 63, 68, 78, 79–82, 86, 88, 90, 94, 154
sanctification, 90, 131, 163, 171, 172, 191, 192, 194, 202, 207, 210, 218
Scripture, xi, 5, 9, 24, 30, 31, 43, 45, 49, 52, 58, 61, 66, 67, 68, 69, 71, 73, 75, 80, 81, 82, 83, 86, 88, 90n, 94, 96–98, 101, 105, 106, 110, 123–24, 133, 138, 139, 140n, 144, 164, 165, 166, 179, 196, 197, 198, 203, 206, 220. *See also* Scripture; Old Testament; New Testament

Subjects and Names

sin, 46, 47, 48, 53,74, 101–3, 112, 128, 205, 211, 215, 216, 217, 219
  carnality, 140, 148,154, 184, 187, 189, 195
  depravity, 24, 69, 100, 102, 106, 107, 112, 118, 121, 129
  Fall of, xiii, 22, 50 51, 55, 57, 60, 66, 70, 76, 77, 100, 112, 113, 129, 132, 133, 134, 172, 192
  guilt, 69
  original, 80, 101–3, 104, 134
  spiritual senses, 65–66, 67, 193, 207
  status purorum naturalium, 107, 112
  synergism, 56, 62, 203, 211
  Swiss theology. *See* Swiss church
  telos, xii, 58, 59, 86–87, 204, 222
  The Apostles Creed, 11
  The Nicene Creed, 11
  Trinity, of, vi, xii, 8, 11, 72, 79, 88–93, 99, 176–80, 192, 193, 198, 199
  appropriation, 61, 91
  truth, 56, 82, 85, 187
  works, 5, 55, 99n, 112–14, 121, 125, 127, 128, 129, 131, 139
  writings, xii, 5, 7, 9, 21, 23, 45, 57, 155, 189
  via media, 10, 24, 25, 50, 72, 124, 137, 158
Fletcher, Mary (née Bonsanquet), xxi, 1n, 2, 6 (as biographer), 19n, 72n, 147, 147n, 151n, 190, 190n, 205, 206n
Fletcher, W. Brian, 3, 4
Flick, Stephen, xvi, xx, 6, 6n, 7n, 62n, 79n, 93n
Fuhrman, Eldon Ralph, 7, 75n, 108n, 148, 148n, 159n
Formula Consensus, 20, 21
Forsaith, Peter, xvi, 1n, 6, 6n, 9n, 10n, 13n, 53n, 153n, 155, 155n, 170n
France, 19, 41
Fraser, M. Robert, 3, 4, 4n, 9 5n, 165n, 167n, 181, 181n, 191, 191n, 203n
Frazier, J. Russell, 6, 7n, 131, 131n, 161, 162n, 170n, 201n

free will, 71. *See also* Fletcher's theology, free will.

Gardner, Don, xvi
Gargett, Graham, 16, 16n
Garrett Evangelical Divinity School, xvi
Geneva, xv, 1, 12, 13n, 14, 15, 18, 19, 20, 21, 22, 24, 95, 97
General Board of Discipleship of the United Methodist Church, xv
General Commission on Achieves and History of the United Methodist Church, xvi
Gentil, 17. *See also* Fletcher's theology, dispensations, Gentilism
geology, 41
Glas, John, 64
God. *See also* Fletcher's theology, God
  accommodation, 11, 14, 16, 17, 18, 77
  Creator, 50, 53, 77
  governance, 27, 39
  immanence, 94
  knowledge of, 16, 32, 51, 53
  providence, 29, 37, 39, 55, 101
  Redeemer, 11, 77
  reign of God, 27
  transcendence, 94
  unity of, 10, 30
  will, 76
Goltz, Hermann de, 14n
González, Justo L., 11n
Goodwin, John, 85, 168
gospel, 26, 85–86
Gnosticism, 10, 11
grace, 12, 17, 26, 27, 40, 55, 56. *See also* Fletcher's theology, grace
  free grace, 31, 70
Grace and Truth Vindicated, 31, 31n, 32n, 33n
Graham, Bill and Elaine, xvi
Greathouse, William, xvi, 201n
Green, John, 31–33, 31n, 32n, 33n
Gregory, Benjamin, 40, 73, 73n, 74
Grider, J. Kenneth, 3n

Hammond, Geordan, xv

Subjects and Names

Hatton, Miss, 151
Hazard Community and Technical College, xvi
heathen, 16, 99–115. *See also* Fletcher's theology, dispensations, heathen.
Heitzenrater, Richard P., 196n, 208, 208n, 209n
hell, 16, 32, 49, 127, 219
Helvic Consensus Formula, 20
Henry, Matthew, 55, 55n
Herefordshire Record Office, xvi
hermeneutics, 5, 63, 80n.
Hervey, James, 64, 64n
Hill, Richard, 53, 54, 54n, 69, 69n, 83, 83n, 94, 95, 105n, 106, 107, 121, 125, 125n, 131n, 134, 134n, 148, 150
historical theology, 8, 25
history, 37, 63, 75, 80. *See also* salvation history
holiness, vi, xiii, 2, 3, 28, 209
holiness movement. *See* Wesley-holiness
Holy Spirit, 32, 40, 54, 77, 88
Holland, 19
Hopper, Christopher, 74
Hosman, Glenn Burt, 81, 81n
Houghton, Russ, xv
Huguenot, 9n
humanity, 11, 16, 17, 70, 77
humanism, 13, 15, 18, 19, 21, 95
Huntingdon, Selina Hastings, xviii, 22n, 31, 64, 64n, 146n, 164, 166, 167n, 168, 168n, 169, 169n, 170, 170n, 186
Hymns for Whit-Sunday, 45

Ingham, Benjamin, 64–65
Ingham, Margaret, 64
infidelity, 22, 96, 191
infralapsarian, 61, 61n, 116, 126, 133, 134
Institutes of the Christian Religion, 13, 13n, 14, 16n, 94n
Instruction Chrétienne, xxi, 15–18, 19, 22
Irenaeus of Lyons, 11–12, 92n

Ireland, 184
Ireland, James, 23n

John Rylands University Library of Manchester, xv
Judaism, 10, 16, 17, 33, 49
justification, 64, 122. *See also* Fletcher's theology, justification.
 eternal justification, 26
 forensic justification, 121

Kant, Immanuel, 37
kingdom of God, 29
Kinghorn, Kenneth Cain, 5, 5n, 13n, 151, 151n
Klauber, Martin, xvi, 14n, 16n
Knickerbocker, Waldo Emerson, 2n, 43n, 97, 97n, 98
Knight, John, 2n, 3, 4, 50, 51n, 52, 52n, 58, 58n, 62n, 63, 63n, 69, 70, 71, 71n, 73, 73n, 82, 82n, 82, 84n, 86n, 94n, 95, 95n, 96n, 97n, 129n, 162, 162n, 175, 175n, 198, 198n, 209, 209n
Kudo, Hiroo, 51n

latitudinarianism, 18
Laud, William, 24
law, 12, 13, 17, 22, 26, 28, 46, 120. *See also* Fletcher's theology, law.
Lawton, George, 6, 13n, 21n, 23, 23n, 24, 24n, 45n, 79n, 81, 81n, 143n
Lees Campus Library, xvi
Letters on Theron and Aspasio, 64, 64n
Lettres Physiques et Morales sur Histoire de la Terre, 41
liberalism, 22
Locke, John, 36, 38
London, xv, xvi, 31, 153, 186n
Lockhart, Wilfred C., 5n
Lovely Lane Museum, xvi
Loyer, Ken, 43n, 90n, 91n, 92n
Lyon, Robert W., 3n

Maciver, Donald, xv
Maddox, Randy L., 3, 4
Madeley, xi, 1, 6, 23, 23n, 30, 101, 125, 126, 143, 155, 156. *See also*

289

Subjects and Names

Fletcher, John William, Madeley parish
Madeley Library, xv
Madison, New Jersey, xvi
Manchester Wesley Research Centre, xv
Marcion, 11
Marseille, 205
Matthews, Rex Dale, 39n
McDonnell, Kilian, 88, 88n, 89
McDonald, H. D., 35, 35n, 36, 36n, 38n, 71n, 76, 76n
McGonigle, Herbert, xv, 3n
McGrath, Alister E., 11n, 47n, 53n, 88n, 91n
McKim, Donald K., 94, 94n
Messer, Don, xvi
Methodist Archives and Research Centre, xv
methodist/Methodist, xi, 1, 2, 4, 5, 6, 9, 23, 24, 26, 28, 37, 64, 67, 70, 71, 95, 100, 104, 128, 134, 185, 189, 190, 199, 210, 213. *See also* Fletcher, John William, methodism (connection to)
  Conference Minutes, xii, 1, 22, 28, 31, 53, 55, 83, 92, 104, 105, 120, 121, 122, 125, 128, 130, 159, 169, 185, 190n
meteorologist, 41
Milton, John, 29-30, 29n, 75, 97
missiology. *See* Fletcher, John William, theology, practical
Monk, Robert C., 26n, 28n
Monod, Isaac François, 1n
More, Henry, 44
moralism, 22, 87, 112
morality, 39, 41, 80
Morgan, Irvonwy, 27n
Morris, Henry, xvi
Muller, Richard, 50
Murray, John, 25, 26n

Nash, Ronald H., 37n, 80
Nashville, Tennessee, xv
National Library of Wales, xvi
nature, 27, 36, 38, 39, 40, 41, 45, 46, 51, 53

natural light, 16
natural religion, 15, 17, 36, 38, 39, 41, 41n, 50-52, 51n
Nazarene Theological College, xv
Neff, Blake J., 3, 4
New Room, xv
New Testament, 10, 11, 17, 18, 30, 38, 65, 96, 116, 123-24, 133, 154, 164, 197. *See also* Scripture
Newton, Isaac, 38, 46
Nockles, Peter, xv
Norwood, 31
Nyon, xvi, 1, 1n, 9n, 23

Oath of Association, 20
Oath of Religion, 20
O'Brien, Glen Ashley, 7n, 176n, 192n
Old Testament, 10, 11, 12, 17, 18, 38, 65, 96, 98, 116, 123-24, 133, 140, 196, 197, 206. *See also* Scripture
Olson, Mark, 175, 175n, 190n
ontological 50, 88, 91, 92,
ordo salutis, 115, 122. *See also* Fletcher's theology, ordo salutis
orthodoxy, 14, 18, 39
Osborn, George, 45n
Ostervald, Jean Frédéric, 14
Outler, Albert, 88, 88n, 93
Owen, John, 28
Oxford, xvi, 163, 164, 165n, 190n, 191n
Oxford Brooks University, xvi

pastoral theology, 8, 170, 208. *See also* Fletcher's theology, practical
Packer, James I., 26n, 27, 27n
Paradise Lost, 29
peace, 12, 19, 20, 41, 47, 74, 150, 154, 165, 171, 174, 187, 193, 196, 199, 200, 202, 218, 219
Pelagian, 54, 94, 134
Pentecostal Grace, 24, 24n, 151n, 175n, 201n
Pentecost, 4, 32, 61
Pentecostalism, 2, 3, 203
Percy, Eustace, 13, 13n
perfection, 17, 32

290

Subjects and Names

Perkins Library, xvi
Perkins School of Theology, xvi
Perronet, William, 23n, 199
philosophes, 16, 18, 19
philosophy, 36, 41, 42, 43, 46
Plymouth Brethren, 79,
polemic, 15, 122, 131
Polier, Georges, 20
post-modern, xii
Powers, Marvin E. xvi
predestination, 13, 20, 20n, 21, 25, 75, 92, 93–95, 99, 100, 104, 115, 168n. *See also* Fletcher's theology, predestination
Priestly, Joseph, 90n, 125, 149,
Protestantism, 5, 10, 14, 19, 25, 35, 50, 80, 94, 96, 111, 116, 120, 121, 194, 192. *See also* Fletcher's theology, Protestantism
Prothero, Rev. 145n,
providence, 29, 37, 39. *See also* Fletcher's theology, God, providence
Puritans, 11n, 25–30, 33, 34, 36, 122, 168
Purkiser, W. T., 201, 201n
Ptolemaeus, 11

Quakers, 36, 37, 143–44, 156n, 182, 192, 203

Rainey, David, xv, 88n, 89n, 198, 199n
Ranters, 36
Ramus, Peter, 26
rationalism, 15, 19, 35, 36, 37, 67, 73, 193
Rayleigh, xvi
Reading, Berkshire, 31
reason, 13, 16, 16n, 18, 19, 35, 36, 37, 38, 39, 40, 52, 53, 66, 67, 71–73, 75, 87, 96, 102, 102n, 108–9, 161, 166n, 171, 220. *See also* Fletcher's theology, reason
Reasoner, Victor P., xvi, 3, 3n, 4, 201n
Rees, D. A., 37, 37n
Reformers, 5, 13, 18, 21, 25, 35, 38, 112, 120
regeneration, 77, 115. *See also* Fletcher's theology, regeneration

religion, 9, 15, 16, 17, 21, 24, 36, 38–40, 41, 41n, 81, 87, 90, 103, 123, 130, 149, 155, 168, 221n
Renty, Gaston Jean Baptiste de, 199,
revelation, doctrine of, xi, 11, 13, 16, 16n, 17, 18, 19, 25, 35, 36, 37, 38, 39, 40, 41, 51, 73, 77, 90. *See also* Fletcher's theology, revelation, doctrine of
general revelation, 16
progress, 33, 38, 40, 60n
Richardson, Hannah, 178n, 179n
Ritchie, Betsy, 29, 32n
righteousness, 120, 121. *See also* Fletcher's theology, righteousness
imputation, 28, 121, 128
Roman Catholicism, 5, 6, 10, 30, 35, 94, 96, 116, 120, 121, 194
Roney, John B., 14n
Rose, Daniel, 143,
Runyon, Theodore, 66, 66n, 67, 67n
Rutherford, Samuel, 26

Saint Michael's Church, xvi
Salop, 101
sanctification, 122
Sandeman, Robert, 64, 64n, 67, 68, 193
Santa Barbara, California, xvi
Saltmarsh, John, 26, 28
salvation, 21, 35, 77, 120, 122. *See also* Fletcher's theology, salvation or salvation history
finished, xii, 16, 28, 37, 38, 40, 82, 93, 121, 192,
salvation history, 10, 11, 12, 13, 14, 16, 17, 27, 28, 29, 37, 38, 39, 77, 93. *See also* Fletcher's theology, salvation or salvation history
tripartite view, 27, 28,
sanctification, 32, 40. *See also* Fletcher's theology, sanctification
Saumur, 13, 14, 27
Schlimm, Matthew R., 123, 123n, 124
scholasticism, 14, 18, 25, 50, 83
Scottish theology, 13
Scripture, 18, 31, 35, 36, 38, 39, 88, 90. *See also* Fletcher's theology, Scripture; sola Scriptura

291

unity of Old and New Testament, 10, 11, 12, 13, 17, 18, 38, 133,
Scylla and Charybdis, 36, 72
Seaman, John, xvi
Second Helvetic Confession, 21
Seekers, 36
seekers, 202n, 214, 215, 216–17
sermon, 38, 38n, 76, 12, 153, 154, 159, 164, 174, 178, 178n, 179n, 185, 191, 195, 197, 203, 204, 206, 208
Servetus, 21
Severn River, 46
Seymour, Aaron Cropley Hobart, xxii, 31, 31n, 168n
Shirley, Walter, 46, 168, 169, 170, 180, 181
Simeon, Charles, 44n
sin, 16, 27, 77, 80, 121. See also Fletcher's theology, sin
noetic effects of, xii, 77
Shakers, 36
Shipley, David Clark, 2n, 5, 5n, 13n, 28n, 71, 71n, 72, 72n, 74, 74n, 102, 102n
Shropshire, xv, xvi, 46, 53n
Shropshire Magazine, xvi
Smisby, 213
Smith, David Rushworth, 13n
Smith, Timothy, 2n, 3, 4
Smith, William Robertson, 25
Socinianism, 21, 22, 125
sola fide, 10, 15, 16, 17, 18, 64, 120, 121n, 125. See also Fletcher's theology, faith
sola gratia, 120, 122
sola Scriptura, 120
Sorkin, David, 15, 15n, 18n, 19
Spross, Daniel, xvi
spiritual, 36
Stafford, xvi
Staffordshire Record Office, xvi
Staples, Rob, 3, 4, 163n
state, 20
Stillingfleet, Edward, 24,
Streiff, Patrick, 1n, 5, 5n, 7n, 9n, 15n, 19, 19n, 42, 42n, 64n, 130n, 132, 143, 143n

supralapsarian, 60, 60n, 93, 129, 134, 137
Swiss church, 2, 14, 19–22, 23, 40
Switzerland, xi, 1, 2, 7, 14, 20, 21, 23, 40, 53n, 191

Taylor, Clive, xv
Taylor, Jeremy, 24
Taylor, John (of Norwich), 125
Telford, John, 186n
The Doctrine and Discipline of Divorce, 29, 29n
The Enchiridion, 12
The Federal Theology of Johannes Cocceius (1603–1669), 59, 59n, 81n
The Finishing Stroke, 53
The Folly of Atheism and Deism, 35
The Holiness Pilgrimage, 63, 63n
The Knowledge of God in Calvin's Theology, 76
The Reasonableness of Christianity, 36
Theological Roots of Pentecostalism, 3, 3n, 4, 181n
theology, 36, 37. See also Fletcher's theology
middle way, 19, 25, 36, 50, 124, 137
Theology of Love, 70, 70n
Theron and Aspasio, 64, 64n
Thirty-Nine Articles. See Fletcher's theology, Anglican theology
Thompson, Claude H., 13n
Thurnscoe, Yorkshire, 31
Tillotson, John, 24
Tindal, Matthew, 36, 38, 39
Tyerman, Luke, 2, 2n, 6, 13n, 19n, 44n, 166n, 169n, 170n, 184n, 188n, 206n
Trevecka College, 163–70, 175, 199
Trinity, 14, 39, 90. See also Fletcher's theology, Trinity and Fletcher's theology, dispensations, Trinitarian
Tronchin, Théodore, 16n
Turrettin, Jean-Alphonse, 14, 18, 20

United Library, xvi
Université de Genève, xv. See also Académie de Genève

Subjects and Names

Université de Lausanne, xv
University of California, Santa Barbara, xvi
Upper Room Chapel and Museum, xv
Ussher, James, 24

Valentinus, 11
van Asselt, Willem J., 59–60, 81n
Vaud, Pays de, 20, 21
Vernet, Jacob, 15–19, 15n, 16n, 17n, 22, 22n, 33
via media, 10, 24, 26
von Hofmann, J. C. K., 92n
Vuilleumier, Henri, 20, 20n

Wendel, François, 13n
Werenfels, Samuel, 14
Wesley, Charles, xviii, 1, 2, 23, 28, 28n, 31, 45, 46n, 65n,74n, 93, 96, 96n, 125, 125n, 149n, 159n, 166n, 167, 167n, 168, 168n, 176–79, 183, 184, 184n, 185, 185n, 198, 199, 199n, 210, 222
Wesley, John, xi, xii, 1, 2, 3, 4, 5, 6, 7, 13n, 20, 21, 23, 28, 29, 29n, 30, 31, 31n, 32n, 37, 44, 45n, 52n, 54n, 55, 66, 69, 70, 75, 76, 78, 81, 86n, 89, 90, 101, 105, 121, 123, 128, 130, 131, 141, 142, 145n, 153n, 154, 159, 161, 163, 164, 165, 165n, 169, 175, 177, 180–191, 196, 197, 197n, 199, 200, 201, 206, 208, 209, 210, 213, 221, 222
Wesleyan, 3, 8, 54, 69, 70, 71, 74, 100, 104, 107, 122, 137, 201, 203
Wesleyan-holiness, xiii, 2, 3, 4, 7, 161, 201, 203, 209, 210
Wesley Center, Oxford, xvi
Wesley Chapel, xvi
Wesley College, xv
Wesley Historical Society, xvi
Wesleyan Theological Journal, xxii, 2
Westminster College, xv
Westminster Confession, 115
Westminster Institute of Education, xvi
Whitefield, George, 31
Whitefield's Tabernacle, 31
Wiggins, James Bryan, 5, 5n, 7n, 41, 41n, 63n, 68, 68n, 82n, 132, 132n, 140, 140n, 193, 193n
Williams, Anne, 78, 78n, 81, 81n
Williams, Daniel, 26
Williams, 168
Wilson, David R., xvi, 6, 6n, 7n, 155, 155n, 210n, 212n, 221n
Wood, Laurence W., xvi, 3, 4, 7n, 24, 24n, 59n, 79n, 92n, 151n, 152n, 163, 168n, 175n, 188n, 189n, 196n, 197n, 198n, 201n, 204n
Wood, Arthur Skevington, 51, 51n
Wynkoop, Mildred Bangs, 70, 70n

Zinzendorf, Nicolaus, 188

293

Scripture

Genesis
28:17	42

Numbers
16:20–34	48

2 Kings
2:20–21	54

Psalms
46:8	48n
148	40

Proverbs
20:27	37

Isaiah
9:6	204, 204n
35:3	221
45:5,7	69

Joel
	169, 181

Haggiah
2:7	109, 209n;

Matthew
3	202n
5:20	155, 155n
11:11	141, 150
14:26–27	217, 271n
18:3	174
25:46	113n,

Mark
16:16	74

Luke
12:48	50
12:50	202, 202n
14:25	29
15:7	216–17, 220–221
16:9	55
16:10–12	56
16:11	55

John
1:5	77n
1:9	72, 108
1:12	213, 213n, 215, 216n
3:7	174, 219
3:8	197n
3:18	107
6:44	102n
7:38	204
7:39	160

Scripture

10:16	110
14:2	33
14:6	108, 85
14:7	219
14:15	181
14:16	177
14:16–17	178
14:17	153, 164, 175–76
14:26	161
15:4	155n
16:7	160
16:8	128

Acts

	167, 202, 206
1:5	209
2	169
2:38	209
4:33	201
5[:42]	215
8:15	196
19:2, 6	144

Romans

1	41
1:20	44n
2:14	47
5:5	208, 210
5:18	55, 107, 133
5:20	107
7	148–49
7:1–7	139
7:24	217–19
8:9	209
8:15	179
10	52
11:5–6	126
14:17	193, 199

1 Corinthians

2:14	213, 218
3	187
3:2	222
6:19	209
7:39	139
8:13	221

2 Corinthians

3	161
3:9	78n, 137
3:11	140
5:17	209, 174
6:2	150

Galatians

2:19	139
3:3	154
3:8	126, 221, 222n
3:19	172
4	117
4:5	144, 203
5:6	156
5:18	209

Ephesians

3:8	63
3:19	104, 104n
5:14	67
5:26	156

Colossians

3:4	156

1 Thessalonians

5:14	221

Hebrews

4:12	67
6:1ff.	32
9:23	44
11:3	44

James

1:25	135
2:12	135–36

1 Peter

3:21	144
3:21	156

2 Peter

1:4	179
3:14	213n, 216, 216n

1 John

2:12ff	184–85

Jude

[14]	158

Revelation

14:6	105

www.ingramcontent.com/pod-product-compliance
Lightning Source LLC
Chambersburg PA
CBHW050623300426
44112CB00012B/1624